Oriental Medicine

Contributors

Jan Van Alphen
Ethnographic Museum, Antwerp, Belgium

Cai Jing-Feng
China Institute for the History of Medicine and Traditional Literature, Beijing, PRC

Chen Bin-Chern
China Medical College, Taiwan, ROC

Cyong Jong-Chol
Oriental Medicine Research Center, The Kitasato Institute, Tokyo, Japan

Kenneth Holmes
Rokpa, Samye Ling Tibetan Centre, Eskdalemuir, Scotland

Kim Jung Jae
Department of Traditional Medicine, Kyung Hee University, Seoul, Korea

Claudia Liebeskind
The Wellcome Institute for the History of Medicine, London, UK

Ram Manohar
Foundation for the Revitalisation of Local Health Traditions, Bangalore, India

Fernand Meyer
Centre International de la Recherche Scientifique, Ecole Pratique des Hautes Etudes, Paris, France

Nguyen Van Thang
Vietnam National Institute of Traditional Medicine, Hanoi, Vietnam

Ineke Van Put
Catholic University Louvain, Belgium

Darshan Shankar
Foundation for the Revitalisation of Local Health Traditions, Bangalore, India

Robert Svoboda
Ayurvedic Institute, Albuquerque, USA

Khenpo Troru Tsenam
Traditional Tibetan Hospital, Lhasa, Tibet

Dan Vercammen
Taoist Studies Centre, Antwerp, Belgium

Charles Willemen
Ghent University, Belgium

Dominik Wujastyk
The Wellcome Institute for the History of Medicine, London, UK

Oriental Medicine

An Illustrated Guide to the Asian Arts of Healing

General Editors
Jan Van Alphen & Anthony Aris

Field Photography
Mark De Fraeye

Introduction
Fernand Meyer

Shambhala

Boston
1996

Shambhala Publications
Horticultural Hall
300 Massachusetts Avenue
Boston, Massachusetts 02115

Published by arrangement with Serindia Publications, London.

9 8 7 6 5 4 3 2 1

First Shambhala Edition

Printed in Hong Kong

Distributed in the United States by Random House, Inc.,
and in Canada by Random House of Canada Ltd

Library of Congress Cataloging-in-Publication Data

Oriental medicine: an illustrated guide to the Asian arts of healing—
general editors: Jan Van Alphen and Anthony Aris; field photography, Mark De Fraeye.
p. cm.
Includes bibliographical references and index.
ISBN 1-57062-175-6
1. Medicine. Oriental. 2. Medicine, Oriental—Pictorial works.
I. Alphen, J. Van (Jan)
R581.075 1996 95-22120
610'.95—dc20 CIP

Contents

List of Objects Illustrated

164 *Xiuzhen Tu*. The Development of Truth. Stone rubbing from the Baiyunguan Temple, Beijing. 115.2 x 53.2 cm. Collection: Dan Vercammen, Antwerp.

166 *Bagua*, the 8 trigrams around the yin yang symbol. Lacquer and gilt wood. H: 26 cm. x W: 29 cm. Collection: Mark De Fraeye, Belgium.

168 Page from a Korean shaman manual. Collection: Mark De Fraeye, Belgium.

171 Two compasses for geomantic and astrological calculations. Wood, lacquer work, glass and iron. Above: from Japan, early 19th century, collected between 1823 and 1829 by Philipp Franz von Siebold, diam: 11.7 cm; Acc.1-3285 and, below, from China, 19th c., D: 25.1 cm; Acc.1-4812. National Museum of Ethnology, Leiden.

171 Set of 33 Chinese surgical instruments. Science Museum, London. Science & Society Picture Library. A624558.

172 Ivory female diagnostic figure. 19th c. L: 26 cms. Private Collection, Belgium.

173 Two figures illustrating skin diseases. Wellcome Institute, London.

174 Two illustrations from the *I-tsung chiu-chien*, 'The Golden Mirror of Medicine', a compendium of medical works edited by Wu Chien and first published in 1742. Chinese Collection No. 71b. The Wellcome Institute, London.

179 Chiropodist inspecting the leg of his patient. Watercolour by Zhou Pei Qun, from *Chinese Trades and Professions*, early 19th century. L.5099B. Wellcome Institute, London.

184 Village doctor treating a peasant with moxibustion. Detail from a reproduction of a painting by Li Tang of the Sung Dynasty (10th-13th century). 67.5 x 56.5cm. National Palace Museum, Taiwan.

184 Set of medical instruments. Lacquered wood, copper, metal alloy with a high silver content. Japan, early 19th century, collected between 1823 and 1829 by Philipp Franz von Siebold, W: 24.9 cm x H: 4.7 cm. National Museum of Ethnology, Leiden, Holland. No.1-618.

184 Modern acupuncture set from Korea. Collection: Mark De Fraeye, Belgium.

185 The treatment of cataract by acupuncture, from *Shen-Shih yao-han* compiled by Fu Jen-Jü, a compendium of opthalmology first published in 1644. Wellcome Institute, London.

185 Watercolour of a seated man, showing acupuncture points. Wellcome Institute, London, V 18491B.

186- Chinese acupuncture charts showing the loci for the front, back, side, and internal organs. 1906. Wellcome Institute, London.

199 'Bare -foot doctor' astride a galloping horse. Chinese title: *pao ma song yi*, "a race by horse to bring medicines". Guangdong, Shiwan Glazed stone ware. H: 25 x W: 31 cm. National Museum of Ethnology, Leiden. 4743-19.

227 Medicine chest, *yak-chung*, for storing herbs, with 77 small and 3 large drawers. c.1880. brass fittings. H:118 x W: 87 x D: 26 cm. Collection M. De Fraeye, Belgium.

228 Bronze pitcher for boiling medicine *chu do*. Shilla period, 9th century. 12.8 x 26 cm. Han-Dok Medico-Pharma Museum, Korea.

228 Bronze pitcher with handle used for dispensing liquid medicine. Koryo period, 11th century. 25.7 x 25 cm. Han-Dok Medico-Pharma Museum, Korea.

228 Celadon pitcher for decocting medicinal herbs. Choson period, 13-14th century. 12 x 24.5 cm. Han-Dok Medico-Pharma Museum, Korea.

228 Celadon mortar for medicinal preparations. Koryo period, 13th century. 9.2 x 20.5 cm. Han-Dok Medico-Pharma Museum, Korea.

229 Medicine chest of the traditional Korean 'pillow' type. Choson period, 18th century. 18 x 40 cm. Han-Dok Medico-Pharma Museum, Korea.

230 Advertisement for a proprietary remedy for intestinal problems, '*Wakyōgan*'. Coloured woodcut print, anonymous. Japan, c.1870. 49.6 x 34.4 cm. National Museum of Ethnology, Leiden. B226-310.

236 *Hashika yōyō no kokoroe*. Dietary advice for patients with measles. Ukiyo-e woodcut print by Kunimasa, 1885. Naito Museum of Pharmaceutical Science and Industry, Gifu, Japan. E2498.

237 *Inshoku yōyō*. The Rules of Dietary Life. Reproduction of a Ukiyo-e woodcut print by Kunisada Utagawa, c. 1850. Naito Museum of Pharmaceutical Science, Gifu.

238 *Hashika karukusuru hō*. Advice for the relief of measles. Ukiyo-e woodcut diptych by Oju, 1862. 36 x 26 cm. Naito Museum of Pharmaceutical Science and Industry, Gifu, Japan. E2491, E2492.

239 Johannes Pompe van Meerdervoort with two legendary medical heros. Detail from scroll painting, ink on paper, possibly by Kuoshoshi. Japan, 1865, 132,5 x 56,6 cm. National Museum of Ethnology, Leiden. 5094-1.

239 Drawing of the asparagus plant from a 17th century herbal or 'Kruydboek'. Japanese Ms 2142, 1620. Wellcome Institute, London.

239 Title page of a work by Joh. Valverde on anatomy based on the drawings of Andreas Vesalius. Printed by Plantin in Antwerp in 1568. Museum Plantin-Moretus, Antwerp.

239 Title page from *Kaitai Shinsho*, the *New book on Anatomy*. Published in Japan in 1774. Staatsbibliothek zu Berlin Preussischer Kulturbesitz.

240 Acupuncture model collected by Philipp Franz von Siebold. Wood, wood pulp, colouring and ink. H: 77.5 cm. National Museum of Ethnology, Leiden. 1-3496

240 Japanese painting of the meridians and loci for acupuncture after a Chinese original of 1474, from a work of the same title by Sun Simiao (died 682). Watercolour on paper. Early 19th century, 121.8 x 49.4 cm. National Museum of Ethnology, Leiden. 360-7751.

241 Lacquer box for moxa instruments with polychrome mother-of-pearl inlay illustration of a moxa-doctor with female patient. Japan, early 19th century, collected by Philipp Franz von Siebold. W: 18.1 x H: 3.6 x D: 7.7 cm. National Museum of Ethnology, Leiden. 1-640.

241 Two inros. Left: signed Kansai , 2602-38, 6.8 x 5.5 cm. Right: unsigned, Somada School, 2602-23, 8.5 x 5.8 cm. National Museum of Ethnology, Leiden.

242 Ivory netsuke of a human skull with two character inscription 'Toko'. H: 4.6 x W: 3.9 x D: 5.0 cm. Science Museum, London. A641324. Science & Society Picture Library.

242 Ivory netsuke depicting a Buddhist Arhat (*rakan*) massaging the shoulders of a demon (*oni*). Japan 17th century. H: 3.8 x L: 4 cm x W: 3 cm. Science Museum, London. A38879. Science & Society Picture Library.

242 Signboard for a proprietary stomach medicine, *Kumanoi mokkōgan*. 84 x 41 cm. Naito Museum of Pharmaceutical Science and Industry, Gifu, Japan. E7533.

242 Votive tablet, *Chichi shibori ema*, 'to make the milk flow easily'. Japan, 20th century. 9 x 15 cm. Naito Museum of Pharmaceutical Science and Industry, Gifu, Japan. Z1400.

243 Portable medicine chest. *Oshinyo hyaku mi dansu*. 20 x 40 x 49 cm. Naito Museum of Pharmaceutical Science and Industry, Gifu, Japan. E1758.

258 Shennong, the Chinese deity of medicine, pharmaceutics and agriculture. Water-colour, Shanghai, 1920. 27.5 x 17.5 cm. Wellcome Institute, London. ICV 18873.

260 Bhaiṣajyaguru, the Medicine Buddha. Tibetan thangka, 14th century. H: 95.5 x 79.5. Musée National des Arts Asiatiques-Guimet. Paris. MA5959.

264 Gilt bronze statue of a standing Bhaiṣajyaguru. Korea, 9th century. H. 25.1 x W. 9.5cm. 9th century. National Museum of Korea, Seoul.

265 Bhaiṣajyaguru, the Medicine Buddha, accompanied by two monk attendants. Tang dynasty (2nd half of the 9th c.) painting on silk recovered from Dunhuang by Paul Pelliot. 84 x 49.1 cm. Musée National des Arts Asiatiques-Guimet. Paris. MG23078.

Acknowledgements

Our thanks are due to the photographer Mark De Fraeye who first had the idea for this book, and who made available to the General Editors his extensive archive of field photographs taken over a number of years of travelling throughout the length and breadth of Asia. Besides the interest and beauty of his photographs, we believe that they actually help to evoke these ancient civilisations with great sympathy, and at the same time to situate their medical traditions in their contemporary contexts. Working exclusively with Agfa film and with Hasselblad cameras, Mark De Fraeye is able to record delicate situations with sensitivity and an unobtrusive skill.

This book was made possible by the financial help of Janssen Pharmaceutica of Belgium, especially through the enthusiastic interest of Gus van Kesteren. Not only were some of the field trips of Mark De Fraeye and Jan Van Alphen financed by Janssen, but their generous assistance with production costs enabled the publishers to enlarge the visual scope of the book with a rich balance of images from the traditional iconography of these Asian medical systems.

Our seventeen contributors are drawn from all over the world and are represented by eight languages; with only three exceptions they have not even met. Inevitably, with contributions deriving from the perspectives and value systems of both western academics as well as that of physicians working within the individual Asian medical systems, there will be certain discrepancies in terminology and approaches between the essays which we trust the reader will tolerate and understand. We have not imposed a structure for the contributors to follow but rather preferred them to speak in their own voices about the subjects that are their particular interest or concern.

Fernand Meyer, biomedical physician and orientalist, bridges the conceptual and scientific gap between our two groups of contributors and we owe him a great debt of gratitude for agreeing to provide the introduction, for the chapter on the Theory and Practice of Tibetan Medicine, as well as for sympathetic guidance on the contents and scope of this book.

The task of translation and editing has not been light and our most grateful thanks are especially due to Maria Phylactou for her thoughtful editorial assistance and to Veronique Martin and Marie-Laure Aris for the translations from French. Our contributor Ineke Van Put kindly agreed to tackle the index. Robert Beer supervised the design of this book.

The curators and staff of the following museums and institutions were helpful with advice in the selection of objects and paintings to illustrate this book and its accompanying exhibition; Brooklyn Museum, New York; Ethnographic Museum, Antwerp; Han-Doc Medico-Pharma Museum, Korea; Heinrich Harrer Museum, Hüttenberg; Musée National des Arts Asiatiques-Guimet, Paris; National Museum, Copenhagen; National Museum of Ethnology, Leiden; Naito Museum of Pharmaceutical Science, Gifu; The British Library, London; Science Museum, London; Topkapi Palace Museum, Istanbul, and The Wellcome Institute for the History of Medicine, London. This book has also been enriched from the private collections of John Barnett, Mark De Fraeye, Sam Fogg, Mimi Lipton, Dan Vercammen, Muriel and Jack Zimmerman, and others wishing to remain anonymous.

Without the enthusiasm and skills of the staff of our Dutch-language copublishers, Lemniscaat of Rotterdam, especially Frances van den Hoek, Irma van Welzen and Gerolf T'Hooft, this book would have been difficult to achieve.

As with traditional art the world over, the names of the painters, sculptors and artisans responsible for the magnificent works presented herein are mostly unknown to us, but it is to them that our final thanks must go, for they have preserved for us and for the future the very heart of these ancient medical traditions, thus providing a point of entry to appreciating the civilisations that gave them birth.

Foreword

The tremendous growth of interest in alternative therapies in the West in recent years, allied with a general and popular disaffection for conventional medicine, has caused many to look to the traditional medical systems of Asia for new sources of healing. A recent study in the United States has estimated the number of annual visits to alternative therapists at an astonishing figure of 425 million with an estimated cost of $10.3 billion a year, as against 388 million visits to primary care physicians with $12.8 billion spent out of pocket annually for all hospitalisation. There is an undeniably widespread notion throughout the West that the kind of conventional medicine and treatments available to the sick today are not adequate to the late twentieth century, or at least to the New Age, and that we must look to the East to meet those of our needs which are not easily satisfied by pills and conventional advice.

The intention of this book is to present these traditional medical systems of Asia in such a way that they will provide the general reader, whatever their interests may be, with the necessary tools to understand their basic history, their main theories, and their diagnostic and therapeutic methods. This is not a celebration of their curative powers, a sort of rediscovery of lost efficacy, nor does it seek to compare one system with another, or even to advocate alternative or complementary medicine. It is a celebration of the actual persistence and in some cases revival today of these ancient and learned, that is codified, bodies of knowledge by identifying the special features that distinguish them, and to provide pointers to how they approach and resolve the universal human concerns of what actually constitutes health and sickness. These may eventually help us to understand and interpret our own.

For this purpose we have gathered together both Western scholars who specialise in the main streams of Indian, Tibetan and Chinese medicine, together with physicians working from within each of these systems, and who are mostly concerned with the actual problems of adaption to and integration with Western biomedicine. We hope that what will become apparent is that the medical systems presented here may be perceived as intellectually coherent bodies of knowledge. They may appear exotic and consist of strange beliefs and practices, but they have an underlying logic supported frequently by empirically verifiable concepts of pathophysiology and therapeutics.

All the same, it is not possible to understand these systems outside the main stream of history as if they were frozen in time. Not much is known about how one tradition influenced another but it is clear that the Indian, Tibetan and Chinese systems did not evolve out of vacuums nor were any insulated from the influences that have connected Asia over the centuries with the rest of the world. Moreover, these systems have never been static and what has become apparent over the two years this book has been in preparation is that there is a burgeoning interest in dialogue between the medical systems of Asia and modern biomedicine which is now influencing the direction each of these traditional systems are taking. By translating and defining the key concepts of these systems, we hope that this book will help with this dialogue, encouraging the development of a truly cosmopolitan medicine, the strengths and weaknesses of each being duly recognised, in the knowledge that "a science if badly handled, destroys its user like a poorly handled weapon destroys its inept user, while the same science or weapon when rightly handled becomes a source of succour".

We have defined the scope of this book in terms of the worlds of Indian, Tibetan and Chinese medicine because these countries are the inheritors of a great corpus of learned texts still used today, and our interest has been to provide the reader with some access to them by translating and defining key concepts of theory, diagnosis and actual practice contained therein. But in some ways it may have been more appropriate to classify these systems according to the religions with which they are so intimately linked—Islamic, Hindu, Buddhist or Taoist—for each of them embody both a world view and a concept of the body that defined the vital character and direction of each medical system. A major concern of all religions, but especially that of Buddhism, was the relief of all suffering, be it spiritual or physical, and the different systems presented here are so embedded with their own individual religious symbols that it is often not possible to unravel the science from the religion.

Another approach is to classify the systems by a main feature, such as the requirement to restore balance (i.e. humoral and Taoist medicine), or to expel sickness (i.e. Tantric) or by what actually works empirically (i.e. pragmatic). In the end we wonder how useful this may be when, for instance, the syncretic medical system of Tibet can fit into all of these classifications.

Six of the essays presented here are concerned with how these medical systems situate and define themselves in the present and in their relation to modern biomedicine. It is a matter of great regret that we have as yet been unable to investigate how this is happening in the countries of South-East and Central Asia, where all these traditional systems are also still found today. There is certainly scope for a revised edition in the future which would include them.

It is clear that traditional medicine throughout Asia is now moving out of the herbalist's shop, away from the core texts, and into the biochemical laboratories. Thousands of plants are today being screened for their pharmaceutical properties and their medically active ingredients isolated and used to design new and more powerful drugs. Already medicinal plants of Asian origin are being used to alleviate the side effects of cancer therapy, as well as in treating such chronic problems as malaria and eczema. There is even the hope that with a boost from Western science, some solution may be found for curbing the AIDS epidemic. One certain advantage of isolating the medicinally active ingredients of herbs and developing them into synthetic drugs will be to protect the fragile ecology of the plants themselves, much threatened today by a global demand.

Although we have tried to assist the reader through a maze of epistemology, we hope that the bare bones of theory, diagnosis and therapeutics of these systems, are brought to life with the illustrations of traditional medical iconography. It is no surprise that some of the finest oriental sculpture, artifacts and paintings, present subjects of medical interest. Sometimes the purpose is didactic, as with the famous series of seventeenth century Tibetan medical paintings which serve as *aides-mémoires* for training doctors, or it may be utilitarian as with the early celadon medicinal vessels from Korea or the exquisite inro from Japan, or superbly illustrative, such as the masterpiece of Mughal painting from the Hamza-nameh and the Company style paintings from India presented here. Then finally there is the religious art. We conclude the book with an appropriate icon for the relief of suffering; a splendid ninth century painting recovered from Dunhuang in the deserts of Serindia, of the Medicine Buddha accompanied by his two attendant monks, striding across the watershed of civilisation between India and China.

Jan Van Alphen
Anthony Aris

Introduction

FERNAND MEYER

To this day Asia has kept alive those great learned and codified medical traditions which arose over the centuries, not only its own, but even the Galeno-Hippocratic system of ancient Greece which disappeared in the west during the eighteenth century as it gave way to modern biomedicine.

Over a long and as yet little-known history these various medical traditions have given rise to a vast body of literature while perpetuating at the same time their own rich oral traditions. Despite an apparent continuity, they have actually undergone profound changes over the centuries, and have given birth to various schools of interpretation regarding their original texts, basic principles, their theories or practices. These learned medical systems, along with other cultural features, have often spread far beyond the lands where they had originated. They have continuously provided a valuable resort against illness, together with other therapies offered by various specialists or belonging to common popular knowledge. Generally, it was social environment which determined the prevalence or choice of one method of care for the sick over another. For instance, learned medicine was generally more accessible in towns than in the remote countryside and it is apparent that most of the methods of treating illness were not those offered by the learned medical systems. Moreover, we have no way of knowing to what extent these various traditional therapies, including those of the learned medical systems, had any impact on the overall epidemiological situation. The vitality of these medical traditions, despite the widespread competition of biomedicine, bears witness to the satisfaction they continue to provide, and hence to their effectiveness which, as we shall see later, is not limited to the biological domain.

The learned medical traditions of Asia are sets of beliefs and practices which have been integrated into distinct systems, themselves based on specific principles, methods and aims. On the other hand, they are also constantly found in intimate contact, overlapping or interacting with other cultural or social fields, be they learned or popular. Medical theory also speaks of the world and society, just as politics, philosophical speculations and religious views may hold certain medical implications. Beyond their apparent exoticism, which might be attractive to some, and provided that they are not only viewed as potential sources of empirical treatments, these medical systems shed light on a universal anthropological question: how different societies, including our own, interpret and relate to health and illness. Before considering the subject of traditional medicine, whether written or oral, from this angle, let us first examine certain concepts such as medicine and illness which appear to us so familiar and ordinary that we tend to regard them as being both obvious and universal.

Patients, diseases; healers and medicine

The notion of medicine as commonly understood—a body of knowledge and specialised practices intended for the treatment of somatic disorders and used by a specific socio-professional group—does not necessarily apply to all societies. Indeed, in many traditional societies, explanations and therapies used when dealing with the sick cannot be confined to the above definition alone, either because their aim is not necessarily confined to dealing with somatic disorders, or because they may be the responsibility of other types of specialists—soothsayers, priests, shamans—whose range of skills greatly exceed those of doctors. Thus we should abandon the ethnocentric and limiting presumptions that take medicine *per se* as the object of study. Disease, a universal event and an empirical fact, should provide the focus instead. But first of all, it is important to be aware of the various connotations which the term 'disease' conceals under its apparent ordinariness, as well as its general usefulness as a tool for our anthropological analysis.

The term 'disease' has three distinct meanings: a concrete event affecting a person (disease-event), a term of classification in pathology (disease-entity), and the abstract notion of a state which is opposed to that of good health.

The general notion of disease carries no positive connotations and tends to be defined as a deviation from a norm which obviously varies from one culture to another. Moreover, the two notions, health and disease, are entangled in a circular reasoning each being defined in relation to the other. In many societies without a written tradition, the general and abstract notion of disease is not clearly distinguished since disease may be assimilated with the more general categories of evil and misfortune. Furthermore, even when this notion is distinct, disease is still considered as an ill-fated event, among others, affecting social relations. Just as illness may be considered a form of misfortune, health can be seen as an aspect of the harmonious order which governs man's relationship with others and the world in which he lives.

Of the three aspects of the term disease, that of disease as a pathological event is primary. Before a disease is identified and classified as a nosological entity—say, as diabetes in biomedicine, or the depletion of yin in the kidneys in Chinese medicine, or the aggravation of vital wind in Indian Ayurveda—it first manifests as a particular psychosomatic event affecting a given person who, as a result, becomes ill. Like birth and death, illness is both an individual and a social event imposed by man's biological nature. However, unlike birth and death, disease is generally more or less spontaneously reversible—a fact which tends to confirm the effectiveness of the chosen method of treatment—and likely to recur throughout a person's life.

Because it is rooted in a suffering body and because it threatens the integrity and survival of both the individual and society as a whole, illness is an event characterised by an ability to mobilise strong emotions, and to trigger social processes into complex interactions. Disease is the manifestation and awareness at a personal level of a psychosomatic change experienced as unpleasant and incapacitating.

The threshold of perception of the illness and the relative importance given to certain symptoms over others are strongly conditioned by cultural environment. This most personal and subjective experience of the illness already presents a social dimension. But the first stage of illness becoming a social event as such is when the sick person states his condition to those around him, verbally and through certain types of behaviour which are generally culturally codified. The subject therefore takes on the sick role which exculpates him from this specific form of deviation, that is, disease, by recognising his involuntary incapacity to perform the social duties normally required.

The noxious, unexpected and apparently selective nature of illness, compels the afflicted person, with the support of those around him and eventually with the help of experts, to seek an explanation and to undertake the course of action deemed most efficient. It consists of a dynamic and not necessarily coherent process, following a therapeutic itinerary using many different approaches successively or simultaneously. The level of explanation sought and selected, and the social implications of the therapeutic itinerary itself, depends upon biological, psychological and social factors.

For the sick person and for those around him, as well as for many healers, diagnosis—in other words, the application of explanatory models to the signs manifested by a particular pathological event in order to interpret their cause and/or to define them as a given nosological entity—must satisfy a quest for meaning rather than a need for knowledge as such. What makes a diagnosis meaningful is not so much its scientific or even empirical accuracy, but its coherence with the sick person's subjective experience and with his conception of his relation with others and the world. In general the interpretation or diagnosis of a pathological event rests on at most four categories of questions: 1. To which nosological entity does it correspond?; 2. What is its pathogenic process?; 3. Who or what caused it?, and finally, 4. Why is that person afflicted at that particular time?

All four questions are not necessarily posed, nor do they always follow a specific order, and the answers provided do not necessarily have to fit into an all-encompassing coherence. Moreover, in many societies, these four 'diagnostic' questions and the resulting methods of treatment they entail belong to different domains. The first two relate more to the realm of common empirical knowledge or to traditional and biomedical doctors. The last specifically concerns more particularly soothsayers, mediums, and religious specialists. The third question belongs to both categories depending on whether the search for the cause is 'personalistic': "Who caused it?" (ancestor, sorcerer, demon, etc.), or 'naturalistic': "What caused it?" (climate, lifestyle, diet, etc.).

It would seem that throughout the history of humanity, man afflicted by illness, a crisis both individual and social, has preferred in his search for meaning causal explanations over those models directed towards the pathogenic process. Man was especially attracted to those explanations involving beings of evil intent because they best provided a notion of an individual meaning to each sick person's spontaneous and anxious feelings of persecution: "Who resents me?", "Why me?", "What have I done wrong to deserve this?" This type of pathogenic cause is revealed through divination or trance rather than from the clinical observation of symptoms.

As learned traditional medical systems appeared, the explanatory models applying to illness as an event shifted more and more towards naturalistic causes, in other words impersonal, non-intentional, and universal (such as those causes to do with climate, diet, lifestyle, emotional disposition etc.), and also towards the pathogenic process itself (humoral imbalance, clogging or deviation of bodily fluids, decomposition of the bodily juices etc.). This split represented an important epistemological step which went towards the more spontaneous and 'archaic' tendency and personalist interpretations mentioned above. These explanatory models, however, have not altogether disappeared from collective and individual consciousness—like a geological stratum that has been covered but not eliminated by another and is therefore likely to reappear on the surface—for they continued to answer certain needs, expressed or latent, which continued to be satisfied by non-medical specialists. Moreover, even though learned medical traditions offered essentially naturalistic models of interpretation for certain pathological categories, they still tended to incriminate gods, demons and other evil spirits for certain pathological categories such as children's diseases, behavioural and psychic disorders, epidemics etc. In addition, many physicians combined learned medical tradition in their writings and especially in their practice, with ideas and techniques pertaining rather to the religious world.

As we have previously mentioned, a pathological event calls for an explanation (diagnosis) and an efficient course of action (therapy). In most medical systems strictly speaking, diagnosis consists in applying an explanatory model to the illness which will lead to its identification as a disease-entity. It can then be said that the person has such and such a disease. It is important to stress, although we tend to think otherwise, that diseases-entities whether listed in traditional medical systems or in biomedicine are not natural entities having a proper existence, like animal or plant species. They are the result of a singularising process conditioned by culture and applied to the complex, dynamic and fluctuating sociobiological reality of disease-events. This classifying system is built according to a selective process which, founded on recurring associations of ideas, select certain features deemed meaningful, such as causes, symptoms, etc. If elementary symptoms are indeed transcultural, this cannot apply to their classification as nosological entities. It is thus very difficult to establish direct equivalents between different nosological systems, except when the association of symptoms is so obvious that it is universally recognised.

For traditional learned medical systems, pathology usually represents a disruption of the normal physiological functions. Practitioners within these traditions tend therefore to consider disease-entities as reference points on a continuous nosological grid which directs their course of action, rather than as absolute entities in themselves. These traditions may also sometimes refer to a disease in terms which confer an ontological reality, sometimes so marked as to evoke that of evil spirits.

The explanatory models of the learned traditional medical systems tend to be naturalistic, i.e. impersonal, general and abstract. This tends to diminish their capacity to convey a personalised meaning to the subjective experience of the patient, unlike the interpretations of a more popular or religious nature. These models still retain a strong power of suggestion and therefore of significance and involvement for the sick because they are based on largely shared holistic or even cosmological concepts, and because they necessarily take into account the patient's subjective complaints during diagnosis. Indeed, the concepts of traditional medicine and the metaphors used to describe them, such as the flows of energy or fluids, the precarious balance of opposing entities, images relating to cooking and purification, the correlation between macrocosm and microcosm, etc., evoke for their users a whole variety of experiences relating to their body, their cultural and social integration and their relation to the natural environment (symptoms). These concepts and metaphors relate also to the imaginary world, the position within society and culture and the relation to natural environment.

From this point of view, traditional medical systems contrast strongly with modern medicine, which, by basing itself on science, has become more concerned with the universal rather than the particular. Furthermore, modern medicine has developed highly specific methods and concepts which satisfy its demand for objectivity, implying an objectification of disease and a verifiable accuracy imposed by the scientific ideal. For this reason, its paradigms are expressed in a technical language which has lost the multiple meanings and suggestive power of traditional metaphors. At the same time, thanks to technological progress, its diagnostic systems rely less and less on personal information from the patient, which is subjective and therefore suspect. Diagnosis now aims to attain the objectivity offered by biological, histological, chemical or microbiological facts which no longer form part of the patient's personal experience. The emergence in the West during the nineteenth century of this biomedical model led to a considerable progress in medical theory and practice. But at the same time, because of its very nature, it neglected the non-biological aspect of illness which explains why it is often perceived by patients as limiting, dehumanising and aggressive, by contrast with the milder and holistic approach ascribed to traditional medicine or to alternative therapies.

The learned medical traditions of Asia

The healing systems presented in this book deserve to be called medical in the strict sense of the word since they are exclusively concerned with the prevention, diagnosis and cure of that particular form of misfortune which is disease.

The term 'learned' as used here is not intended as a value judgement, but to indicate that these systems are based on a written corpus. This feature is important since writing not only ensures the material survival of the knowledge it transmits, it actually modifies its very nature by allowing a greater degree of abstraction, whereas orally-transmitted knowledge remains dependent on circumstantial statements.

These medical systems are called traditional not from an outside 'modern' perspective, but because they themselves continuously claim and reassert the value of tradition, that is the ideally faithful transmission of a heritage viewed as the unfolding of all the potentialities already contained in the original texts. Nevertheless, this ideal importance accorded to tradition has not condemned these systems to remain unchanged as we tend to believe. On the contrary, they have been continuously enriched and have undergone many transformations throughout history.

The most ancient learned medical systems emerged gradually over the same period around the Mediterranean, in India and China in the centuries preceding our era. These traditions ascribed their origins to a series of texts which are generally the oldest to have reached us but obviously not the most ancient. Indeed, their composite character testify to the existence of previous medical currents from which their respective traditions evolved. These texts appear to be heterogeneous compilations involving various schools rather than works of individual authorship, even though they have been attributed to historical or legendary figures who subsequently became the emblematic founders of these traditions: Hippocrates in the Greco-Roman world, the Yellow Emperor in China, Caraka or Suśruta in India. The medical theories which were more or less coherently formulated and integrated into these writings borrowed their fundamental concepts from the speculations of contemporary philosophical schools concerning the universe, nature, man, the socio-political order or the epistemology.

During the following centuries, these medical theories were systematised and sometimes reinterpreted in various treatises which, alongside the original corpus, became the classical works of reference for these traditions.

Although these medical traditions may differ in the detail of their theories and practices, they do share a number of fundamental features. They are all more concerned with the functions of the body, which they tend to attribute to the circulation and transformation of ubiquitous humoral fluids, than with the anatomical parts. Physiological, pathogenic, or therapeutic processes are explained in terms of perceptible qualities, often expressed in contrasting pairs: hot/cold, dry/wet, active/passive, light/dark etc. These qualities are applied to different registers: bodily components, mental or emotional states, environment and climate etc., and thus integrate man with the spacio-temporal universe. While biomedicine assimilated, in its objectification of disease, the dualism of body and mind which evolved out of Descartes' philosophy, traditional systems conceive body and mind as two interdependent poles of the same somatic and psychic continuum. Furthermore, this body-mind, the world and society, are interrelated, reflecting one another in a complex system of polysemy, parallels and metaphors.

These learned medical traditions have produced a great number of specialised writings: general treatises, numerous commentaries, pharmacopoeias, prescription formularies, handbooks devoted to particular diagnostic or therapeutic techniques, etc., whose history continues to remain obscure, especially as far as Asian medical systems are concerned. For instance, in China 10,000 medical works are said to have survived. Moreover, all these medical traditions have spread beyond their land of origin, generally in the context of larger cultural borrowings, be they religious, philosophical and scientific. Thus, Chinese medical trends spread with the rest of Chinese classical civilisation to Korea, Japan and Vietnam. With the expansion of Buddhism, Indian medical traditions reached Sri Lanka, South East and Central Asia. From the seventh century onwards in Tibet, Indian medical trends merged with other foreign influences, notably Chinese, to create a syncretic, indigenous medicine which was in turn transmitted to the Mongols almost 1000 years later. Furthermore, the Greco-Roman heritage adopted by the Arab-Islamic world from the seventh century onwards spread to India by way of the Islamic conquests. All these great medical traditions have influenced one another to various degrees, especially in their practice and their use of *materia medica*.

The medical texts which have reached us, particularly those which have been studied until the present, were generally written by learned doctors often in close contact with the religious or political authorities. Hence they do not reflect the full spectrum of medical theories and practices of their time. Indeed, medicine was practised by a great variety of specialists, from the learned court physician down to the village healer. Although they claimed to be of the same medical tradition, they never, until recently, formed a homogenous socio-professional group. Moreover, there existed no authority able or willing to impose a general standard of knowledge and practice.

Between the sixteenth and eighteenth centuries the first western merchants, travellers and missionaries brought back information on the Asian medical traditions and were generally favourably disposed towards them as they seemed to present a number of similarities or equivalent concepts with traditional Western medicine, such as humours, pneuma, vital heat, vital spirits, natural faculties, etc. For example, the Jesuits in China decided to translate the texts devoted to pulse diagnosis for the use of western doctors, as the fundamental theories did not seem incompatible with those of Galenic sphygmology. Furthermore, the greater sophistication of the Chinese techniques appeared to yield better results. In addition, the Asian medical systems possessed vast pharmacopoeias with certain products of high repute since ancient times that could be added to those of the west. With the breach in epistemology which marked the disappearance of Galenic medicine and the emergence of biomedicine and its successes at the beginning of the nineteenth century, the western perspective on traditional Asian medical systems changed. The colonisers, whose technological achievements attested to the triumph of science, now considered these traditions as obsolete, exotic, primitive and incomprehensible. Gradually, traditional Asian medical systems came into contact and competition almost everywhere with biomedicine. After a period of decline and discredit in the eyes of the new indigenous elites who were influenced by modern western values, these traditions have enjoyed in our century a revival thanks to the return to national values advocated by decolonisation movements. Contrary to the promise of a decline which had been assured to them in the name of progress, not only have these traditions retained an important position, now often officially recognised, within their own cultural environment, but they have also been the subject of a growing interest from both practitioners and patients in quest of alternative methods of treatment. Thus, their recent history is marked by profound and rapid changes—theoretical adjustments, secularisation, professionalisation and institutionalisation—for which Western biomedicine often served as a model.

Until recently, research on the learned medical traditions of Asia was based primarily on the study of their texts—according to the tradition of classical orientalism—or on their theories and practices in the sole view of their actual usefulness. These studies have generally tended to present these medical systems in the light of their classical theories, in other words, as monolithic and unchanging systems isolated from their cultural, social and political context. However, in the last twenty years the study of Asian medical systems has been characterised by new methods of research, new perspectives and by an opening to other disciplines. New important works concerning the history of these medical traditions enable us to perceive more clearly the heterogeneity of their original texts, the diversity of their schools and the historical changes behind the apparent continuity of their terminology. Nosology and *materia medica* have acquired with time new entities while others were abandoned or reinterpreted. This is equally true of diagnostic and therapeutic techniques. Besides these historical developments, recent studies reveal the regional diversity of these systems, especially in the identification of drugs or the preference for certain therapeutic methods over others. Moreover, a growing number of researchers in their study of Asian medical systems, historical or present-day, now take into account their cultural, social, economic and political contexts.

Indeed, beyond a purely practical interest for their healing potential—in the elaboration of adapted models for clinical or pharmacological evaluation—traditional Asian medical systems deserve to be known and studied for their own sake and in all their aspects within their respective contexts. Such an approach would not only account for the coherence and vitality of the medical systems but would also contribute to an understanding of how we relate collectively or individually to health and illness.

वैद शहाब विलइती आए हिंदुस्तान देषे पंडित हिंदु के तासों कीयो मिलान ॥६॥
चरक आदे तै ग्रंथ सभ देषे उदधं समान मरजीयें की भात ज्यों रतन गहे तिन जान ॥७॥

A Persian physician came to India, to confer with the Hindu Pandits.
Together they studied the Caraka Saṃhitā and all other medical texts.
They realised that the medical texts are like an ocean,
and they were like pearl-divers who plunged into the ocean to grasp the pearls.

From *Kavi-taraṅga* by Sītārāma, Ambala District, Punjab, 1703.

The World of Indian Medicine

Liṅga shrine to the Hindu god Śiva at Walkeshvar, Bombay. The Liṅga or phallus was venerated at the time of the Indus Valley civilisation (4000-2000 BC) and later became the main icon of Śiva. It is the symbol of life-giving power and embodies the nature of the cosmos.

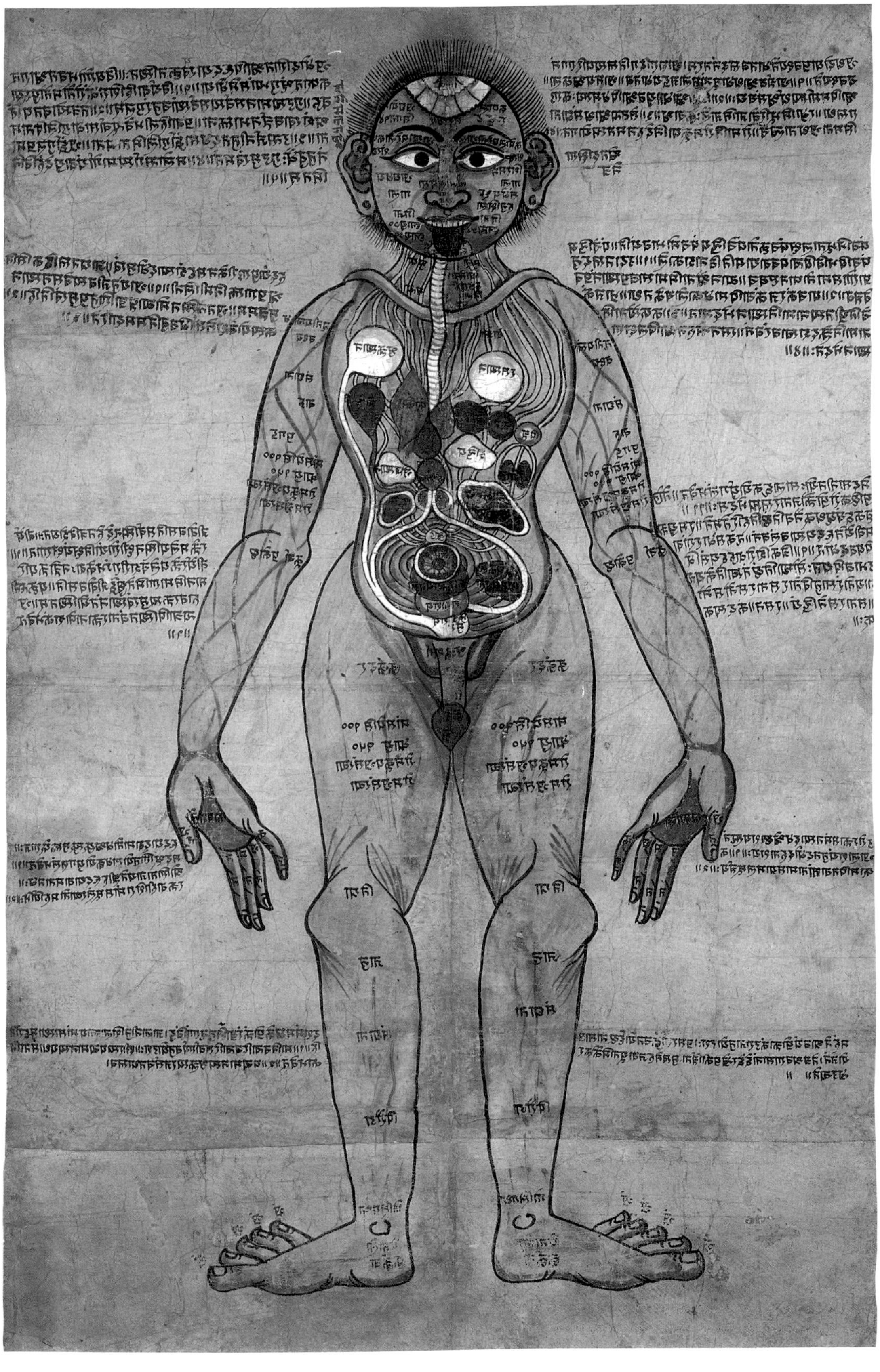

Anatomical painting with Sanskrit medical annotation. Despite the enormous number of manuscripts concerned with medicine, India has no known tradition of illustrated medical texts. This Nepalese painting is one of the only known examples. Wellcome Institute for the History of Medicine, London.

Medicine in India

Dominik Wujastyk

Prehistory and the Indus Valley

There is extensive archaeological evidence from all parts of the South Asian peninsula for the presence of man from the Lower Palaeolithic Stone Age onwards. The first settled agricultural communities seem to have appeared at the end of the Pleistocene, about ten thousand years ago. A marked increase in the use of grains of cereal type is indicated in eastern Rajasthan from about 7000 BC, accompanied by the development of mud-brick architecture, and the domestication of cattle, sheep and goat.

Mesolithic (15,000-6,000 BC) rock paintings were discovered in the late 1950s at Bhimbetka, Madhya Pradesh by V.S. Wakankar. This painting may depict surgery being performed on a subject's head or eye.

During the second half of the fourth and the early part of the third millenium BC, developments took place around the course of the Indus river which were to lead to the Mature Indus civilisation, which flourished during the middle and late third millennium. Archaeologists have pointed to the concurrence of three factors which brought the Indus civilisation to its maturity: the pre-existence in the region of many incipient urban trading communities; the rich natural environment offered by the Indus river system, a great river flowing through a desert which inevitably reminds us of Egypt and Mesopotamia; and finally the stimulus of contacts with other societies outside the Indus system, including those of Central Asia and Mesopotamia.[1]

Excavations of the impressive Indus cities of Harappa, Mohenjo-daro, and Lothal have revealed an elaborate and refined civilisation, and continuing archaeological work shows that the Indus culture stretched across a far greater area of northern India than was once realised, through a system of smaller villages and settlements that were linked to the cities by trade and shared artefacts. The period of the Mature Indus civilisation shows us an evolved urban society with clearly drawn class divisions and roles. No doubt healers of some type existed, perhaps coinciding with the religious functionaries. However, the script of this civilisation remains undeciphered at the present time, in spite of many promising attempts using modern techniques of decipherment, and the lack of access to the surviving written records impedes interpretation of the archaeological facts.

One may point to the large, central water tanks or communal baths that exist in the main cities and postulate religious or secular rites of cleansing. It certainly seems that hygiene was highly regarded, since the houses in Harappa, Mohenjo-daro, and Lothal often have separate bathrooms with drainage to covered culverts that run beneath the city streets. Several statues, toy models, and images survive, representing plants, animals, and presumed deities and in many cases it is tempting to draw parallels with later Vedic developments in the historical period. For example, there are images of what looks like a Pipal (Skt. *pippala*, *aśvattha*) leaf, which was of importance in the *materia medica* of later Indian medicine.[2] But while the Indus script remains unread, such conjectures concerning cultural continuity must remain tentative in the extreme.

During the middle of the second millennium BC, the Indus civilisation declined. The cities seem to have fallen into disuse, and the populations to have migrated to outlying villages. The causes for this decline are subject to strenuous debate today by archaeologists, geologists, linguists, and historians, but they probably include environmental changes affecting the river courses and the climate,[3] and perhaps the collapse of an over-rigid hieratic system of centralised government in the face of declining economic prosperity.

Medicine in the Vedic Texts

During the latter part of the second millennium BC, the eastward migrations of the Indo-European peoples reached South Asia.[4] The sacrificial liturgy of these peoples was memorised wholesale by families of hereditary priests (*brāhmaṇa*). By extraordinary feats of memory and tradition these hymns have reached us today in much the same form as they existed *circa* 1200 BC. This body of Sanskrit liturgical literature is called *veda*, 'the knowledge'.

The subject matter of these hymns is religious and includes the praise and worship of the gods, and prayers for health, long life, and many sons. From these hymns, we are able to deduce obliquely some information about health and healing in these early times. It must be stressed that there is no such thing as 'Vedic Medicine' in any unified sense. All we can do is scour the surviving liturgical texts for insights into the healing practices of the time.[5]

The picture that emerges is—perhaps unsurprisingly given the nature of our sources—one of a magical and religious approach to the causes of disease and to remedies. Several deities were ascribed particular healing powers, including the Aśvins, twin horsemen and divine physicians, cognate with the Roman Dioscuri. Diseases could be caused by evil spirits or by external accident, and rituals involving incantations (*mantra*), penances, and prayers were used to placate the suprahuman beings who brought disease upon mankind. Plants too were recognised for their healing powers. In general, internal diseases like *yákṣma* (consumption) and *takmán* (fever, particularly associated with the onset of the monsoon) were believed to have magical and demonic causes, while broken bones, wounds, and other external afflictions were ascribed to their more obvious mundane causes. Poisons were evidently known and used.

A superficial knowledge of anatomy is revealed. Vedic rites included animal and human sacrifice, and in this connection the ritual texts include some lists of anatomical parts.

A simple form of surgery is described, in which a reed was used as a catheter to cure urine retention.[6] Cauterisation with caustic substances and resins was used to prevent wounds from bleeding. In many places, the texts refer to water as a potent healing substance, but it is unclear whether it was to be drunk, sprinkled on the patient, or used for bathing.

Medicine and the Early Heterodox Ascetics

The religion of Vedic ritual continued to embody the orthodox religion of north India in the latter half of the first millenium BC, and it has continued to do so to some extent even today. However, a number of other religious groups sprang up in opposition to what was seen as a sterile, mechanistic religion. Generally speaking, these heterodox groups sought to internalise religious values to a greater extent than was demanded by Vedic ritual, and to live a life of ethical, rather than solely sacramental, integrity. The best known such group was the Buddhist *saṅgha* (community), founded by Gautama Śākyamuni, but there were others such as the followers of Mahāvīra (later called the Jains), and of Makkhali Gosāla (the Ājīvikas, now extinct), as well as many independent ascetics (*śramaṇa*). Amongst these groups a new kind of medical practice evolved. The evidence we have comes mainly from the Buddhist canonical texts which contain important medical information.[7]

The monastic rule governing Buddhist monks (Pāli *vinaya*) laid down that their few possessions should include five basic medicines: clarified butter, fresh butter, oil, honey and molasses.[8] As the Buddhist *saṅgha* evolved, the list of medical prerequisites grew to include numerous foods and a large pharmacopoeia. There is archaeological evidence from about the fourth century AD that some Buddhist monasteries included a sick room, which may have evolved into a more formal hospital.[9] Initially, the monks' healing activities were aimed at the care of their fellow monks, but by the middle of the third century BC the monasteries were beginning to serve the lay community.

Of particular interest for the history of Indian medicine are the close similarities that exist between the Buddhist texts and the later Ayurvedic texts in some lists of herbs, salts and other medicines, as well as in specific treatments. This is in contrast to the medicine of the Vedic texts, which is not generally similar to Ayurveda. The evidence points to the

Ayurvedic texts having grown, at least partly, from the ascetic milieu.[10] This seemingly simple fact has long been obscured because scholars have taken at face value the Ayurvedic texts' own strenuous assertions that they are derived from the Vedic tradition. But something quite complicated seems to have happened to this tradition, and research has not yet cleared up all the issues. Recent work has discerned in the classical compendia of Caraka and Suśruta a core of world-affirming, pragmatic realism amounting to an early scientific attitude, which has been subjected to a secondary process of religious over-coding.[11] Texts which were originally dedicated wholly to the accurate observation and description of disease, and to healing by whatever means were effective, have been recast in the framework of a dialogue between certain primeval Hindu sages and gods, and a pedigree has been clumsily prefixed to these works which traces the descent of the science of medicine back to the gods themselves.

Some of these ideas are still, perhaps, somewhat speculative. But the role of the ascetic communities of the fourth century BC onwards, and in particular of the Buddhist *saṅgha*, must now be recognised as a vital part of the early evolution of Ayurveda.

Ayurvedic Medicine

The classical system of Indian medicine is called, in Sanskrit, *āyurveda* 'the knowledge (*veda*) for longevity (*āyus*)'. An ancient etymological definition runs as follows:

> *It is called* 'āyurveda' *because it tells us* (vedayati) *which substances, qualities, and actions are life-enhancing* (āyuṣya), *and which are not.*[12]

Ayurveda is a broad system of medical doctrines and practices, with both preventive and prescriptive aspects. It consists of a great deal of excellent practical advice concerning almost every imaginable aspect of life, from cleaning the teeth, to diet, exercise and regimen. Ayurveda's theoretical foundation is a doctrine of three bodily humours (wind, bile and phlegm), somewhat analogous to the ancient Greek teachings of Hippocrates and Galen, and seven bodily constituents (chyle, blood, flesh, fat, bone, marrow and semen). Its medicines are mainly herbal and it teaches a broad range of therapies including enemas, massage, ointments, douches, sudation and surgery. From the end of the first millenium AD, metallic compounds began to come into medical use, but these remained on the periphery of the Ayurvedic pharmacopoeia; opium too was introduced, probably from Islamic sources, as an effective cure for diarrhoea. Throughout the classical texts the emphasis is on moderation: whether it be in food, sleep, exercise, sex, or the dosage of medicines, it is vital to stay within the limits of reasonable measure and balance.

Dr. Kabiraj Siddhi Gopal represents the twenty-first generation in a long lineage of Ayurvedic Vaidyas (physicians) in Patan, Nepal. The medical treatises of Caraka and Suśruta in front of him still form the basic medical literature after almost 2,000 years.

Source texts

The textbooks of Ayurveda are written in the classical Sanskrit language, although many are today available with translations into modern Indian languages (especially Hindi), and some have been translated into European languages. The earliest surviving texts date from the first centuries of the Christian era, although, as we have seen, there is evidence that a system which could be called Ayurveda was developing from perhaps as early as the fourth century BC. However, extravagant claims that Ayurveda dates from thousands of years BC can be firmly discounted. Such claims are frequent, and arise from nationalism, religious fundamentalism, a partisan attachment to romantic ideas of India's spiritual heritage, and other such causes. They are not supported by scholarly historical research. Likewise, several English translations, intending to glorify India's past achievements, only make it seem ridiculous by falling into the trap of presenting both ancient and medieval Indian medicine as though it foreshadowed all modern discoveries. Ayurveda's real history is impressive enough and does not benefit at all from proleptic scientism.

There are numerous Sanskrit texts devoted to expounding the traditional system of Indian medicine, Ayurveda. The earliest of these texts, by many centuries, are the *Caraka Saṃhitā* and the *Suśruta Saṃhitā*. The Sanskrit word *saṃhitā* means 'compendium', and Caraka and Suśruta are proper names. So these titles translate as 'Caraka's Compendium' and 'Suśruta's Compendium'. A third ancient text, the *Bheḷa Saṃhitā* has survived up to modern times in only a single damaged manuscript,[13] and it has as yet to be critically edited and translated.

The tradition of the *Caraka Saṃhitā* is associated with northwestern India, and in particular the ancient university of Takṣāśilā. Chinese sources place Caraka at the court of the famed first-century Scythian king, Kaniṣka; the *Suśruta Saṃhitā* is said to have been composed in Benares. We do not know the exact date of composition of these two works. Prior versions of these works may date as far back as the time of the Buddha, that is, the early fourth century BC.[14] At the end of several chapters, the texts themselves explicitly declare that they have been supplemented, edited, and partially rewritten by later authors, whose dates run up to about the eighth century AD. The published Sanskrit texts available today represent the works in the form which they had reached during the latter half of the first millenium AD.

The *Caraka Saṃhitā* and the *Suśruta Saṃhitā* are both long texts: one continuous English translation of the former is over 1,000 pages long,[15] and a translation of the latter is over 1,700 pages long.[16]

These two texts form the cornerstone of Ayurveda. Although there are many other texts on Ayurveda, these two provide the foundation of the system, and are constantly referred to and paraphrased in other texts.

Later texts of great importance include the *Aṣṭāṅgahṛdaya Saṃhitā* of Vāgbhaṭa (*c.*AD 600), the *Rugviniścaya* of Mādhavakara (*c.*AD 700), the *Śārṅgadhara Saṃhitā* of Śārṅgadhara (*c.* early fourteenth century) and the *Bhāva-prakāśa* of Bhāvamiśra (sixteenthth century). Mādhava's work broke new ground in its rearrangement of medical topics according to pathological categories, and set the pattern of subject arrangement that was followed by almost all later works on general medicine. Śārṅgadhara is important as the first author to discuss in Sanskrit several new foreign elements, including the extensive use of metallic compounds, an idea of respiration, diagnosis and prognosis by pulse, and opium.

There is some variation between north and south India regarding the popularity of Ayurvedic texts. Broadly, the *Caraka Saṃhitā* is more popular in the north, while the *Aṣṭāṅgahṛdaya Saṃhitā* is more popular in the south. This regional variation is revealed both by the geographical distribution of surviving manuscripts, and by the location of surviving living traditions of orally transmitted medical literature, such as the tradition of the *aṣṭavaidya* brahmins in Kerala.[17] A small medical digest called the *Vaidyajīvana*, written by Lolimbarāja in the late sixteenth century, became extraordinarily popular all over India, perhaps because of the beauty of the ornate classical metres in which its verses were cast: it has a dozen Sanskrit commentaries, and has been translated into many modern Indian languages. A well-known aphorism, 'a doctor by a hundred stanzas' refers jocularly to the fact that anyone can become a doctor by learning the *Vaidyajīvana*.[18]

Basic tenets

Both the *Caraka Saṃhitā* and the *Suśruta Saṃhitā* emanate from a single tradition of medicine, that is, their general views and doctrines are in consonance, and the theoretical basis of medicine presented in the texts is identical. The *Caraka Saṃhitā* is distinguished by its long reflective and philosophical passages: why twins are not necessarily identical (4.2),[19] what evidence there is for the doctrine of reincarnation (1.10), definitions of causality (3.8), etc. The *Caraka Saṃhitā* has proved to be of great interest to historians of India's philosophical traditions, since it contains doctrines associated with the philosophical schools of *sāṃkhya* and *vaiśeṣika*, yet predates the standard texts of these philosophical schools.[20] The *Suśruta Saṃhitā* contains extensive descriptions of sophisticated surgical techniques: eye operations (6.1-17), removal of foreign bodies (1.26), plastic surgery on the face (1.16), etc., which either do not appear in the *Caraka Saṃhitā* at all, or not in such detail.

The *Caraka Saṃhitā* (and similarly the *Suśruta Saṃhitā*) contains a vast accumulation of medical and indeed general information, including:

the merits of a measured diet and of smoking herbal mixtures (1.5, 3.2);
the pharmacological characteristics of a huge range of plants and vegetables (1.27, 3.1);
aetiology and characteristics of various diseases (2.1, 3.6-7);
epidemics (3.3);
methods of examination of the patient (3.4, 3.8);
anatomy (3.5, 4.7);
nosology (3.6-7);
philosophical topics about human life and spirit (4.1, 4.5);
conception, embryology, the care of the newborn, and growth (4.2-4, 4.6, 4.8);
prognosis (5.1-12);
stimulants and aphrodisiacs (6.1-2);
description and treatment of fever, heated blood, swellings, urinary disorders, skin disorders, consumption, insanity, epilepsy, dropsy, piles, asthma, cough and hiccup, etc. (6.3-18);
cupping, blood-letting and the use of leeches (6.14, 29);
proper use of alcohol (6.24);
disorders of paralysis, lock-jaw, rheumatism (6.27-29);
properties of nuts, vegetables and other *materia medica* (7.1-12);
the use of enemas (8.1-7, 8.10-12).

This heavily abbreviated list is intended just to give a feel for some of the topics covered.

The medicines described in the *Caraka Saṃhitā* and the *Suśruta Saṃhitā* contain a broad array of animal, vegetable and mineral substances. An estimate of prescribed items in the *Caraka Saṃhitā* shows 177 substances of animal origin (including snake dung, fumes of burnt snake, the milk, flesh, fat, blood, dung or urine of several animals such as horse, goat, elephant, camel, cow and sheep, the eggs of sparrow, pea-hen and crocodile, bees' wax and honey, soup of various meats, etc.), 341 substances of plant origin (including seeds, flowers, fruit, tree bark, leaves, etc.), and 64 items of mineral origin (including ash, various gems, silver, copper, salt, clay, tin, lead, gold, glass, orpiment, sulphur, etc.).[21]

It is worth noting in this context that several substances in these lists, such as dung and urine, are not necessarily considered shocking in the Indian rural context. To orthodox Hindus, the consumption of meat or wine (both also recommended in the texts) would be a far more horrifying prospect than the admixture of animal dung in a medical recipe. The

Medicinal herb garden of the Ārya Vaidyaśāla, a foundation for the study of traditional medicines in Kottakal, Kerala. As a result of a new scientific interest in Indian medicinal herbs, several books on Ayurvedic materia medica have been recently published.

cow, in particular, is a holy animal for Hindus, and all its products, including milk, urine, and dung, are considered auspicious and purifying. It is normal practice in Indian villages for a housewife to begin the day by smearing the floor of her home with cow-dung, which is seen as having disinfectant properties.[22] Cow-dung is also commonly used as fuel for cooking fires. Furthermore, in three cases out of four, animal dung is prescribed for external use (including fumigation); urine is prescribed externally about twice in every three recipes.

The *Caraka Saṃhitā* contains several passages extolling the virtues of the good doctor:

> *Everyone admires a twice-born [i.e., brahmin] physician who is courteous, wise, self-disciplined, and a master of his subject. He is like a guru, a master of life itself. On completing his studentship a physician is said to be born again: the title 'doctor' [vaidya] is earned, not inherited. On completing his studentship a spirit, be it divine or heroic, enters firmly into him because of his knowledge: that is why the physician is called 'twice-born'. For someone being dragged into death's realm by savage diseases, no benefactor, either religious or worldly, can match the person who holds out life. There is no gift to compare with the gift of life. The practitioner of medicine who believes that his highest calling is the care of others achieves the highest happiness. He fulfills himself.*[23]

and condemning quacks:

> *Attired in doctors' outfits, they wander the streets looking for work. As soon as they hear that someone is ill, they descend on him and in his hearing speak loudly of their medical expertise. If a doctor is already in attendance on him, they constantly harp on that doctor's failings. They try to ingratiate themselves with the patient's friends with jokes, confidences, and flattery. They put it about that they won't want much money ... but when they fail to avert the illness they point out that it was the patient himself who lacked equipment, helpers and the right attitude.*[24]

Caraka also presents an 'Oath of Initiation' which has often been compared with the Hippocratic Oath. During a rite of initiation at the beginning of a pupil's tutelage in Ayurveda he had to swear to live a celibate life, to speak the truth, to eat a vegetarian diet, to be free of envy and never to carry arms; he was to subject himself to his teacher completely, except where this would bring him into conflict with higher ethical values; he was to work day and night for the relief of his patients, and was never to desert them, nor take advantage of them sexually; he was to withhold treatment from enemies of the king, wicked people generally, and from women who were unattended by their husbands or guardians; he was to visit the patient's home only in the company of a mutual acquaintance, and moreover, was to treat as totally confidential any privileged information acquired concerning the patient's household.[25]

In practice

The diagnostic and practical aspects of Ayurveda depended on a thorough knowledge of the Sanskrit texts. The good physician (*vaidya*) memorised a vast amount of material, which consisted largely of medical verses giving correspondences between the three humours, wind, bile and phlegm (*vāyu*, *pitta*, *śleṣman*) and the different symptoms, diseases, herbs, and treatments. When confronted with a patient, the *vaidya* examined the patient and his or her symptoms, and verses would spring to his mind which encapsulated the condition confronting him. These verses would trigger the memory of further verses which contained the same key combinations of humoral references, and presented a prognosis and treatment.[26] The *vaidya* was operating in a rich semantic field of correspondences, offering innumerable possibilities for diagnosis and treatment. The Ayurvedic schemes of substances, qualities, and actions offered the physician an excellent combination of the freedom to act and a structure within which to exercise choice. It is important to see the practice of Ayurveda in the context of oral traditions, in which vast amounts of memorised textual material is 'recreated' orally to suit particular circumstances, while remaining true to the fundamental meaning of the text.[27]

Of course Ayurveda had (and has) its poor practitioners and the texts face up to the problem of bad doctors. To be good at Ayurveda required not only years of training as a youngster, but also native intelligence and sensitivity.[28] But in the absence of a centralised system of qualification and testing, *vaidyas* were judged by reputation alone, and Sanskrit literature contains sharply satirical passages about dangerously ill-qualified physicians.[29]

Surgery

The *Suśruta Saṃhitā* tends to be known for its extensive chapter on surgery, which retains its power to impress even today. Caraka too has brief descriptions of surgical techniques, but the *Suśruta Saṃhitā* goes into much greater detail, describing how a surgeon should be trained, and exactly how various operations should be done. There are descriptions of ophthalmic couching, cutting for stone, removal of arrows and splinters, suturing, the examination of dead human bodies for the study of anatomy, and much besides. Suśruta claims that surgery is the most ancient and most efficacious of the eight branches of medical knowledge.[30] It is certain that elaborate surgical techniques were practised in Suśruta's circle. But there is little evidence to show that these practices persisted beyond the time of the composition of the text. Some of the techniques may have survived as caste skills, isolated from the maistream of Ayurvedic practice. For example, a description of the couching operation for cataract survives in the ninth-century *Kalyāṇakāraka* by Ugrāditya,[31] and texts based on the *Suśruta Saṃhitā* copy out the sections on surgery along with other material. But there is no evidence from other historical sources that the sophisticated surgery described by Suśruta was actually practised by *vaidyas*.[32] Medical texts do not contain any development of surgical ideas, nor do any genuinely ancient or medieval surgical instruments survive. Surgery is not described in literary or other sources, except as science fiction. It may be that as the caste system grew in rigidity through the first millenium AD, taboos concerning physical contact became almost insurmountable and *vaidyas* may have resisted therapies that involved cutting into the body. Against this it may

Occulist (sathiyā) treating a patient, with specialist instruments laid out before him. Company artist, 1825. The British Library, London.

Earpicker, specialist in removing wax, (Kan mal walāh) with his instruments laid out before him. Company artist, 1825. The British Library, London.

be argued that the examination of the pulse and urine gained in popularity, as did massage therapies. But whatever the reasons, the early efflorescence of sophisticated surgical knowledge seems to have been an isolated phenomenon.

There is, however, one famous historical event which is often cited as evidence that Suśruta's surgery was widely known even up to modern times. In March 1793, an operation took place in Poona which was to change the course of plastic surgery in Europe. A Maratha named Cowasjee,[33] who had been a bullock-driver with the English army in the war of 1792, was captured by the forces of Tipu Sultan, and had his nose and one hand cut off. After a year without a nose, he turned to a man of the brickmakers' caste, near Poona, to have his face repaired. Thomas Cruso and James Trindlay, British surgeons in the Bombay Presidency, witnessed this operation (or one just like it), and appear to have prepared a description of what they saw, together with a painting of the patient and diagrams of the skin graft procedure. These details, with diagrams and an engraving from the painting, were published at third hand in London in 1794.[34] The description showed that the anonymous brickmaker had performed a magnificent skin graft and nose reconstruction, using a technique that was superior to anything the English surgeons had ever seen. The technique was taken up in Europe and is still known as the 'Hindu method' today.

The first known published description of plastic surgery in the west accompanied this engraving of a subject with a reconstructed nose by skin graft, after a painting by James Wales, commissioned in 1794 by two British surgeons, James Trindlay and Thomas Cruso. Wellcome Institute, London.

This would at first sight seem to be a triumphant vindication of the historical persistence of Suśruta's surgery. But there are several puzzling elements to the story which belie this initial impression. One of the most important is that the rhinoplasty operation is not described in any detail in the *Suśruta Saṃhitā*. The Sanskrit text says:

> *Now I shall carefully describe how to repair a severed nose. Take the leaf of a tree, of the same measure as his nose, and append it. The same size should be cut from the side of the cheek. Now it is attached to the end of the nose. With care the physician should scratch it and then swiftly tie it up with a clean bandage. After checking that it is properly joined, he should raise it and attach two reeds. Then he should powder it with sandalwood, liquorice and collyrium. Covering it completely with white cotton he should sprinkle it several times with the oil of sesame seeds. Once his digestion is over, the man should be made to drink ghee, anointed and purged, according to the rules. That repair should become healed; if there is half of it left, it should be cut again. If, however, it is small, one should try to stretch it, and one should even out any excess flesh.*[35]

The Sanskrit text of this passage is brief and laconic, and certainly not detailed enough to be followed without an oral commentary and practical demonstration. Also, no surviving manuscript of the text contains any illustration. In fact, there is no tradition of anatomical manuscript illustration in India at all. In other words, it would not be possible for the tradition to have persisted purely textually.

Furthermore, as a member of the brickmakers' caste, the surgeon who performed the Poona operation was not a traditional physician or *vaidya*, and probably knew no Sanskrit at all. He had the skill in his hands, not in his head. And the skill that he had would probably have been specific to his caste, or even family. Indeed, maybe it was an extraordinary survival of a technique from Suśruta's time, but in that case it was transmitted by means wholly outside the learned practice of traditional Indian physicians. There is also no clear evidence from any other historical sources that such operations were ever performed in medieval times. Indeed, the contrary is true.

Whatever the not inconsiderable complications that surround this case, it demonstrates the presence of a major

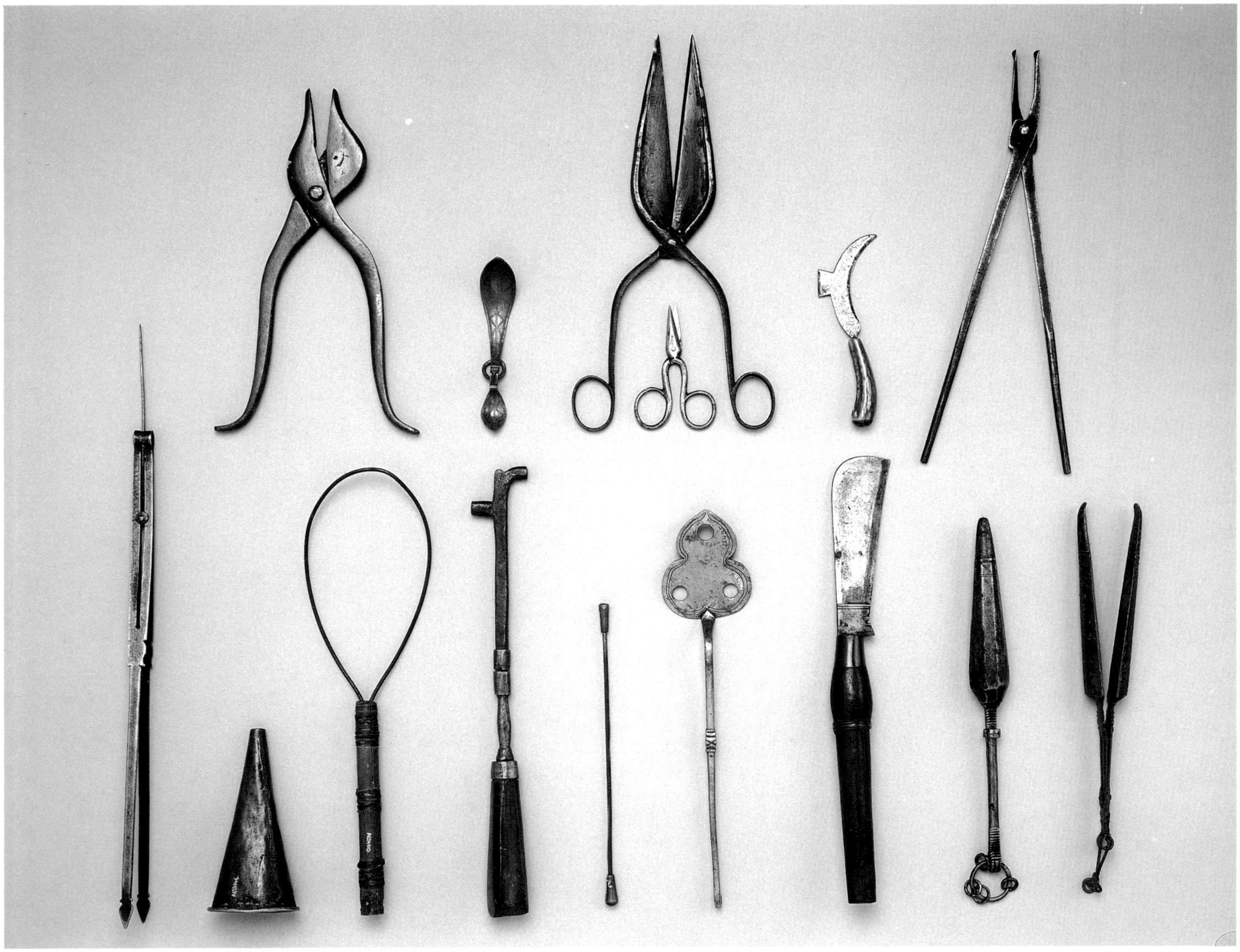

Medical and surgical implements of 19th century Indian origin. Although surgery was extensively described in the Suśruta Saṃhitā, its practice seems to have survived only in isolated castes of non-physicians during the 19th century (see page 43). According to Suśruta there were 101 instruments classified as either 'blunt' or 'sharp', but he recognised the main implement as the hand. Science Museum, London.

medical practice in the late eighteenth century appearing apparently from nowhere, millennia after being invented and laconically sketched out in the ancient texts.

Inoculation

Before the twentieth century, inoculation—the deliberate infection of a healthy patient—was the only means of protection from smallpox. The patient was prepared beforehand to be in the best possible health, and was kept quarantined and in a controlled environment, in the hope that the smallpox episode would be mild. If the patient survived, and many did, he or she would thereafter be immune to smallpox. The practice of inoculation first became known to European science after Lady Mary Wortley Montague observed market women practising inoculation in Constantinople. She had the courage to have her own children inoculated, and then returned to England in 1717 to preach the new technique. It was to provoke a terrific controversy which took on political and theological overtones, and grew stronger until Edward Jenner's discovery of vaccination in 1796 rendered the practice of inoculation obsolete. Nevertheless, for a considerable amount of time, inoculation, with all its inherent risks and dangers, was the only known defence against smallpox.

Inoculation was current in Turkey in the early eighteenth century; there is evidence that it may have been brought to Turkey from China. It is interesting, then, to find a detailed account by a renowned English surgeon in 1767, describing the widespread practice of inoculation in Bengal.[36] There is also some evidence to push the Indian practice of inoculation back further, to 1731.[37] Once again, there is a historical paradox here: there is not the slightest trace of this important and effective treatment in any of the Sanskrit medical treatises. Smallpox was certainly recognised in Ayurvedic texts, where it is called *masūrikā* ('lentil' disease) and was treated after a fashion. But of inoculation there is absolutely no mention. The link between theory and practice is broken once again.

After smallpox vaccine was introduced to India in 1802, a rumour was started in 1819 by an article in *The Madras Courier*, a popular daily newspaper, to the effect that there existed an ancient Sanskrit text describing in detail the process of vaccination. This proved, it was argued, the superiority of ancient Indian science, and that 'there is nothing new under the sun'. Unfortunately, this rumour gained currency and was republished in books and encyclopaedias across Europe all through the nineteenth century, and it even surfaces today. Careful literary research has shown, however, that no such Sanskrit text exists, and that the whole affair was almost certainly triggered by the excessive zeal of British vaccination propagandists, who composed tracts on vaccination in local languages and probably in Sanskrit too. One of these tracts was so convincing that the belief was born of an ancient Indian knowledge of the technique.[38]

These cases, the rhinoplasty and the inoculation, demonstrate that in the history of Indian medicine, all is not what it seems. Techniques in the texts fell into disuse, while new discoveries were widely practised apparently without impinging on the traditional medical establishment. Perhaps this situation is not entirely unlike that of today, with the growing popular acceptance of alternative medicine which is often ignored by the medical establishment.

This is not to deny that there was a strong core of continuity throughout the tradition. A great deal of what is practised by Ayurvedic physicians in Indian villages today is derived directly from the classical schools of medicine which were so creative nearly two thousand years ago, and this practice has been the basis of healthcare in India in all that time. Yet time affected the Indian medical tradition, as it affects all things.

Change and continuity

It has long been presupposed by historians of Indian medicine that the Ayurvedic tradition was static, that later texts merely elaborated a unified theory already present in the earlier texts, the *Caraka Saṃhitā* and the *Suśruta Saṃhitā*. This view of Ayurveda was partly due to the fact that these two texts present themselves as timeless bodies of celestial knowledge, containing no programme for development or change, and partly because it conformed to uncritical ideas of India as the home of timeless truths. The idea that Ayurveda never evolved also flourished for the simple reason that the research needed to discover evidence of change in the tradition is very difficult, and very detailed. It requires that a vast body of medieval Sanskrit medical literature be read, and that detailed indexes of diseases, therapies and diagnostic techniques be compiled.

While the most famous texts of the system, mentioned above, are indeed homogeneous to a great extent, Meulenbeld's recent pioneering researches into the history of Sanskrit Ayurvedic literature have revealed that many authors refused to submit to the orthodox point of view, and stuck to their own ideas.[39] Many new diseases were identified and described in the course of time. For example, from the sixteenth century we find syphilis (*phiraṅgaroga*, 'foreigners' disease') described in texts like Bhāvamiśra's *Bhāvaprakāśa*; it was treated with mercury. From the eighteenth century onwards we find texts including descriptions of diseases clearly borrowed from Western medicine. Other diseases that were described in early texts disappear from the literature.

Developments also took place in the field of diagnostics. The detailed and systematic examination of urine (*mūtraparīkṣā*) is a relatively late development, dating from about the eleventh century. The examination of the pulse (*nāḍīparīkṣā*) is never found in Sanskrit texts before about the thirteenth century, but it subsequently became a diagnostic method of first resort. A diagnostic technique called 'examination of the eight bases' (*aṣṭasthānaparīkṣā*), which meant a routine for examining the pulse, urine, faeces, tongue, eyes, general appearance, voice, and skin of the patient began to appear in texts from the beginning of the sixteenth century.

New prognostic methods also came into use. For example, from about the sixteenth century, a technique developed whereby a drop of oil would be placed in the surface of a patient's urine. The remaining span of the patient's life would be read from the way the oil spread out.[40]

In therapy, one of the most noticeable changes over the centuries was the explosive growth of standardised compound medicines (*yoga*). A yoga normally consists of a large number of ingredients, and is described in terms of its effect against a particular disease or ailment. Its therapeutic use speaks against the view that each patient was treated holistically, as a person in relation to his or her environment, with certain habits, disposition, etc. Although such ideas are certainly present in the early texts, the growth of the use of yogas speaks for much more standardised therapeutic methods, with generalised medicines targeted at diseases, over the heads of the patients, so to speak. This development has continued today with the growth of a large pharmaceutical industry devoted to the manufacture of standardised Ayurvedic medicines. Most Ayurvedic medicines today are of this type, and it is rare to find a practitioner who will prescribe and prepare a medicine specific to a particular patient, as the old texts recommend. Also noticeable is the increasing use in the tradition of astrological, alchemical, and magical methods of healing.

Finally, the enormous Indian pharmacopoeia was subject to far-reaching changes. Meulenbeld has categorised these changes as follows:[41]

- the decline of knowledge with respect to the identity of medicinal substances;
- the change of identity of plants designated by means of a particular name;
- the appearance of new names and synonyms;
- the use of substitutes for drugs which had become rare;
- the introduction of new drugs.

The study of this subject is beset by difficulties, but many examples of all these cases can be cited. Indian Ayurvedic medicine certainly changed over the centuries, and in non-trivial ways. The study of these changes is still nascent, but promises to be full of interest.

An Ayurvedic drugstore in Kathmandu, Nepal. Although traditional drugstores in Kathmandu sell proprietary medicines from Ayurvedic pharmaceutical companies, most pharmacists will prepare drugs according to physicians' prescriptions.

Ayurveda is the 'great tradition' of indigenous Indian medicine, the Sanskritic, literate system that received royal patronage. There are other 'great' traditions in this sense: the Siddha system of the Tamils, and the Unani system of Islam. There is also a whole range of therapies traceable in the subcontinent, from folk medicine and shamanism through astrology to faith healing. I can do no more than mention some of these.

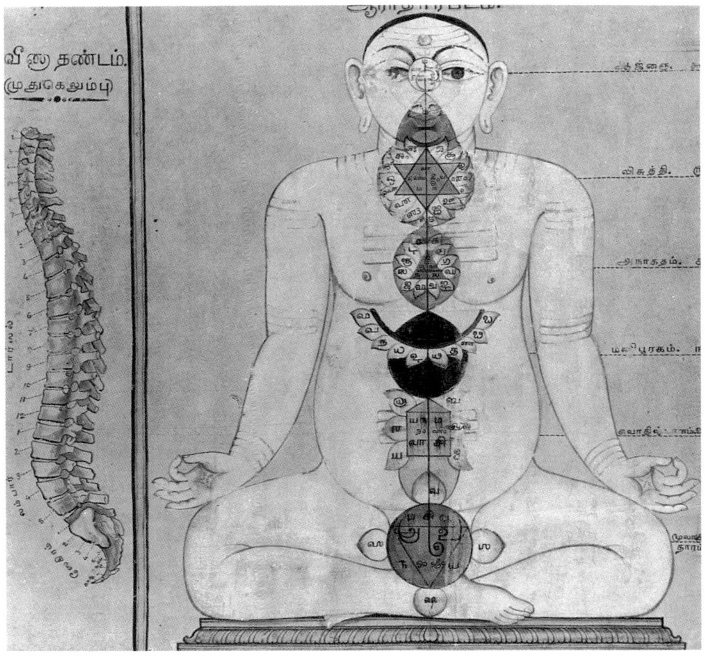

The six cakras of the 'Subtle Body'. In tantric yoga the inner central column of the spine is identified with the axis of Mount Meru or the cosmos. In this painting the position of the cakras is related to an anatomically correct spine as well as to various divinities. Tanjore, Tamil Nadu, 19th century. National Museum, New Delhi.

Siddha Medicine

In south India, a system of medicine evolved in the Tamil-speaking areas that was different in certain conceptions from Ayurveda. Known as Siddha medicine (Tamil *cittar*), this was—and is—primarily an esoteric alchemical and magical system, apparently strongly influenced by tantric thought and Ayurveda, about which very little has been written.[42] It is marked by a greater use of metals, in particular mercury, than is the case in Ayurveda, and holds particular reverence for a substance called *muppū*, which is believed to hold potent powers, for both physical and spiritual transformation.[43] Taking the pulse is more prominent as a diagnostic procedure in Siddha medicine than in Ayurveda, and it has been suggested that Ayurvedic pulse diagnosis—which is not common before the late thirteenth century—was borrowed from Siddha medicine.[44] The semi-legendary founders of Siddha medicine include Bogar, who is believed to have travelled to China, teaching and learning alchemical lore. Other legends include stories of a Siddha called Rāmadevar 'who travelled to Mecca, assumed the name Yakub, and taught the Arabians the alchemical art'.[45]

Siddha is very popular in contemporary Tamil south India, offering a heady mix of mysticism, medicine, and magic. Siddha practitioners draw partly on a developed literary tradition of early Tamil writings on medicine and spirituality, and partly on folk traditions. The medicines that a Siddha may offer are considered uniquely potent, and often contain metals such as mercury. A Tamil Siddha is believed to be able to cure innumerable diseases, to remedy barrenness or sterility, to appear to someone at a distance to warn them against imminent danger, to change female children into male, to control people, animals, and inanimate objects at a distance, to know another's thoughts, to live without food, drink or sleep, and to feed a multitude with a single portion of food. As such, the Siddha system combines elements of medicine, religion, yoga, and tantra that are found separately elsewhere in Indian tradition.

Astrological Medicine

From the earliest times, Ayurveda treated a range of children's diseases as being due to the malign influence of celestial demons (*graha*, 'seizer') who were believed to attack children and to afflict them with a range of symptoms.[46] The Sanskrit word *graha* was later used to mean 'planet', and although *grahas* are clearly described as celestial beings in the *Suśruta Saṃhitā*, the later evolution of rites for planetary propitiation are clearly aimed at the same types of influence.

The literatures of Indian astrology (*jyotiḥśāstra*) and religious law (*dharmaśāstra*) include texts for pacifying the planets, as well as prognostications regarding such matters as pregnancy, the sex of unborn children, the interpretation of dreams, sickness, and death.[47] Private booklets containing invocations for pacifying the planets, as well as prayers and rituals for safeguarding children were not uncommon.[48] As an ancient and influential treatise on law and conduct says:

> *One desirous of prosperity, of removing evil or calamities, of rainfall (for crops), long life, bodily health and one desirous of performing magic rites against enemies and others should perform a sacrifice to planets.*[49]

A work exemplifying the close relationship between medicine and astrology as therapeutic systems is the *Vīrasiṃhāvaloka* by Vīrasiṃha, composed in AD 1383, probably in Gwalior. It treats the aetiology and therapy of groups of

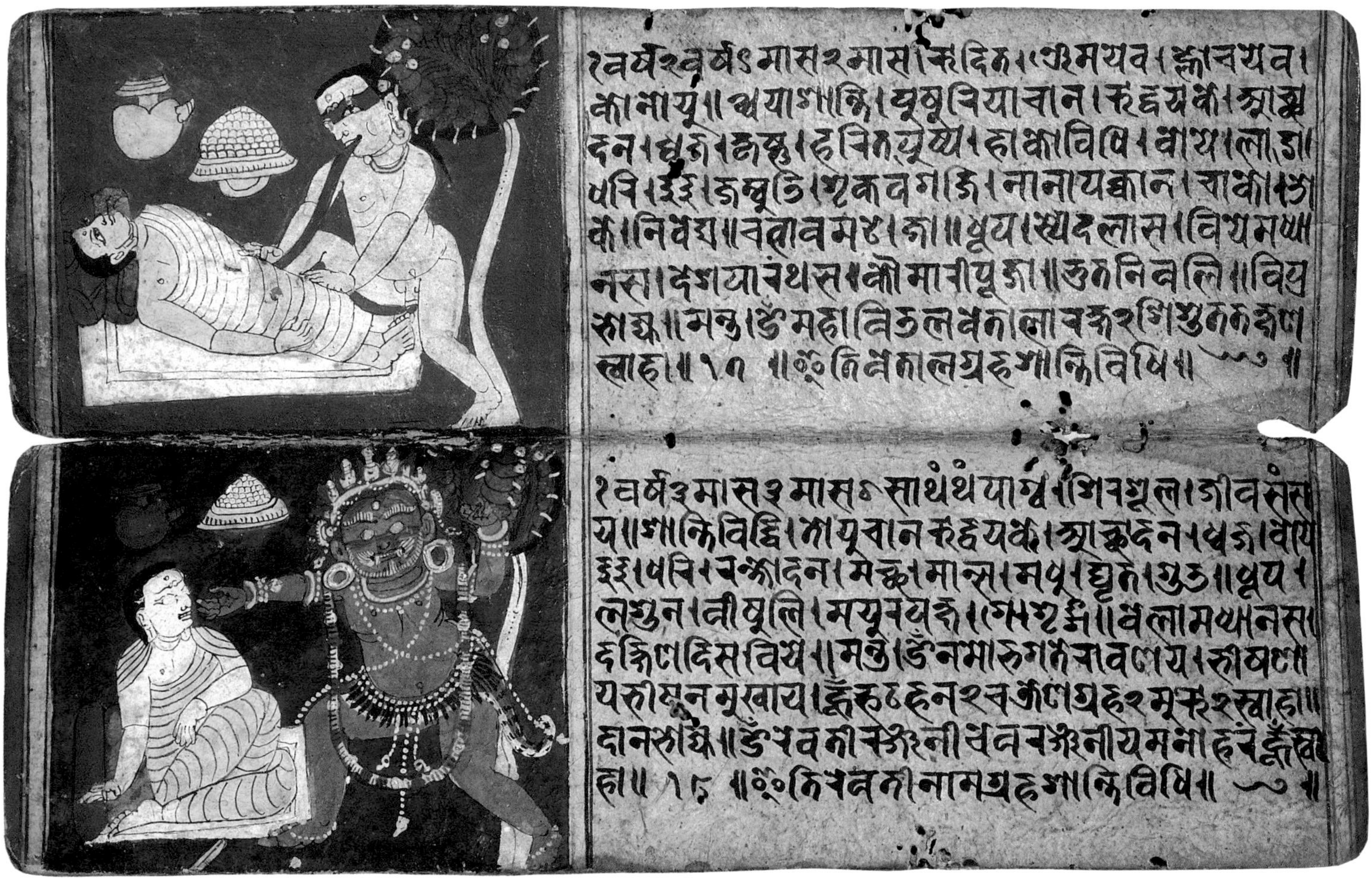

Medico-astrological text: Graha Śānti Vidhi. This illustrated manuscript shows how to avoid the malific influence of 'grahas' (demons) that attack children at certain stages (days, months and years) of life. Nepal, 17th century. Collection: Muriel and Jack Zimmerman, New York.

diseases from three distinct points of view: that of astrology, that of religion,[50] and that of medicine.

Even today, Indian astrologers and physicians are expected to provide charms and prayers to ward off evil influences from the planets and elsewhere. The parts of the body are conceptually equated with the constellations and planets in a complex scheme of relationships and influences, and the astrolger 'reads' this structure of symbols in order to understand his patient's problem and to suggest such remedies as amulets, penances and prayers, as well as herbal decoctions.[51] A breathtaking variety of omens has formed a compelling element in the daily life of Indians for millennia, and many of these omens have to do with health and sickness.[52] Bookshops in India frequently stock numerous texts on astrology and healing for popular consumption.[53]

It is worth noting that the Bower manuscript, one of the oldest surviving Indian codices, contains not only important examples of fifth-century medical literature, but also a text on divination by dice.[54] Considered as a cluster of related texts, the Bower manuscript shows us a cross-section of the concerns of a fifth-century healer: he was specially interested in medicinal uses of garlic, elixirs for eternal life, the treatment of eye diseases, herbal medicines, butter decoctions, oils, aphrodisiacs, the care of children, and spells against the bite of the cobra, as well as the aforementioned divinations.

Shamanistic Healing

Sudhir Kakar has written engagingly of a number of shamanistic and folk healers in modern India, and it is certain that such practices have been common in India since earliest times.[55] In fact, there are clearly elements within Ayurveda itself that stem from such folk traditions. Patients with a range of beliefs about devils and spirit possession visit such practitioners. It is interesting to note that shamans are not opposed to recommending patients to cosmopolitan medical clinics if they recognise an ailment such as an ulcer or high blood pressure.[56]

Foreign Influences

The coming of Islamic medicine

Unani *tibb* (medicine) is the name given to the medical practice brought to India with Islam, which began to have a major impact on India starting with the Afghan invasions of Gujarat in the early eleventh century. The word *ūnānī* (sometimes spelt *yūnānī*) is an Indian representation of the name 'Ionian'. Unani medicine is the system founded on that of Galen, and in particular as interpreted in Avicenna's (AD 980–1037) work *Al-Qānūn fi l-ṭibb*. Unani medicine is still very much alive in India today, and it is fascinating to consider that a fundamentally Galenic medicine is still in contemporary practice.

As might be expected, Unani medicine and Ayurveda have influenced each other, especially in the realm of *materia medica*. Although the primary languages of Unani medicine are, of course, Persian and Arabic, there are even Sanskrit texts on Unani. For example, the eighteenth century work *Hikmatprakāśa* was written in Sanskrit by the pious Hindu, Mahādevadeva.[57] Unani medicine postulates four basic humours, as opposed to Ayurveda's three, and Unani medicine is more oriented towards the treatment of patients in hospitals. The major difference between these systems, however, is in their clientele. Broadly, Unani physicians treat Muslim patients and Ayurvedic physicians treat Hindus.

The Portuguese and Dutch

In the first half of the sixteenth century, the Portuguese arrived in Goa. The first medical book printed in India—and only the third book printed in India—was the *Coloquios dos simples, e drogas he cousas mediçinais da India ...* or *Colloquies on the medical simples and drugs of India* by Garcia d'Orta, printed in Goa in 1563. D'Orta gathered a mass of material from the local physicians, and learned as much as he could of their methods, even competing with them for rich clients.[58] There was a free and fertile exchange of medical ideas between the Portuguese and the Indians for much of the rest of the sixteenth century. But despite this promising beginning, the relationship declined and during the early decades of the seventeenth century the Portuguese introduced restrictions that effectively outlawed Hindu physicians.

The Dutch East India officials showed great interest in the local flora and fauna of the Malabar coast from the end of the seventeenth century onwards. Heinrich van Rheed, who was appointed Governor of the Dutch possessions in 1667, prepared a magnificent series of 12 folio volumes, published between 1686 and 1703 in Amsterdam, which contained nearly eight hundred plates of Indian plants, a work much admired by Sir William Jones. Other works of a similar scale were produced, including the work of van Rheed's appointee to Ceylon, Paul Herman, whose herbarium and *Museum Zeylanicum* were major sources of Linnaeus' 1747 *Flora Zeylanica*.[59]

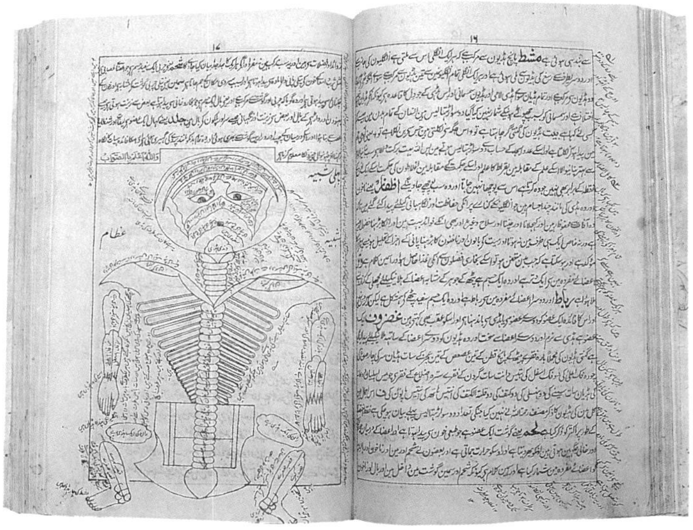

Medical textbook showing the skeletal system. Dissection of the human body was not allowed under Islamic law and for anatomical knowledge Muslims had to rely on Galen's concept of anatomy supplemented with their own observations. Library of the Nizamia General Unani Hospital, Hyderabad.

The British

The British arrived in India at the beginning of the seventeenth century, in the form of the East India Company. The influence of 'John Company' grew steadily over the succeeding years until a flurry of battles and political acquisitions at the start of the nineteenth century projected the Company into the position of de facto government in large parts of India. In 1858 the Company was dissolved, and India was placed directly under the British crown.

The history of British medicine during this period belongs to the larger context of colonial and imperial medicine and the birth of tropical medicine, but some remarks should be made here about the interaction between British and indigenous physicians.

During the seventeenth century, there were relatively small numbers of English traders in India, and like the

Opposite: Classical Ayurvedic literature contains many references to yoga. The Śarīra-sthāna chapters of the Suśruta Saṃhitā are intended 'for the very purpose of the men of medical profession and the members of yogic discipline'. The anatomy of the body in yoga is explained with the help of Ayurvedic terms. Today, the beneficial effect of yoga on body-mind is generally admitted. Three miniatures of yogic postures (āsanas) accompanied by explanations in Brajbhasa verse from an early nineteenth century album containing 84 Hatha-yoga postures and twenty-four asanas. The British Library, London.

Portuguese and the Dutch before them, they faced a completely new set of health problems in India. They were keen to learn from the local *vaidyas* and *hakīms*, and local remedies and regimens were often adopted. Missionaries were particularly active in both teaching and learning from indigenous practitioners, a task made easier by their mastery of local languages. For their part, the Indians were particularly interested in British surgeons since, in spite of the early evidence of the *Suśruta Saṃhitā*, surgery had passed almost completely out of practice amongst *vaidyas*. The French traveller Tavernier reported in 1684 that once when the King of Golconda had a headache and his native physicians prescribed that blood should be let in four places under his tongue, nobody could be found to do it, 'for the Natives of the Country understand nothing of Chirurgery'.[60] Two hundred years later, Sir William Sleeman observed:

> *The educated class, as indeed all classes, say that they do not want our physicians, but stand much in need of our surgeons. Here they feel that they are helpless, and we are strong; and they seek our aid whenever they see any chance of obtaining it...*[61]

A persistent factor encouraging the British physicians to adopt Indian methods was the sheer difficulty and expense of shipping medical supplies from Europe. When the *British Pharmacopoeia* was formalised in 1858, the idea of a formal and legally enforceable standard for drugs took hold, and caused many British physicians in India to grow increasingly critical of the crudeness of indigenous drugs. Yet in the 1860s economic pressures forced the Medical Department of the Bengal Presidency to declare that indigenous drugs should be used wherever possible.[62] In the longer term, feelings against Indian medicine hardened, in common with attitudes to all indigenous skills and sciences, and after official government support for Indian medicine ceased in 1835, Ayurvedic and Unani physicians were thrown back on their own private resources for training and practice.[63]

Tapakara āsana

Ayurveda continued to be the main system of professional healthcare in India under the British Raj, which initially encouraged its study alongside British medicine when medical colleges were founded in Bengal and elsewhere. But with the change of British educational policy, after Lord Bentinck's educational reforms of 1835, and the end of Ayurvedic teaching in state-funded medical colleges, government support for Ayurvedic training ceased. Ayurvedic practitioners continued to practise however, although their training was reduced to the traditional family apprenticeship system, and privately sponsored colleges.

Contemporary Pluralistic Medicine

With the rise of the Indian independence movement, all indigenous traditions received strong support from nationalists. Since Independence in 1947, the Indian Government has oscillated between a commitment to modern cosmopolitan medicine, and the necessity of grappling with the unavoidable fact that Ayurvedic medicine is widely accepted in

Parasarām āsana

Vaspamudrā

India, especially in rural areas. Furthermore, Ayurveda remains strongly identified with Indian nationalistic sentiments.[64] The Indian Government has sponsored a number of commissions and studies regarding national health care provision, with widely varying outcomes.

The current situation is complicated but the basic fact is that after much debate over several decades the Indian Government recognises a place for Ayurvedic medicine in its overall health policy. It has become clear that modern cosmopolitan medicine has not been very successful in penetrating the countryside, and that by contrast Ayurvedic practitioners are more likely to work in villages. This view was encouraged by the Ramalingaswami report of 1980 which promoted several ideas along the lines of the Chinese 'barefoot doctor' schemes, and was accepted as Government policy.

Today, Government-accredited colleges and universities provide professional training and qualifications in Ayurveda. This training includes some basic education in Western cosmopolitan methods, family planning and public health. Graduates of such institutions are recognised by the Government in so far as they may be employed as the third medical officer at Primary Health Care Centres, and as community health volunteers. Many run successful clinics in urban as well as rural settings. Private Ayurvedic practitioners also prescribe modern cosmopolitan medicines and treatments, often at the insistence of their patients, and this tends to happen with varying degrees of impunity.[65]

Government control of indigenous medicine—where it exists at all—continues to be highly pragmatic and based on local political decisions. The idea that Ayurvedic physicians deal purely in innocuous herbs, roots and therapeutic massage is a grossly simplified representation of what really happens in indigenous medical circles today.

In contemporary India, the patient, or indeed the healthy person, may take any of many available paths towards greater health. There exist physicians of cosmopolitan medicine, Ayurveda, and Unani, as well as homoeopaths, naturopaths, traditional bone-setters, yoga teachers, massage and enema therapists, faith healers, famous gurus, traditional midwives and the wandering specialists who remove the wax from the ears. The variety is overwhelming, both as a subject of study, and as a subjective experience.

Notes

1 Bridget and Raymond Allchin 1982, pp. 221 ff.
2 *Ibid.*, p. 215.
3 Herman Kulke and Dietmar Rothermund 1990, pp. 30-3.
4 For an excellent discussion of these migrations see Colin Renfrew 1989.
5 See K.G. Zysk 1985.
6 K.G. Zysk 1985, pp. 70-1.
7 J. Mitra 1985; K.G. Zysk 1991, chapters 2 and 3.
8 K.G. Zysk 1991, p. 40.
9 *Ibid.*, p. 44 ff.
10 *Ibid.*, pp. 117-9 *et passim.*
11 D. Chattopadhyaya 1977.
12 *Caraka Saṃhitā* 1.30.23.
13 A.C. Burnell 1880, p. 63b.
14 For recently revised judgements concerning the date of the Buddha, see Heinz Bechert 1982, p. 10, 29 ff.
15 Shree Gulabkunverba Ayurvedic Society, *The Caraka Saṃhitā ... with Translations in Hindu, Gujarati and English*, vol. 5: *English Translation*, Jamnagar, Gulabkunverba Ayurvedic Society, 1949.
16 Bhishagratna, Kaviraj Junja Lal, *An English Translation of the Sushruta Samhita, Based on Original Sanskrit Text*, 3 vols., Calcutta, Bhaduri, 1907-1916.
17 F. Zimmerman 1989, pp. 40-8 *et passim.*
18 The aphorism (*śataślokena paṇḍitaḥ*) is reported by M. Seshagiri Sastri 1898, p. 26.
19 References are to the chapters (*sthāna*) and sections (*adhyāya*) of the texts.
20 See, for example, A. Comba 1991, chapter 1 'Medicina e Filosofia', pp. 35-77.
21 See Priyadaranjan Rây and Hirendra Nath Gupta 1965, tables 1-3.
22 See Julia Leslie 1989, pp. 59-61.
23 *Caraka Saṃhitā* 6.1, pāda 4, verses 51-3, 60-2.
24 *Caraka Saṃhitā* 1.29, verse 9.
25 *Caraka Saṃhitā* 3.8.13-14.
26 F. Zimmerman 1987, chapter 5 'Logic and cuisine'; and 1989, chapter 4, 'Ethnoscience et rhétorique'.
27 A.B. Lord 1960.
28 Guido Majno 1975, pp. 271-304, presents several interesting vignettes reconstructing the *vaidya* at work.
29 For example, the *Narmamālā* of Kṣemendra (2.68-81) cited by A.L. Basham in C. Leslie 1976, pp. 30-1.
30 *Suśruta Saṃhitā* 1.1.15-19.
31 Cited in G.J. Meulenbeld 1984, p. 67, n. 76.
32 Robert Henry Elliot 1917, describes couching operations which were carried out by traditional practitioners at the beginning of the twentieth century. Elliot admits that he never saw the operation himself, and all his material is at second hand. Nevertheless his reports suggest that the operation was indeed practised, though not by *vaidyas*.
33 Puzzlingly, this is a Parsee name.
34 *The Gentleman's Magazine and Historical Chronicle*, vol. 64(2), October 1794, pp. 883, 891, 892.
35 *Suśruta Saṃhitā* 1.16.28-33.
36 J.Z. Holwell 1767.
37 Letter of February 10, 1731, from Ro. Coult in Calcutta to Dr. Oliver Coult giving 'An Account of the Diseases of Bengall'. Ff. 271 v-272r of Add. MS 4432 of the Royal Society Papers in the British Library, published in Dharampal 1971, 141 f., 276.
38 D. Wujastyk 1987, pp. 139-67.
39 See G.J. Meulenbeld 1984, pp. 37 ff, and his forthcoming opus, *A History of Sanskrit Medical Literature*, Royal Asiatic Society.
40 This practice was reported at the end of the seventeenth century by John Ovington 1696, pp. 351 ff.
41 G.J. Meulenbeld 1984, pp. 48-56.
42 S.V. Subramanian and V.R. Madhavan 1983; Guy Mazars 1984, pp. 123-9; K.V. Zvelebil 1973.
43 K.V. Zvelebil 1979, pp. 1-9; D.M. Bose, S.N. Sen and B.V. Subbarayappa (eds.) 1971, pp. 335-8.
44 E.V. Daniel 1984, pp. 115-26.
45 D.M. Bose, S.N. Sen and B.V. Subbarayappa (eds.) 1971, p. 318.
46 *Suśruta Saṃhitā* 6.27-37, 60-2.
47 D. Pingree 1974, pp. 110 ff.
48 For example, Wellcome MS Sanskrit 456.
49 Nārāyaṇa Rāma Acārya (ed.) 1949, 1.295, p. 103; cited in P.V. Kane 1977, chapter 21: 'Individual Śāntis', pp. 748-814.
50 Actually, *karmavipāka*, the ripening of deeds performed in former lives.
51 J. Pugh in E.V. Daniel and J. Pugh (eds.) 1984, pp. 85-105.
52 D. Pingree, *op. cit.*, chapter 4.
53 Such texts as J.N. Bhasin 1986, and J. Rao 1972.
54 A.F.R. Hoernle (ed. and tr.) 1893-1912. The dicing text appears to be in a different handwriting from the medical tracts, but this does not necessarily mean that it was not part of a single handbook.
55 S. Kakar 1984; see also O.P. Jaggi 1973.
56 The first case is described in Kakar 1984, p. 97; the second is a personal observation.
57 Described in G.J. Meulenbeld, forthcoming (see note 39).
58 T.J.S. Patterson in D. Wujastyk and G.J. Meulenbeld (eds.) 1987, p. 120.
59 D.M. Bose *et al.* 1971, p. 401.
60 J. Tavernier 1684, book 1, part 2, p. 103.
61 W.H. Sleeman 1893, vol. 1, p. 130.
62 P. Bala 1990, 1.171.
63 See B. Gupta 1976, p. 369 f.
64 See the strongly supportive remarks on Ayurveda published by the Government of India in its *Report on the Sanskrit Commission*, 1956-57, Delhi, Govt. of India Press, 1958, pp. 214-16.
65 For example, many people regard the injection as a powerful, almost magical cure for most ailments. Separate vernacular tracts exist extolling the virtues of 'injection therapy' (see S. Gupta 1983), and the physician is often under pressure from his patients to provide injections, even if only of water.

References

Allchin, Bridget and Raymond. *The Rise of Civilisation in India and Pakistan*, Cambridge, Cambridge University Press, 1982.

Bala, P. 'State policy towards indigenous drugs in British Bengal', *Journal of the European Āyurvedic Society*, 1990.

Basham, A.L. 'The practice of medicine in ancient and medieval India', in C. Leslie (ed.), 1976.

Bechert, Heinz. 'The date of the Buddha reconsidered', *Indologica Taurinensia*, 1982.

Bhasin, J.N. *Medical Astrology: A Rational Approach*, New Delhi, Sagar, 1986.

Bhishagratna, Kaviraj Junja Lal. *An English Translation of the Sushruta Samhita, Based on Original Sanskrit Text*, 3 vols., Calcutta, Bhaduri, 1907-1916.

Bose, D.M., Sen, S.N., and Subbarayappa, B.V. (eds.). *A Concise History of*

Science in India, New Delhi, Indian National Science Academy, 1971.
Burnell, A.C. *A Classified Index to the Sanskrit MSS. in the Palace at Tanjore*, London, Trübner, 1880.
Chattopadhyaya, Debiprasad. *Science and Society in Ancient India*, Calcutta, Research India Publications, 1977.
Comba, Antonella. *La Medicina Indiana (Āyurveda)*, Torino, Promolibri, 1991.
Daniel, E. Valentine. 'The pulse as an icon in Siddha medicine', in *Contributions to Asian Studies*, vol.18: *South Asian Systems of Healing*, E.V. Daniel and J.F. Pugh (eds.), Leiden, Brill, 1984, pp. 115-26.
Daniel, E.V., and Pugh, J. (eds.). *South Asian Systems of Healing*, vol. 18 *Contributions to Asian Studies*, Leiden, Brill, 1984.
Desmond, R.*The European Discovery of Indian Flora*, 1994
Dharampal. *Indian Science and Technology in the Eighteenth Century*, Delhi, 1971.
Elliot, Robert Henry. *The Indian Operation of Couching for Cataract*, London, H.K. Lewis, 1917.
Gupta, Brahmananda. 'Indigenous medicine in nineteenth and twentieth century Bengal', in C. Leslie (ed.), 1976.
Gupta, Śivadyālu. *Sacitra-Ādhunika Injekśan Cikitsā* [Illustrated Modern Injection Therapy], Vārāṇasī, Kṛṣṇadāsa Akādamī, 1983.
Hoernle, A.F.R. (ed. and tr.). *The Bower Manuscripts*, Archaeological Survey of India, Calcutta, 1893-1912.
Holwell, J.Z. *An Account of the Manner of Inoculating for the Smallpox in the East Indies*, London, 1767.
Jaggi, O.P. *Folk Medicine*, Delhi, Atma Ram, 1973.
Jeffery, Roger. *The Politics of Health in India*, London, University of California Press, 1988.
Jolly, Julius. *Indian Medicine*, 2nd revised edition, New Delhi, Munshiram, 1977.
Kakar, Sudhir. *Shamans, Mystics and Doctors: A Psychological Inquiry into India and its Healing Traditions*, London, Unwin, 1984.
Kane, P.V. *History of Dharmaśāstra (Ancient and Medieval Religious and Civil Law)*, vol. V, part II, second edition, BORI, Pune, 1977.
Kulke, Hermann and Rothermund, Dietmar. *A History of India*, London, Routledge, revised edition 1990.
Leslie, Charles (ed.). *Asian Medical Systems: A Comparative Study*, Berkeley, University of California Press, 1976.
Leslie, Julia. *The Perfect Wife*, Delhi, Oxford University Press, 1989.
Lord, A.B. *The Singer of Tales*, Cambridge MA, Harvard University Press, 1960.
Majno, Guido. *The Healing Hand: Man and Wound in the Ancient World*, Cambridge, Harvard University Press, 1975.
Mazars, Guy. 'Les textes médicaux tamouls', in G.J. Meulenbeld (ed.), 1984.
Meulenbeld, G.J. 'The surveying of Sanskrit medical literature', in G.J. Meulenbeld (ed.), 1984.
___ (ed.). *Proceedings of the International Workshop on Priorities in the Study of Indian Medicine*, Groningen, University of Groningen, 1984.
___ *A History of Sanskrit Medical Literature*, London, Royal Asiatic Society, forthcoming.
Mitra, Jyotir. *A Critical Appraisal of Āyurvedic Material in Buddhist Literature*, Varanasi, Jyotirlok Prakashan, 1985.
Nārāyaṇa Rāma Ācārya (ed.). *Yājñavalkyasmṛtiḥ*, Nirṇayasāgara-mudraṇālaya, Bombay, fifth edition, 1949.
Ovington, John. *A Voyage to Suratt in the Year 1689*, London, Jacob Tonson, 1696.
Patterson, T.J.S. 'The relationship of Indian and European practitioners of medicine from the sixteenth century', in D. Wujastyk and G.J. Meulenbeld (eds.), 1987.
Pingree, David. *Jyotiḥśāstra: Astral and Mathematical Literature*, Wiesbaden, Harrassowitz, 1974.
Pugh, J. 'Concepts of person and situation in north Indian counseling: the case of astrology', in E.V. Daniel and J. Pugh (eds.), 1984, pp. 85-105.
Ramalingaswami, V. *Health for All: An Alternative Strategy*, Report of the Indian Council of Social Science Research and Indian Council of Medical Research Joint Study, 1980.
Rao, Jagannath. *Principles and Practice of Medical Astrology*, New Delhi, Sagar, 1972.
Rây, Priyadaranjan, and Gupta, Hirendra Nath. *Caraka Saṃhitā (A Scientific Synopsis)*, New Delhi, National Institute of Sciences of India, 1965.
Ray, P., Gupta, H., and Roy, M. *Suśruta Saṃhitā (A Scientific Synopsis)*, New Delhi, Indian National Science Academy, 1980.
Renfrew, Colin. *Archaeology and Language: The Puzzle of Indo-European Origins*, 2nd edition, London, Penguin Books, 1989.
Seshagiri Sastri, M. *Report on a Search for Sanskrit and Tamil Manuscripts for the year 1896-97*, no. 1, Madras, Govt. Press, 1898.
Sharma, Priya Vrata. *Caraka Saṃhitā: Agniveśa's Treatise Refined and Annotated by Caraka and Redacted by Dṛḍhabala*, 3 vols., Varanasi, Chaukhambha Orientalia, 1981-85.
Shree Gulabkunverba Ayurvedic Society, *The Caraka Saṃhitā ... with Translations in Hindu, Gujarati and English*, vol. 5: *English Translation*, Jamnagar, Gulabkunverba Ayurvedic Society, 1949.
Sleeman, W.H. *Rambles and Reflections of an Indian Official*, London, Constable, 1893.
Subramanian, S.V., and Madhavan, V.R. *Heritage of the Tamil's Siddha Medicine*, Madras, International Institute of Tamil Studies, 1983.
Tavernier, Jean-Baptiste. *Travels in India*, London, 1684.
Wujastyk, D. 'A pious fraud: the Indian claims for pre-Jennerian smallpox vaccination', in D. Wujastyk and G.J. Meulenbeld (eds.) 1987, pp. 139-67.
Wujastyk, D., and Meulenbeld, G.J. (eds.). *Studies on Indian Medical History*, Groningen, Forsten, 1987.
Zimmerman, Francis. *The Jungle and the Aroma of Meats: An Ecological Theme in Hindu Medicine*, Berkeley, University of California Press, 1987.
___ *Le discours des remèdes au pays des épices: enquête sur la médicine hindoue*, Paris, Payot, 1989.
Zvelebil, Kamil V. *The Poets of the Powers*, London, 1973.
___ 'The ideological basis of the Siddha search for immortality', in *Sources of Illness and Healing in South Asian Regional Literatures*, vol. 8 of *South Asian Digest of Regional Writing*, Heidelberg, University of Heidelberg, 1979.
Zysk, K.G. *Religious Healing in the Veda*, Philadelphia, American Philosophical Society, 1985.
___ *Asceticism and Healing: medicine in the Buddhist Monastery*, New York, Oxford, 1991

The Nizamia General Hospital in Hyderabad, a traditional Unani hospital and medical school.

Unani Medicine of the Subcontinent

CLAUDIA LIEBESKIND

THE THEORY OF UNANI MEDICINE

In the early Islamic period Muslims took over the medical system of the Greeks. This is reflected in the name this system received in the subcontinent, Unani, which stands for Ionian or Greek.[1] It was based on the humoral theory developed by the Hippocratic school and further refined by Galen. According to this theory there were four humours, *akhlat*, in the human body: blood (*dam* or *khun*), phlegm (*balgham*), black bile (*al mirra al sawda*) and yellow bile (*al mirra al safra*). Each humour was qualified by natures and elements; the natures being cold, dry, wet and hot, and the elements being water, earth, air and fire. Thus blood was thought to be hot and wet and was related to air; phlegm was wet and cold and related to water; black bile was cold and dry and related to earth; and yellow bile was dry and hot and related to fire. According to the Hippocratic concept, health depended on all the humours being in complete balance with each other. In Galen's view, however, there was no such perfect equilibrium and every person tended towards a particular type of humoral imbalance, which then characterised his temperament. People were thus sanguine, phlegmatic, melancholic or choleric. The predominance of one humour could be brought about by external factors like climate, age or way of life.

The four bodily humours were produced by digestion. It was thought that on reaching the stomach food was 'boiled' into separate substances by the body's natural heat. The humours were then processed a second time in the liver and transported by the blood to the various organs and parts of the body, while the residue was excreted. But to live man needed more than humours. The humour-mixture was only the receptacle for the spirit, *ruh*, which descended from God and was the intermediary between the body and the force of life from the world above.[2] There were three spirits: the vital spirit located in the left ventricle of the heart and by nature hot and dry; the natural spirit located in the liver, hot and wet; and the psychic spirit, cold and wet, located in the brain. The vital spirit was responsible for the growth, reproduction and movement of the body, it moved in the arteries; the natural spirit was concerned with food, growth and reproduction, it moved in the veins; the psychic spirit was responsible for sensation and movement, it moved in the nerves.

Since health, according to Galen, consisted in the relative harmony of the humours, illness meant a disruption of that harmony. To cure an illness caused by the increase or decrease of a particular humour the previous balance had to be re-established. To cure a 'cold' disease 'hot' medicines were given, and to cure a 'wet' disease 'dry' remedies were prescribed. Drugs were categorised according to the same criteria as the humours: dry and cold; dry and hot; hot and wet; cold and wet; and since a 'cold' disease meant, for example, an excess of black bile, a medicine classified as 'hot' was given to restore the normal healthy balance. External factors, like climate, food, level of activity, emotional upheaval and others, could also influence the humoral balance and a physician always tried to establish a patient's circumstances in order to prescribe the correct remedy. Unani medicine had a holistic approach; health did not simply mean balancing the humours internally, it also meant living in harmony with the environment.[3]

THE PRACTICE OF UNANI MEDICINE

The circumstances under which Unani medicine was taught and practised have remained remarkably similar over time. Once a student had studied the traditional Islamic curriculum and decided to become a doctor or *hakim* (literally 'a sage or philosopher', the term only later came to denote a physician), he apprenticed himself to an established doctor. Very often that physician would be a close male relative and it was

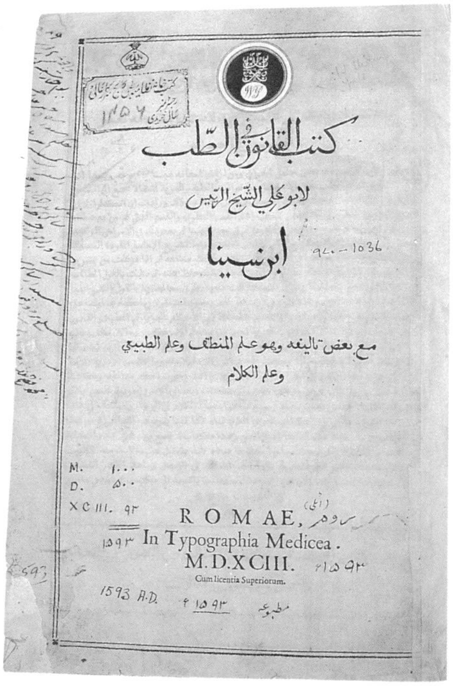

The Canon of Medicine 'Kitab al Qanun fi l tibb' by Avicenna (972-1036), published in Rome in 1593, is still used as a manual by the medical students of the Unani Medical College in Hyderabad.

not unusual for families to be involved in medicine for many generations. The medical textbooks in India were mostly in Arabic and Persian and only came to be translated into the vernaculars in the nineteenth century. They were taught either in a private circle at a physician's home or in specially established schools. Since the textbooks conveyed only technical and theoretical knowledge, it was imperative for the student to observe his guide dealing with patients, as often as possible. All the intricacies of the trade, the individual examination of patients, the diagnosis, subsequent prescription and manufacture of drugs, the surgical operations undertaken on serious cases, had to be learned by observing and following the example of a practising *hakim*. Trainee *hakims* were sent to hospitals to learn about clinical medicine, surgery and proper bedside manners. Most of the hospitals had teaching rooms attached to them. Those students who had mastered the field of Unani medicine, or *tibb*,[4] in its complexity either passed an examination set by their teachers, or by a government official, and thereby gained a licence which stated what they had achieved and allowed them to practise on their own.

Hakims usually worked in one of three different settings although these were not mutually exclusive: they worked in hospitals in big cities; at the court of the ruling dynasties; and in their own, urban-based, practices. Since the *hakims* had to be educated, and most of them depended on the patronage of the educated upper classes, Unani medicine was very much a feature of urban areas.

The *hakim* who worked on his own did so either from home or from a separate practice, where he would be visited by his male patients. He would determine their illness by questioning them about the events of the preceding days, taking their pulse and examining their urine. Some physicians prided themselves on being able to identify a patient's illness simply from the pulse. Generally, however, there was a six-point checklist of external factors which also influenced a person's well-being, and which the *hakim* took into account in making his diagnosis. The six points were: climate; food and drink; level of physical activity and rest; sleep; emotional upheavals; excretion and retention.

Each patient needed a personally designed treatment because not only did he possess a unique temperament, that is personal humour-mixture, but his life was also influenced by a unique combination of external factors. As the medical textbooks only stated the general principles of how to tackle a particular illness, *hakims* had to be skilled in the field of logic to be able to adapt the general outlines to individual cases. In many cases the *hakims* themselves, or the students apprenticed to them, prepared the drugs for their patients not trusting pharmacists to follow the correct procedures. Those patients who did not want to come to the *hakim*'s clinic were visited at home. The code of practice of the Unani physician based on the Hippocratic oath advised him to treat poor people free of charge, although this could only be undertaken on a large scale by those with independent means.[5]

The female patient presented something of a problem area for *hakims*. Conservative Muslim families would not have allowed a woman to be examined by an unrelated male doctor, and there were very few women doctors in Unani medicine. If a doctor were allowed to visit a female patient, he would usually find access to her restricted by a veil or screen, and an examination was often no more than a taking of the pulse. Thus sick women did not often receive treatment from a doctor. Nor were *hakims* normally involved in childbirth, which was left to midwives who might have been trained by a Unani physician.[6]

The institution of the hospital, *bimaristan*, was one of the features taken over from the Persians in the early Islamic period. The first 'state-of-the-art' hospital built by an Arab ruler was in Baghdad in the eighth century AD, although more specialised institutions, for lepers and for the blind for

Servant & Hakeem with medicine bags.

Country doctor seated amongst his medicines, his servant beside him, by a western Indian artist, c. 1856. The British Library, London.

example, had been constructed prior to that. Hospitals came to be established throughout the Islamic world, from India to Morocco and Andalusia, and from Turkey to Egypt. The most notable were found in the bigger cities: in Baghdad, Raiy, Damascus, Cairo and Marrakesh. In India, hospitals were built in various places, for example in Delhi and in Agra. Generally a hospital was divided into two separate areas for men and women. These were further subdivided into separate halls for people suffering from different diseases. There was additional space for out-patient treatment and the storing of medicines. Special segregation was exercised for cases of infectious diseases and mental disorders. Some of the hospitals had an in-patient capacity of several thousand. Apart from the wards there were likely to be a mosque, libraries and administrative quarters. Despite the separation of male from female patients, all staff were male.[7]

Another institution popular throughout the Islamic world was the traditional public bath, the *hammam*. Besides its ritual and social significance, the public bath, equipped with hot and cold water, hot steam, and professional masseurs, had important medicinal qualities which were mentioned in the classical medical texts. These baths still play a role, albeit a less medicinal one, in many Muslim countries.[8]

The Branches of Unani medicine

Anatomy and physiology

In both anatomy and physiology Unani medicine was fairly indebted to Galenic concepts. Under Islamic law the dissection of human bodies was forbidden, and physicians only occasionally dissected animals. For many centuries there was therefore no advancement on Galen's theories. The human body was believed to contain 248 bones, and to be permeated by a system of nerves, veins and arteries, with broadly similar functions. They were routes through which the three different spirits—psychic, natural and vital—flowed from their point of origin to other parts of the body. The nerves were believed to originate in the brain, the veins in the liver and the arteries in the heart.[9]

A major advance was made by ibn Nafis (d. 1288) who identified the blood circulation between heart and lungs. Refuting the Galenic idea that blood passed from the right to the left ventricle through a 'passage' in the heart, he stated that it flowed from the heart through the pulmonary artery into the lungs where it mixed with air 'to purify', and then back through the pulmonary vein to the left ventricle of the heart to receive the vital spirit. Unfortunately this discovery of the minor circulation of blood was not recognised as the major breakthrough it represented, and remained virtually unknown until the twentieth century.[10]

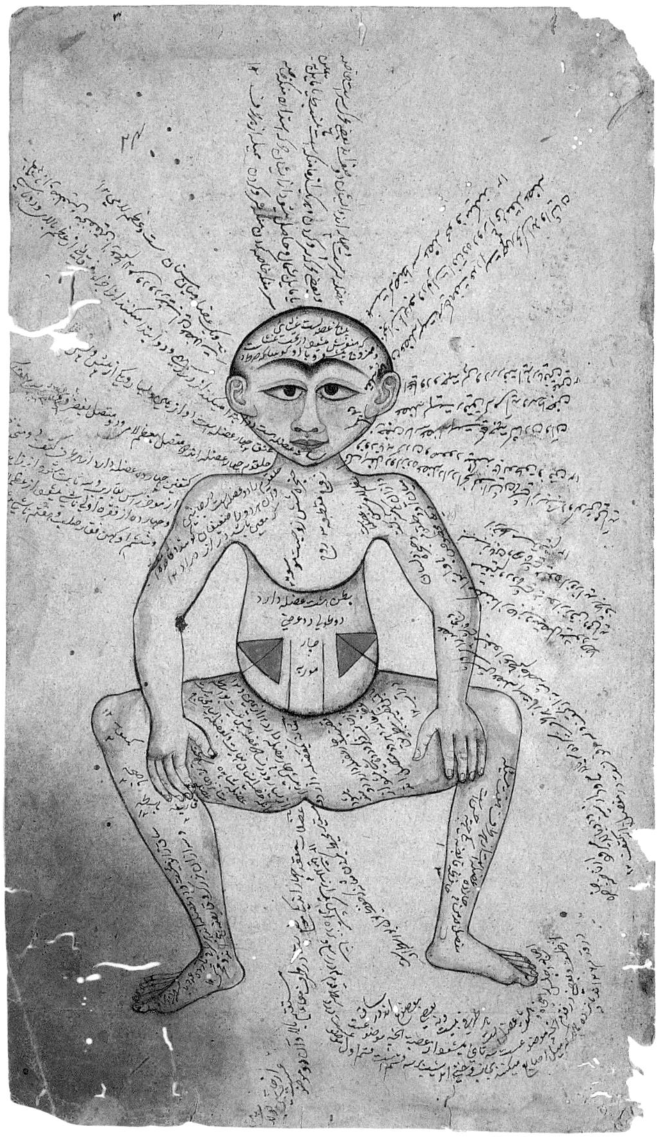

Anatomical drawing showing the muscular system of the body with a commentary in Persian (part of a series of four illustrations, see pages 33 and 44). Mughal, 17th century. Collection: Sam Fogg Rare Books, London.

Surgeon (jarrāh) attending to the leg of a patient, by a company artist 1825. The British Library, London

Surgery

Surgery was inseparably linked with a detailed knowledge of the make-up of the human body. The prohibition on the dissection of bodies obstructed the development of such knowledge and ultimately hindered major advancements in the surgical field. In its approach to treatment, Unani medicine was not geared to drastic, that is surgical, interventions but endeavoured, instead, to assist the body's own mechanisms to combat illness. Surgery tended, therefore, to be seen only as a last resort.

This is not to say that surgery had no role; it was mostly concerned with bone-setting, cauterisation and bloodletting. Disjointed or broken bones were set by the application of external pressure, and not through operations. This was done so successfully, that the skill has continued to this day. Cauterisation was used for a variety of circumstances which ranged from the treatment of infected wounds, to dealing with haemorrhoids and tumours. Blood-letting was a very widespread practice usually employed for one of three reasons: because of an over-production of blood; to divert the blood flow; or, 'to allow free movement of the blood and the vital spirits'.[11] Surgeons also undertook more complicated medical interventions like Caesarian operations, the removal of tonsils, or operations on the bowels. A further field of surgical expertise was dentistry. Unani physicians were concerned with oral hygiene and conducted a variety of dental activities: operating on the gums, filling teeth, fixing or extracting loose ones, and providing replacements. Cauterisation was also used on teeth and gums.

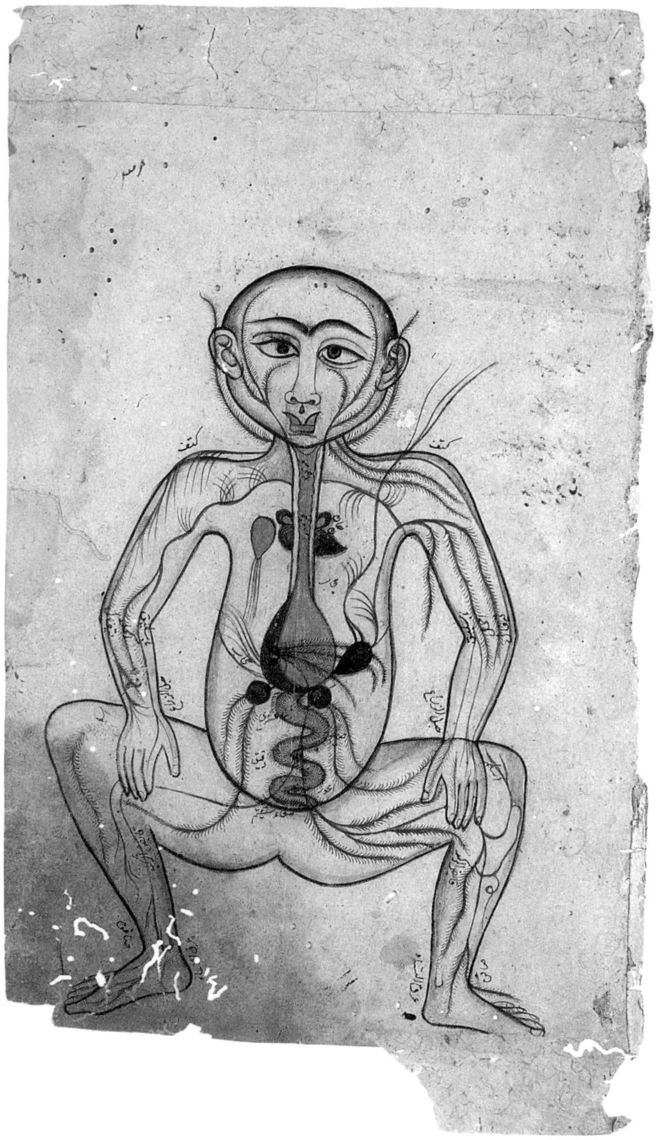

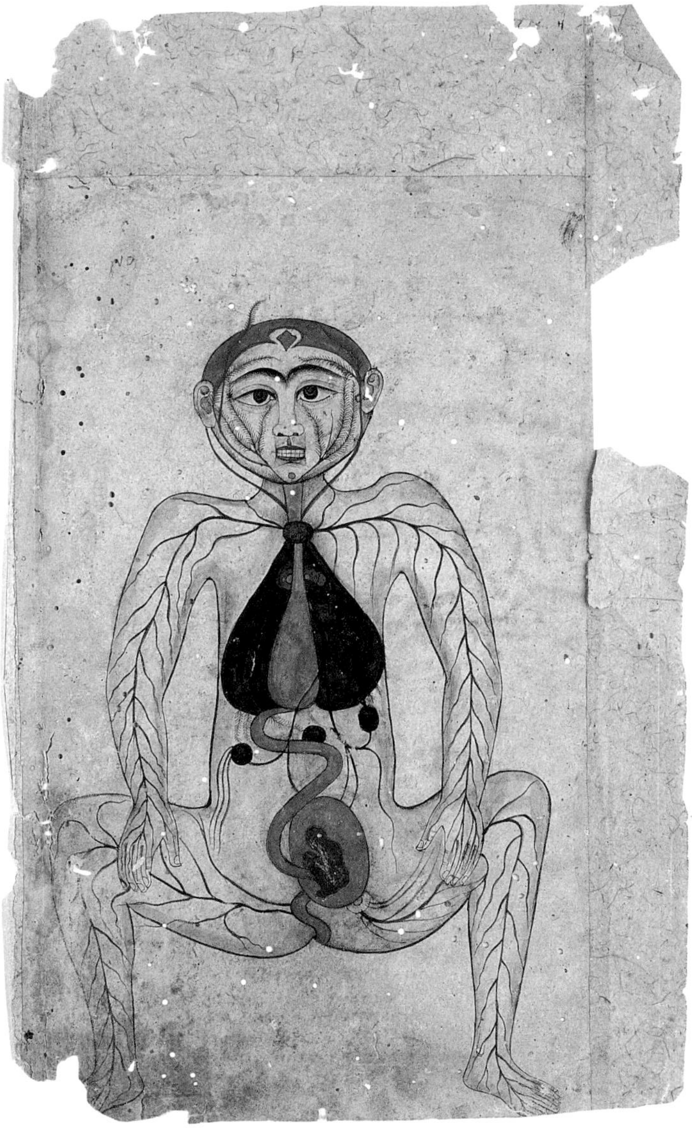

Two anatomical drawings out of a series of, usually, four (see pages 33 and 42). Depicted above is the intestinal system with the veins, and to the right, a human embryo in the uterus. The anatomical series contained as a rule, illustrations of the skeleton, muscles, nerves, blood vessels and intestines. These were always shown as overall systems and not in detail. Additionally, all the drawings exhibited similar features: a squatting figure, a relatively round head and the face turned forwards or backwards. Mughal, 17th century. Collection: Sam Fogg Rare Books, London.

For both bodily and oral surgery *hakims* had at their disposal many different surgical instruments. In his writings al Zahrawi (Albucasis, d. 1013) included approximately 200 drawings of surgical instruments which he had designed himself. These instruments continued to be used throughout the history of Unani medicine. Muslim physicians were also among the first to use narcotic drugs in surgical procedures. Opium, or one of its derivatives, was used as an anaesthetic. Many of the minor surgical operations were undertaken by barbers, while the rest were done by surgeons. The social standing of surgeons (as in the Galenic tradition of Europe) was generally well below that of general practitioners.[12]

Ophthalmology

It was in the field of ophthalmology that the Muslims made some of their greatest advances. Diseases of the eye were common in the Middle East, most probably due to the dusty and sandy environment in which people often lived. Research in this area was thus particularly stimulated. From the ninth century onwards scholars produced works on ophthalmology which initially relied heavily on the Greek theoretical models, but which were increasingly modified by their own experiments and observations.

The first author in this field, Hunain ibn Ishaq (d. 873) believed the crystalline lens in the centre of the eyeball to be the central organ of vision. Following the Greek concept, he believed the optic nerve to be hollow so that the visual spirit could travel along it. The lens was where the visual force from the brain and the image of the object from without met. Ibn al Haitham (Alhazen, d. 1039) corrected the Greek version of the nature of vision. He showed that the rays of light came from the external object to the eye and not, as previously believed, from the eye to the object and back. He also demonstrated that a person's sense of vision could be deceived depending on the course taken by rays of light when they were refracted or reflected.[13] In the tenth century, al Razi too concluded that the eyes were not radiators of light, and was probably the first to describe pupillary reflexes.

Under the Arabs the treatment of cataract was particularly advanced. The cataract was seen as the pouring out of humour into the eye. To improve the vision of the affected person the lens had to be moved. 'Ammar bin 'Ali al Mawsili (ninth/tenth century) introduced the technique of suction removal of the lens, for which he used a hollow needle: a method of couching still used in India today. Not until the mid-nineteenth century was this technique used in Europe.[14]

Internal medicine

The basic foundation of Islamic medicine was that health, and not illness, was the natural condition of the body. The human body thus had an inbuilt propensity to correct any humoral imbalance, and to restore the balance necessary for well-being. Medication together with the other external factors, climate, food, etc., only assisted this internal mechanism. The importance assigned to the digestive system in internal disorders was evident from the large number of purgatives used.

Many illnesses were described and charted for the first time by Arab physicians. One of the earliest and most famous works was that by al Razi on smallpox. In it he listed all the characteristics of smallpox, its diagnosis, treatment, varieties of occurrence, and how to distinguish it from measles. Among the other diseases identified for the first time were whooping cough and meningitis.[15]

Medicine of the Prophet and the Imams

The development which became known as 'Medicine of the Prophet', *tibb al nabi* or *al tibb al nabawi*, was based on statements concerning health found in the Quran and the traditions of the Prophet Muhammad, the *hadiths*. Into these were incorporated certain Galenic concepts such as humoral theory, whilst other concepts, like the importance of a balanced diet and the digestive system, featured in both.[16] Prophetic medicine, however, was always religious in character. The *hadiths* dealing with medicine were based on bedouin folk medicine, and often expressed in such maxims as, 'Travel! It keeps you healthy'. Remedies suggested by the Prophet included cupping, the use of honey, of black grain (possibly black cumin), camel's milk and urine. Amulets were commonly given as a cure for the evil eye and evil spirits. Quranic verses were written on paper which was either worn by the patient or washed out in water and then drunk.[17]

Prophetic medicine was aimed at a different audience from the technical Galenic texts. Whereas Unani medical writings were only appreciated by a small educated elite, *hadith*-based prophetic medicine appealed to the common man. Moreover, whilst Unani *tibb* was predominantly urban-based, the overwhelming majority of the population lived in the countryside.

Within Shia Islam the *tibb al a'imma*, the 'Medicine of the Imams' or leaders of the Shia community, developed. Sayings of the Imams, especially of the first, sixth and eighth Imams, concerning medical topics were collected and acted upon. Both medical traditions, that of the Prophet and of the Imams, achieved great popularity; many books were devoted to these subjects first in Arabic and later Turkish, Persian and Urdu.[18]

Astrology and Medicine

Astrology was widely regarded as an integral part of medical science. The stars were seen as directly influencing the condition and well-being of human beings on earth. Many *hakims* believed in the importance of the position of the planets in treating their patients. It was believed that the position within the zodiac at any time of seven planets—Saturn, Jupiter, Mars, Venus, Mercury, Sun and Moon—affected human beings. The survival of a baby born before the normal period of gestation was completed, for instance, was believed to depend to some extent on the planet in ascendancy at the time of its birth.

> *The twelve signs of the zodiac were divided into three groups: the four elements (fire, earth, air and water); the four humours (blood, phlegm, black bile and yellow bile); and the four qualities of temperature and humidity (cold, hot, moist and dry).*[19]

This cosmic make-up clearly conformed to, and reflected, the principal concepts of Unani medicine.

Development of Unani Medicine up to 1200: Important Physicians and their Works[20]

With the spread of Islam, Muslims came into contact with centres of medical expertise in southwest Persia or Alexandria in upper Egypt, where migrants from Greece had settled. Among them were families who had practised Greek medicine over generations. In the eighth and ninth centuries a vast translation movement set in to make the Greek texts available to Arabic- or Syriac-speaking audiences. Over time, more and more hospitals, centres of medical progress, were built all over the Islamic world from Andalusia in the west to Baghdad in the east. Despite the vast distances between these medical institutions, knowledge and discoveries were freely interchanged.

The key figures in the advancement of Unani medicine, some of whom will be described below, had all gained their medical experience through managing one of the numerous hospitals. Their works were translated into Latin in the Middle Ages, and provided the basis of medical understanding in Europe until the seventeenth century.

The physician Hunain ibn Ishaq al 'Ibadi (808-73/77) was, together with his team, the most productive translator of Greek medical texts. He came originally from al Hira and was the son of a pharmacist. During extensive travels he perfected his Greek, and on his return to Baghdad was the court physician of the Caliph al Mutawakkil. Like his teacher Yuhanna ibn Masawaih (*c.* 777-857), who had run the hospital in Baghdad, written medical works in Arabic and translated Greek texts into Arabic, he too had been a Christian.

Hunain translated more than a hundred Greek texts, and among them a whole medical curriculum, the *Jawami' al Iskandaraniyin* (Alexandrian Summaries). His method of translation was very scientific; in order to establish the original text he gathered together as many manuscripts of a particular work as possible. By means of his translations Hunain helped to develop a scientific vocabularly in Arabic. Apart from these translations he also wrote medical texts. He was a renowned physician and ophthalmologist as is reflected in his works: the *Kitab al 'Ashr maqlat fi l 'ain* (Book of Ten Discourses on the Eye) and the *Kitab al Masa'il fi l 'ain* (Book of Questions concerning the Eye), both of which combined the knowledge of Antiquity with his own personal observations. Works on general medicine included his *Kitab al Masa'il fi l tibb* (Introduction to Medicine) which was the most authoritative textbook of his time, not only in its Arabic but also in its Latin translation.

By the beginning of the tenth century most of the Greek medical texts had been translated, and they provided a relatively solid foundation from which to advance medicine through new observations and experiments.

This was undertaken by Abu Bakr Muhammad bin Zakariya al Razi (Rhazes, 865-925) whose position in Unani medicine has been compared to that of a second Galen. Born in Raiy, he spent his youth studying music, philosophy, literature and alchemy, and did not embark on medicine until the age of thirty. His career included managing the hospitals in Raiy and Baghdad. After travelling extensively

Perfumers (gandhi or attār) were also known to be accomplished pharmacists and familiar with the preparation of certain formulas to cool the mind or excite the passions. Here one is shown surrounded by shelves of bottles in his shop. Company artist 1825. The British Library, London.

he went blind in his old age. Al Razi's writings indicate a reliance on his own clinical observations; the incorporation of his own practical experiences rather than a mere reiteration of known facts. The most well known of his 56 medical texts were: the *Kitab al Mansuri*, his treatise on internal and clinical medicine; the *Kitab al Jadari wa l hasba*, on smallpox and measles; and, the *Kitab al Tibb al ruhani*, which examined the psychological dimension of illness. The *Kitab al Hawi*, his posthumously compiled, 25-volume medical encyclopaedia, was a mixture of quotations from Greek, Indian and Arabic authors, and al Razi's own medical case studies. Although al Razi relied heavily on his Greek predecessors especially Galen—many of his texts had the same titles as Galen's—he was not afraid to criticise or correct the Greek texts wherever he found them wanting.

The first physician to make use of Indian Ayurvedic sources, in addition to Greek and Syriac ones, was 'Ali ibn Rabban al Tabari (*c.* 810-55). A Christian born in Merw, he held a court position in Tabaristan and was forced to flee to Raiy after his ruler's dethronement. His work, the *Kitab al Firdaws al hikma* (Paradise of Wisdom), was dedicated to the Caliph al Mutawakkil, who also caused him to convert to Islam. Subsequently, he also wrote two polemical tracts against Christians. In the *Firdaws*, which dealt with psychology, astronomy, astrology as well as most branches of medicine, al Tabari also devoted a section to the principles of Ayurveda. For this he relied on translations of the basic Ayurvedic source texts: the books of Caraka; of Suśruta; of Vāgbhaṭa; and of Mādhavakara.

One of the most important medical works, second only to ibn Sina's *Qanun*, was the *Kitab al Malaki*, or *Liber Regius* as it became known in its Latin translation, of 'Ali ibn al 'Abbas al Majusi (Haly Abbas, d. 994), originally from Ahwaz. The *Kitab al Malaki* provided a comprehensive overview of Islamic medicine as it was known in the tenth century. Divided into two parts, one dealing with the theory, the other with its application, it offered a clear and logical treatment of all branches of Unani *tibb*. Al Majusi had gained his personal experience through running a hospital. He was the first to use a tourniquet to stop the flow of blood through an artery.

The tenth and eleventh centuries saw two more important specialists; al Zahrawi for surgery and 'Ali ibn 'Isa for ophthalmology. Abu l Qasim al Zahrawi (Albucasis, *c.* 940-1013) lived in Cordoba in Andalusia, and was the greatest Muslim surgeon of his time. His book, the *Kitab al Tasrif li man 'ajiza 'an al ta'lif* (Book of Concessions), was a medical textbook which covered all branches of medicine but of which the section on surgery was the most famous. It was the most comprehensive and systematic treatment of surgery and the first to include illustrations of surgical instruments, more than two hundred, many of which al Zahrawi himself had invented. This section acted as a manual for surgeons down the centuries.

'Ali ibn 'Isa (Jesu Haly, d. tenth century) worked in Baghdad, and his *Kitab Tazkirat al kahhalin* (Treasury of Ophthalmologists) had an impact similar to that of al Zahrawi's *al Tasrif*. Divided into three parts and relying on Hunain's and Galen's findings, it was one of the most important books of the period on ophthalmology.

In the twelfth century, there were two more outstanding physicians who came from Andalusia; ibn Zuhr and ibn Rushd. Abu Marwan 'Abd al Malik ibn Zuhr (Avenzoar, d. 1162) belonged to a family of physicians from Cordoba. He found employment with the ruling dynasties of Andalusia and North Africa, was imprisoned in Morocco, but was eventually made *wazir* (minister). Among his works was the first book on diet composed in the Muslim world, the *Kitab al Aghziya*. Apart from dietary matters it dealt with hygiene, including sexual hygiene. Abu l Walid Muhammad ibn Ahmad ibn Muhammad ibn Rushd (Averroes, 1126-98) was also born in Cordoba. He was trained in law and concerned mostly with philosophy; he was considered to be the most important defender and interpreter of Aristotle in the Middle Ages. He wrote the *Kitab al Kulliyat*, latinised *Colliget*, in which he covered the whole medical field in abridged form. While conforming to most of his predecessors' precepts in his writings, he defended Aristotle's ideas in physiology and attacked Galen's theory. Such criticism was also evident in his numerous commentaries on Galen.

The Unani physician with the most far-reaching and enduring impact in the Islamic and Western worlds was Abu 'Ali al Husain ibn 'Abd Allah ibn Sina (Avicenna, 980-1037). Born in Bukhaṛa, he studied philosophy and medicine; at the age of eighteen he had completed the latter. He travelled very widely. During his life he also became *wazir* of Hamadan, but generally tried to avoid court positions. He was widely considered to have been the greatest philosopher of the Islamic world. He was best known for his work the *Kitab al Qanun fi l tibb*, latinised *The Canon of Medicine*. His other work included the *Maqala fi Ahkam al adwiya al qalbiya* (Tract on Cardiac Drugs), and his *Al Arjuza fi l tibb* (Medical Poem), which was to help students memorise the medical principles

Babur (1483-1530) being treated by physicians during a serious sickness, most probably a trismus which prevented him from opening his mouth. Detail of a miniature from a Babur Nameh, c.1590. The British Library, London.

through its verse form. Ibn Sina's importance for Unani medicine in South Asia will be discussed in the next section.

A second physician whose influence was felt in India was Saiyid Zain al Din Isma'il al Husaini al Jurjani (d. 1136). He was the author of the first medical encyclopaedia in Persian, the *Zakhira-i Khwarizmshahi* (Treasury of the King of Khwarizm), as well as the *Yadgar-i Tibb* (Medical Memoranda), and the *Aghrad al tibb* (Aims of Medicine). The *Zakhira-i Khwarizmshahi* was heavily influenced by ibn Sina's *Qanun*, on which it had been modelled. Within the Persian-speaking world it helped spread the fame and importance of ibn Sina down the centuries.[21] Just as Hunain was crucial for the creation of a new scientific vocabulary for Arabic, so was al Jurjani for a Persian one.

The Development of Unani Medicine in South Asia up to 1800 [22]

Little work has been done on the history of Unani medicine in South Asia, and the information which is available is at best sketchy if not sometimes contradictory. For some periods all we have are the names of *hakims* and the number of hospitals supported by the different rulers. Any overview has therefore to be somewhat vague and disjointed.

In the twelfth century the advancing Muslim armies and rulers brought the Unani system of medicine with them to India. It began to spread out gradually over the subcontinent, depending heavily on the patronage of Muslim rulers. The various dynasties of the Delhi Sultanate (1206-1526), the different rulers of the Mughal Empire (1526-1858), as well as the regional and local ruling Muslim dynasties in north and south India, all supported to various extents the advance of Unani medicine in the subcontinent.

Since patronage came from the court Unani medicine was, in the main, urban-based. Rulers supported hospitals, medical libraries, schools and important *hakims*. The first centre of Unani medicine in South Asia was set up in Lahore in the 1160s under the patronage of the son of the last Ghazni king.[23] According to the medieval historian Firishta (1552-1623), there were 45 prominent *hakims* in court employment during the reign of Sultan 'Ala al Din Khilji (regn 1295-1315). During the reign of Muhammad bin Tughluq (regn 1325-52), there were around 70 hospitals in Delhi, while 1,200 *hakims* found employment through the state. In times of peace rulers generally continued the work of their predecessors while adding new medical buildings and committing more resources in their own name. This pattern continued under the Mughals who, beginning with Akbar (regn 1556-1605), established hospitals in many places, in Delhi and Agra for example. Hospitals were also built in the provinces; Aurangzeb (regn 1658-1707) tried to construct, or have his nobles construct, hospitals in the smaller towns of his empire. Rulers outside the Mughal sway followed similar policies. When the city of Hyderabad was planned by the Qutub Shahi dynasty of Golkonda in the late sixteenth century, one of the first buildings to go up was the hospital, which had a capacity for 4,000 in-patients. Many resources were spent on building and maintaining hospitals, and on employing *hakims*. And yet, on the whole, Unani medicine remained in the towns, scarcely reaching the countryside. Only during Sher Shah's brief reign (regn 1540-45) was an attempt made by the state to fund *hakims* outside the important towns. Sher Shah attempted to place a Unani physician in all way-stations on the caravan routes under his control.[24]

The spread of Unani medicine was helped by the availability of many medical works in Persian. Not only was a translation movement introduced to make Arabic books available in Persian, but more and more books were actually written in Persian. The earliest Unani medical textbook which can be found in India is the *Tibb-i Firuz Shahi* by Shah Quli written in 1281/2, which deals with the medical treatment of hunting birds.[25] Important work was composed in Kashmir in the fourteenth and fifteenth centuries by Mansur bin Muhammad Yusuf bin Ilyas. He wrote the *Kifayat-i Mujahidiya*, which dealt with concepts of general medicine, drugs and treatment. He also wrote *Tashrih-i Mansuri*, a widely used anatomical treatise on the curriculum of many *tibbi* colleges in India. The most prominent physician-writer of Aurangzeb's time was Hakim Muhammad Akbar Arzani (d. 1722), who first worked in the Deccan and only later came to Delhi.

Opposite: Amr is disguised as the doctor Musmahil, a subterfuge in order to gain entrance to the fort of Zummurrud Shah in order to rescue captives. This rather agitated scene from the Hamza-nameh (around 1570) shows Amr taking the pulse of a sorcerer while sick people and children seem to be waiting anxiously for treatment. In the midst of scattered medicine bags, a servant pounds herbs in a mortar. Brooklyn Museum, New York.

Important among his seven books were the *Mizan-i Tibb*, a book on the general principles of diseases and their treatment, and the *Tibb-i Akbar*, in which the diseases of the body were explained organ by organ, and the different treatments set out.[26] Another unique treatise was written by Hakim Hidayat Allah in the period of Nasir al Din Muhammad (regn 1719-48). His *Yusr al 'ilaj* was composed in 1731 and contained a detailed collection of drugs and prescriptions. The importance of the collection was twofold: firstly, all the drugs mentioned in it were cheaper though just as effective as others available; secondly, it contained the suggestion that at least one person in each family should be knowledgable about *tibb* so that female family members could be examined and treated without embarrassment, and the family could save money. Indeed the title of the treatise translates as, 'Cheap and Easy Treatment'.[27]

Unani medicine did not make any huge advances or new discoveries during the medieval period in India. It was most notable for its continuous efforts in systematising medical knowledge, for the large number of compilations of the different ways of treatment and for the translation of Unani textbooks into Persian.

The influence of Persia

The development of Unani medicine in India and Persia were closely entwined. The Persian language was common to both countries and at various times since the early thirteenth century, political, social and economic circumstances led *hakims* and scholars to move to India in search of work. The patronage of the Sultanate, but even more so of the Mughal court, beckoned invitingly to the *hakims* from Persia. But it was not only the north Indian courts which attracted Persian *hakims*. Some of the Deccan kingdoms made a point of employing Persian scholars, and later on many *hakims* of Persian origin could be found in Hyderabad.

The important centres of learning in Persia which supplied *hakims* to India were Gilan, Tabriz, Isfahan and Shiraz. Some practitioners stayed only during their employment and returned later to Persia, while others remained with their families in India, and continued to serve the courts over generations. An example of one such family was that of Mawlana 'Abd al Razzaq Gilani whose four sons: Hakim Abul Fath Gilani, author of commentaries on the *Qanun* and the *Qanuncha*; Hakim Najib al Din Humam; Hakim Nur al Din Qarawi; and Hakim Lutf Allah Gilani, and various grandsons: Hakim Fath Allah; Hakim Haziq; and Hakim Khushhal Khan, all played a part at the courts of Akbar (1556-1605), Jahangir (1605-27), and Shah Jahan (1628-57).[28] Another widely known Persian *hakim* was Hakim Muhammad Hashim Shirazi known as Hakim 'Alawi Khan. He came to India towards the end of Aurangzeb's reign and continued to work under his successors. He wrote a number of books, mostly on drugs and forms of treatment. The invading Nadir Shah of Persia carried 'Alawi Khan off with him to Persia, but the *hakim* managed to return to India, via Mecca.[29] Of course there were also Indian *hakims* who went to Persia for their medical training and later returned. The flow of Persian *hakims* to India only diminished in the nineteenth century due, in part, to the decline of financial rewards and official court positions.

The influence of ibn Sina

The medical history of Muslim India has been dominated by the work of ibn Sina. His writings, the *Qanun* in particular, influenced the development of Unani medicine in South Asia more than the work of any other author. The medical theories of ibn Sina remained in use right up to, and including, the twentieth century, and featured prominently in the curricula of various Unani medical colleges.

The *Qanun*, a medical encyclopaedia of some 1,000,000 words, was divided into five books:

- (i) general principles of medicine which included the philosophy of medicine, anatomy and physiology, hygiene and the treatment of diseases;
- (ii) *materia medica* or simple drugs;
- (iii) particular theory: disorders of each internal and external organ of the body;
- (iv) general therapy: illnesses which affect the body in general and were not limited to a single organ or limb;
- (v) formulary or compound drugs.

Ibn Sina incorporated many of his own observations into the *Qanun*, including his discovery of the spread of epidemics, his identification of meningitis, and the recognition of the contagiousness of tuberculosis.[30] But its main significance lay in the ordering and systematising of the available medical knowledge of the period.

The *Qanun* in its entirety has been translated into Latin, Uzbek, Turkish, Hebrew, Persian and Urdu. In its Latin version it was the key text in European medieval medical schools and continued to be produced in new editions up to

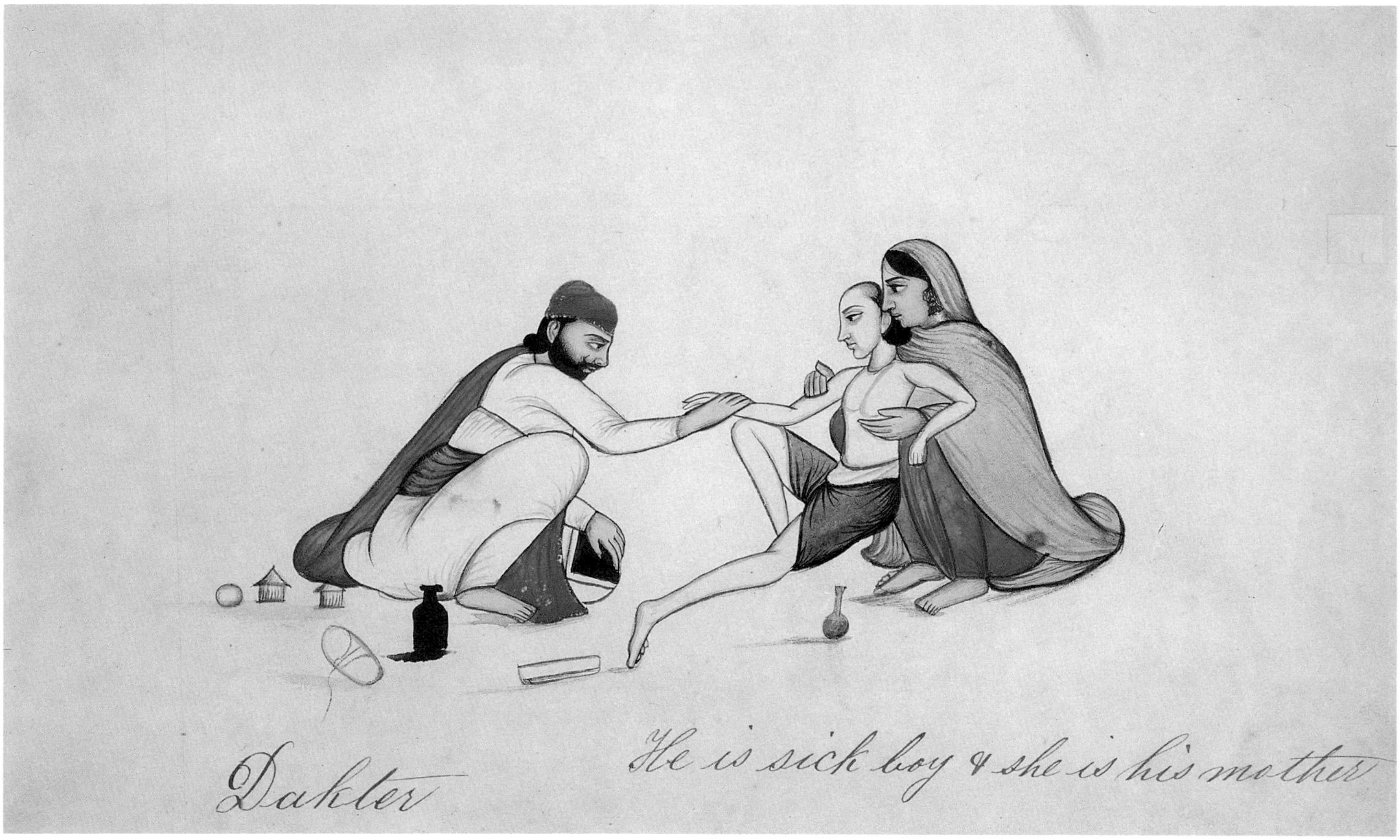
Dakter
He is sick boy & she is his mother

Doctor examining a sick boy in the arms of his mother. Company artist, Lahore, c. 1860. The British Library, London.

the seventeenth century. The Latin *Canon* was one of the most frequently printed works in the sixteenth century. There was a large number of Persian and Urdu translations.[31] The *Qanun* has also been commented upon, almost since its inception. One of the more important commentaries in the Indian region was the *Sharh-i Qanun-i Ibn Sina* by Hakim 'Ali Gilani (d. 1609), which is considered an extremely authoritative book and is still used today. The *Qanun* was also abridged by different authors. Over time, these abridged versions became sufficiently important in themselves to be translated and become the subject of commentaries. An example is the *Mufarrih al Qulub* of Hakim Muhammad Akbar Arzani, a Persian translation-cum-commentary on the *Qanuncha*, one of the more famous abridgements of the *Qanun*.[32] Of the two main Unani medical traditions of the nineteenth and twentieth centuries, one drew heavily on the work of ibn Sina.

Unani medicine and Ayurveda[33]

When Unani medicine came to India another medical system was already in place there, Ayurveda. Like Unani *tibb* Ayurveda was humour-based. To Unani's four humours (blood, phlegm, black and yellow bile) Ayurveda had three (phlegm, bile and wind). Both systems emphasised the necessity of a humoral balance for the well-being of the patient. Both systems were based on a 'holistic' approach to health; they considered man in his totality within a wide ecological spectrum. There were also a number of similarities in the practice of both medical systems. They were based, in the main, on medical texts written centuries earlier which provided only the general principles and left the individual treatment to the doctor in charge. The training of students was similar in both systems. Students were taken into the family setting of the practitioner and learned from him by following his example. The systems of diagnosis benefitted also from each other. For instance, pulse examination began to play a much greater role within Ayurveda after the arrival of Unani medicine.[34]

Ayurvedic texts had first been translated into Arabic in the ninth century but with the coming together of the two systems in India it became desirable and necessary to make more of the Ayurvedic system available to the Unani *hakims*. The first Unani medical text written in India which contained a separate chapter on Ayurveda was the *Majmu'a-i Ziya'i* (Collection of Ziya), composed in 1313 by Ziya Muhammad Mas'ud Rashid Zangi 'Umar Ghaznawi. The book, while revealing the state of Unani medicine at the time, also indicated the influence exerted on it by Ayurvedic medicine. A second important text is dated 1512, the *Ma'din al shifa'-i Sikandar Shahi* (Mine of Cures of Sikandar Shah), by Hakim Bahwa Khan. He wrote:

> *... by experience I found that Unani medicine did not suit the temperament of the people living in the changed climatic conditions of India. Secondly, the names of the medicines were either in Persian or Unani (Greek) language and they were not known to the people of India. Often the Unani physicians could not get what they wanted. So there was no alternative except to translate the books of the Indian physicians.*[35]

Bahwa Khan thus compiled his selection of the most effective Ayurvedic drugs and prescriptions in Persian. In 1474 the *Aṣṭāṅgahṛdaya* became the first Ayurvedic text to be translated into Persian. Entitled *Tibb-i shifa'-i Mahmud Shahi*, it was the product of the translation department set up by Sultan Mahmud Shah of Gujarat.

Muhammad Qasim Firishta (1552-1623) who lived at the court of the Adil Shahi dynasty in the Deccan (but was originally from Persia), wrote *Ikhtiyarat-i Qasimi*, or *Dastur al atibba'*. It gave a detailed exposition of the Ayurvedic system of treatment and drugs. The *Tibb-i Dara Shukohi*, written in 1645 by Hakim Nur al Din Muhammad 'Abd Allah, was an important collection of the medical knowledge of the Arab and Indian physicians of the time. There were many scholars and *hakims* who through their work tried to make Ayurveda accessible to the Unani *hakims*, and who tried to integrate the two systems for maximum benefit. And during their period of co-existence the pharmacopoeia and therapeutics of both systems changed through their interaction.[36]

The Development of Unani Medicine from 1800 to the Present

The impact of Western medicine and the modern state on Unani medicine

The arrival of Western medicine in India presented no immediate threat to Unani medicine. It simply meant one more medical system joining the fray. When the Europeans arrived in the subcontinent from the sixteenth century onwards, they set up court like other regional potentates. In the main they employed European doctors, but resorted also to indigenous practitioners.[37] Western medicine as practised in India until the beginning of the nineteenth century was very similar to Unani medicine. Both systems were based on the same classical Greek texts which had come to Europe via the Middle East and via Unani medicine; both systems were therefore based on humoral theory. The gulf between them was only created by the advances in Western medicine made in Europe in the nineteenth and twentieth centuries. A refinement in medical equipment and the commercialisation and standardisation of the drugs market, combined with major advances in bacteriology, anatomy, surgery, pathology, nosology and diagnosis, allowed Western medicine to be more effective.[38]

With the rise of British power in India during the first half of the nineteenth century and the consequent decline of Indian rulers, Unani medicine lost much of its court/state patronage. Unani medicine was taught in government institutions at the Native Medical Institute in Calcutta between 1822 and 1835, and at Lahore University up to 1907.[39] The government, too, employed *hakims* in the Punjab in a supportive role within rural health care, but not with a view to further developing Unani medicine.[40] Apart from this there was not much encouragement from the state for the spread and advance of Unani *tibb*. Western medicine became entrenched in the central and provincial ministries, gaining a monopoly over public expenditure and public sector employment in the medical sphere. Further disadvantages for Unani medicine stemmed from the medical registration acts which came into force all over British India in the 1910s. These measures were designed to give additional protection to Western medicine, and they legitimised only Western doctors in any official context. The state also controlled the recognition of medical schools and colleges and the degrees they conferred.[41]

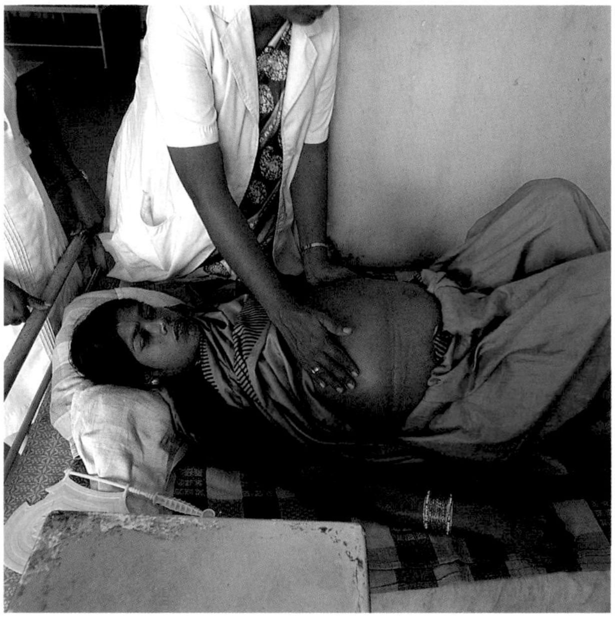

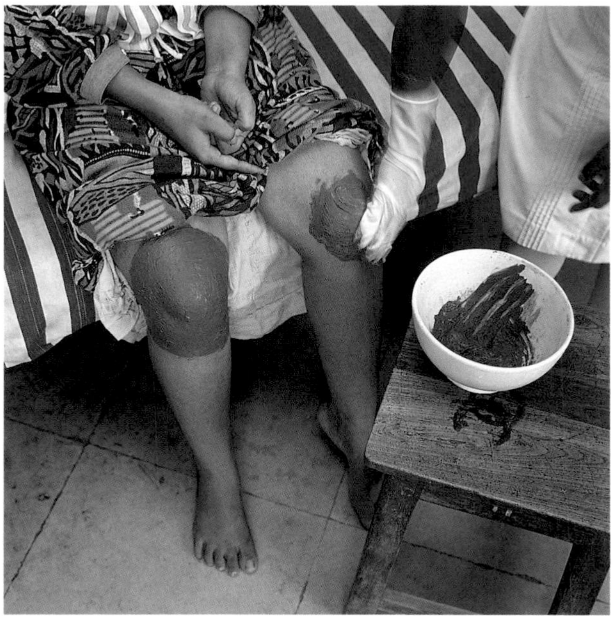

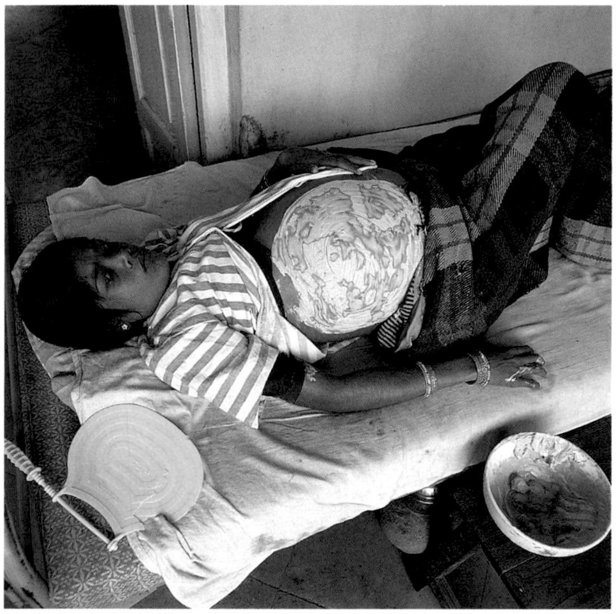

A patient in the women's department of the Nizamia Unani Hospital, Hyderabad, receives treatment for a swelling caused by a dysfunction of the liver.

Ointments made from herbal substances are much favoured in Unani medicine. Cases of knee arthritis and toe paralysis are here treated at the Nizamia Unani Hospital, Hyderabad.

As a result of the Montagu-Chelmsford reforms of 1919, Indian politicians became actively involved in the running of the various Indian provinces. It was then within their power to channel funds towards Unani medicine. Many provinces instituted committees of inquiry into the situation of indigenous medicine which often led to the establishment of Ayurvedic and Unani colleges as well as dispensaries and hospitals.[42] Unani medicine received some measure of support. In those areas, like Bhopal and Hyderabad, which had remained independent Indian states during British rule and which were governed by Muslims, Unani medicine and its necessary infrastructure were actively supported. Their rulers also contributed to private medical enterprises in British India. After Independence the state encouraged research into Unani medicine and set up more Unani colleges. An ongoing dispute within the colleges was whether Unani *tibb* should be taught in its 'pure' form, or in a version 'integrated' with Western medicine. After Independence most government-funded Unani colleges ran 'integrated' or mixed courses.[43] Some central organisations relating to Unani and Ayurvedic medicine have been set up by the government, the Central Council for Indian Medicine and the Central Council for Research in Indian Medicine, mirroring those already in existence for Western medicine. The increased state interest in, or responsibility for, Unani *tibb* and Ayurveda has led to a dual system of institutions of medical education and medical relief. Yet in spite of its increased interest in the traditional medical systems, the state did not envisage them as being equal to Western medicine.[44]

When Western medicine arrived Unani *tibb* was well established in most towns of the Indian subcontinent. Due to its nature Unani medicine was mainly urban-based and had not penetrated the countryside successfully. The impact which Western medicine had on Unani *tibb* was evident in two areas: patients and state patronage. As far as patients were concerned, it was not until the twentieth century that Western medical practitioners began to compete with *hakims* in any serious measure. Until then doctors had been mainly employed by the state and had had their patients provided for them. The impact of Western medicine was felt much more, however, in terms of state patronage. The loss of government support was compensated by turning towards fee-paying clients from the middle class market as well as the aristocracy. This middle class which began to play a significant role, medically, around the end of the nineteenth century consisted of 'the educated, English-speaking elite ..., the increasingly successful small traders, large landowners and emerging industrialists'.[45] This shift towards a market orientation was reflected in the increasing professionalisation and bureaucratisation of Unani medicine. The rapid professionalisation which Western medicine had undergone in the nineteenth century served as an example for Unani *tibb* too. *Hakims* began to set up private Unani medical colleges 'with paid staff and fixed requirements to replace the personalistic informal settings of family homes and apprenticeship'.[46] These schools and colleges had boards of governors and fixed curricula to ensure a certain medical standard. A good example was, and is, the Ayurvedic and Unani Tibbiya College in Delhi, founded by Hakim Ajmal Khan (d. 1927), and inaugurated in 1921. Designed to 'impart complete education, theoretical as well as practical, in Indian medicine',[47] it has become affiliated to Delhi University and awards degrees recognised by the government. *Hakims* also formed national organisations like the Tibbi Conference, now the All-India Unani Tibbi Conference, founded in 1906 also by Hakim Ajmal Khan. It was designed to represent the Unani interest with government, and to seek state recognition for the profession of *hakim*.[48] In the wake of the revival of Ayurveda at the end of the nineteenth century Unani medicine also experienced a certain revival. The nationalist movement declared itself to be the champion of indigenous medicine maintaining that it was more suitable for the Indian character and climate.

Thus Unani medicine was stimulated by the advances of Western medicine and the revival of Ayurvedic medicine to consider its own further development. There were two basic strands of thought. One sought to advance Unani *tibb* through further integration with other systems of medicine, Ayurvedic or Western. The case for mixing Unani and Western medicine was a strong one. Surgery, which was the one field in which *tibb* lagged behind considerably, was well advanced in Western medicine. There were attempts to find 'systematic, generalisable' scientific principles in Unani *tibb* that were compatible with Western medicine.[49] It was further argued that new diseases existed in the modern world, and that Unani *tibb* could learn about their treatment from Western medicine. The group of *hakims* advocating this integrated system came from what can be called the Delhi school which was represented by the Tibbi College of Hakim Ajmal Khan.[50]

The second group was determined to advance Unani medicine from within, and not to resort to outside help. Their view was that *tibb* should have the freedom to work and progress within its own conceptual framework. There should be no assimilation of medical concepts conflicting with it. Unani medicine might make use of some modern subjects and modern equipment, but only in moderation, so that the original theoretical principles were not distorted. This group represented the Lucknow tradition associated with the Takmil al Tibb College of Hakim 'Abd al 'Aziz (1855-1911).[51]

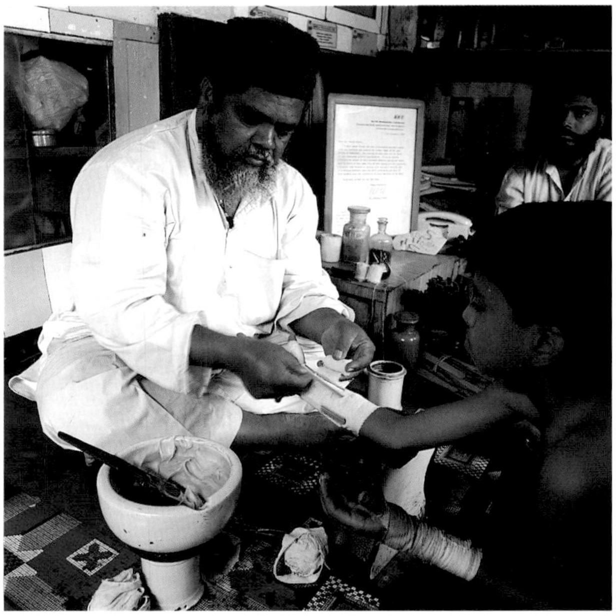

Bone fractures and dislocations have been successfully handled for many centuries in Unani medicine. Some orthopaedicians, such as Dr. Hakim Gulam Rasool, an expert bonesetter in Hyderabad, have gained a nationwide reputation.

The 'Azizis of Lucknow: a family of *hakims* in the modern period

The history of the 'Aziz family is a good illustration of the development of Unani medicine in the modern period. The 'Aziz family started practising medicine at the beginning of the nineteenth century and five generations or forty-four *hakims* later, at the end of the twentieth century, many of its members were still immersed in *tibb*.

The family history can be divided into three phases. In the first phase the *hakims* were either employed by rulers of the Indian states or ran their own clinics, mostly both. The founder of the family medical tradition was Hakim Muhammad Ya'qub (1790-1870) who set up his clinic in the Jhawai Tola quarter of his natal town of Lucknow. After completing his studies he continued the teaching tradition of his teachers. He divided his time between his students, his clinic and attending to various members of the Awadh court.

Two of his four sons worked as court physicians outside Lucknow in lieu of their father. One went to Rampur and became Head of the State Medical Department as well as attending upon the Nawab. He was succeeded in both capacities by his own son, Hakim 'Abd al 'Ali (d. 1905). After the Nawab's death, Hakim 'Abd al 'Ali attended upon the last Nawab of Awadh in exile in Calcutta and then became Head of the State Medical Department in Hyderabad. Other descendants of Hakim Muhammad Ya'qub through the female line also worked in Rampur and Hyderabad either as Heads of the State Medical Department, or as court physicians. The other son of Hakim Muhammad Ya'qub went to Calcutta with the wife of the last Nawab of Awadh to look after her. The remaining two sons stayed in Lucknow, and Hakim Muhammad Isma'il (d. 1886) took over the clinic after his father's death. He was also a consultant to several rulers of princely states. This part of the family continued in the traditional mode of employment of Unani physicians; they attended upon Muslim rulers all over India.

In the second phase, the family followed the need for professionalisation of Unani medicine. Hakim Muhammad

'Abd al 'Aziz (1855-1911), after whom the family is named, felt that medical education needed to be standardised and institutionalised. In 1902, he founded the Takmil al Tibb School, later to become a college and now affiliated to the University. Hakim 'Abd al 'Aziz provided the infrastructure for the school, while other members of the family taught at the school without pay. Early on, Hakim 'Abd al 'Aziz had recognised the importance of surgery and anatomy, which had fallen somewhat into neglect in Unani medicine. He had two of his sons, 'Abd al Rashid (1879-1920) and 'Abd al Hamid (1884-1940), instructed in these subjects by the Civil Surgeon of Lucknow. This emphasis was also reflected in the school's curriculum. Takmil al Tibb offered a three year course with theoretical and practical parts which included surgery, anatomy, physiology and chemistry among its subjects. A teaching hospital was also attached to the school. The main emphasis of the school was the teaching of ibn Sina's *Qanun*. After Hakim 'Abd al 'Aziz's death, his two eldest sons took over the running of Takmil al Tibb. Hakim 'Abd al Rashid set up an executive committee for the school in 1911, and he became its first secretary. During his leadership the number of patients went up from 9,692 in 1911 to 23,032 in 1920. New buildings were added to the school, and the number of students also rose. Following his death, Hakim 'Abd al Hamid became secretary of Takmil al Tibb. The improvements at the college continued under his guidance. Still, for financial contributions the college depended on the patronage of many Indian rulers.

Hakim 'Abd al Rashid and Hakim 'Abd al Hamid were both involved in local and national organisations of Unani practitioners, government boards and many advisory committees of other Unani colleges. In 1911 the *hakims* of Lucknow founded the Anjuman-i Tibbiya, the Medical Society, whose general aim was the advancement of Unani *tibb*. Hakim 'Abd al Rashid became the secretary. Hakim 'Abd al Hamid was involved in the All India Ayurvedic and Tibbi Conference, and was active during a period of government inquiries into Unani medicine and the consequent setting up of many colleges. He was a member of the UP Board of Indian Medicine in 1926, on the selection committee for the new medical school of Aligarh Muslim University, and on the syllabus committee of the Tibbi College in Hyderabad. He was also a member of the All India Sanitary Conference (1914), on the board of the Allahabad Persian and Arabic and Tibbi examiners (1927), and a member of the Provincial Board for the Prevention of Epidemics (1929). Other family members continued to be involved in teaching at, and running, Takmil al Tibb, and also to be members on Government boards as well as on various advisory committees.

The third phase of the family stemmed directly from the second. Family members moved beyond the Takmil al Tibb institution in Lucknow and were involved in other medical schools and colleges. After setting up his own medical school Hakim 'Abd al Halim (1905-54), the fourth son of Hakim 'Abd al 'Aziz, became principal of another medical institution in Lucknow over whose development and subsequent merger he repeatedly presided until 1951.

Both Hakim 'Abd al Latif (d. 1970) and Hakim 'Abd al Hasib (1917-74) were involved in the Tibbiya College of Aligarh Muslim University. 'Abd al Hasib received some of his education at Aligarh Muslim University and later returned to serve as principal of the Tibbiya College, where he improved the research facilities. With the introduction of postgraduate training in medicine in Aligarh he became its first professor. Hakim 'Abd al Latif joined the College on its inception in 1927 as a teacher, and worked as its principal from 1949 to 1961. He was also on many advisory committees of *tibbi* institutions from Patna to Hyderabad.[52]

The movements of the 'Aziz family indicate clearly the different phases of Unani medicine. While the first family members worked according to the traditional mould, the activities of the following generations revealed the increasing bureaucratisation and professionalisation of Unani medicine. Schools and colleges with institutional structures were set up and took over medical education. With that followed hospitals and dispensaries. The state also provided bureaucratic structures through which the circumstances of Unani medicine could be influenced. Those concerned about the fate of Unani *tibb*, like the 'Azizis, made use of these modern structures to safeguard the future of the precious medical knowledge they had inherited from the past.

Pharmacology

Theory and sources

The theory of Unani pharmacology corresponded to the Galenic medical theories. Just as people had specific temperaments, so did drugs. They too were characterised as hot, cold, dry and wet, or any combination thereof. Drugs were further graded according to four degrees of potency, the first being the mildest and the fourth degree the strongest. The effect of a drug on a healthy, well-balanced person provided the standard by which the temperament of a drug was decided. This categorisation was by nature somewhat vague since the effects produced might vary from person to person; hence different compilers of pharmacopoeia classified the same drugs differently. Since each drug and each patient had their own temperaments, they had to be matched carefully by the *hakim*. A practitioner never prescribed a drug of the fourth degree at the beginning of treatment. He would start off with a drug of a lower grade and, depending on its effects, adjust the treatment accordingly. In the course of a single treatment, the drugs given to the patient could therefore be changed several times. Some restrictions on food consumption or living habits had also to be imposed, since the effects of relatively mild drugs could otherwise be neutralised by food with the opposite qualities. The same caution had to be exercised in the composition of compound drugs so that their different elements did not cancel each other out. Every drug prescribed or made up in Unani medicine was chosen uniquely for each patient according to his temperament.[53]

Pedanius Dioscorides of Cilicia, here shown teaching, is considered the father of scientific pharmacology. His De Materia Medica *in five volumes was written about 77 BC and describes the medicines found in their raw state in the mineral, vegetable and animal realms, their treatment and everything relating to the preparation and preservation of the drugs. It was copied again and again during the later Greco-Roman and Byzantine periods, and later used by the Arabs as the basis for their pharmacology. Right hand title page miniature from* De Materia Medica *dated 626 AH (AD 1229). Topkapi Palace Museum, Istanbul.*

The sources of Unani pharmacology were to be found in the Greek, ancient Persian, and Indian traditions. Persia and especially India had access to a rich fauna and flora which was reflected in the pharmacological literature produced in these two countries. The most important source text for Unani pharmacology was Dioscorides' *de Materia Medica* which was translated in the ninth century by Istafan ibn Basil and Hunain ibn Ishaq. Known as the *Kitab al Hasha'ish fi hayula l tibb*, it became the main reference book for pharmacologists in Unani medicine.The text consisted of five volumes dealing with plant, mineral and animal drugs. Dioscorides' *de Materia Medica* was translated again and again from the Greek into Arabic, Syriac and later Persian. Almost all the subsequent pharmacological compilations have cited him, or used his text as a model. Other important source materials were a text of Galen in which he explained the effectiveness and usefulness of different drugs, and other Greek writers like Paul of Aegina.[54] But Unani pharmacology was influenced, more so than any other medical discipline, by sources from India and Persia.

Simple and compound drugs

Drugs used in Unani medicine were derived from plants, minerals and animals. The classical division made in Unani pharmacology was between simple and compound drugs. Sections on drugs were found in many of the medical text-books, such as al Tabari's *Firdaws al hikma*, al Razi's *al Hawi*, al Zahrawi's *al Tasrif*, and, of course, ibn Sina's *Qanun* which had two of its five volumes devoted to the subject. 'Ali ibn 'Isa's work on ophthalmology, the *Tazkirat al kahhalin*, contained a chapter on drugs useful for diseases of the eye. Apart from these, there was a huge range of books devoted entirely to simple and compound drugs.

Books on simple drugs were often entitled, or had as part of their title the phrase, *Kitab al Adwiya al mufrada* (Book on Simple Drugs). Most of them were similar in content, since later authors usually copied and used the materials of their predecessors. The major difference between the various compilations was in the number of drugs they listed and how they were ordered. In some texts, like the *Kitab Quwa l adwiya al mufrada* (The Powers of the Simple Drugs) by ibn Abi l Ash'at, the drugs were listed by name according to the Arabic alphabet. In some they were listed by name according to the *abjad* alphabet,[55] an example being the *Kitab al Jami' li aqwal al qudama' wa l mutahaddithin mina l atibba' wa l mutafalsifin fi l adwiya al mufrada* (Collection of Views on Simple Drugs of Ancient and Modern Physicians and Philosophers) by Abu Bakr Hamid ibn Samajun written in tenth century Cordoba. In some, like the *Kitab al Musta'ini* by Yusuf ibn Ishaq ibn Biklarish composed in the late eleventh/early twelfth century, the drugs were ordered according to the Maghrebian alphabet. Some compilations of simple drugs were arranged into sections dealing with the different substances (seeds, leaves, flowers, grains, oils, minerals etc.). An example of this can be found in the second part of al Majusi's *Kitab al Malaki*. In some texts the drugs were divided into sections according to their degree of potency. This is the case in the *Kitab al I'timad fi l adwiya al mufrada* (Book of Confidence concerning Simple Drugs) of ibn al Jazzar (d. *c.* 1004), which was also translated into Latin. Ibn Sina in his *Qanun* was the first to put all the known data about drugs into tables. In some books the drugs were ordered according to the organs and symptoms which they were to heal, as in the *Kitab al Mughni fi l adwiya al mufrada* of Ziya al Din Abu Muhammad 'Abd Allah ibn Ahmad called ibn al Baitar (d. 1248), and in some books according to the illness they were supposed to cure, as in the

As with most Unani hospitals, the Nizamia General Unani Hospital in Hyderabad runs an extensive drug laboratory. Here, the drug-prescriptions for the patients are prepared daily by highly trained pharmacists. Much attention is paid to each step in the preparation of drugs.

Opposite: In this folio from an Indian copy of 'De Materia Medica' by the Greek Pedacius Dioscorides, three different bamboo plants are depicted. Although missing here, the accompanying text must have described the healing qualities of these varieties. Deccan, dated 1595. Collection: Howard Hodgkin, London.

Kitab al Tazkira of 'Izz al Din Abu Ishaq Ibrahim ibn Muhammad ibn Tarkhan al Suwaidi (1204-96).

The first Arabic text on simple drugs is said to have been written even before the Dioscorides translation. This is the eighth century *Kitab Quwa l 'aqaqir wa manafi 'iha wa mazarriha* (On the Power, Benefits and Ill-Effects of Drugs) by Masarjis, now lost. The first treatise composed in Persian was the *Kitab al Abniya 'an haqa'iq al adwiya* by Abu Mansur Muwaffaq in the tenth century. The most famous work on simple drugs was the *Kitab al Jami' li mufradat al adwiya wa l aghziya* by ibn al Baitar. It is a compilation citing 260 earlier works, in which ibn al Baitar edited his predecessors' findings and corrected their mistakes. The *Jami'* was copied, translated and used as a model for further pharmacological compilations.

Compound drugs comprised a completely separate branch of pharmacology. These are drugs which are made up of different components, each ingredient possessing individual characteristics. By being mixed together certain temperaments of the components will be enhanced while others will be suppressed. Compound drugs may have more than 150 ingredients, but also as few as two. Compound drugs are dealt with in a separate section of the literature, which generally consists of collections of formularies. These were called *aqrabadin* or *qarabadin*, meaning lists of drugs. This branch of pharmacology was heavily influenced by Galen's writings and all books on compound drugs have followed him in that the drugs were either ordered according to the organ to be treated, or according to the type and substance (powder, cream, plaster, etc.) of the drug. The most important texts on compound drugs were those of Sabur ibn Sahl (d. 869), of Ya'qub ibn Ishaq al Kindi (d. 870), of Amin al Dawla Abu l Hasan Hibat Allah ibn al Tilmiz (d. 1154 or 1165), volume five of ibn Sina's *Qanun,* as well as two collections of al Razi and of Najib al Din al Samarqandi (d. 1222). The two most comprehensive compilations were those of Badr al Din Muhammad ibn Bahram ibn Muhammad al Qalanisi (late twelfth/early thirteenth century), and of Abu l Muna ibn abi Nasr al Kuhin al 'Attar al Isra'ili (thirteenth century). The latter was more widely used than the *Aqrabadin* of al Qalanisi.

Unani pharmacology had to deal with the problem of finding replacement drugs when a substance became too expensive or unavailable. The theory dictated that one drug could be replaced by another if the second had the same temperament and was of the same degree of strength. Many of those who wrote on drugs either composed separate texts on substitute drugs, or included sections on them in their main work. Another difficulty which had to be overcome was the wide divergence of plant names. In translating from the Greek, Indian, Persian or Arabic pharmacological texts, the plants mentioned had to be identified and a name had to be found for them in the language into which the text was being translated. This problem was overcome by the creation of lists of synonyms. When writing about medical drugs, an author would often include the name of the substance he was dealing with in a variety of different languages, in different dialects, and in folk terminology. Since the same textbooks were used from Andalusia to India, many language barriers had to be overcome. A number of works were created specifically for this purpose. The most comprehensive was the *Kitab al Simat fi asma' al nabat* of 'Izz al Din al Suwaidi. In it al Suwaidi listed the Greek, Syriac, Persian, Castilian and Berber names next to the Arabic entry. The different variants of the Arabic name used in Egypt, Palestine, Spain and Cyprus, were also given. Substitute drugs and lists of synonyms allowed Unani pharmacology the flexibility it needed in adapting to the various countries it was introduced to.[56]

Pharmacology in the Indian environment [57]

From the outset, Unani pharmacology was heavily influenced by Indian sources. In India it found a country with a plant and mineral world much richer than any previously encountered. Unani physicians steadily increased their knowledge and use of Indian drugs by borrowing from Ayurvedic sources and undertaking their own research. It was through such research, for example, that Hakim Ajmal Khan, founder of the Tibbiya College in Delhi, discovered the medical uses of the plant *Rauwolfia serpentia*. It is used for neurovascular and nervous disorders such as hypertension, schizophrenia, hysteria, eclampsia, insomnia and psychosomatic conditions. The alkaloids in *Rauwolfia serpentina* were named after Ajmal Khan hence: Ajmaline, Ajmalinine, Isoajmaline, Neoajmaline, etc.[58] The development of Unani pharmacology in South Asia involved an adaptation to and an exploration of a different fauna and flora.

The earliest pharmacological book written in India was a Persian translation of the *Kitab al Saidana fi l tibb* by Abu l Raihan Muhammad ibn Ahmad al Biruni (d. 973). The translation was undertaken by Abu Bakr ibn 'Ali ibn 'Uthman Asfar al Kashani, who lived at the court of Sultan Iltutmish (1211-36). The book deals with *materia medica* and, besides lists of substitute drugs, it contained lists of synonyms from the Greek, Syriac, Persian, Indian and Hebrew traditions.[59] In the sixteenth century Rustam Jurjani, who had settled in the Deccan, compiled a pharmacological dictionary along the lines of ibn al Baitar's *Jami'*. Later this work became more popular within India than the book of ibn al Baitar. Known as the *Zakhira-i Nizam Shahi* (Treasure of Nizam Shah) it deals with simple and compound drugs and includes information on drugs used in India. As already mentioned, Firishta's *Dastur al atibba'* had a section on drugs which listed hundreds of substances widely used in Ayurvedic and Unani medicine at that time. Two *Alfaz-i adwiyas* (Vocabulary of Simple Drugs) were compiled by Hakim Shams al Din 'Ali Shirazi (d. 1595) and his son Hakim Nur al Din Muhammad 'Abd Allah. In the South Asian context the latter collection was especially important and it was one of the few works translated into English. The pharmacological compendium of the Mughals was *Ganj-i badaward* written by Hakim Aman Allah Khan (d. 1637). It was an extensive treatise dealing with simple and compound drugs used within both Ayurveda and Unani *tibb*. An important later work was that of Hakim A'zam Khan (d. 1903). His Unani pharmacopoeia, *Muhit-i A'zam*, was a compilation of simple drugs found in Unani, Ayurvedic, and some Western medical books. Hakim A'zam Khan listed the drugs with their natures and degrees as well as synonyms and substitutes.[60]

Many compilations of compound drugs were produced in India, especially during the Mughal period. Hakim Shaikh Jalal al Din Amrohi (eighteenth century) wrote *Qarabadin-i Jalali*; Hakim Iskandar Khan (eighteenth century) wrote *Qarabadin-i Hakim Sikandar*; Hakim Abdus Salam Burhanpuri (d. 1799) wrote *Qarabadin-i Salami*; and Hakim A'zam Khan wrote *Qarabadin-i A'zam*. The most outstanding, however, was the *Qarabadin-i Qadri* of Hakim Muhammad Akbar Arzani. It is a compilation of some 500 pages in which formularies were listed by organ. Many of the drugs mentioned in it were exclusively of Indian origin.[61]

The process of adaptation to the Indian environment has led to the further development of Unani pharmacology in South Asia. Unani drugs are widely used today by the Indian population, perhaps even more extensively than within Unani medicine itself.

The Contemporary Picture

In conjunction with other 'traditional' medical systems Unani medicine has experienced a marked revival over the last few years. It has benefited from the disaffections and problems associated with Western medicine. The enormous costs involved in training its practitioners and in manufacturing and purchasing its drugs together with the inability of Western medicine to find cures for many 'modern' illnesses, like cancer or AIDS, and the many side-effects of its pharmaceutical products have led to a degree of disillusionment. On the other hand Unani medicine while keeping its traditional principles and theories has adopted modern medical techniques. It uses modern diagnostic instruments, like x-rays and ultrasound, and its pharmaceutical industry is using increasingly modern technology. The drugs it produces have become patient-friendly in that they are sold as fine powders, capsules, tablets and syrups. The Indian Government has put funds towards further research into Unani medicine; it set up the Central Council for Research in Unani Medicine. Unani medicine has proved to be successful in treating leucoderma, rheumatism and arthritis, sinusitis, jaundice and elephantiasis. Further research today is directed towards cholesterol control, myocardial infarctions and leucoderma.[62]

For the patient Unani medicine is one of the many medical systems on offer. For the *hakim* it is a living tradition which has adapted itself to the changes of the twentieth century. And for the state Unani medicine is one of the indigenous medical systems able to provide some relief for large numbers of the Indian population. Unani medicine remains a vibrant tradition in the twentieth century; many different paths have developed in taking it forward, and its decline, once predicted, is not in sight.

Notes

1 Outside South Asia, this medical system is usually referred to as Islamic or Arabian Medicine. Here, for the sake of consistency, the term Unani has been used throughout the text.
2 Seyyed Hossein Nasr 1976, p. 160.
3 See Manfred Ullmann 1970, pp. 97-8; Seyyed Hossein Nasr 1976, pp. 159-62; O.P. Jaggi 1977(a), pp. 37-48.
4 *Tibb* means 'medicine' and from it are derived the forms *tibbi*—'medical', *tabib*—'medical doctor', *atibba'*—'medical doctors'. The noun *tibbiya* also means medicine, and is used in names of organisations and institutions in South Asia.
5 J.Christoph Burgel 1976, pp. 48-51; Seyyed Hossein Nasr 1976, pp. 154-5.
6 Sami K. Hamarneh 1983, p. 180; R.L. Verma and N.H. Keswani 1977, p. 281.
7 Seyyed Hossein Nasr 1976, pp. 155-6; O.P. Jaggi 1977(a), pp. 31-4; Sami K. Hamarneh 1983, pp. 178-9.
8 Seyyed Hossein Nasr 1976, pp. 157-9.
9 *Ibid.*, pp. 162-4; O.P. Jaggi 1977(a), pp. 56-9.
10 Seyyed Hossein Nasr 1976, pp. 180-1; O.P. Jaggi 1977(a), p. 55.
11 O.P. Jaggi 1977(a), p. 58.
12 Seyyed Hossein Nasr 1976, pp. 167-8; O.P. Jaggi 1977(a), pp. 56-9; Sami K. Hamarneh 1983, pp. 198-200.
13 O.P. Jaggi 1977(a), p. 63.
14 Seyyed Hossein Nasr 1976, pp. 166-7; O.P. Jaggi 1977(a), pp. 61-4; Sami K. Hamarneh 1983, pp. 179-80.
15 Seyyed Hossein Nasr 1976, p. 166; Sami K. Hamarneh 1983, p. 176.
16 Michael Dols gives the following definition of *tibb al nabi*:
a blend of three distinct elements ... : the folk medicine of the Arabian bedouin, the borrowing of Galenic concepts that had become common parlance (such as humours, temperaments, and qualities), and the over-arching principle of divine or supernatural causation.
(M.W. Dols 1988, p. 421; quoted in A.J. Newman 1988, p. xvi)
17 J. Christoph Burgel 1972, pp. 54-9.
18 For a sympathetic discussion of these medical traditions see Andrew J. Newman (ed.) 1991, pp. vii-xxiii. For a critical discussion see J. Christoph Burgel 1972, pp. 50-61.
19 Sami K. Hamarneh 1983, p. 189.
20 See Manfred Ullmann 1970.
21 Seyyed Hossein Nasr 1976, p. 182.
22 See O.P. Jaggi 1977(a).
23 Tazimuddin Siddiqi 1978, p. 185.
24 John C. Hume 1977, p. 218.
25 S. Zillurrahman 1986-7.
26 Tazimuddin Siddiqui 1981, pp. 170-4, 199-214.
27 The idea of devolving Unani treatment onto each family was aided, in the nineteenth century, by the translation of many books into Urdu, then the most widely used vernacular in Muslim north India. The idea of empowering a member of each family with a basic knowledge of medicine was made use of again in the women's education literature of the late nineteenth century. One of its most famous examples was Mawlana Ashraf 'Ali Thanawi's *Bihishti Zewar* which had a chapter devoted to the principles of Unani medicine as they could be used by the women of a family.
28 Nayyar Wasti 1978, p. 267-70.
29 *Ibid.*, p.280.
30 Seyyed Hossein Nasr 1976, p. 179.
31 For an overview see Hakim Abdul Hameed and Hakim Abdul Bari 1984.
32 Tazimuddin Siddiqui 1981, pp. 174-82.
33 See O.P. Jaggi 1970(a).
34 N.P. Rai, S.K. Tiwari, S.D. Upadhya, and G.N. Chaturvedi 1979.
35 Quoted in O.P. Jaggi 1977(a), p. 114.
36 Barbara D. Metcalf 1985, p. 5.
37 Roger Jeffery 1979-80, pp. 60-1.
38 Poonam Bala 1991, pp. 143-4.
39 Roger Jeffery 1979-80, p. 62; Poonam Bala 1991, pp. 41-8.
40 John C. Hume 1977.
41 Roger Jeffery 1979-80, p. 64; Poonam Bala 1991, pp. 85-8.
42 O.P. Jaggi 1977(b).
43 Roger Jeffery 1988, pp. 185-6.
44 Roger Jeffery 1979-80, pp. 66-7.
45 *Ibid.*, p. 63.
46 Barbara D. Metcalf 1985, p. 4.
47 Tazimuddin Siddiqui 1980, p. 152.
48 *Ibid.*, p. 154.
49 Barbara D. Metcalf 1985, p. 5.
50 Tazimuddin Siddiqui 1980.
51 S. Zillurrahman 1978; S. Zillur Rahman and S. Siddiqi 1983; Abdul Halim Sharar 1989, pp. 97-8.
52 See S. Zillurrahman 1978; S. Zillur Rahman and S. Siddiqi 1983.
53 O.P. Jaggi 1977(a), pp. 40-1; Hakim Mohammed Said 1990, pp. 47-8.
54 Seyyed Hossein Nasr 1976, pp. 185, 187; Manfred Ullmann 1970, pp. 256-64.
55 *Abjad*—an alphabet which gives numerical value to letters.
56 See Manfred Ullmann 1970, pp. 257-313.
57 See O.P. Jaggi 1977(a).
58 Tazimuddin Siddiqui 1980, pp. 147-8.
59 Manfred Ullmann 1970, pp. 272-3.
60 M. Azeez Pasha 1974.
61 Tazimuddin Siddiqui 1981, pp. 184-98.
62 Roger Jeffery 179-80, pp. 66-8; Ramesh Menon with Kai Friese 1994.

References

Bala, Poonam. *Imperialism and Medicine in Bengal*, New Delhi, London & California, Sage Publications, 1991.

Burgel, J. Christoph. 'Secular and Religious Features of Medieval Arabic Medicine', in Charles Leslie (ed.), *Asian Medical Systems: A Comparative Study*, Berkeley, Los Angeles & London, University of California Press, 1976.

Dols, Michael W. 'Islam and Medicine', a review of Fazlur Rahman, *Health and Medicine in the Islamic Tradition*, in *History of Science*, 26, 1988.

Hamarneh, Sami K. 'The Life Sciences', in John R. Hayes (ed.), *The Genius of Arab Civilization*, 2nd edition, MIT Press, 1983.

Hameed, Hakim Abdul and Bari, Hakim Abdul. 'Impact of Ibn Sina's Medical Work in India', *Studies in History of Medicine*, 8:1 & 2, 1984, pp. 1-12.

Hume, John C. 'Rival Traditions: Western Medicine and Yunani Tibb in the Punjab, 1849-1889', *Bulletin of the History of Medicine*, 51, 1977, pp. 214-31.

Jaggi, O.P. *Medicine in Medieval India*, Delhi, 1977(a).

___ 'Indian Systems of Medicine during British Supremacy in India', *Studies in History of Medicine*, 1:4, 1977(b), pp. 320-47.

Jeffery, Roger. 'Indian Medicine and the State', *Bulletin of the British Association of Orientalists*, 11, 1979-80, pp. 58-70.

___ *The Politics of Health in India*, Berkeley, Los Angeles & London, University of California Press, 1988.

Leslie, Charles. 'The Professionalization of Ayurvedic and Unani Medicine' *Transactions of the New York Academy of Science*, 30, 1968, pp. 559-72.

Menon, Ramesh, with Friese, Kai. 'On the Way to a Healthy Revival', *India Today* (International Edition), March 31, 1994, pp. 92-7.

Metcalf, B.D. 'Nationalist Muslims in British India: The Case of Hakim Ajmal Khan', *Modern Asian Studies*, 19:1, 1985, pp. 1-28.

Nasr, Seyyed Hossein. *Islamic Science: An Illustrated Study*, World of Islam Festival Publishing Co. Ltd.,1976.

Newman, Andrew J. (ed), *Islamic Medical Wisdom: The Tibb al A'imma*, London, The Muhammadi Trust, 1991.

Pasha, M. Azeez. 'Muheet-A-Azam (A Great Unani Pharmacopeia)', *Bulletin of the Indian Institute of the History of Medicine*, 4, 1974, pp. 19-25.

Rai, N.P., Tiwari, S.K., Upadhya, S.D., and Chaturvedi, G.N. 'The Origin and Development of Pulse Examination in Medieval India', *Studies in History of Medicine*, 3:2, 1979, pp. 110-24.

Said, Hakim Mohammed 'Islamic Medicine and the Art of Drug-Making: A Historical Perspective', *Hamdard*, 33:1, 1990, pp. 43-57.

Shankaranand, B. 'Unani and Other Systems of Medicine in Health Care', *Hamdard*, 26:2, 1983. pp. 55-9.

Sharar, Abdul Halim. *Lucknow: The Last Phase of an Oriental Culture*, translated and edited by E.S. Harcourt and Fakhir Hussain, Delhi, OUP, 1989.

Siddiqi, Tazimuddin. 'Unani Medicine in India during the Delhi Sultanate', *Studies in History of Medicine*, 2:3, 1978, pp. 183-9.

Siddiqui (*sic.*), Tazimuddin. 'Hakim Ajmal Khan: A Champion of Indian Medicine', *Studies in History of Medicine*, 4:1, 1980, pp. 145-76.

___ 'Hakim Muhammad Akbar Arzani', *Studies in History of Medicine*, 5:3, 1981, pp. 167-214.

Thanawi, Ashraf 'Ali. *Bihishti Zewar*, Sadhaura, 1905.

Ullmann, Manfred. *Die Medizin im Islam*, Leiden/Koln, E.J. Brill, 1970.

Verma, R.L., and Keswani, N.H. 'Women's contribution to Unani Medicine in India', *Studies in History of Medicine*, 1:4, 1977, pp. 279-84.

Wasti, Nayyar. 'Iranian Physicians in the Indian Subcontinent', *Studies in History of Medicine*, 2:4, 1978, pp. 264-83.

Zillurrahman, S. *Tazkira-i Khandan-i 'Azizi*, Aligarh, 1978.

___ 'Tibb-i Firoz Shahi by Shah Quli', *Studies in History of Medicine and Science*, 10-11, 1986-87, pp. 1-16.

Zillur Rahman (*sic.*) S., and Siddiqi, Tazimuddin. 'The 'Azizi Family of Physicians', *Studies in History of Medicine*, 7:1, 1983, pp. 1-93.

As part of the pañcakarma treatment (see pages 89-91) patients may attend specialised departments in Ayurvedic hospitals for different kinds of body massage. Podar Ayurvedic Hospital, Bombay.

Theory and Practice of Ayurvedic Medicine

Robert Svoboda

Ayurveda in History

Healing and healers have probably been a part of Indian civilisation from its earliest beginnings. While the technologically-advanced civilisation of Harappa, which arose around or before 3000 BC, is likely to have possessed therapists, it is currently impossible to know how their art related to Ayurveda, the system of medicine which developed from the ancient books of wisdom known as the Vedas. Diseases and remedies are mentioned in many parts of the Vedas, but most often in the *Atharva Veda*, the fourth of the four Vedas. The Ayurveda that we know at present began life as an *upaveda*, or subsidiary body of knowledge, for the *Atharva Veda*, which is basically a manual of magic, and Ayurvedic therapeutics during the Vedic era is likely to have been significantly ritualised.

The regard that physicians enjoyed during the early Vedic period faded as later changes in social organisation excluded physicians from much religious ritual. The ritual impurity doctors incur by handling blood, pus, and other body substances eventually so downgraded their social status that they were impelled to professionalise. Cast out by the priestly caste, many doctors sought service with royalty or with affluent merchants, aiming thereby to re-establish good reputations while being well recompensed for their work. Among the noteworthy texts composed during this period to train these professionals are two of Ayurveda's three most famous treatises: the *Caraka Saṃhitā* and the *Suśruta Saṃhitā*. The overall success of this more business-like approach to medicine may have been one factor which caused the spread Ayurveda during this era. One factor of undeniable sigificance was the enthusiastic support many Buddhist rulers showed for the practice of medicine as an active means of showing compassion to living beings.

Much Ayurvedic knowledge and many Ayurvedic practitioners were lost during the Muslim invasions which swept over India during the first half of this millenium. While reeling from this blow Ayurveda was challenged by the Unani (Greco-Arabic) medicine that the Muslim invaders brought with them, and by the time these two systems had reached a *modus vivendi* the British had begun to administer roughly half of India, and to strongly influence the other half. At first many Europeans seemed interested in Ayurveda, just as Alexander the Great had shown interest when he entered India in the fourth century BC, but by 1835 the British government had decided not to support Ayurveda. Only after the start of the Indian independence movement did Ayurvedic institutions again begin to regenerate, and one of the fruits of political agitation in the early part of this century was the founding of many new colleges of Ayurveda.

Political calculations have continued to influence Ayurveda's development, in particular the ongoing dispute of tradition versus progress. Many Ayurvedists, practitioners and educators alike, are convinced that Ayurvedic doctrines are so fundamentally archaic that Ayurveda can only be saved as a medical system by extensively integrating the tenets of modern medicine into its structure to form an 'integrated' medical system. Those authorities who support *śuddha* (pure) Ayurveda are equally convinced that the fundamentals of Ayurveda are superior to those of modern medicine, and that only certain useful technological advances need be considered for adoption into the Ayurvedic armamentarium. Integrated practitioners try to position themselves as innovators who battle against blind orthodoxy, while the 'pure' faction sees itself as fighting a rearguard action to prevent the destruction of the Indian cultural environment while remaining open to worthwhile innovation.

After my arrival in 1974 at the Tilak Ayurveda Mahavidyalaya, an Ayurvedic college, in Poona, I was quickly and unwillingly drawn into this controversy. Few students could understand why I had come to study Ayurveda at all, when our medical system in the USA was so much more 'advanced', and few could appreciate that there are heavy prices to pay for all such 'advancement'. I admired many of my teachers from both camps; I was particularly impressed with both the knowledge and the ethics of the purists. While it was force of circumstance that placed me in the 'pure' camp at first, it soon became clear to me that most of the students and faculty who claimed to support 'integrated medicine' actually planned to welcome only a few fragments of Ayurveda into their system. The fight over Ayurveda's modern definition has already been decided in Sri Lanka, where the term 'Ayurveda' now signifies integrated medicine, and the 'pure' system has taken an alternative name. Until recently it seemed that the integrationists held the stonger hand in India as well, but the current surge of popularity for Ayurveda in other countries has by and large strengthened the 'purists'. The battlelines in India are now no longer clear, and the matter remains unresolved.

The following exposition of Ayurveda's basic principles has been strongly moulded by the influence of those of my instructors who most captivated me with their visions of what Ayurveda can be. The strongest influence of all these experts on my image of Ayurveda has been that of my mentor, the Aghori Vimalananda. He was heir to a Tantric tradition of scientific wonderment at the workings of the universe which, inspired by the Vedas, teaches its disciples to press the whole world, and their own lives, into service as their laboratories. It is his vision and his tradition which continue to inspire me today.

Ayurveda: An Eternal Tradition

> *This science of life is declared to be eternal, because it has no beginning, because it deals with tendencies which proceed innately from Nature, and because the nature of matter is eternal. For at no time was there a break either in the continuity of life or in the continuity of intelligence. The experience of life is perennial. ... At no time can it be said that the science of life sprang into existence having been non-existent before, unless the dissemination of knowledge by means of receiving and imparting instruction be considered as creation of such knowledge.* (Caraka Sūtrasthāna 30/27)

The fountainheads of Hindu culture are the four ancient books known as the Vedas, and the foundation of Vedic teaching is the principle that the entire cosmos which is our reality is just a small part of one singular 'absolute reality' which is often referred to as the *paramātmā* 'supreme self' or *puruṣa* 'ultimate person'. This *puruṣa* can only ever be represented in part, for 'Truth is singular; the wise speak of it in various ways'. Inspired by their visions of the absolute, Vedic seers called *rishis* (*ṛṣi*) visualised various ways to utter its truth. Their limited expressions of the unlimited reality became the Vedic hymns.

Classical Ayurveda is one such limited expression of reality. Like the Vedas themselves its texts are reputed to have been 'seen', not composed, by seers. Each sage who incarnates the spirit of Ayurveda is the creator and life-bringer for the cosmos of living knowledge which is his text, and each text is an inspired expression of the nature of life itself. By collecting together the dead, dry 'facts' of life and transmitting their own life force into this raw material, sages create living texts which transmit to those who study them something of the flavour of reality. Ayurveda itself is eternal, being an integral part of the universal reality, but it is unusable by ordinary humans until a seer, Prometheus-like, brings some of it down to earth.

As soon as Ayurveda was born as an *upaveda* it began to be taught and learned. Era by era knowledge accumulated until, in classical times, the collected wisdom was compressed into pithy texts, several of which are still studied in Ayurvedic colleges. Though thousands of years old they remain useful, their descriptions of human realities still fresh and practical, because they focus on principles, not details; details are provided by a guru's commentary. Texts tend to be handed down essentially intact, and it is the accumulated inferences of innovative physicians down the years which has continually updated the textual principles, equipping them to cope with changing conditions. Only when enlivened by the commentary of an expert mentor can an Ayurvedic text be reborn within a physician. When enhanced in this way an Ayurvedic treatise contains sufficient detail for the ordinary practitioner to use to practise successfully, and provides enough clues for the intelligent physician to use to infer what has remained unmentioned. The text

Opposite: *The Attainment of Samādhi. This splendid miniature illustrates yogic attainment as a cosmic figure representing the universe. From an early nineteenth century album containing 84 Hatha-yoga postures and twenty-four asanas. (See also pages 34 and 35) "This volume is stated by Major Jerome to have been obtained from the library of the Ranee of Jhansi, at the sacking of that place in April 1858. ..." The British Library, London.*

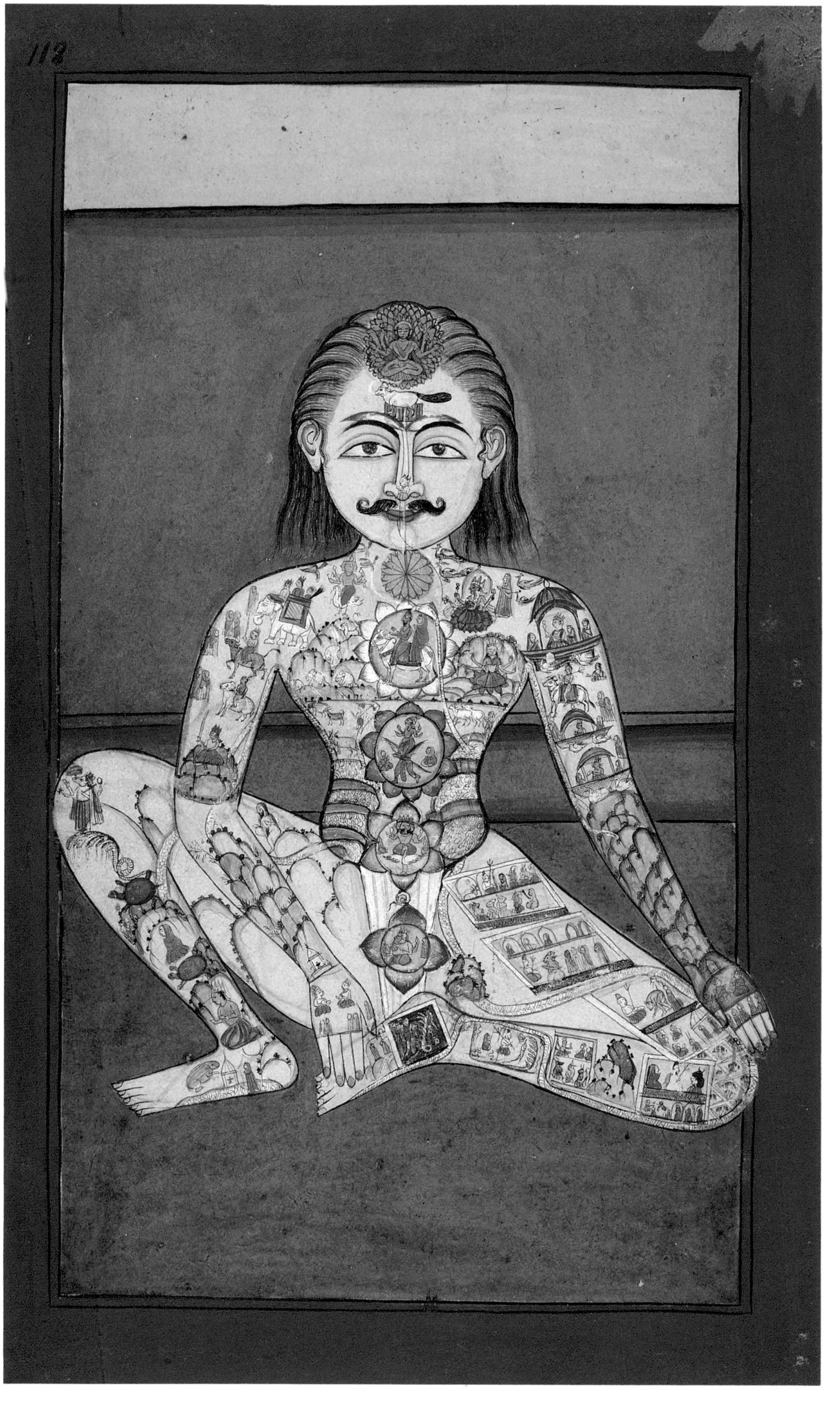

preserves the seed of the knowledge, which flowers whenever it is sown by a proficient gardener in a fertile pupil.

A student learns theory from a text and practice from a tradition. Only that inspiration which is obtainable through a living tradition can give life to the corpse that is the theoretical framework; the spark of life that is passed down through the lineage is the soul of the learning. All texts do not agree in every detail, for each Ayurvedic text is a unique expression of the reality of embodied life as expressed by an individual seer. All teachers who teach the same text teach the same theory, but their teaching is personalised according to their individual ability and their tradition's capacity. The authentic text in any living tradition is the living text an authority on the subject creates, moment by moment, by living his practice, which is his personal commentary on the theory; to walk the walk *is* to talk the talk. Many have been and are Ayurveda's traditions, some more literary and some wholly oral, some wholly materialistic and others mostly spiritualised; but all such traditions which have endured have been directly passed down in unbroken line from mentor to disciple. Without tradition there is no Ayurveda.

Theoretical Bases

One widely-accepted description of the nature of the *paramātmā* 'supreme self' is *sat-cit-ānanda*: the absolute reality exists (*sat*) and is aware (*cit*) of its existence, and this awareness fills it with bliss (*ānanda*). While everything in the universe arises from the *puruṣa*, the *puruṣa* 'the ultimate person' or 'world soul' appears in the manifested universe most purely in the form of awareness. Every celestial object, every terrestrial rock, and every natural force in the cosmos possesses some form of consciousness, however rudimentary, as does each cell in the human body. In this worldview consciousness does not evolve from matter; matter rather evolves from consciousness. The *puruṣa* lives, and enjoys its life, when it takes on a body. It externalises itself in order to experience itself, and the production of matter is one of the consequences of this externalisation. Life is awareness, and as consciousness projects into matter life ceaselessly strives to develop new and better organs of sense and action. The human body is the best instrument for the expression of consciousness in matter that nature has yet developed after billions of years of evolution.

It is taught that everything that exists in the vast external universe, the *macrocosm*, also appears in the *microcosm*, the internal cosmos of the human body. Though the universe is eternal and without beginning, it periodically projects outward from singularity into multiplicity, remains multiple until its trajectory is spent, and then resolves again into unmanifestation. A human being, created in the image of the cosmos, originates when consciousness locates a zygote, a single cell containing all his or her potentialities. The zygote then projects explosively into a physical form which grows and develops, stabilises, decays, and dies. A human being is a living replica of the universe, and every part of the universe is as alive as every human cell. The parts need the whole, and the whole needs its parts. Although it sometimes seems capricious, the universe is well-ordered, and all beings who tenant it must act in accordance with the cosmic order in order to enjoy a long and satisfying life. The study of how to establish and preserve a harmonious relationship between between the great and singular macrocosm and the many individual microcosms is the proper study of Ayurveda.

Sāṅkhya

Classical Ayurvedic theory is related to the Sāṅkhya philosophy, which details the evolution of awareness into a number (*sāṅkhya*) of material evolutes. Sāṅkhya postulates that before creation occurs there is no universe; all that exists is *puruṣa*, the 'absolute reality' of *sat-cit-ānanda* which is homogenous spirit beyond time, space, and causation. All potentialities exist within the *puruṣa*, but none manifest until within this single point without magnitude the desire to produce individuals who might perceive and know reality arises, spontaneously. This moment of primeval desire is the instant when the cosmos catapults into existence. Each atom that arises in that instant is a fragment of that *puruṣa* who desired to experience, and that desire to exist and experience is present in each of those atoms. Desire may be minimal in 'inert' matter and maximal in humans, but like consciousness it lurks everywhere. Desire is the basis for both macrocosm and microcosm; the craving which causes two people to unite sexually is but a reflection of that original desire which caused duality to arise from unity.

In Sāṅkhya philosophy we cannot speak of the cosmos separate from the *puruṣa*, nor of the *puruṣa* separate from the cosmos; *puruṣa* is cause, and cosmos is effect. In no way can we explain cause as separate from effect; they flow into one another, because they are two time-varied states of the same thing. The first Sāṅkhyan evolute which evolves when desire disrupts the absoluteness of the absolute is *prakṛti*, or 'nature', the matrix of the manifested universe. Nature is a seamless consciousness which differs from *puruṣa* only in the conviction that *she* is different. When *prakṛti* senses *her* separateness *she* evolves into undifferentiated transcendent intelligence (*mahat*). This intelligence atomises into individual bundles of *ahaṃkāra*, the 'I-creator', the force which produces 'I-ness' in an organism. Without *ahaṃkāra* there would be no living beings, for there would be no sense of individuality to permit them to differentiate into discrete units.

Ahaṃkāra has three *guṇas*, or attributes: *sattva* (equilibrium), *rajas* (activity) and *tamas* (inertia). *Rajas* ('I' as action) represents kinetic energy, and *tamas* ('I' as unconscious being) produces particles of potential energy (i.e. matter). The objectivity of *tamas* evolves into the five objects of the senses—sound, touch, form, taste and odour—which in turn produce the 'five great elements' (*pañca mahābhūtas*) which make up the physical universe: space, air, fire, water and earth. These elements make up the physical body of living beings, the sheath of matter which embodies the mind and spirit. *Sattva* ('I' as conscious being) is the subjective consciousness which resides within the body, perceiving and manipulating objective matter and energy. *Sattva* develops into the mind and the ten senses: the five senses of cognition—hearing, touch, sight, taste and smell—through which we take in information from the world, and the five senses of action, with which we express ourselves in the world: speech (which symbolises all forms of communication), hands (which symbolise creative action), feet (locomotion), genitals (reproduction) and anus (elimination). Of *ahaṃkāra*'s three attributes it is *sattva* which most fully expresses consciousness.

For Sāṅkhya, embodied life is the functioning as one unit in one place at one time of the five great elements, the five cognitive senses and the five active senses, the thinking mind, *ahaṁkāra*, and the intellect, enlivened by the individual soul, the witness without whom all the other components remain inert. All the Sāṅkhyan principles which compose the universe thus also appear in an embodied being. The individual soul, which is a personalised counterpart of the cosmic *puruṣa*, is also called *puruṣa*. The consciousness which is the individual *puruṣa* is firmly fixed in the body, and depends on the body's health or ill-health for the quality of its expression. In fact, one word for health in Sanskrit, *svastha*, means 'established in oneself'.

To understand the body one must understand the five great elements which make up the body. All matter in the universe is made up of these elements: earth, water, fire, air and space. Earth represents the solid state of matter, water the liquid state, air the gaseous state, fire the power to change the state of any substance, and space the field which is simultaneously the source of all matter and the space in which it exists. These elements are stages in the manifestation of matter, space being the most rarefied and earth the most solid. The author Caraka defines a human as the assemblage of these five elements plus the 'immaterial self':

> *The earth is represented in man by hardness, water by moisture, fire by heat, air by the vital breath* (prāṇa)*, space by the interstices and the self by the indwelling spirit.*
> (Śārīrasthāna 5/5).

Without that immaterial self, the body is but a corpse; in fact, one way of saying in Sanskrit that people have died is to say that they have 'gone to fiveness', that is, gone to the state where all that remains of them are the five *mahābhūtas* which made up the physical aspect of their existence.

From the Ayurvedic perspective bodily health should be an individual's primary objective:

> *An intelligent man should therefore specially devote himself to those endeavours which assure the body's well-being. The body is truly the support of one's well-being, since humans are established in the body. Leaving everything else one should take care of the body, for in the absence of the body there is the total extinction of all that characterises embodied beings.*
> (Caraka Nidānasthāna 6/6-7)

Body, mind, and longevity

Body evolves from mind, but mind is dependent on body. Ayurvedists have focused much attention on the seeming paradox that there is both a fundamental difference between, and a fundamental identity of, mind and body. The striking verse which begins the first chapter of *Aṣṭāṅgahṛdaya*, a famous compilation (*c.* AD 600) of the texts of Caraka and Suśruta, reflects this mind-body reciprocity. The chapter is entitled *Āyuṣkāmīya*, the 'Desire for Life', or 'Desire for Longevity':

> *Obeisances to that unique physician who has utterly destroyed all diseases, beginning with desire* (rāga)*, which are innate to the body and pervade it, producing agitation* (autsukya)*,*

delusion (moha), *and dissatisfaction* (arati).
(Vāgbhaṭa Sūtrasthāna 1/1)

Caraka is famous for his exposition of internal medicine, and Suśruta is known as Ayurveda's most famous surgeon. Vāgbhaṭa's claim to fame is his *Sūtrasthāna* (Section on Aphorisms), which succinctly expresses the essence of Ayurveda in rhythmic verse. Traditionally every student of Ayurveda was expected to memorise word-for-word the text they studied, and many thousands of Ayurvedic students have thanked Vāgbhaṭa for making his tome so easy to commit to memory. Vāgbhaṭa placed his *Sūtrasthāna* at the beginning of his work because it is the epitome of all that follows it. Since this first chapter of the *Sūtrasthāna* is the first chapter a student would learn, Vāgbhaṭa ensured that it succinctly epitomises the whole *Sūtrasthāna*, which thus makes it a worthy summary of the entire science. A leisurely stroll through this chapter can therefore provide a reasonable overview of Ayurvedic theory.[1]

Because the scripts used for Sanskrit have no capitalisation and little punctuation, position becomes an indicator of importance. *Rāgādi* (beginning with *rāga*), which is the first word of this first chapter, is therefore particularly emphasised. *Rāga* (which is closely related to the English word 'rage') means desire, passion, and heat. When desire for life—the fundamental cause for both macrocosm and microcosm—mutates into uncontrolled passion it disrupts contentment and drags the mind away from balance. This is what makes it the first of all diseases. Desire perturbs the primeval equilibrium to permit the cosmos to evolve, and enables disease to evolve by perturbing an individual's equilibrium. Satisfaction creates calmness, and so coolness, in the consciousness; agitation generated by dissatisfaction, especially with regard to selfish desires, causes that abnormal heat of passion which disturbs all layers of the organism.

The word *Āyurveda* means 'the science of life', or 'the knowledge of longevity'. Longevity is not expressed in lifespan alone; a long but unhappy, unhealthy, destitute life may not be worth living. Ayurveda values quality far more than it values quantity, and Ayurveda's concept of longevity is a life well-lived, month by month and year by year, an unending succession of 'good days'. When life is well lived you have longevity, no matter how long your earthly existence may last. Living well is possible only when mind and body are in harmony, and when the individual cosmos is in harmony with the external universe. This first chapter is entitled 'Desire for Longevity', and its first verse warns clearly that there is no longevity in the absence of satisfaction.

Whether desire and passion lead to healthy enjoyment or to disease is partly a matter of degree. *Autsukya* can mean both 'anxiety, uneasiness, attachment' and 'ardent desire, eagerness, zeal'; *moha* can mean 'insensibility, perplexity, confusion, folly, infatuation, affliction, pain' or it can mean 'wonderment'; *arati* indicates all the states (including languor, anxiety, regret, agitation, and discontent) which arise from the longings of love. The line between satiation and excess is a fine one, and because human beings tend to be overwhelmed by the power of passion, it is common for the heat of *rāga* to inflame the organism, and metamorphose into the diseases which begin with desire (*rāgādi*); among these are lust, anger, greed, arrogance, envy, hatred, fear, and disgust. This emphasis on the pathological face of desire, and on its associated negative emotions, is one way of saying that the body is ruled by the very consciousness which is established within it and dependent upon it. The body and the mind can no more be separated from one another than smoke can be separated from its fire, and there can be no health when these two essential components of embodied existence refuse to co-operate.

Longevity and Ayurveda
Here is verse 2 of the chapter entitled 'Desire for Life':

Those who desire longevity, which is the means by which dharma, artha, *and* sukha *are obtained, should place the utmost faith in the teachings of Ayurveda.*
(Vāgbhaṭa Sūtrasthāna 1/2)

Desire for existence is the ultimate foundation of both the internal human cosmos and the external universe, and the vast majority of human actions arise from some species of desire. While the most fundamental of all human desires is desire for longevity, in the next rank of importance come three goals: *dharma*, *artha*, and *sukha*. *Dharma*, which some translate as 'duty', is really 'doing what you were born to do', doing what best fits your individual aptitude in the context of your familial and societal responsibilities. *Dharma* is that path through life which when followed causes you to achieve your destiny, which is that which you were born to achieve. *Artha* means 'wealth' or 'resources', and represents all material means, including both money and knowledge, needed to live life fully in pursuit of *dharma*. A long but impoverished life is too often a wretched life. Wealth earned through one's own right livelihood lends dignity to life, and advances the cause of *sukha*. *Sukha* is 'happiness', which is the achievement of your *dharma*-aspirations by means of your *artha*-resources. *Sukha* includes both *kāma*, the pleasure of sensory enjoyment, and the bliss of *moksa*, or 'liberation', which is freedom from bondage to the mind and the senses.

Sukha, which is usually translated as 'happiness', literally means 'good space', and *duḥkha* (misery) means 'bad space'. In the bodily context 'space' means the spaces within which things flow. When there is 'good space' things will flow well, and life will be uncomplicated; 'bad flow' indicates obstruction, frustration, and imbalance. *Sukha* and *duḥkha* also mean 'health' and 'ill-health' respectively; people who are truly happy are usually also healthy, and the miserable of mind are usually miserable in body as well. 'Good space' in body and mind creates health and happiness, while 'bad space' produces disease and distress.

Verses 1 and 2 of this chapter promise that although disease is innate to the body and pervades it, both physical disease and its mental counterparts can be removed by those who follow the path blazed by the *rishis*. This assertion was revolutionary in its time, for many of the ancients believed that sickness and health were determined by fate, and that one ought not tamper with destiny by trying to cure disease. Ayurveda boldly refutes that position by asserting that nothing happens without cause because cause and effect are two time-varied states of the same thing, and that what is fate today is merely the result of previously performed actions. Ayurveda teaches that suffering is caused, and that health can be caused.

Verses 3 and 4 provide a mythical lineage which links the student, of whatever era, to those seers who recognised that both disease and its cure are inherent in embodied life. Caraka tells us that Ayurveda appeared in our world when a number of great sages met together and, motivated by compassion for those town and city dwellers whose lives were being disturbed by disease, said to themselves,

> *Health is the supreme foundation of* dharma, artha, kāma, *and* mokṣa, *while diseases are the destroyers of health, of the good in life, and of life itself. How can we remedy this great impediment to humanity's progress?*
> (Caraka Sūtrasthāna 1/15b-17a)

Meditating on this problem they obtained Ayurveda from the celestials and translated this divine knowledge into human language. They used the Sanskrit language for their treatises because of its proven ability to join fragments of knowledge together into living structures.

> Kāya, Bāla, Graha, Ūrdhvāṅga, Śalya, Daṃṣṭrā, Jarā, *and* Vṛṣa *are the eight limbs of Ayurveda in which treatment is embodied.* (Aṣṭāṅgahṛdaya Sūtrasthāna 1/5b-6a)

Ayurveda, which is living wisdom, incarnates its theory in texts like *Aṣṭāṅgahṛdaya*, and its practice in individual practitioners. Like all other living beings it possesses limbs, which are: internal medicine, gynaecology/obstetrics/paediatrics, psychology, eye-ear-nose-throat, surgery, detection of poisons, geriatrics/ rejuvenation, and virilisation. These limbs of practice all sprout from the same theoretical tree.

The three *doṣas*

> *In short,* vāta, pitta, *and* kapha *are the three* doṣas; *when abnormal they destroy the body, while they sustain it when not abnormal.* (Aṣṭāṅgahṛdaya Sūtrasthāna 1/6b-7a)

Here is the trunk of that theoretical tree: the three *doṣas*. *Doṣa* is derived from the root *duṣ*, which is equivalent to the English prefix 'dys': dys-function, dys-trophy, dys-plasia, and so on. A *doṣa* is any fault or error, any transgression against the rhythm of life which promotes chaos. Though we could speak of any number of *doṣas*, and later commentators on the surgical authority Suśruta talk of four (they include 'blood'), since antiquity the Ayurvedic mainstream has used three. The three *doṣas* of the microcosm—*vāta*, *pitta* and *kapha*—are active, hard-to-control condensations of the five great elements, created by nature to satisfy some of the peculiar requirements of living matter. *Vāta* arises from air and space, *pitta* from fire and water, and *kapha* from water and earth, and their tasks are to manipulate those elements within the context of the microcosm. While every substance in our world is made up of the five elements and can be classified according to their predominant element, it is usually more meaningful, when discussing the life of living beings, to speak in terms of the *doṣas*, the forces which manipulate the elements within the microcosm.

Vāta is in charge of all motion in the body and mind; everything that moves, from a molecule to a thought, moves because of *vāta*, and every motion of any kind influences every other motion. *Pitta* is in charge of all transformation in the organism; it digests food in the gut, light in the eyes, and sensory data in the brain. *Kapha* is the stabilising influence in the living being; it lubricates, maintains, and contains, and its various activites, like those of *vāta* and *pitta*, are all interrelated. Life is inconceivable without these three activities: movement, metabolism, and stability, or kinetic energy (*vāta*), potential energy (*pitta*), and regulatory energy (*kapha*). No one of these forces can singly sustain life; all three must work together, each in its own way, for health to result.

When balanced these energies cause the body's elements to cohere together and function together healthily; only when they are unbalanced do they prevent cohesion, disturb function, and create chaos among all the organism's other constitutents. When they do go out of balance disease is almost inevitable, for it is their nature to vitiate. This is why Vāgbhaṭa states that they sustain the body 'when not abnormal', instead of 'when normal', for the three *doṣas* are not 'normal'. They are flaws in the organism, waste products produced when the body replenishes its elements. When a being is healthy its digestion is powerful and little metabolic waste is produced; during ill-health, waste prevails. Like the body's physical wastes the *doṣas* support the body only so long as they continuously flow out of it, and in fact proper elimination of urine, faeces and sweat helps to maintain healthy levels of the *doṣas* within the body.

Kapha generally expends its force by projecting itself into the production of the lubricant substances which are its vehicles. So long as the right amount of *kapha* is produced and, after doing its job, is expelled from the body, all will be well. Excess *kapha* causes mucus and its other vehicles to be overproduced and to accumulate within, creating conditions of excess, while insufficient *kapha* leads to problems of their deficiency. Even the proper amount of *kapha* may cause disease if some obstruction prevents its expedient excretion. *Pitta* produces substances like bile which are also useful to the system so long as they are continuously excreted from the body. Overproduction of *pitta* leads to an excess of bile and its ilk, creating 'hot' conditions like anger and acidity. Obstructed *pitta* may also cause these and other problems, and insufficient *pitta* can cause cold illnesses. *Vāta* does literally produce gas in the body, but its more important substrate is the 'wind' of nervous energy. Excessive or insufficient nervous impulses, or nervous energy which becomes blocked, inevitably leads to distress.

Pitta is the more reactive form of the flame of life, called *tejas* or *agni* in Sanskrit, *vāta* is the unstable form of *prāṇa*, and *kapha* the more inert, 'dead' form of *ojas*, or *soma*. *Prāṇa*, *tejas* and *ojas* are the essences of the air, fire and water elements as applied to embodied life. *Prāṇa*, the 'life force' which Chinese medicine calls *qi*, strings body, mind and spirit together like beads on a strand of breath. *Prāṇa* is not air, though oxygen is one of its vehicles; *prāṇa* is the power which forces an individual body, mind and spirit to function together in one place at one time for one purpose. *Tejas* creates the interfaces which permit body, mind and spirit to nourish, influence, and communicate with one another in spite of their differing planes of existence. *Ojas* is the subtle glue which seals those interfaces, integrating these three fundamentally identical but effectively discrete things into a functioning individual.

When an organism functions at peak efficiency the three *doṣas* are produced in quantities just sufficient to meet physical needs; in systemic imbalance the *doṣas* are overproduced or underproduced at the expense of the body's vitality, adaptability and immunity. When digestion is strong the *prāṇa* contained within the food is efficiently imbibed into the system, and only a little *vāta* is produced; when digestion is weak only a little *prāṇa* can be assimilated and much *vāta* is generated. When *vāta* is excessive all the healthy *prāṇa* which should invigorate each cell evolves instead into nervous energy, which is useless for most bodily functions and must be burned away. Likewise, a superabundance of *pitta* instead of *tejas* produces inflammation of body or mind, and plentiful *kapha* loads the system with sticky toxins when *ojas* is inadequate.

Though *vāta*, *pitta* and *kapha* are associated with respiration, digestive juices, and mucus respectively, and though they resemble in certain ways the humours of Greek medicine, they cannot be translated as 'wind, bile and phlegm'. Wind, bile and phlegm are vehicles for the *doṣas*, substances which host the *doṣas* within the body. The three *doṣas* are invisible forces which can only be demonstrated in the body by inference. When you pour iron filings onto a sheet of paper beneath which is a magnet, any movement of the magnet will move the filings around. We must not confuse the less-than-material *doṣas* with their material vehicles, even though these conveyances are produced by the *doṣas*, just as we must not misidentify the iron filings with the magnetic force field which invisibly moves them.

The *doṣas* in the body

> *Though they pervade the body,* vāta *predominates in the area below the navel,* pitta *in the zone between the heart and the navel, and* kapha *in the region that is above the heart.*
> (Aṣṭāṅgahṛdaya Sūtrasthāna 1/7b, in expanded form)

The three *doṣas* pervade the body, working in every cell of every tissue every moment of the day, concentrating themselves in those tissues in which they are particularly required. *Vāta* accumulates below the navel to help counteract the force of gravity by pumping blood, lymph and wastes from the lower parts of the body back into the torso; *kapha* accumulates above the diaphragm to keep *vāta* from moving upward too strongly, and to ensure lubrication for those organs which most need it (the heart, lungs and alimentary canal); and *pitta*, the mediator and fulcrum between *vāta* and *kapha*, occupies the region between the diaphragm and the navel, near the body's center of gravity. Otherwise, *vāta* is concentrated in the brain and nervous system, heart, colon, bones, lungs, bladder, pelvis, thighs, ears, and skin; *pitta* in the brain, liver, spleen, small intestine, endocrine glands, skin, eyes, blood, and sweat; and *kapha* in the brain, joints, mouth, head and neck, stomach, lymph, thorax (especially lungs, heart and oesophagus), and fat.

Because Ayurvedic anatomy is more concerned with the overall organisation of living systems than with the details of their many tiny parts, an Ayurvedic 'organ' usually includes but is not limited to what we think of as that organ. For instance, Ayurveda regards the 'heart' as the centre of circulation of blood and *vāta*, and the seat of the mind, intellect and consciousness. 'Heart' disease is not limited to disease of the pumping muscle; it also includes disorders of the forces and substances of the chest region which may involve the pumping muscle only secondarily. Abdominal disorders such as distention of the colon with gas, which can disturb the heart by exerting pressure on it through the diaphragm, is therefore considered in Ayurveda to be a form of 'heart' disease; so are 'heartache' and 'heartbreak'.

There is actually only one *vāta*, one *pitta*, and one *kapha*, but according to the specific duties they perform each is divided into five aspects. The five *kapha*s manifest in specialised body lubricants: stomach mucus, pleural and pericardial fluid, saliva, synovial fluid, and cerebrospinal fluid. The five *pitta*s appear in transformative substances: digestive juices, haemoglobin, melanin, rhodopsin, and various neurotransmitters. The five *vāta*s divide the body into spheres of influence: *prāṇa vāta*, the 'forward-moving air', extends from the diaphragm to the throat; *udāna vāta*, the 'upward-moving air', from the throat to the top of the head; *samāna vāta*, the 'equalising air', from the diaphragm to the navel; and *apāna vāta*, the 'downward-moving air', from the navel to the anus. *Vyāna vāta*, the 'pervasive air', pervades the entire body from its seat in the heart.

The *doṣas* in time

> Vāta *predominates during the final stages of the lifespan, the day, the night, and digestion,* pitta *during the middle stages of these processes, and* kapha *during their initial stages.*
> (Aṣṭāṅgahṛdaya Sūtrasthāna 1/8a, in expanded form)

Any kind of recurring time cycle creates a set of 'seasons': childhood, adulthood, and old age are the three seasons of life; dawn, midday, and dusk the three seasons of day; and so on. The nature of embodied life is such that the force of *kapha* is always enhanced at the beginning of a cycle (like spring), when development occurs; the force of *pitta* becomes particularly strong during the cycle's zenith (like summer); and the force of *vāta* accelerates during its decline (like fall). Women have yet another season, the menstrual (monthly) cycle; *kapha* dominates during its initial portion (between the end of the flow and ovulation), *pitta* during the succeeding portion (between ovulation and the commencement of the flow), and *vāta* during its terminal phase (during the period of flow). Ayurveda tells us that diseases are generated at the 'junctions of the seasons', the moments when one season changes into another. Every adaptation to changed circumstances that a system must make increases the likelihood of disease. Adolescence and menopause, for example, are the junctions of life, times when there is a potential for many sorts of disorders.

Personal constitution

> *By them are produced* viṣamāgni, tīkṣṇāgni, *and* mandāgni *respectively, while* samāgni *is produced by their equilibrium.* (Aṣṭāṅgahṛdaya Sūtrasthāna 1/8b)

Everything which enters a human being must be operated on in order to transform that thing into a form which the human organism can utilise. Food, water, air, sunlight, touch, odours, tastes, sights and sounds and even thoughts and emotions from the outer world enter the inner world and alter it, forcing it to adapt. How well an organism responds to these challenges and adapts to new conditions, how well it 'digests' its experiences, is an expression of its innate equilibrium, its immunity to imbalance, its degree of coherence relative to the external chaos, a chaos which too is relative, composed as it is of innumerable intelligences all trying to order things to suit themselves. Whenever an experience remains 'undigested' the microcosm loses its coherence and develops a disease. If it is the balance and or lack of balance of the *doṣas* which creates health and disease, the degree of *doṣa* balance is due to the relative strength or weakness of the organism's digestive ability, which Ayurveda calls its 'digestive fire' (*āgni*). Well-balanced *doṣas* produce a strong, well-balanced digestive fire (*samāgni*). When *vāta* is in excess this digestive fire becomes erratic and unpredictable (*viṣamāgni*), excess *pitta* makes this fire intense (*tīkṣṇāgni*), and an overabundance of *kapha* causes dullness of the digestive fire (*mandāgni*).

> *The* koṣṭha *created by each is* krūra, mṛdu, *and* madhya *respectively, and when the* doṣas *are balanced it is also* madhya. (Aṣṭāṅgahṛdaya Sūtrasthāna 1/9a)

Koṣṭha is an individual's 'bowel predisposition'. When *vāta* is in excess the bowel becomes *krūra* (cruel), leading to a tendency either for constipation or for erratic and unpredictable bowel movements. Excess *pitta* makes for a *mṛdu* (gentle) bowel, which tends to respond with loose stools when it is overstressed. When *kapha* predominates in an individual, or when a person's *doṣas* are balanced, stress to the intestines is not likely to lead immediately either to constipation or diarrhoea. Vāgbhaṭa mentions bowel health here to emphasise how very important to good health is the proper digestion of food.

> *The three types of* prakṛti *(human constitution)—the* hīna, madhya, *and* uttama—*arise from the respective predominance of each (of the three* doṣas*) which are present in the* śukra *and* ārtava *at the time of conception, just as poisonous worms arise from poison. That constitution which arises from the equal proportion of all of them is the* samadhātu prakṛti, *which is ideal, while those arising from a combination of two* doṣas *are* nindya. (Aṣṭāṅgahṛdaya Sūtrasthāna 1/9b-10)

Digestive fire and bowel predisposition are two of the most significant of the many traits which make up an individual's 'personal constitution' (*prakṛti*). While in Saṅkhyā philosophy *prakṛti* indicates the macrocosm, Ayurveda uses the term to indicate those innately characteristic physical and mental tendencies which predominate in an individual organism as a systematised expression of that microcosm. *Prakṛti* must be distinguished from *vikṛti*, the moment-by-moment condition of the organism. Usually, but not always, an individual's personal *vikṛti* will conform to the type of *doṣa* imbalance promised by the *prakṛti*. *Prakṛti*, which is the first reaction that an individual's body and mind show to stress, is fixed at the moment of conception, determined by conditions in the parents' bodies and minds at the time of coitus. These conditions affect the foetus by influencing the sexual fluids of the father and mother (*śukra* and *ārtava*, respectively). Whatever qualities are to be found in the body will also be found in its product, the offspring, just as worms that grow up in poison will themselves become poisonous under its influence. This is why Ayurveda prohibits, up to the moment of conception, exposure of both parents to any influences which might damage the foetus .

The three basic microcosmic constitutional types are fundamentally identical with the three basic macrocosmic types of climate: arid (*vāta*), torrid (*pitta*), and humid (*kapha*). While the 'climate' of your microcosm affects you much as the climate of your homeland affects you, internal influences are much more difficult to shut out than are external ones. Constitutional typing shows how an organism prefers to utilise its matter and energy. People in whose constitution *vāta* predominates generally have little ability to retain either matter or energy within themselves, and *kapha* people have too great a tendency to retain both. Only *pitta* people have an innate knack for managing both well, and too often they overmanage. *Vāta* makes people erratic, *pitta* makes them intense, and *kapha* relaxes or over-relaxes them.

Of the eight principal *prakṛti* types—*vāta*, *pitta*, and *kapha* each predominating alone; two of the three *doṣas* predominating together; all three *doṣas* tending to imbalance; and all three *doṣas* tending to balance—the last is ideal, but very rare. Most people have double predominance, which Vāgbhaṭa says is *nindya* (blameworthy) because two predominant *doṣas* each ever ready to be vitiated will create exponentially more problems than will one *doṣa* alone. Of the indidual constitutional types the *vāta* type is the easiest to imbalance (which is why it is called *hīna*, 'deficient') and the *kapha* type is the easiest to maintain in a state of health (and so it is *uttama*, 'best'). Those in whom all three *doṣas* predominate tend to be classified as ever-sick.

Qualities

We have now seen that these *doṣas* can, by being excessive or insufficient, imbalance the organism and initiate illness. Verse 18 tells us how they become excessive or insufficient:

> *Heavy-light, dull-intense, cold-hot, unctuous-dry, smooth-rough, solid-liquid, soft-hard, stable-mobile, subtle-gross, clear-sticky are the ten pairs of qualities.*
> (Aṣṭāṅgahṛdaya Sūtrasthāna 1/18, in expanded form)

Heavy and light are extremes of weight, cold and hot extremes of temperature, oily/moist and dry of emolliency, slow/dull and acute of intensity, and so on. Each pair of attributes can also be extended to other fields of activity; for example, dull-intense can represent slow-fast in the context of velocity; subtle-gross can also mean small-large, or rarefied-dense; clear-sticky can indicate unslimy-slimy or unsmearable-smearable. Moreover, these physical qualities can also be extended to apply to mental and emotional states.

Anything on which a quality resides is either a substance or an action. The soul, mind, time and direction (spatial orientation) are all substances, because each possesses qualities which affect the life of living beings. A nervous impulse is a substance; it has a name and can be described, it has a form, albeit unstable, and it has qualities. Sleeping during the day and staying awake at night are actions whose qualities affect their performers (the first increases *kapha*, the second, *vāta*). Some qualities are innate to the substance or action and so inseparable from it, while others are superadded, remaining only for some time. When any substance or action, including time and space, impacts upon you, its qualities, innate and added, influence your system for better or worse.

Qualities are important because we humans are qualitative beings. A hot chilli pepper will not make a thermometer's mercury rise, but all of us know it to be 'hot'. Everyone does not respond to the same stimulus by experiencing the same quality; the same room that may feel 'cold' to one person may be 'hot' to someone else. Ayurveda is concerned to know how easily the qualities of the objects we imbibe through our senses will be digested and how they will affect us, so that we can know which objects to enjoy, and which to avoid, in order to strengthen our bodies, our digestive fires, and our minds.

> *Increase of all of them* (doṣas, *tissues, and wastes) is caused by the use of similars, and [their decrease] occurs by the use of dissimilars.* (Aṣṭāṅgahṛdaya Sūtrasthāna 1/14a)

This rule, 'the law of like and unlike', governs the interaction between an organism and its environment. It is a simple principle: like qualities causes increase, and unlike qualities causes decrease, of the constitutents of the body and mind. Your body becomes warm when you lie in warm sunlight because the warmth it takes in from the sun increases its own warmth. When you go out on a winter's night without a coat the cold of the environment flows into you by sucking out your heat, which makes you feel cold. Everything you experience increases the parts of your being which possess similar qualities, and decreases those parts which are unlike it. Every thought you have changes your physiology, according to its qualities, and every fluctuation in your biochemistry affects the qualities of the mind. While a beneficial habit gives you qualities which will resonate with and reinforce the harmonious aspects of your being, bad habits reinforce the unhealthy, selfish parts of you. You are what you eat, what you think, and what you do; repetition and resonance create your reality. Knowing what is good and what is not so good for your own personal self enables you to make informed decisions in your life and to act on those choices. What you put into yourself today will determine what you become tomorrow; you are what you eat, and see, and hear, and think.

> Vāta *is dry, light (in weight), cold, rough, subtle, and mobile (or unstable).*
> Pitta *is slightly unctuous, intense, hot, light (in weight), malodorous (a raw-meat-like smell), free-flowing, and liquid.*
> Kapha *is unctuous, cold, heavy, dull, smooth (and soft), slimy, and static.* (Aṣṭāṅgahṛdaya Sūtrasthāna 1/11a-12a)

Like all other substances the three *doṣas* also possess qualities, and their increase or decrease in the system depends upon the similar or antagonistic qualities of everything ingested. All substances and all activities increase and decrease the three *doṣas* according to their qualities, and when one of the *doṣas* is increased in a living being that individual will experience, in body, mind or both, an increase in the qualities which characterise that *doṣa*.

The doṣas in space

> Deśa *is of two types:* bhūmi *(terrestrial) and* deha *(physiological). Terrestrial habitat is of three kinds:* jāṅgala, *in which* vāta *predominates;* anūpa, *in which* kapha *predominates, and* sādhāraṇa, *in which all the* doṣas *are balanced.*
> (Aṣṭāṅgahṛdaya Sūtrasthāna 1/23-24a)

The two types of *deśa* (land) are that which is found on earth in the outer world, and that which makes up the territory of the inner world, namely the body's tissues and wastes. The habitat of the internal world is the *prakṛti*, or personal constitution (see above). Its external counterpart can be arid, humid, or balanced. The arid qualities of *jāṅgala deśa* will aggravate the *vāta* in the bodies of those who live there, just as the humidity of *anūpa deśa* will aggravate *kapha* in the bodies of its denizens.[2] It is reasonable to assume that Ayurveda's seers saw no need to express the obvious—that a torrid climate will increase *pitta*—since the greater part of the Indian subcontinent is hot most of the year.

Ordinarily it is best not to live in the sort of habitat that increases the primary *doṣa* in your constitution. For instance, people with *vāta prakṛti* who live in arid climates will always find *vāta* increasing in their internal environments, no matter how carefully they observe strict diets and healthy habits, because the climate will continuously dry them out, and dryness always increases *vāta*, which is the only dry *doṣa*. It would be much better for a *kapha* person to live in an arid climate, so that the external weather would, by its inherent qualities, always exert an antagonistic, and so balancing, effect on the internal humidity.

Tissues and wastes

> Rasa, *blood, flesh, fat, bone, marrow, and* śukra *are the seven* dhātus. (Aṣṭāṅgahṛdaya Sūtrasthāna 1/13a)

The products of digestion are the seven tissues, or *dhātus*, which anchor mind and spirit firmly in the physical body (the word *dhātu* comes from a root meaning 'to support'). The grosser body tissues act as raw materials for the subtler. The nutritional essence of each *dhātu* is extracted by the next, the essence being progressively concentrated until *ojas*, the ultimate product of metabolism, results. At each stage are produced *upadhātus* (secondary tissues which undergo no further transformation) and wastes, each of which has its own job to do as it is expelled from the body. Faeces, for example, provide temporary strength to the colon; urine maintains body fluid balance; and sweat lubricates the skin, controls heat and fluid balance, and promotes growth of body hair.

Nutrition of the body begins when the first 'juice' is extracted from the food and is converted by the digestive fire into *rāsa*. In its largest sense *rāsa* (its root means 'to move') is every juice which makes life possible and worth living, and can mean, according to context, liquid, potion, sap, the expressed juice of fruit, leaves or other plant parts, meat soup, nectar, essence, semen, the element mercury, the minerals used in alchemy, melodious sound, aesthetic appreciation, artistic delight, and emotion. In the physical body *rasa* is chyle or plasma, the body's 'sap', the nutrient liquid which moves ceaselessly throughout the body bathing each cell in its fertilising flow. Nourishment of body and mind, and the exaltation which ensues therefrom, is its task. The same sort of bliss you feel after a truly satisfying meal is felt by every little cell of your body when they are immersed in fresh *rasa*.

Rasa nourishes *rakta* (blood), which invigorates the organism. Blood nourishes *māṁsa* (flesh), which is in charge of 'plastering' the skeleton to contain and protect everything within. Flesh nourishes *medas* (fat), whose job is *snehana*, which means both lubrication and love. Fat's essence goes to nourish *asthi* (bone), the only tissue in which *vāta* predominates, filled as it is with spaces. Bone supports the body and gives 'backbone' to the personality. Bone's essence nourishes *majjā* (marrow), the tissue which 'fills' the bones, which includes the brain and spinal cord as well as the red and yellow varieties of bone marrow. Marrow's essence creates *śukra* (the reproductive fluids of both male and female). The action of a very subtle form of digestive fire on *śukra* generates *ojas*, the glandular secretion which buffers the individual against potentially imbalancing external influences.

Ojas is the finest refinement of 'sap' the body produces, and when *ojas* is firm and 'plump' mind and body are firm and 'plump' as well. *Rasa* is the foundation and *ojas* the apex of the body's nutrition pyramid. *Ojas* permits *tejas* to project into the physical body, where it appears as the digestive fire; this makes *ojas* both the cause and the effect of good digestion. Because *ojas* controls the immune system and generates the body's aura—the lustrous halo which projects the essence of one's being out into the world to act as a subtle shield against the entry of dangerous ethereal forces—the conservation of *ojas* is essential to good health.

> *These seven, plus the wastes, which are urine, faeces, sweat, etc., are the* dūṣyas. (Aṣṭāṅgahṛdaya Sūtrasthāna 1/13b)

The tissues and wastes taken together are the *dūṣyas*, the things which are vitiated by the *doṣas*. Diseases exist in the *dūṣyas*, and though the three *doṣas* are the instruments through which disease is created, they remain always separate from the diseases which are their effects. Indiscretions in diet and activity promote disease by encouraging the *doṣas* to invade the *dūṣyas*. Removal of the *doṣas* from the *dūṣyas* will alter the disease, but may not be sufficient to eliminate it.

> *Sweet, sour, salty, bitter, pungent, and astringent are the six tastes. These six reside on substances, and each strengthens the body more than the one which follows it.*
> (Aṣṭāṅgahṛdaya Sūtrasthāna 1/14b-15a)

Of all the substances and actions which contribute to health and disease, food is the most important:

> *The life of all living beings is food, and all the world seeks food. Complexion, clarity, good voice, long life, understanding, happiness, satisfaction, growth, strength and intelligence are all established in food. Whatever is beneficial for worldly happiness, whatever pertains to the Vedic sacrifices, and whatever action leads to spiritual salvation is said to be established in food.* (Caraka Sūtrasthāna 27.349-350a)

Of all the ways in which food affects us its three primary qualities are taste, potency, and post-digestive effect. The most commonly used of the several systems of Ayurvedic flavour classification is that of the 'six tastes'. Although these tastes apply to each sense organ, they are called tastes (*rasas*) because their most important influence is on the makeup of the *rasa* tissue in our bodies. The characteristics of the environment in which *rasa*, the tissue which nourishes all the other tissues, is formed impregnate *rasa* and generate its 'flavour'. Your personal experience of life, its flavour, is generated from this 'sap' which pervades your existence and your consciousness. This flavour is your reality; it is the environment in which you live your life, the factor which makes your personality sour or salty, your existence bitter or sweet, blissful or miserable. When your *rasa* is sweet, you will be satisfied and happy, and the harmony in your life will multiply. While self-controlled people find all the bliss they need within themselves, the rest of us must extract the flavours we require from the food, drink, medicine, activity, climate, seasons and other 'substances' that we consume, cooking these 'things' within ourselves to satisfy our souls with their soup. Everyone's body craves the taste it lacks within; whether or not the mind will allow the body to obtain that taste is another matter, for the mind often craves those tastes which are most detrimental to the body.

Taste, potency, and post-digestive effect

> *The first [three] of these decrease* vāta; *the three beginning with bitter decrease* kapha; *astringent, bitter, and sweet decrease* pitta; *and the others cause their increase.*
> (Aṣṭāṅgahṛdaya Sūtrasthāna 1/15b-16a)

Sweet, sour and salty decrease *vāta* and increase *kapha*; bitter, pungent and astringent decrease *kapha* and increase *vāta*; and sour, salty and pungent increase *pitta*. The sweet taste, whether obtained from food or from Mozart, strengthens the body more than sour, which is more strengthening than salty, and so on. The least strengthening of the tastes, whether obtained from fear, cold, or unripe persimmons, is astringent, the taste which makes your mouth pucker.

> *Substances are of three kinds: those which calm the* doṣas, *those which aggravate the* doṣas, *and those which help to maintain health.* (Aṣṭāṅgahṛdaya Sūtrasthāna 1/16b)

Whatever nourishes the organism is food, whatever disturbs it is poison, and whatever balances it is medicine.

> *Hot and Cold, the powerful qualities, are the two potencies (*vīrya*) of substances.* (Aṣṭāṅgahṛdaya Sūtrasthāna 1/17a)

The three most powerful pairs of qualities, the strong potencies (*vīrya*) which are mainly responsible for a substance's action in the body, are hot-cold, heavy-light, and unctuous-dry. Their importance derives from the fact that *pitta* is the only hot *doṣa*, *kapha* the only heavy *doṣa*, and *vāta* the only dry *doṣa*. The most important *vīrya* is hot-cold. 'Hot' food enhances the fire available to the body, while 'cold' food reduces that fire. 'Hot' food usually, but not always, increases digestion; when it increases *pitta*, it can disturb the digestive fire. 'Cold' food usually weakens digestion; the 'colder' the food, the more digestion will be weakened. Sweet, bitter and astringent foods are usually 'cold', and sour, salty and pungent foods are usually 'hot'.

> *The post-digestive effect (*vipāka*) is threefold: sweet, sour, and pungent.* (Aṣṭāṅgahṛdaya Sūtrasthāna 1/17b)

Vipāka is the end product of digestion, the result of everything which has been done to it. It is a measure of both the natural qualities of the food ingested and the strength of the digestive process which ingests them. Taste is the effect of the food on the body after ingestion and before digestion; *vīrya* is the effect the food exerts during digestion; and *vipāka* is the expression of a food in the system after it has been digested and assimilated. Foods with sweet *vipāka* tend to build up the tissues, promote *kapha*, and increase body weight; those with sour *vipāka* tend to increase *pitta* and may burn the tissues; and those with pungent *vipāka* tend to increase *vāta* and dry out the tissues. Sweet and salty foods ordinarily produce sweet *vipāka*, sour food sour *vipāka*, and bitter, pungent and astringent foods pungent *vipāka*.

Most substances have qualities which closely agree with this theory; most foods with the sweet taste, for example, usually have cold *vīrya* and sweet *vipāka*. Many of the most useful foods and medicines, however, have unusual qualities. *Āmalakī* (*Emblica officinalis*), for example, the chief ingredient in the famous rejuvenative jam *cyavanaprāśa*, contains five of the 'six tastes' (all but salty), of which sour predominates. Its potency is cold; and its post-digestive effect is sweet. These characteristics make it useful for reducing *vāta* (being sour and sweet), *pitta* (being cold and sweet), and *kapha* (being bitter, pungent, and astringent), though it is mainly used to reduce *pitta*. Many of the most useful substances possess *prabhāva*, an action which cannot be explained on the basis of its qualities no matter how you try. Though *tulasī* (*Ocimum sanctum*) is pungent in taste, hot in potency, and pungent in post-digestive effect, all qualities which increase *pitta*, its *acintya prabhāva* (inexplicable power) is to reduce fevers, many of which are caused by *pitta*.

The *doṣas* of the mind

> Rajas *and* tamas *are the* doṣas *of the mind.* (Aṣṭāṅgahṛdaya Sūtrasthāna 1/21b)

The quality of your awareness depends upon the functioning within your consciousness of *sattva*, *rajas* and *tamas*, which work by mutual suppression: whichever is strongest at any one instant expresses itself and suppresses the others. No ultimate distinction can be drawn between subject (*sattva*), object (*tamas*) and action (*rajas*) as all are manifestations of *ahaṁkāra*; they appear to differ only because of their relative positions. Who is subject and who object in any particular situation depends upon perspective, and can only be expressed accurately by reference to all three aspects: the figure, its background, and the relationship existing between the two. *Rajas* and *tamas* are the mind's *doṣas* because whenever an individual's mind becomes too fixed on external sense objects (*tamas*) or too fixed on action (*rajas*) they rob energy and attention from subjective consciousness (*sattva*), thereby preventing *sattva*, which is the mind's natural state, from functioning efficiently.

Crimes against wisdom

> *While the inadequate, improper, and excessive contact [of the individual] with seasons, sense objects, and activities are the chief causes of diseases, their proper association is the chief cause of health.* (Aṣṭāṅgahṛdaya Sūtrasthāna 1/19)

Having described the *doṣas* and *dūṣyas* and how they are vitiated, explained the personal constitution, and delineated the qualities of the various substances which are good or bad for each, Vāgbhaṭa now explains why people get sick. This answer though merely creates a new question: why is it that people who know what to do to be healthy do not follow through by doing it? Why do they permit themselves to become ill?

The mental attitude which permits an organism to act contrary to its own self-interest is known in Sanskrit as *prajñāparādha*, which literally means 'crime against wisdom'. On the most obvious level *prajñāparādha* is a 'violation of good sense', both mental and physical, as for example failing to protect yourself against the cold or the rain when you go outside. Such failings are due to allurement, the selfish desire of a microcosm to try to ignore that transcendent wisdom (*prajñā*) arising from the inherent rhythm of the macrocosm.

> *Whatever act is done by one who is deranged of understanding, will, or memory is to be regarded as a volitional transgression* (prajñāparādha). *It is the inducer of all pathological conditions.* (Caraka Śarīrasthāna 1:102).

'Perversity of mind' is the ultimate cause of every disease; it can affect any activity of speech, mind or body directly, or it can work indirectly through improper sensory enjoyments or inattention to diet and lifestyle changes necessitated by the evolution of the seasons. *Prajñāparādha* is a sort of weakness of the mental digestion, caused by overabundance of the two mental *doṣas*, *rajas* and *tamas*, which weakens, directly or indirectly, the physical digestion. No sense of guilt need be attached to *prajñāparādha*; it is an impartial assessment of your unwillingness or inability to remain in a state of harmony with the cosmos. Prosperity and health come to you when you co-operate with nature, and penury and disease become your lot when your conduct is otherwise. Nothing is more important in Ayurveda than your relationship with your environment.

This attitude must not be confused with the New Age prevarication that 'everything that happens to you is your own creation'. Ayurveda believes that those who are wise will constantly try to avoid all causes of disease which are avoidable, and will not lament overmuch when pathogenic factors which no one can avoid may temporarily lay them low. It is only when you willfully permit yourself to deteriorate that you are guilty of a 'crime against wisdom', and this is as true for society as it is for individuals. If a good government helps to make a nation healthy, an evil government sickens that nation's workplaces, schools, homes, and even the land itself. A corrupt, heartless government corrupts those it governs; people pattern themselves after their rulers, even when such patterning may be fatal to them. Like those they lead, village, municipal, national and international leaders are led into wrongdoing by the force of *prajñāparādha*. Their unrighteousness generates epidemics, insect plagues and other catastrophes. When the ruled imitate the ruler's failure to follow the path indicated by the cosmic rhythm, environmental disorder (cosmic lawlessness) supervenes, disturbing the winds, the water, the land and the seasons, resulting in droughts, floods, earthquakes, epidemics, wars, and affliction by diabolic powers.

Disease classifications

> *Diseases are of two types: those which arise from within, and those which arise from without. Their sites are also two: the body and the mind.* (Aṣṭāṅgahṛdaya Sūtrasthāna 1/20-21)

In exogenous disease (arising from without), which includes epidemics, occupational disorders, iatrogenic disease, accidents, adverse planetary positions and possession by spirits, the symptoms arise first, followed the imbalance of the *doṣas*; endogenous diseases (arising from within) commence with *doṣa* imbalance. Of the seven main types of diseases—genetic or hereditary, congenital, metabolic, traumatic, temporal (failure to follow daily or seasonal regimens), divine, and natural (hunger, thirst, sleep, fatigue, other urges, decay, senescence, and death)—only the metabolic type is directly due to the machinations of the *doṣas*. From another perspective there is only one type of disease, the type which comes from within due to *prajñāparādha*. According to this theory even such seemingly uncontrollable events such as accidents are caused by long-term acccumulating stress which periodically releases itself into the consciousness, like an earthquake, and causes one to put oneself, knowingly or unknowingly, into harm's way.

All diseases express themselves predominantly either through the body (as may asthma), or through the mind (as does anxiety), or both; constipation, for example, may be a purely mental condition, caused by intense mental attachment and 'tightness'. Mental disease can arise due to imbalance in either the mental *doṣas*, *rajas* and *tamas*, or in *vāta*, *pitta* or *kapha*, or because of intense emotions, or misuse of intoxicants. Mental diseases can be transformed into physical conditions, and vice versa. The gravest and most difficult to treat of the many diseases listed in the Ayurvedic texts were the eight *mahāgadas* (great illnesses): fever, *raktapitta* (haemorrhagic diseases), *gulma* (phantom tumours), diabetes and other urinary disorders, skin diseases (especially leprosy), consumption (including but not limited to pulmonary tuberculosis), insanity, and convulsions (including epilepsy). Each of these was attributed, directly or in-directly, to the corrupting influence of intense negative emotions: greed, malice, and anger—the diseases beginning with *rāga*.

Diseases are also classified according to severity, curability, aetiology (especially cold versus hot), symptoms, location, time (e.g. worse during the day or night or during a certain season or stage of digestion), prognosis, and management. Iatrogenic disease, which is caused by the therapy administered for another ailment, is a separate category. Diseases may be primary (arising independently) or secondary (occurring as a complication of some pre-existing disease); sometimes one disease eliminates itself in giving rise to a new disease, while at other times it causes a new disease and continues to co-exist with it. All diseases are due either to *undernourishment* (drying out the body) or *overnourishment* (making it too wet). Because most of the diseases of the affluent are due to excess, this 'wetness-increasing quality' (*abhiṣyandī*) is a primary cause of ill health, particularly among those who try to maximise their indulgences by suppressing acute disease for years at a time. Diseases which thus result will be chronic almost from their outset, including especially gout, obesity, and diabetes, the so-called 'diseases of affluence'. These diseases of overnutrition arise in people who have too much of everything.

Finally, though, there are as many diseases as there are patients, and the detailed descriptions of various syndromes which have been preserved for centuries in Ayurvedic texts were never meant to be exhaustive. Ordinary practitioners should use them as memorised, and intelligent physicians should use them to infer the specific nature of the particular case in question.

The Practice of Ayurveda

Diagnosis

> *The patient should be examined by* darśana, sparśana, *and* praśna. (Aṣṭāṅgahṛdaya Sūtrasthāna 1/22a)

Ayurveda's diagnostic tests concentrate on investigating the 'state'—the pattern of relationships existing among the various parts of the body and mind—of the individual as a unitary whole. Ayurvedic diagnosis evaluates where you are now, how much and in what direction you are changing, what influences are affecting that change, and what can be done to make your state harmonious and your life momentum rhythmic. A good physician tries to first discover patients' strengths before plumbing their weaknesses, hoping to use the former to counteract the latter. All physicians must at all times, especially during the diagnostic process, broadcast curative energy toward their patients, for diagnosis can no more be divorced from treatment than effect can be divorced from cause. Since diagnosis can either initiate the healing process or foreclose on it, faith and hope, the physician's allies, must be continually reinforced.

Diagnosis should begin with an examination of how 'excellent' the body's tissues are. Each tissue has its own signs of excellence. By adeptly performing their physical and psychological functions excellent tissues generate harmony in the microcosm, which produces happiness, good fortune, power, pleasures, prosperity, intelligence, knowedge, health and cheer, and long life. These excellences are a good measure of a person's strength and vitality, and are used to prevent the deception of appearances. Major diseases may seem minor in people who have 'richness of spirit, vitality and body', while minor disease will seem major in a patient with 'poverty' of those things.

Strong memory, devotion, gratitude, wisdom, purity, great energy, skill, courage, prowess in battle, freedom from sorrow, firmness of tread, deep intelligence and character show excellence of mind. People with strong minds often appear unaffected even when afflicted by severe ailments, while those with moderate mental power compose themselves by seeking consolation. Weak minds cannot be calmed and composed either by themselves or by others, and are rarely able to endure even small ailments stoically. Mental strength is the chief factor determining an individual's ability to 'digest' life experiences and emerge stronger from them. Medical anthropologists distinguish between *disease*, which is objective—what the physician perceives—and *illness*, which is subjective—what the patient feels. Because there is often a substantial difference between the two, examination must be done from both points of view, just as we must always inspect the imbalance of an organism from the points of view of both the body and the mind.

A physician can use any of four methods to thoroughly know a patient's condition. The first and best method is direct perception (*pratyakṣa pramāṇa*), which is sometimes not possible, and other times unreliable, due to defects of perception. Whatever cannot be known directly must be elicited through the other means: logical inference (*anumāna*), analogy (*upamāna*), and the testimony of experts (*āptopadeśa*). All the physician's sense organs (except, usually, the tongue) are used to evaluate the patient. The senses provide direct perceptions for logic and intuition to process, particularly as applied to the eight important diagnostic factors: faeces, urine, tongue, sound, touch, sight, face, and pulse. Good physicians, who usually become expert in one or two of these methods, encourage whatever information they can accumulate to coalesce into an image of the patient's past, present, and possible futures.

Darśana

Inspection (*darśana*) involves the examination of all parts of the patient that can be seen, including even the aura. Diagnosis by using the patient's natal horoscope is also a kind of inspection. After inspecting the tissues and the skin, the physician should inspect the 'nine doors' (two eyes, two ears, two nostrils, mouth and throat, anus, and penis or vulva) and their secretions, paying particular attention to the tongue, which discloses the state of the digestive fire, the load of toxins in the body, the efficiency of *vāta's* movements or lack of these, and the conditions of the channels in the body through which 'things' flow. Faeces examination provides further information on the condition of the digestive tract, especially the presence or absence of *āma* (see below). A few physicians specialise in urine examination even today.

Sparśana

All diagnostic methods which involve touch are included under *sparśana* (palpation), including examination of the pulse, estimation of the body's relative heat or coldness, and testing of the hardness, softness, or roughness of the skin. Pulse diagnosis is the most important of these, and some traditional Ayurvedic physicians refuse to ask questions of their patients, preferring to silently take the pulse and then inform the patient of his or her symptoms. Examination of the pulse is examination of the movement of *prāṇa* in the body. Each *doṣa* has its own gait through the body, and all gaits are due to *vāta*, the only mobile *doṣa*. Pulse diagnosis is the examination of these gaits, and, though generally used to detect disease, it can also disclose other consequences of the movement of *vāta* and *prāṇa*. While any of the body's arteries can be used for pulse diagnosis, the most commonly used is the radial pulse. The accuracy of pulse diagnosis depends entirely on the sensitivity and objectivity of the practitioner.

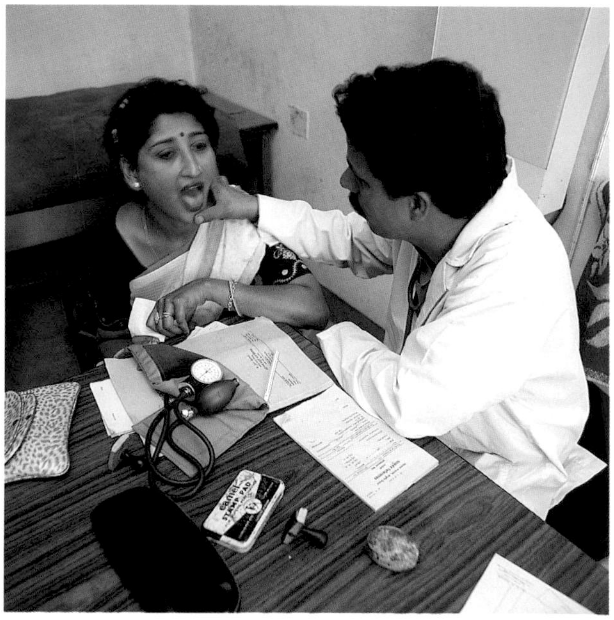

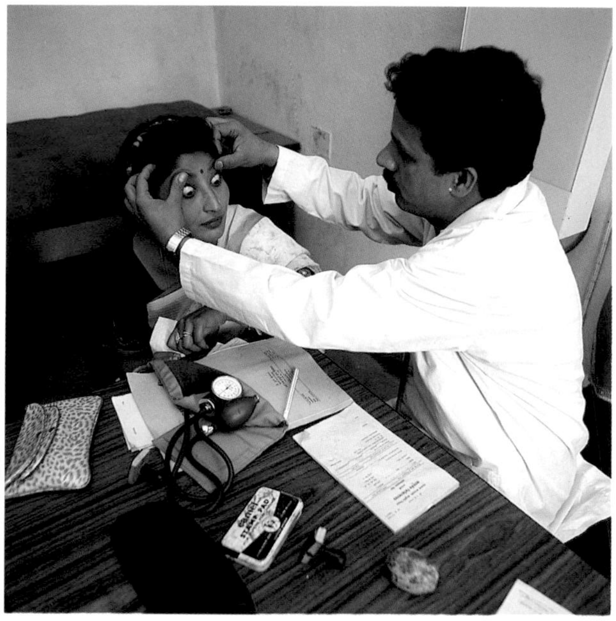

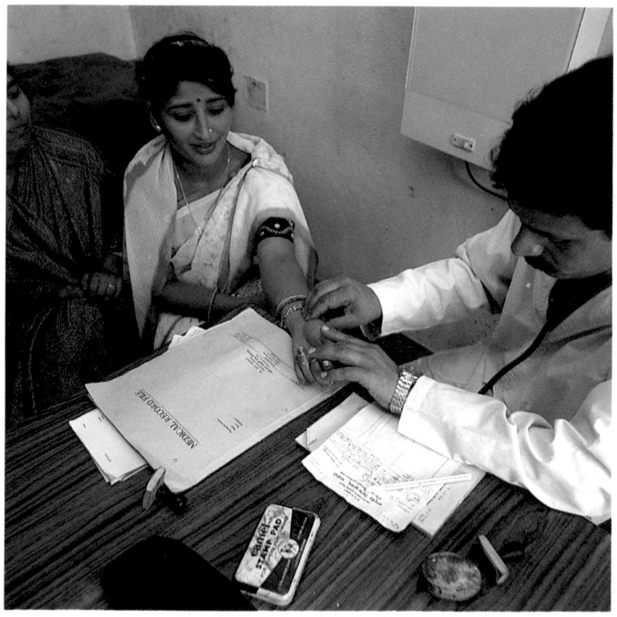

Diagnostic techniques in Ayurveda investigate the condition of different body tissues. Pulse-taking (top) is part of sparśana or palpation. Depending on the patient's complaints, all or some of the 'nine doors' of the body are inspected (here, the eyes). As with sparśana, the investigation of the tongue (below) provides much information to an experienced Ayurvedic physician. Dr. R.R. Koirala, Tribhuvan University, Kathmandu, Nepal.

Praśna

Praśna (interrogation) includes listening to body sounds, the heartbeat, the breathing sounds, and any sounds of injury or disease (like crepitus). Auscultation is a sort of interrogation of the body parts. Verbal interrogation elicits medical history, causative factors, and past and present symptoms. Some doctors diagnose solely by the tone of the patient's voice, and by the words the patient uses to describe his or her condition. A doctor who can read body language and hear the messages between a patient's words will not be misled about the true state of the organism. *Praśna* can also indicate diagnosis through the use of a horoscope cast for the moment the patient meets the physician.

> *The disease should be examined [by its] aetiology, prodromal symptoms, clinical features, test treatment (*upaśaya*), and pathology.* (Aṣṭāṅgahṛdaya Sūtrasthāna 1/22b)

Disease aetiology in Ayurveda is the study of all the factors which have caused the *doṣas* to go out of balance. The clinical features are the specific signs and symptoms which permit us to positively identify a specific disease. Prodromal symptoms are those which appear before the typical symptom complex, as heralds of the coming crisis. One example of prodromal symptoms is the polydipsia (excessive thirst) and polyuria (excessive urination) which often presage the onset of diabetes mellitus.

Test treatment (*upaśaya*) becomes useful when a physician is unclear on which of two possible diseases a patient may be suffering from. *Upaśaya* is performed by administering to the sufferer the treatment which is appropriate for one of those possible conditions. If the patient improves, the diagnosis was correct; if there is no improvement, then another diagnosis must be sought and confirmed.

Regarding pathology, all diseases are due to *agnimāndya*, weakness of the digestive fire (except for a single disease condition in which the digestive fire becomes exceptionally intense). While some sorts of stress can be beneficial to the organism, all sorts of dys-stress lead to *agnimāndya*, which generates *āma* (raw, uncooked, unripened). *Āma* is a generic term for food which is absorbed into the system without having first been properly digested. Such partly-digested material cannot be used by the system, and acts mainly to clog it and to elicit rejection reactions from the indignant immune system. *Āma* provides a culture medium for every parasite in the neighborhood; it is the juice which nourishes disease, just as *rasa* nourishes its fellow tissues. Mental *āma* arises when the mind, unable to come to grips with disorienting sense perceptions, thoughts, emotions or opinions, leaves mental nutrients sitting undigested, polluting the mind with *prajñāparādha*. Both forms of *āma* reinforce one another: selfish thoughts pollute the body, and the polluted body disturbs the consciousness. *Āma* is the immediate cause of most human afflictions; exposure to disease-causing microbes results in disease only in those people whose internal conditions are ripe for colonisation, for microbes cannot grow without support. The fundamental cause for all *āma* is indigestible desire.

The usual process by which disease develops is known as 'obstruction to the pathways' (*mārgāvarodha*). It begins with *prajñāparādha*, which leads to inappropriate behaviour, which results in digestive weakness, which generates *āma*, which obstructs some or all of the channels of body and mind, which prevents *vāta* from moving in its normal direction. *Vāta* then circulates in all directions through the tissues and wastes, often accompanied by *pitta* and *kapha*, until it finds a weak point where it can settle and generate a 'disease being'. *Vāta* can also undergo aggravation and create disease by two processes known as 'wasting of the tissues' (*dhātukṣaya*) and 'emptiness of the reservoir organs' (*āśayāriktatā*).

All illnesses caused by whatever relative influence of the *doṣas* follow a six-step programme of development, beginning with:

Accumulation — exposure to causative factors causes one or more of the *doṣas* to accumulate in its 'seat' (the stomach for *kapha*, the small intestine for *pitta*, and the colon for *vāta*). Because the *doṣas* are easiest to remove from the system at this stage, this is the best stage at which to 'conquer' them. Regular seasonal purifications protect health by removing the accumulations of the *doṣas* which naturally arise due to the inherent qualities of the various seasons. Untreated accumulation is usually followed by:

Aggravation — literally 'rage', a stage in which, continuing to increase, the *doṣas* put pressure on their reservoir organs, intensifying the previously-produced symptoms. It is still fairly easy to remove the *doṣas* even at this stage, but now while treating them their reservoirs, which have been stressed by their ire, need also to be strengthened. If aggravation is permitted to proceed unchecked, it results in:

Overflow — The digestive tract, its wastes, and the tissue *rasa* are usually the first structures to be affected by the *doṣas*, but if the *doṣas* are not expelled by active purification or reduced in strength by more conservative treatment at the stage of overflow they change their direction (*gati*) and start to flow into instead of out of the body, entering the other six tissues. Now the *doṣas* escape their homes, wandering about the body like vagabonds searching for a house to squat in and wreck. All previous symptoms worsen, and new ones commence. If the imbalance is further suppressed at this stage both *āma* and the *doṣas* may dive deeper into the tissues and enter the vital organs.

Whatever their direction and momentum in whichever part of the organism the *doṣas* eventually discover a convenient locale for their depredations. Then begins the stage of:

Location — which usually happens in a previously weakened body region. When the circulating *doṣas* find the right location in which to concentrate themselves they accumulate, initiating the specific disease process by physically or functionally obstructing the local channels of flow. No matter how intensively the tissues or wastes may be involved they are not the immediate cause of the ailment; every disease is caused by the presence in the tissues or wastes of aggravated *doṣas*, just as a burn received by touching a hot iron ball is due to the ball's heat and not to the ball itself. All diseases, even those known to be due to pathogenic organisms, are classified in Ayurveda according to the underlying causative *doṣa*. At this stage the prodromal or premonitory symptoms begin.

Once the *doṣas* have settled somewhere the disease can develop fully and display its qualities; it undergoes:

Manifestation — the stage at which a disease is recognisable as such; for example, when an incipient boil finally selects a spot in which to develop. The specific variety of the disease arises due to:

Specialisation — which is usually indicated by the predominance of the *doṣa* involved. For example, oedema is a swelling of the skin, flesh or other tissues due usually to accumulation of fluid. Oedema due mainly to *kapha* pits on pressure; that due to *vāta* does not do so; and *pitta* oedema is very tender. Most diseases have several varieties.

Therapeutic timing

> *That time which is relevant to therapy is of two kinds: moments and the like (*kṣaṇādi*), and stage of the disease (*vyādhyavasthā*).* (Aṣṭāṅgahṛdaya Sūtrasthāna 1/24b)

While *kṣaṇādi* time is external, objective, and measured by the clock, *vyādhyavasthā* time is internal, subjective, and measured by the disease's life expectancy. Every disease has its own independent personality; like a shadow brought to life it lives a temporary, parasitic existence, feeding off your physical and mental wastes, until it dies, sometimes dragging you along with it. The strength of a disease is proportional to how well it possesses you; a good 'fit', which happens when your own personality does not 'fit' well in your body, makes it easier for the disease to enter and remain inside you, its consciousness possessing your consciousness and skewing the way you think, feel and act. When a disease possesses you it also takes over your internal clock, and shifts your awareness to 'disease time', which is the time it takes for the illness to be born and live within you before it dies. While therapies may be externally scheduled by the clock, they must also be internally scheduled. A treatment like lancing a boil, which may be curative at the stage of the disease when the boil has ripened, would delay ripening, increase pain and inflammation, and possibly spread the infection if attempted during the ripening stage.

Palliation and purification

> *Therapy is, essentially, of two kinds: purificatory and palliative.* (Aṣṭāṅgahṛdaya Sūtrasthāna 1/25a)

Because the ideal medicine is prevention of disease, Ayurveda details daily and seasonal routine activities which can keep the *doṣas* from going berserk. These routines are part of *svasthavṛtta* (establishing oneself in good habits), and its salient principle is moderation. Harmony and health are possible only when everything in life is enjoyed at the proper moment in the proper amount; excess in everything must be firmly rejected. Unfortunately, since desire lies in wait for all of us, creation—moderate people are usually made—not born—and good habits must be inculcated. The process of increasing desirable qualities, reducing negative qualities, and introducing previously absent qualities into any substance, even a living being, is called *saṃskāra*. *Saṃskāra* (literally, 'doing well') is the 'lending of other properties to a substance'. Herbs, animal products and minerals undergo *saṃskāras* when they are processed into medicines; in a 'cold' thing there is always a little heat which can be enhanced, and a 'hot' thing can always be cooled. The study of medicine is the study of how to create new realities, new character traits and tendencies, in living beings by means of *saṃskāra*. The various daily and seasonal rituals are *saṃskāras*, regularly repeated activities which maintain order in the individual and in society. To neglect such routines is to risk retreat into individual or cultural chaos. Only a life cultured by *saṃskāra* can be truly satisfying and happy.

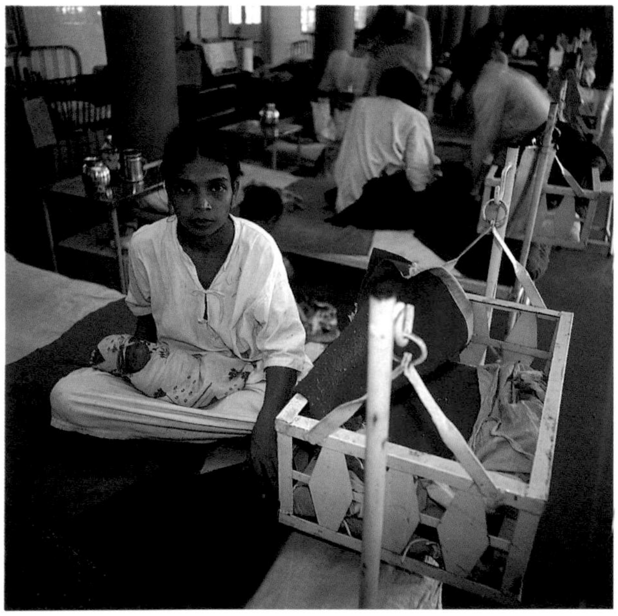

In India birth is usually assisted by midwives and occurs at home. Most Ayurvedic hospitals, however, have maternity departments that offer post-natal care when necessary. Podar Ayurvedic Hospital, Bombay.

Svasthavṛtta should begin before birth, with the *saṃskāras* performed on and by a pregnant woman. Everything an expectant mother eats and does, as well as her milieu, should be wholesome, soft, pleasant and delicate, to reassure and strengthen the growing child, to interfere as little as possible with its self-expression, and to minimise its constitutional predilection for increase in one or more of the *doṣas*. By observing health-promoting routines during her pregnancy a pregnant woman can start the baby off on the right foot in life. After birth an individual is taught appropriate daily and seasonal routines, including changes in diet and activities when the various 'seasons' change, and regular purifications to help protect against potential ailments at the seasonal joints. Many seasonal practices have been institutionalised in India into holiday rituals to make their observance by the general public more automatic.

Because of *prajñāparādha*, however, disease does occur, and should be treated promptly, for as it penetrates progressively more deeply into the system treatment becomes more difficult and success less certain. The effect any particular therapy will have on any particular patient will depend on its dosage, which will depend upon the patient's species, the climate, the *doṣas* involved, the strength of the patient versus the strength of the disease, the patient's age and constitution, the specific syndrome, the patient's social environment, the goal of treatment, the physician's preferred methods of treatment, and so on. Time cycles, including 'disease time' and the 'joints' of the seasons, are especially important because the *doṣas* are controlled differently at different times, depending upon both external time and the disease's 'momentum' within the microcosm. Treatment is supposed to be totally individualised, which means that different diseases may sometimes share a single therapy, while a single disease may be treated differently in different patients according to the 'measure' of the factors involved.

When more than one *doṣa* is involved in a disease's pathology, the most disturbed of them should generally be attended to first. Ayurveda uses all five senses to help balance the *doṣas*, including in context, purification techniques, surgery, drugs, cautery, diet, herbs, minerals, massage and other body work, acupressure, exercises including yoga, music, aromatherapy, flower and gem essences, remedies such as those of homeopathy, colour therapy, meditation, visualisation, chanting, and ritual worship.

Ayurvedic treatment is sometimes *homoeopathic* (administering substances or actions with qualities similar to those which are in excess in the patient and the disease), in such instances as a hot poultice applied to an abcess due to *pitta*, an emetic given to cure vomiting, small amounts of medicinal wine given to treat alcoholism, and shock treatment or threats used on a patient of mania due to *vāta*. Ayurveda usually advocates the *allopathic* approach, however, requiring the use of substances and activites whose qualities oppose those which are in excess. Caraka explains:

This much is evident to us all, namely that we treat a disease-ridden man with disease-removing measures, and the depleted man with impletion. We nourish the emaciated and the feeble,

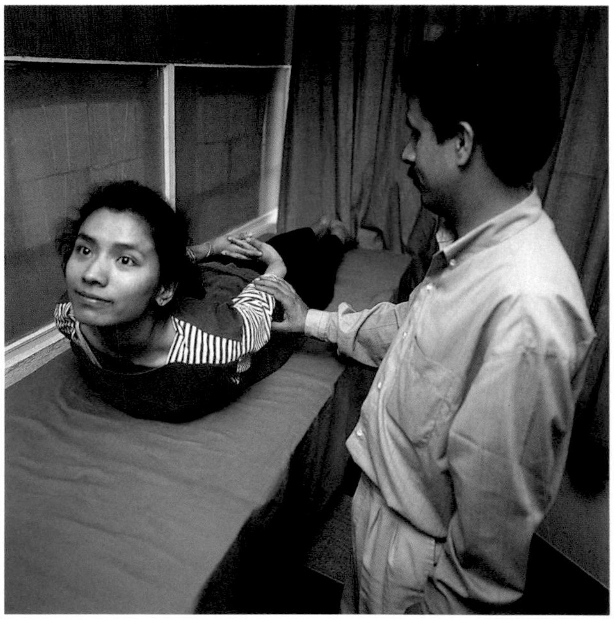

The beneficial effects of certain yoga therapies are now well known all over the world. In the country of origin, therapeutic yoga exercises are often prescribed by alopathic as well as Ayurvedic physicians. Dr. R.R. Koirala in the Ayurvedic Hospital, Naradevi, Kathmandu, Nepal.

> *we starve the corpulent and the fatty. We treat the man afflicted by heat with cooling measures, and with hot things him who is afflicted by cold. We replenish body elements that have suffered decrease, and deplenish those that have undergone increase. By treating disorders properly with measures which are antagonistic to their causative factors we restore the patient to normal. In our hands, administered in this manner, the pharmacopoeia shows itself to the best of its excellence.*
> (Caraka Sūtrasthāna 11.6)

A skillful doctor uses like and unlike substances to increase or decrease a being's elements and rekindle its internal fires. There are three therapies with regard to their location of action: 'scientific' therapy (*yukti vyapāśraya cikitsā*), which uses proper diet, activities and remedies according to season and climate, at the level of the physical body; 'conquest of the mind' (*sattvāvajaya*), which involves restraint of the mind from its desire for unwholesome objects; and 'divine' therapy (*daiva vyapāśraya cikitsā*), which includes all sorts of spiritual rituals and penances, including fire worship and similar sacrifices. Actually, all therapy in any medical system is a sort of penance. A visit to a healer is a pilgrimage to a doctor-guru, a temporary mentor whose rituals help remove the results of the 'volitional transgressions' which have incubated illness. Ayurvedic medical intervention at the physical level is of four types: diet, activity, purification, and palliation. Accumulation of the *doṣas* should be treated with changes in diet and activity; when they become aggravated, palliating or pacifying them with substances of opposite qualities is best. Once the *doṣas* escape their reservoirs, however, it is best to remove them entirely from the system; if this is impossible they must be neutralised with medicine. Should the *doṣas* localise in a weak part of the body, that part will need local treatment as well.

Caraka uses agricultural metaphors to describe this incrementally more invasive approach to treatment. For mild diseases control of the diet, including fasting, is enough, just as a puddle of water is quickly evaporated by sun and wind; for an ailment of medium strength dietary control and pacifying medications are required, just as the adding of sand and ashes to a well or pond helps wind and sun to dry it out. For a strong disease active purification is necessary, just as a flooded rice paddy is easily drained by breaching its retaining wall. Note that these allusions are to the presence of excessive fluid in the system, a condition generated by diet and activities which are 'moisture-producing' (*abhiṣyandi*). This sort of medicine is drainage of the body, comparable to the draining of a swamp to make it fit for cultivation. When the body has been well drained and good seeds are planted in its fields in the right season, and watered with good *rasa*, the result is a bumper crop of health. Diseases due to 'drought' are usually treated by precisely opposite principles, namely nourishing, oiling, and stabilising therapies.

Since 'you are what you eat', dietary control is the most important therapy of all. An appropriate diet is determined by examination of the qualities which are innate to the various foodstuffs, the qualities which are added or removed during their preparation, food combinations, the eater's capacity, the climate, the season (internal as well as external), the rules of eating, and the eater. Your 'capacity' refers not to the volume of your stomach but to the strength of your digestive fire. You can safely eat only that amount of food which you can promptly digest without any impairment of health. You must also follow the rules of eating; these include eating in a congenial, quiet place, either alone or with people who like you, unhurriedly, with concentration, refraining from food when you are not hungry and not failing to eat when you are hungry, and refraining from food when you are physically or emotionally agitated.

Ayurveda favours gradual over sudden cure, including gradual elimination of addictions by substituting less dangerous ones for more dangerous ones and then weaning yourself from those lesser evils. This process, when feasible, is better for the system than is the immediate, 'cold turkey' procedure. There should equally well be gradual escalation of treatment intensity, and gradual weaning from therapy. When change is sufficiently gradual, the result will be return to health without any intervening transformative 'crisis'. Ayurveda tries to avoid the 'healing crises' which some medical systems encourage by inducing managed physical and mental catharsis.

These managed catharses occur during the purificatory procedures called *pañcakarma*. The first step in purification is to ascertain whether or not the patient's body is filled with *āma*. When *āma* is present it must first be digested and expelled from the body by fasting and medication before purification is attempted. Afterwards, or immediately if *āma* is not a major factor, the strength of the patient must be measured against the strength of the disease. If the patient is relatively strong and the disease relatively weak, active purification is indicated. When however the patient is relatively weak and the disease relatively strong active purification is unwise, because all the purification methods temporarily weaken the body to some degree. This weakening, and the emptiness to the reservoir organs which causes it, may increase *vāta*, potentially promoting the disease process instead of resolving it.

After purification, or instead of purification when the disease is strong and the patient weak, or in those people like pregnant women whose bodies are not fit to undergo purification, palliation or pacification of the aggrieved *doṣas* is the route to follow. Seven methods make up the traditional pacification regimen, including 'cooking' the body's accumulated *āma*, enkindling its digestive fire, fasting from food, fasting from liquids, exercise, sun bathing, and wind bathing. Of these fasting is called 'the first and most important of all medicines'. Fasting can be either absolute or done on a number of different foods selected for their utility in treating the condition in question. Acute diseases usually call for brief periods of no food at all, followed by several weeks of a diet tailored specifically for the individual. Every medicine is always given with an *anupāna*, a vehicle which prevents possible side-effects, encourages quick, efficient absorption, and causes a synergistic effect so that the dose of the drug can be reduced. Ayurvedic medicines do not produce their desired effects unless they are given with proper *anupāna* and diet. Hot water is the simplest *anupāna*, and the best *anupānas* is honey. The same drug administered with a variety of *anupānas* can make it effective in a variety of diseases.

If palliation and purification are ineffective, more intensive therapies are sometimes indicated, including the application of alkalis, the use of fire (cautery for wounds, branding for ascites or bone spurs, etc.), and surgery. Fistula-in-ano, in which surgery is often unsuccessful, is treated by insertion of an alkali-impregnated thread into the wound which burns the abnormal tract away. The intensity of treatment usually escalates gradually; for chronic enlargement of the liver and spleen therapy begins with sweating, followed by administration of alkali, then blistering the overlying skin by applying oil of *bhallātaka* (*Semecarpus anacardium*), branding the abdomen thereafter, and, as a last resort, surgery.

After the disease is eliminated from the body a period of convalescence is enforced during which dietary and other restrictions continue for at least the length of treatment. Relapse is possible if any of the rules of convalescence are violated by excess, such as immoderate or forceful talking, travel (especially long distance), excessive walking, continual sitting or lying in one position, overeating (especially when it leads to indigestion), inappropriate diet with wrongful food combining, daysleep (except during summer), and sexual activity.

Pañcakarma

> *Enema, purgation, and emesis are the best [purifying] therapies for the* doṣas *of the body, in order.* (Aṣṭāṅgahṛdaya Sūtrasthāna 1/25b)

Enema is the purification which is generally preferred for disturbances due to *vāta*, purgation with laxatives for *pitta*, and therapeutic vomiting for *kapha*. Like the seasons, sacrificial rituals, and life itself, *pañcakarma* has a clearly defined beginning, middle and end: the preparatory stage, the principal purification, and the post-treatment care. During the preparatory stage the *doṣas* which have overflowed their reservoirs must be returned to their homes before they can be expelled. This return is accomplished by *snehana* and *svedana*. Oleation (*snehana*), the external and internal use of oil, fat, bone marrow or ghee, is the first preparatory step. It is also used as a curative treatment for some *vāta* conditions, especially those caused by emaciation. After oleation the patient must be made to sweat (*svedana*). 'Sweating leads the *doṣas* into fluidity', making it easier for them to leave their locations and flow out of the system. Sweat can be induced by external application of heat (by such means as medicated steam, sun bathing, packs and plasters of hot substances like mustard, and hot baths or showers with medicated oil or water) or by retention of body heat (by exercise, heavy clothes or blankets, fasting, the judicious use of alcohol, or even, occasionally, anger).

After their return special measures are used to bring the *doṣas* into a state of 'excitement', to make them ready and anxious to emerge from the body. Only when the body is ready to be purified should purification be administered; the physician must act only when the time is ripe, not before. After purification, certain procedures are performed to remove any remaining excess *doṣas* (after vomiting, for example, smoking is prescribed) followed by pacification treatment to rebalance the *doṣas* and protect the system until it returns to normal.

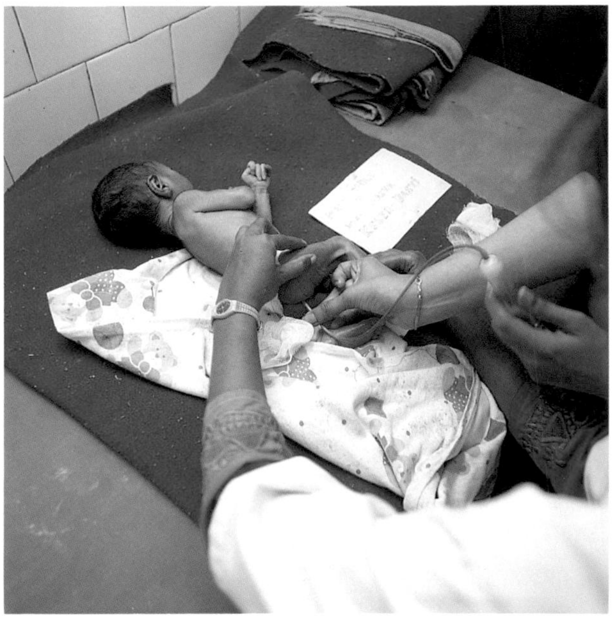

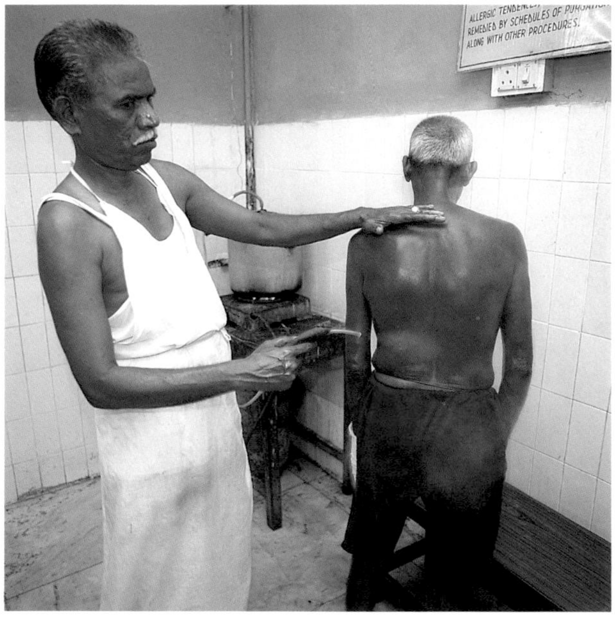

Pañcakarma is a unique Ayurvedic purifying therapy usually conducted in specialised clinics or hospital departments. Enemas or purgations (top) and emesis are the main means used to free the body of excess doṣas. Sweating, which transforms the doṣas into liquid form, is caused by diffusing heat through the body by means of hot baths or saunas (middle), or by applying medicated steam (below). Podar Ayurvedic Hospital, Bombay.

There are two different lists of *pañcakarma* (five actions). Caraka includes vomiting, purgation with laxatives, nasal medication, and two varieties of enema (decoctive and oily) in his list, while other writers including Vāgbhaṭa take both varieties of enema together as one and append blood-letting to the list as the fifth action. *Pañcakarma* is divided into two sorts according to whether it depletes the system (emesis, purgation, evacuative enema, evacuative nasal medication, blood-letting) or nourishes it (oily enema, nourishing nasal drops, and the like). Many possible *pañcakarma* complications are mentioned in the texts including advice on how to correct them.

Some authorities suggest that enema is the only treatment a physician needs to know, and others assert that it is fifty percent of treatment, even for animals. Therapeutic enemas are sometimes given in courses of eight, fifteen or thirty in total, according to the intensity of *vāta*; such courses alternate enemas of oil alone with purifying enemas which contain herbal decoctions. Vaginal douche is also included under the heading 'enema', as is the so-called 'head enema', which involves deluging the scalp with oil.

Nasal medication is the preferred purification for all diseases of the head. It is of various types according to *doṣa*: 'purgative' (using dry powders such as black pepper) for *kapha*, 'nutritive' (using mainly medicated oils) for *vāta*, and 'pacifying' (usually oil or ghee) for both *vāta* and *pitta*. A good daily routine includes the introduction of a couple of drops of medicated oil or ghee into the nose and the massage of its mucous membrane with the little finger.

Suśruta, who opined that half of all surgical problems could be successfully treated by blood-letting, was well aware of its dangers; he mentions twenty types of faulty punctures, and emphasises that excessive blood flow, causing weakness to the patient, must never be allowed. Blood-letting is used only for a few diseases; local ailments are mostly treated with leeches, while venepuncture is reserved for systemic problems.

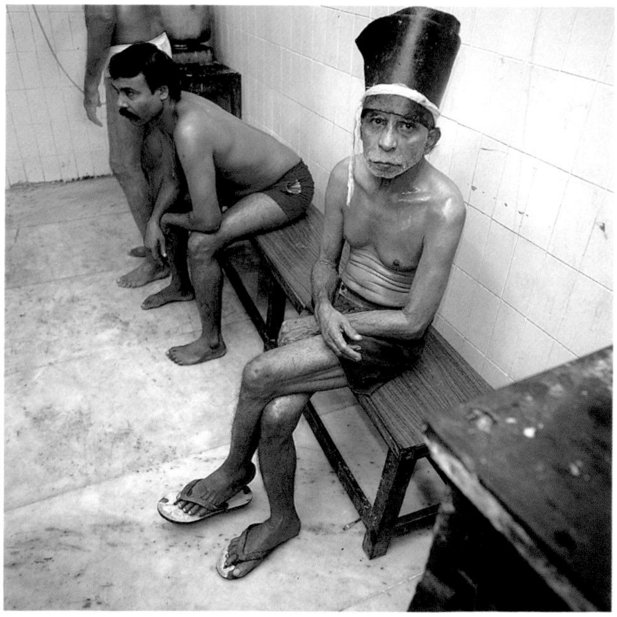

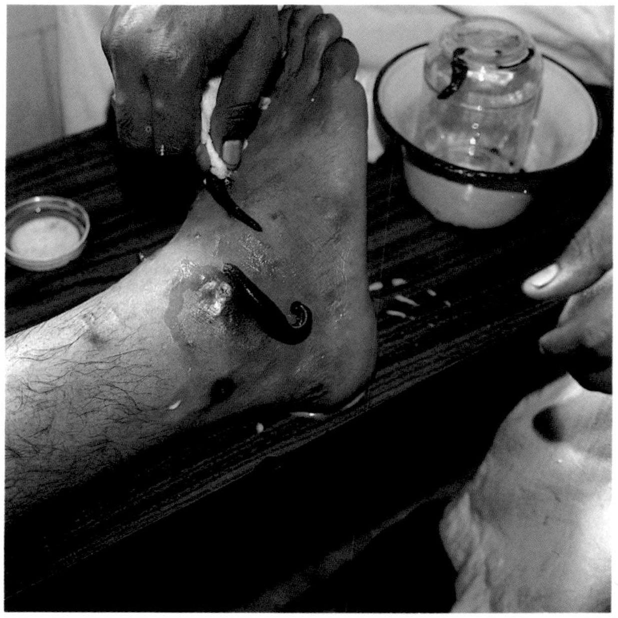

For those diseases which affect the ears, nose, eyes and brain, or for facial paralysis, pañcakarma prescribes a sirovasthi treatment for seven days. Each day, for about one hour, a leather cap is fixed onto the patient's head with the help of blackgram powder. Medicated oil, at a bearable temperature, is poured into the cap (top and middle). For blood-letting, applying leeches is still the most common practice. Ārya Vaidyaśāla in Kottakal, Kerala.

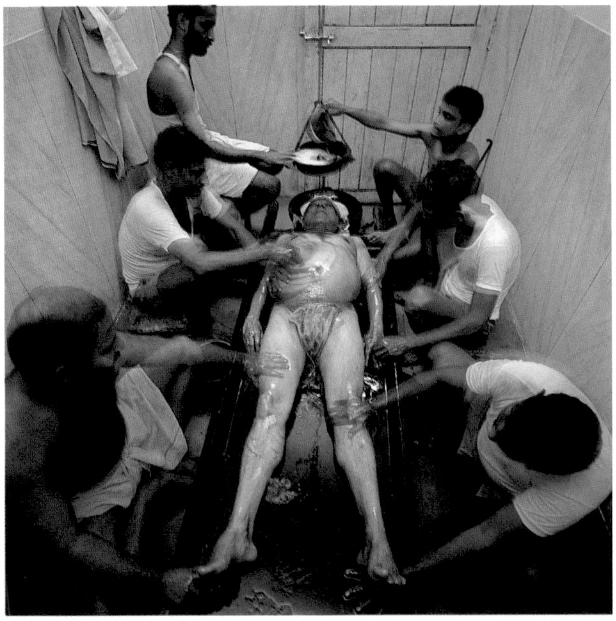

Dhara massage: Two masseurs cause warm medicated oil to stream continuously from a vessel on to the patient's head. Simultaneously, four people gently massage the patient, squeezing warm oil through linen cloth (pizhichil treatment). Ārya Vaidyaśāla in Kottakal, Kerala.

After oleation, a navarakkizhi massage can be performed against neuromuscular diseases or poliomyelitis. Cooked 'navarra' rice is placed in linen towels and heated in cow's milk. The patient is then massaged with heated rice bags. Ārya Vaidyaśāla in Kottakal, Kerala.

Above: *Dharachatti, a vessel to administer medicated oils. This vessel is used in dhara massage treatments to administer medicated oil; a wick is passed through a hole in the base to allow the oil to flow out.* Right: *Droni—massage board. Pañcakarma treatments with medicated oils, decoctions, milk, or other medicated liquids, are administered on this type of board. Ethnographic Museum Antwerp.*

Therapeutic substances

After purification, or instead of it when *pañcakarma* is contraindicated, the patient should consume medicines. If properly prepared and administered every substance (including thought) can be a medicine. Preparing an Ayurvedic medicine is a job for an expert cook, one who has mastered the arts of mixing various substances together and, by judicious use of processing methods (*saṃskāra*), creating a coherently acting, 'tasty' product. Even a small dose of medicine can be made to give a powerful action, and a large dose can be made to give a mild action, by adding assistant, synergistic drugs to or removing them from a recipe, by appropriate processing, and by judicious administration to the patient. An Ayurvedic drug's first and most important duty is to protect the tissues it enters from the attack of the *doṣas*. As such its concern is not with the 'active principles' which modern researchers seek to isolate from medicinal plants and test under laboratory conditions, but with the effects that a substance's innate qualities will have on a living system.

The texts provide sample recipes for the physician of average intelligence to copy, and for the expert physician to use as a guide; the fourth chapter of Caraka's *Sūtrasthāna*, for example, lists six hundred emetic and purgative prescriptions. Soil and climatic conditions, season, and pollution all affect a herb's qualities. Plants selected should be deeply rooted, of normal taste, colour, smell and feel, not attacked by insects or affected by fire, drought, or any other abnormal conditions, and well-tended by shade, sun, and water. Some of the earliest modes of preparation were a group of five methods called the *pañca kaṣāya kalpanā*: expressed juice, paste, decoction, hot infusion and cold infusion, in order from heaviest to lightest for digestion. From these five main methods of preparation other methods developed, including alkalis, distillates, medicated jams, medicinal wines, and pills. Many pills are potentiated by repeated mixing with a liquid and drying in a process called *bhāvanā*, a type of *saṃskāra*. *Bhāvanā* can be given either to enhance or to attenuate a herb's actions. Medicated fats are often potentiated by repeated cooking.

The animal products most commonly used in Ayurveda are animal urines, though the most famous of the animal products is musk, a secretion collected from a small Himalayan deer. Widespread use of minerals in Ayurveda began after the beginning of the Christian era with the introduction of medicines created as by-products of alchemical experiments for achieving physical immortality. Ayurvedically-prepared metals and minerals exert catalytic effects on metabolic processes but do not react chemically, or react very little, with the tissues. Mercury, the most important metal in Ayurvedic therapy, is usually reacted with sulphur to detoxify it. Most other minerals are prepared by incinerating them into ash (*bhasma*). Some *bhasmas* must be repeatedly incinerated in order to optimally potentiate them; mica *bhasma*, for example, requires one thousand incinerations. Because they are tiny but not soluble a well-made *bhasma*'s particles enter the system faster and stay there longer than does an herbal preparation. Metals can also be boiled in water to potentiate the water. The gems used in Ayurvedic therapy are usually either purified and incinerated, or they are immersed in alcohol for a month and the potentiated alcohol is administered.

From the seventh century AD onwards, mercury became the principal ingredient in Ayurvedic alchemy (rasāyana). Mercury is even today prepared from cinnabar (mercuric sulfide, HgS) and detoxified by incinerating in an hourglass-shaped furnace of clay.

Opposite: Bhasma preparation: Above, *a coconut is first perforated and the milk poured away. Medicated minerals are then inserted through the same hole. Middle: the coconut is wrapped in cloth, soaked and then covered with clay. Below: The preparation is then incinerated for twenty-four hours or more. The resulting potentiated ash (bhasma) is further refined and shaped into pills. Banepa Ayurvedic Hospital, Nepal.*

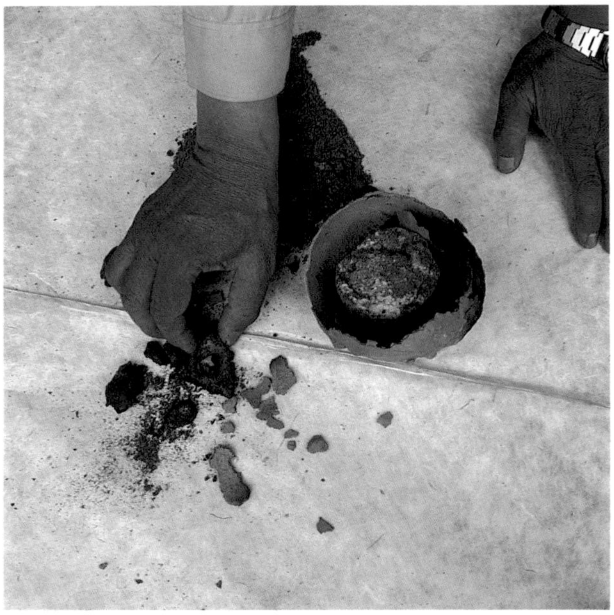

Crude herbs from all over India are gathered, selected and sorted at a drug factory in Kerala. Right, drugs awaiting distillation at the same factory.

Large pestle and mortar used for grinding crude herbs from Kerala. Ethnographic Museum, Antwerp.

Wooden herb container with lid in which herbs are stored as well as pounded. Ethnographic Museum, Antwerp.

Rejuvenation

After disease therapy is successfully completed, rejuvenation therapy should be given to strengthen the body part that was affected by the illness, that it may resist future disorders. *Rasāyana* (rejuvenation) therapy is also sometimes used to protect tissues against iatrotrauma, and to enhance the health and quality of life of the healthy. *Rasāyana* is literally 'the path of juice', a replenishment of the quality and the quantity of the body's fluids, in particular the concentrated hormonal essences which compose *ojas*, which are lost with ageing, physical or mental disease, or trauma. Rejuvenation and virilisation are often considered together because they are both concerned with preservation and maintenance of 'juice'. Sex being one of a human's greatest natural expenditures of 'juice', virilisation (the science of aphrodisiacs) is similarly a juice-repletion procedure.

Rasāyana can be performed either with or without substances. The substance-free variety, called 'behavioral *rasāyana*', involves such restrictions as the avoidance of all intoxicants, especially alcohol; the elimination of all physical or mental conflict and all other negative emotions, beginning with *rāga*; and the daily consumption (with proper digestion and assimilation) of foods in which the sweet taste predominates and salt is absent. Excess indulgence in salt ages the body prematurely, and causes many diseases. A full series of *pañcakarma* purification procedures must be performed before beginning this discipline, which must be strictly followed if it is to work on its own. It is however usual to augment this discipline with a rejuvenating substance. *Rasāyana*'s results depend greatly on preparation, both that of the rejuvenating substance and of the substance's consumer.

> *Discrimination, courage, and knowledge of the soul are the ideal therapies for the mind.* (Aṣṭāṅgahṛdaya Sūtrasthāna 1/26b)

'The essence of treatment is removal of the cause', and the avoidance of causative factors is the best way to stay healthy. Since *prajñāparādha* is the root cause of all disease, its eradication is the ultimate treatment.

> *The remedy for all miseries is the elimination of the allurement of desire.* (Caraka Śārīrasthāna 1/94b).

So long as delusion remains so will disease. Those who can destroy *rāgādi* and its associated delusions can destroy all the ailments over which they have control. While such self-controlled persons are more likely to enjoy good longevity than are the rest of us, even they will occasionally fall victim to those pathogenic factors which it is not possible for anyone to avoid.

The four treatment factors

Verse 27 of the first chapter of Vāgbhaṭa's treatise lists the four factors which are essential for successful medical treatment: a physician, a remedy, a nurse, and a patient. The physician should be expert both in theory and in practice, skillful, and pure in body and mind. Easy availability, appropriateness, utility in a variety of forms, and high quality characterise the optimal remedy. The best nurse is knowledgeable, skillful, sympathetic, and pure. The ideal patient is courageous, able to describe what he or she is feeling, and remembers all the physician's instructions and follows them carefully; all these qualities help the patient get well more easily. Deficiency in any of these factors hinders the therapeutic process. Of these four, the doctor, who must know both the disease and the remedy, must instruct both the nurse and the patient, and must prescribe both the medicine and the dietary regimen, is most important. One of the words for 'physician' in Sanskrit is *kavirāja*, which literally means 'king of poets'. A poet is a being who has been filled with the inspiration of a muse; for a doctor, it is the muse of health. An inspired physician can compensate for deficiencies in the other factors, and an inept physician will prevent successful treatment from occurring even if all else is optimal. Caraka observes that you may survive the fall of a thunderbolt on your head, but you cannot expect to survive the ministrations of an ignorant physician.

Traditional Ayurvedic physicians, who usually expect patients to approach them with full faith, see nothing wrong in neglecting to tell the whole 'objective' truth if 'subjective' truth is more likely to achieve the desired result. In his discussion on the disease consumption Caraka states that if there is a medical need to give the patient a variety of food that he might object to or be disgusted by, such as fried earthworms, the physician should if necessary lie about its true origin and give it anyway, calling it noodles, because of the need to ensure cure.

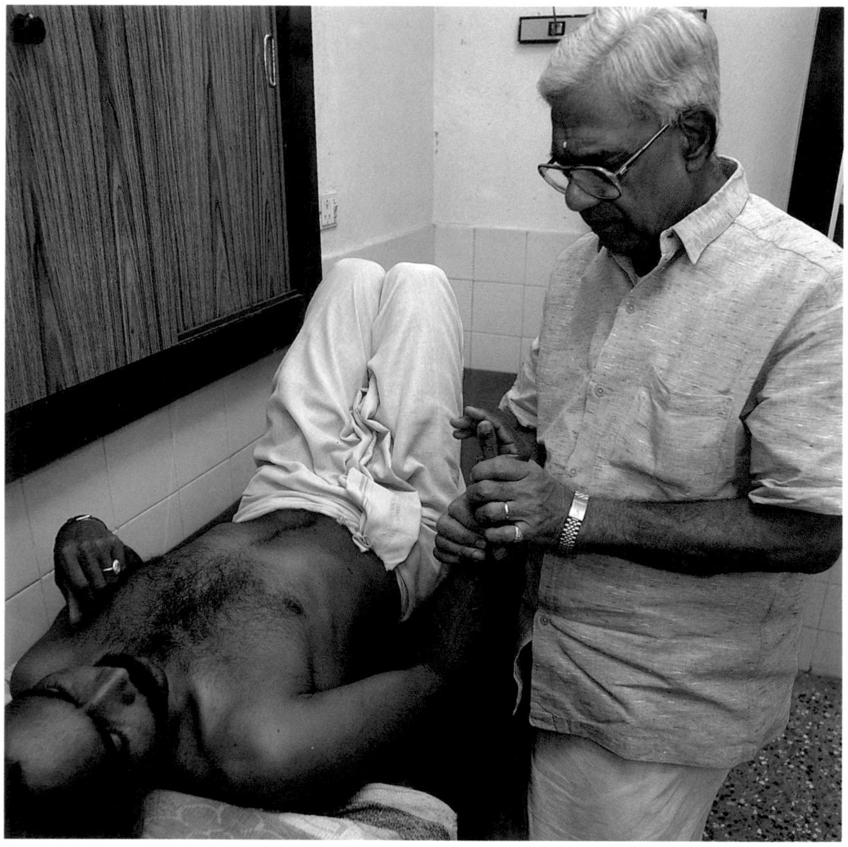

Dr P.K. Warrier of the Ārya Vaidyaśāla in Kottakal, Kottakal, Kerala, which was founded by his family in 1902, taking a patient's pulse.

Prognosis

Verses 29b through 33 of this chapter are devoted to prognosis, which is rightly a part of diagnosis, since once a disease has been identified it is necessary to determine its curability. There are four common prognoses: curable with ease, curable with difficulty, ameliorable (i.e. treatable but not curable), and incurable. When the prognosis is grave the physician must be careful not to shock the patient or the family with the news, particularly if the patient should happen to survive. Most important, when the time for death arrives the patient should be permitted to prepare for death calmly, undisturbed by any heroic measures which might temporarily postpone the inevitable.

> *The physician should reject that patient who hates the physician and the ruler and is hated by them; who hates himself; who lacks the necessities for treatment; who is busy with other activities; who is disobedient; whose life is drawing to a close; who is violent, afflicted with great grief, full of fear; or ungrateful; and who thinks himself to be a physician.* (Aṣṭāṅgahṛdaya Sūtrasthāna 1/34-35a)

While a physician has a moral obligation to try to heal everyone who comes to him or her, there are a few exceptions, most of which are self-explanatory. Doctors are of course encouraged to accept as charity cases as many patients who lack the necessities for treatment as they can—demanding money from the poor as a precondition for treatment is strictly forbidden—but they are not expected to bankrupt themselves in the process; that would not be moderate. Treating those 'whose life is drawing to a close' is discouraged because the dying should be left to die in peace; because such treatment is a waste of the physician's time and the patient's money; and because each person who dies during therapy diminishes the physician's fame. Poor prognosis is also behind the rejection of those patients who are afflicted by intensely negative emotions. The *doṣa*-imbalancing effects of hatred, violence, grief, ingratitude, and all the other derivatives of *rāga* are so much stronger than the body's capability for homeostasis that until the patient is ready to relinquish the passions they will create new diseases just as fast as the doctor can remove the old ones.

A life of sweetness

The last verses of *Āyuṣkāmīya* list all the other chapters of the treatise, beginning with preventative measures and continuing to curative procedures. It is the final three verses of the following chapter, which is dedicated to daily routine, which perhaps most admirably summarise Ayurveda's overall approach to the business of living life:

> *Since for an intelligent person the whole world is a mentor, one should, after carefully considering the implications thereof, emulate [the world]. Good conduct consists of compassion toward all living beings, generosity, control of body, speech, and mind, and attention to the interests of others as if they were your own. Whoever constantly reviews how his day and night are passing will never suffer sorrow.* (Aṣṭāṅgahṛdaya Sūtrasthāna 2/45-47)

Right thoughts and right attitudes actually induce prosperity, for wealth is attracted to that person who approaches it wisely, by the principle of like increases like. The quality of your prosperity will depend upon the means you employ to manifest it, for the end does not justify the means, the end *is* the means. A healthy system is made up of healthy units functioning together in a healthy relationship, and so the well-being of a particular individual cannot be separated from the well-being of the community, the land, the supernatural world or the cosmos. There is no individual so individual that he or she does not interact with the environment. When an individual becomes aligned with the cosmos the lesser universe begins to function as a harmonious unit of the greater, and longevity is secured. When you pass your nights and days in reflection on the transitory nature of existence, examining what is wholesome and what is not for yourself, your family, your country and the world, you will be led to perform only those actions which are beneficial to all concerned. So long as these actions are appropriate to your capacity to act (according to your age, strength, state of health, and so on) neither you nor anyone else will ever have to taste of misery, and you will ensure for yourself a life of sweetness until your dying day.

Notes

1 In the text, all the quotes from Vāgbhaṭa come from Vāgbhaṭa's *Aṣṭāṅgahṛdayam*, vol. 1, trans. Prof. K. R. Srikantha Murthy, Krishnadas Academy, Varanasi, 1991. Those from Caraka come from P. M. Mehta, editor, *Charaka Saṁhita*; Gulab Kunverba Society, Jamnagar, 1949.

2 The English word 'jungle' is borrowed from the Hindi word *jaṅgal*, which is a version of this Sanskrit word *jāṅgala*. While the original word suggested the sort of open savannah with isolated trees that is found in much of peninsular India, it came to be used for any sort of wilderness. Since it was after its use was extended to the rain forests of Malaysia that it was adopted in English, the word 'jungle' signifies a habitat which is precisely opposite from the habitat it originally denoted.

References

Comba, Antonella. 'Caraka Samhita, Sarirasthana I and Vaishesika Philosophy', in (eds.) G. J. Meulenbeld and D. Wujastyk, *Studies in Indian Medical History*, Groningen, 1987, pp. 43-61.

Dash, Bhagwan. *Fundamentals of Ayurvedic Medicine*, Bansal & Co., Delhi, 1978.

Bhishagratna, K. L. *Sushruta Samhita*, Chowkhamba, Varanasi, 1968.

Filliozat, J. *The Classical Doctrine of Indian Medicine*, Munshiram Manoharlal, Delhi, 1964.

Jolly, Julius. *Indian Medicine*, (trans. Kashikar), Munshiram Manoharlal, Delhi, 1977.

Lad, Vasant. *Ayurveda: The Science of Self-Healing*, Lotus Press, Santa Fe, 2nd Edition, 1985.

Mehta, P. M. (ed.) *Charaka Saṁhita*, Gulab Kunverba Society, Jamnagar, 1949.

Mooss, N. S. (ed. & trans.) *Vāgbhaṭa's Aṣṭāṅga Hṛdaya Saṁhita, Kalpasthāna*, Vaidyasarathy Press, Kottayam, 1984.

Murthy, Prof. K. R. Srikanta (trans.), *Mādhava Nidānam*, Chaukhambha, Varanasi, 1987.

— *Aṣṭāṅga Hṛdayam*, Krishnadas Academy, Varanasi, 1991 (Vol. 1) & 1992 (Vol. 2).

— *Śārṅgadhara-Saṁhitā*, Chaukhambha Orientalia, Varanasi, 1984.

Nordstrom, Carolyn R. 'Exploring Puralism: The Many Faces of Ayurveda', *Social Science and Medicine*, Vol. 27 , No. 5, pp. 479-89, 1988.

— 'Ayurveda: A Multilectic Interpretation', *Social Science and Medicine*, Vol. 28 , No. 9, pp. 963-70.

Ray, P., and Gupta, H. N. *Charaka Saṁhita: A Scientific Synopsis*, National Institute of Sciences of India, New Delhi, 1965

Sharma, Pandit Shiv. *Realms of Ayurveda*, Arnold-Heineman, Delhi, 1979.

Svoboda, Robert E. *Prakruti: Your Ayurvedic Constitution*, Geocom, Albuquerque, 1988.

— *Ayurveda: Life, Health and Longevity*, Arkana, London, 1992.

Zimmer, H. R. *Hindu Medicine*, Johns Hopkins Press, Baltimore, 1948.

Zimmermann, Francis. *The Jungle and the Aroma of Meats: An Ecological Theme in Hindu Medicine*, University of California Press, Berkeley, 1987.

Two thousand-year-old Ayurvedic theories and practices are now tested by modern scientific methods. At Zandu Pharmaceuticals, Bombay, the active qualities of herbs are investigated.

Ayurveda Today – Ayurveda at the Crossroads

DARSHAN SHANKAR & RAM MANOHAR

THE INDIAN MEDICAL HERITAGE

India possesses a medical heritage with a long, unbroken history. The traditional health culture of India functions through two social streams. One is the 'codified' stream, which includes well-developed systems of medicine like Ayurveda, Siddha, Unani and Tibetan. The other is the ecosystems-rooted, 'folk' stream.

The 'codified' stream consists of medical knowledge with sophisticated theoretical foundations expressed in thousands of regional manuscripts covering treatises on all branches of medicine and surgery. However, of an estimated 100,000 medical manuscripts lying in oriental libraries and private collections in India and abroad, less than one percent are available and in current use by students and teachers in Indian medical schools. The earliest Ayurvedic texts, the *Suśruta Saṃhitā* and *Caraka Saṃhitā*, are believed to have been written between 1500 and 1000 BC.[1] The main branches of Ayurveda are: *kāya cikitsā* (general medicine), *bāla cikitsā* (paediatrics), *graha cikitsā* (psychiatry), *śālākya tantra* (ENT), *śalya cikitsā* (surgery), *viṣa cikitsā* (toxicology), *rasāyana* (rejuvenation), and *vājikarana* (virilification). Besides these, there are specialised treatises on a range of subjects including pharmacy (*bheṣaja Kalpana*), *materia medica* (*nighaṇṭu*), diagnostics (*nidāna*), special diagnostic techniques like pulse diagnosis (*nāḍī cikitsā*), iatrochemistry (*rasaśāstra*), dietetics (*pathyāpathya*), pharmacology (*dravyaguṇa*) and positive health and preventive medicine (*svasthavṛtta*).[2]

The village-based, ecosystems-linked traditions of folk medicine are purely empirical. They represent a highly decentralised knowledge of healthcare which is community specific, local resource dependent, and hence region specific. According to the Anthropological Survey of India there are 4,639 ethnic communities in India. Except for scattered documentation by anthropologists and ethnobotanists of the ethnomedical traditions of mainly tribal, and fewer non-tribal, communities in different regions, no systematic documentation has been made of the entire spectrum of folk medicine streams of India. Thus the knowledge and resource base of this stream has not been fully documented, or even properly understood.

Millions of households practise home remedies and possess knowledge of local foods and nutrition. More than 600,000 traditional birth attendants manage over 90% of rural deliveries. Thousands of herbal healers, monks, bone-setters, tribal doctors and a host of specialists in various areas attend to a variety of rural health problems. All these local, community-based, actors are the carriers of the folk health traditions. One also comes across startling examples of the incredible depth and range of this tradition in stray reports of medical practices in different regions.

For instance, in 1793 two medical officers of the East India Company—James Trindlay and Thomas Cruso—reported on the practice of rhinoplasty by a potter's community in Pune district in the *Madras Gazette* (and later in 1794 in the London *Gentleman's Magazine*).[3] It was this technical report that led to further developments in Britain of plastic surgery of the nose. In present times, it is well known in south Karnataka that the successful treatment of certain paralytic conditions can be effected by the use of *aṅkola* oil. Ankola is the name of a village; this particular herbal oil is part of its folk medical legacy. There is also the case of the Coimbatore orthopaedic treatment for straightening a club foot by the use of a special herbal oil which softens the bony tissues.

Like other Indian knowledge systems which possess a 'folk' and a 'classical' form (these include music, painting, agriculture, veterinary sciences, architecture, and even theoretical areas like logic, mathematics and linguistics), the 'folk' and the 'codified' or 'classical' streams of medicine have a symbiotic relationship. In all these fields the 'folk' represents empirical experience, whilst the 'classical' has synthesised, generalised and theorised upon it to build up its theoretical foundations.

Thus the Sanskrit language is linked to diverse regional Prakrit languages. Many of the classical *rāgas* in Indian music can similarly be shown to have their origin in regional folk music traditions. Carpenters use simple folk algorithms to make their calculations. In the medical context the classical can often explain the science behind the folk practice and extend its range, depth and application. For example, the nutritive values of vegetables and dietary items in the Ayurvedic classical text *Suśruta Saṃhitā* is based on the existing local practices in different parts of the country.[4]

Whilst they are influenced by the folk traditions, it is equally true that the textual traditions have also influenced and guided the folk traditions, which tend to become rigid and distorted from time to time. Thus we find in the traditional texts discouragement of harmful folk practices adopted to induce delivery.[5] In another instance, it is mentioned that people mistake uterine tumour as pregnancy, and in the event of delivery not taking place in time, they believe that the foetus has been consumed by evil spirits etc.[6]

All folk traditions can be represented by the generic term *prākṛta* and the classical or theoretical streams by the word *saṃskṛta*. *Pra* means primordial; something already—or always—there. *Kṛti* means 'going on' or 'functioning'. So *prākṛta* stands for the unmodified, directly perceived, primordial experiences of human beings. In the word *saṃskṛta*, *saṃ* stands for *saṃskāra* or modification, a refinement, generalisation, or a processing, upon the *kṛt*.

The Contemporary Status of Ayurveda

The contemporary status of Ayurveda is a culmination of the events of the last 200 years of colonial rule, the pre-Independence nationalistic ideology of the Indian National Congress, and the post-Independence health policies of the Government of India. A brief review of these stages reveals more than a century of colonial oppression, as well as distortions imposed on the psyche of the indigenous medical community. These were due to the insistence of Europeans and Indians trained in allopathic medicine (and allied chemical and biological sciences) to interpret Ayurveda in allopathic and modern scientific terms without understanding the fuller epistemological implications of comparing two distinct scientific traditions. Further, although the Government of India's healthcare planning provided an equal status to Ayurveda and other indigenous systems as it did to allopathy in policy, in actual implementation it allocated only a small fraction of the national health budget to traditional systems of medicine.

It is evident from historical records that the first and earliest phase of European response to indigenous medicine in the early seventeenth century was relatively objective, and that it faithfully recorded the state of indigenous medical systems as it was. These records are generally appreciative of the competence of the native doctors.[7] Towards the end of the eighteenth century, however, there was a change in the stance of the British, and the accounts from this period, which reflect the political needs of colonial rule, highlight a deliberate attempt to suppress indigenous talent and achievements. One striking example is the banning in 1804 of the indigenous smallpox inoculation which, according to Dr Holwell FRS, was so extremely effective that, 'when the ... treatment is strictly followed, it comes as a miracle to hear that one in a million fails of receiving the infection or of one that miscarried under it'.[8]

In 1835, the British stopped paying for Ayurveda to be taught at government medical colleges. During the next hundred years of their rule, state patronage of its institutions and practitioners was completely cut off. Thus in the beginning of this century there were no Ayurvedic teaching institutions, and all teaching of Ayurveda was effected through the non-institutional *guru-śiṣya* traditions. Even leading Ayurvedic physicians of the time advised their own children to seek training in Western medicine as that was the only way to get privileged jobs in public health services.

By the middle of the nineteenth century, Western medicine had become the sole recipient of state patronage. Traditional surgery, which in the eighteenth century had won the admiration of Europeans like Colonel Kyd and Dr H. Scott, became literally dysfunctional.[9] The fact that the European world owed to Indian medicine the technique of rhinoplasty seems to have been forgotten.[10] When a national medical register was created in 1912, registration was denied to practitioners of traditional medicine and the morale of traditional practitioners went into a low ebb.

During the pre-Independence phase, which was marked by the political compulsions of establishing a national identity to replace foreign domination, a large number of initiatives were undertaken to promote ISMs (Indian Systems of Medicine). For the first time in 200 years indigenous medicine received political support when the Indian National Congress passed its first resolution in Nagpur in 1920.

Formal colleges of Indian medicine were gradually created. These were modelled on the lines of colleges of allopathic medicine, and the syllabus contained similar prerequisites as modern medicine. Classroom teaching and an examination system replaced the *guru-śiṣya* system. Dispensaries and hospitals similar in design to allopathic OPDs were established. Pharmacies were set up for the smallscale production and marketing of medicines. Professional associations, a board for the registration of medical practitioners, and medical journals were also initiated.

Today there are at least five leading journals for Ayurveda in the country. The number of teaching institutes of ISM—which was 57 at the time of Independence—is now 120. There are over 100 undergraduate institutions teaching Ayurveda, and 24 postgraduate teaching and doctorate granting institutions. The annual capacity for student admissions in all these colleges comes to 3,882.[11]

In 1971, the Central Council of Indian Medicine (CCIM) was established by an act of parliament in order to bring uniformity and maintain standards of education in Ayurveda. In due course the Ayurvedic qualifications were regulated. The three-year Diploma course (DAM) was replaced by the five-and-a-half year BAMS course (Bachelor of Ayurvedic Medicine and Surgery). The BAMS degree course has now been further modified to match the allopathic system, and consists of four-and-a-half years training plus a one-year internship. The main course is divided into three, one-and-a-half year, semesters. The three-year postgraduate course in Ayurveda is known as Ayurveda Vachaspati, MD (Ay), Doctor of Medicine in Ayurveda, and is open to BAMS degree holders. There is also a research degree course of a further two years, at the end of which the candidate is awarded a PhD (Doctor of Philosophy).

The Indian Council of Medical Research (ICMR) was the pioneer in the pharmacological and clinical evaluation of ISM drugs, and the single body responsible for this work between 1960 and 1970. Since 1978, the CCRAS (Central Council for Research in Ayurveda and Siddha), set up by the Ministry of Health, has been the central research agency for Ayurveda.[12] There are now 90—both small and medium—engaged in various research activities all over the country.

Today, of an estimated 400,000 practitioners of ISM, there are 264,800 registered Ayurvedic practitioners. Of these, 108,753 are institutionally qualified, registered medical practitioners. India also has a large number of cottage and smallscale herbal manufacturing units, producing Ayurvedic, Unani and Siddha medicines. There are about thirteen centrally assisted pharmacies, and 4,769 licensed pharmacies for the manufacture of Ayurvedic medicines. There are 1,349 government hospitals, 8,300 government dispensaries, and 16,313 hospital beds. In addition, a number of private nursing homes and clinics have sprung up in response to the demand of the times. About 21 colleges and hospitals give training for Ayurvedic compounders and pharmacists, and have an admission capacity of 858.[13]

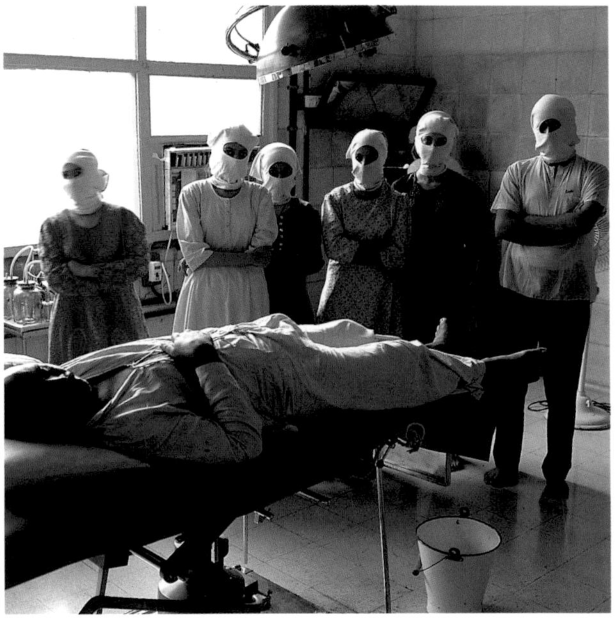

Student surgeons attending a demonstration of the removal of a fistula by means of the famous Ayurvedic medicated thread called Kṣara sūtra at the Podar Ayurvedic Hospital, Bombay.

The picture of Ayurveda in India today therefore appears much brighter than it was in the pre-Independence period. The quantitative profile of contemporary Ayurveda in terms of the above formal parameters may look impressive. However, it must also be noted that in the same fifty year period, the Indian Government allocated less than 4% of the national health budget to Ayurveda, and more than 96% to Western medicine.[14] The mushrooming of Ayurvedic institutions is therefore also a story of the butter being spread very thinly and, although large in number, the new institutions established have been created with sub-critical inputs and resources. As one looks beneath the surface of the above mentioned growth, a weakened state of affairs in the field of Ayurveda becomes evident.

Clear guidelines regarding college infrastructure, the number of staff, laboratory facilities, herbal gardens, hospital beds and number of in-patients for clinical bedside training, are laid down by the CCIM. Yet more than half the Ayurvedic colleges do not have even the basic infrastructure. The majority of colleges produce graduates who are therefore not equipped to diagnose problems along Ayurvedic principles. Many of these colleges are in the private sector and on the verge of closing down.

From 1947 to 1961, Ayurveda was taught on the basis of an integrated syllabus. This instilled fear on the part of both Ayurvedic and allopathic physicians. While the former stated that such an integration would destroy the theoretical foundations of ISM and reduce it to a hybridised version of allopathy, the latter feared that half-baked physicians would be permitted to practise allopathy and compete with their professional monopoly.

This debate is well reflected in the recommendations of the various official review committees on ISMs in the post-Independence period. Finally, in 1961 the Mudaliar Committee strongly recommended the return of ISMs to their *śuddha* or classical form.[15] In some states there was a condensed course in allopathy (equivalent to the MBBS, and open to graduates of traditional systems of medicine), but this was consequently stopped.

Postgraduate education and higher research studies are modelled on the lines of modern science. Students are trained to evaluate Ayurvedic theory according to the parameters of modern medicine and are thus led to accept modern medicine as the more scientific approach. While many scholars of Ayurveda have been talking about the need to evaluate Ayurveda on the basis of its own theoretical foundations, no encouragement is provided to develop alternative research models along these lines.

The field of pharmacy and manufacture of medicines are beset with problems. It has not yet been possible to evolve satisfactory methods for evaluation and standardisation of Ayurvedic drugs. The modern approach of isolating the active principles from the plants is in direct contradiction to the traditional concept of using crude drugs in combination.[16] Pharmacies manufacturing medicines purely on the basis of traditional principles are very few. The trend to imitate modern medicine has led to the emergence of a new breed of patent medicines which are not made strictly on the basis of Ayurvedic principles; these medicines are presented as tablets, syrups and so on.

Medical practice in Ayurveda also oscillates between the two extremes of pure Ayurveda and an untrained use of modern medicines. The practitioners of pure Ayurveda belong mainly to the older generation. A section of the new generation of Ayurvedic graduates are inclined to use modern methods of diagnosis and treatment. To illustrate, during the 1970s, in a study of 59 indigenous practitioners in Punjab and Mysore, researchers were very surprised to find that 75% of the drugs being used were modern cosmopolitan medicines such as antibiotics. The same study uncovered an underground system of healthcare providing the bulk of local medical treatment and a pervasive—but previously unrecognised—system of medical education.

> *The professors are the drug detail men from the pharmaceutical companies. The junior faculty are the pharmacists in the cities. Each pharmacist has a continuing class of practitioners scattered throughout the neighbouring villages. The practitioner will drop into the pharmacist's shop and say, 'I am seeing a lot of conjunctivitis these days. What do you have that's good?' The indigenous practitioners of Ludhiana District had organised an association and monthly meetings to discuss clinical cases and new treatments.*[17]

Thus while there has been quantitative development in terms of the number of Ayurvedic institutions in the post-Independence period, the quality of Ayurvedic medical practice has deteriorated. Although it is present, political patronage for Ayurveda is poorly informed about the difference in the epistemological foundations of Ayurveda, and does not therefore understand the requirements for its proper growth and flowering.

Critical Appraisal

A true revival of Ayurveda could come about only through the strengthening and revival of its epistemological and theoretical foundations. Only then will the system be able to legitimately anchor itself as an alternative medical system in this modern age and rise up in strength to meet the challenges of the times.

There is an urgent need to re-examine the validity of the assumption that Western culture is the most refined in the history of human development, thereby replacing many other cultural expressions, especially in the realm of scientific thinking. A major problem that Asian societies have to contend with in any serious evaluation of their indigenous sciences, and the suitablility or otherwise of modern Western science and technology, is the common claim of all western scientists and philosophers that, after all, science is one, universal and uniquely expressed in Western scientific paradigms. Thus, while it may be possible to conceive of alternative methodologies, theories and practices in other domains such as music, linguistics, logic, art and politics, there is no such possibility with regard to science.

Such claims appear to smack of a dogmatism born out of a Western ethnocentric worldview. An example from the domain of music may illustrate the point. While everybody would grant that Mozart and Tansen were great musicians and composers, nobody would think it meaningful to ask why Tansen did not compose symphonies or sonatas. Yet it is precisely such questions that we seem to encounter in the field of science and technology because of the myth of the exclusively universal and unique nature of modern science and technology.

Beginning with this epistemological position then, it is impossible to initiate a debate on 'alternatives in science' because the very idea is dismissed as an absurdity. Given the continuing domination of the West, Asian societies are left with no option but to accept modern science and technology as the universal, well-established, system and to derive legitimacy for their own traditional system by demonstrating how well the latter conforms to the methodology, theory and practice of the former.

That this is a basically flawed approach to understanding foundationally-distinct knowledge systems is ignored. In order to understand the contemporary picture of Ayurveda, it is essential to be aware of the outline of the foundational debate related to non-Western epistemologies or alternatives in science that has now been running for over a century. In our view, it is this epistemological debate that underlies the entire recent 200 year old history of Ayurveda and its present state of art; its twists and turns have moulded the picture of Ayurveda in India today. Politics and sociology, economics and commerce have built their strategies around this subtle and almost invisible discourse.

The foundational theories, principles, concepts and categories upon which indigenous Indian health science is based are indeed different from Western medical science. While indigenous medical knowledge is built upon a holistic perspective—as seen in the theory of *pañca mahābhūta siddhānta*—Western foundational theory is atomistic. While the former rests on such philosophical foundations as *Nyāya*, *Vaiśeṣika*, *Sāṅkhya* and *Yoga* (Indian systems of knowledge, *darśanas*, dealing with logic and reasoning, study of the phenomenal world, study of evolution of the world and the means to experience ultimate reality through discipline of body and mind),[18] the latter rests on various schools of positivistic thought and Aristotelian logic and its further refinements. The bodies of knowledge that are built upon these different foundations necessarily differ in form, structure, categories and concepts. This foundational difference is reflected in differences in the formulation of theories pertaining to causation of diseases, pharmacology and drug action, dietetics and nutrition, physiology, diagnostics, etc.

In indigenous pharmacology for instance—better known as *dravya guṇa śāstra*—the whole plant or its parts (the leaves, stem, seeds, root, bark, fruit, flowers), is studied as a whole in terms of its *in vivo* effects on such parameters as *rasa* (taste, there are six tastes, each indicative of the composition and properties of the substance), *vipāka* (a post-digestive state of a substance), and *prabhāva* (a unique pharmacological activity of a substance). Modern pharmacology, on the other hand, isolates an active chemical entity from the plant or its parts and studies its *in vitro* and *in vivo* effects on entirely different biochemical parameters. Both approaches undoubtedly have their uses. The difference lies primarily in the fact that in indigenous knowledge systems the category of knowledge known as chemistry is absent. What exists is a holistic category called *dravya guṇa śāstra*. If we believe the absence of chemistry to be a serious lacuna in indigenous science, we would have to concede that the absence of *dravya guṇa śāstra* in modern science is as serious a lacuna. The point, however, is not one of lacunae or gaps in the scientificity of either system, but the fact that these differences arise from fundamental foundational differences which make unintelligible any simple comparison of the form, structure and categories of both systems.

Although measurement and quantification are an important part of indigenous systems of medicine, they differ in form from modern systems. Most measurements in the traditional sciences are made using units normalised to a particular individual. That is, while assessing a person's height or the length of his or her limbs, the measurement is expressed in units of *aṅguli*, the dimension of a finger of the concerned individual, rather than an arbitary standard external to the individual—the international metre. Such normalised units exist not only for measurement of length but also for volume and time. In *yoga cintāmaṇi*, for instance, a *mātra* of time has been defined as the time taken by a sleeping individual to complete one cycle of breath—one inhalation and one exhalation. Although measurement and quantification have their place in ISMs, their importance is somewhat limited as compared to modern systems. In India, it is not the geometry of Euclid but the *Aṣṭādhyāyī* of Pāṇini that is considered to be the supreme example of the construction of theory. Indian sciences are based on the understanding that numbers and symbols are not essential to achieve scientific rigour. Rather, the technical use of natural language—Sanskrit, for instance—has sufficed in highly abstract and technical topics like logic, mathematics and *vedānta*. Recent research has indicated that this method of using natural language to achieve rigour can have powerful applications in computer sciences as well.

Such differences should come as no surprise to those medical professionals aware of the plurality of cultures and their varied scientific expressions. Unfortunately, however, the myth of there being one universal science—modern Western science—dominates the thinking of a large section of the scientific community. In fact, this view has served to block a healthy dialogue in India between those trained in Western allopathic medicine and those trained in the indigenous sciences.

The inner health of Ayurveda today cannot therefore really be understood from an appraisal of its external and formal state. Due to a lack of epistemological defence of Ayurveda and proper research models for validating Ayurveda, all its achievements in the country are reduced to a string of anecdotal accounts of its efficacy in a range of conditions from the common cold to the latest plague of AIDS and cancer. Stray medical success stories from different regions relating to miraculous healing provided by both the folk traditions as well as the codified system abound. Whereas all its achievements can be backed up by indigenous medical theory and principles, naturally they cannot be explained by Ayurvedic physicians in terms of modern medical theories since there is no bio-statistical tradition in Ayurveda. As there are no hard data and statistics, no valid statistical inferences are possible. Moreover, because of the lack of correlation of disease entities in both systems, and the differences in the aetiology and logic of drug action, disease management in Ayurveda also appears to be unrepeatable.

Thus from one perspective, the inner state of Ayurveda is a picture of struggle to establish its epistemological identity and retain its integrity. From another, it is a picture of unhappy compromise with modern medicine seeking justification in terms of modern medical theory and its parameters, and trying unsuccessfully to prove itself to be scientific. In the process, Ayurveda, a great non-Western knowledge system, is being destroyed. Perhaps the only thing that is being partially recovered from this vast treasure-house is its herbal pharmacopoeia and its simplest herbal formulations. A few techniques like acupuncture, acupressure, massage and the like, are also being salvaged because their outcomes are relatively easier to demonstrate and validate according to modern parameters.

However, these herbal drugs and techniques form only a fraction of the knowledge system. Much remains to be discovered in terms of its profound understanding of body and mind relationships, its scheme of systemic diagnosis, its physiology, its indigenous pharmacology, its pharmaceutical principles and a host of specialities. The favourable attitude and policies of the Government of India towards Ayurveda in the post-Independence period have been a necessary—but not sufficient—step towards a revitalisation of the science. The problem lies in the crisis of confidence both within and outside the Ayurvedic community, and it is here that future efforts need to be concentrated in order to effect a revitalisation.

Notes

1 P.V. Sharma 1992, pp. 180, 199.

2 Some of the popular textbooks on these specialised branches are: *Śārṅgadhara Saṃhitā* (pharmacy), *Dhanvantari Nighantu* (*materia medica*), *Mādhava Nidāna* (diagnostics), *Nāḍī Darpaṇa* (pulse diagnosis), *Rasaratnasamuchaya* (iatrochemistry), *Bhojana-kutūhala* (dietetics), *Rasavaiśeṣika Sūtra* (pharmacology), and *Kshemakutūhala* (preventive medicine).

3 Darshan Shankar 1992, p. 140.

4 K.H. Krishnamurthy 1991.

5 *Caraka Saṃhitā*, *Śārīrasthāna*, Chapter 8, Choukhambha Orientalia, Varanasi.

6 *Aṣṭāṅga Saṅgraha*, *Śārīrasthāna*, Chapter 1, Anand Athvale, Pune.

7 Dharampal 1971, pp. 31-5.

8 *Ibid.*, p. 193.

9 *Ibid.*, p. 32.

10 Claude Alvares 1991, p. 67.

11 S.K. Alok 1988 p. 42.

12 Some of its major achievements are listed below (source, S.K. Alok, *ibid.* p. 47):

- number of patents obtained: 16
- formulations for which preliminary standards have been developed: 675
- number of pharmacognostical studies: 135 drugs
- number of chemical studies: 250 drugs
- number of pharmacognostical studies: 305 drugs
- number of forest areas surveyed for medico-botanical work: 250
- number of research projects and time bound enquiries: 98

13 Alok, *ibid.* p. 47.

14 Darshan Shankar 1992, p. 165.

15 *Ibid.* p. 146.

16 The *Caraka Saṃhitā*, the celebrated Ayurvedic text on general medicine, in the section on pharmacy (*Kalphasthāna*, 12th chapter), elucidates the principles of combining drugs to make herbal recipes. A recipe has one main ingredient which performs the main therapeutic action and is assisted by other ingredients which play different roles to effect a balanced curative action on the biological system. This has been compared to the organisation of the state where the king and the courtiers function harmoniously to execute the duties of the state.

17 C.E. Taylor 1985, pp. 77-89.

18 The entire first chapter of *Śārīrasthāna* in *Caraka Saṃhitā* dealing with the development of the human body and its relation to the development of the universe, is based on the principles of *Sāṅkhya* and *Yoga*. The eighth chapter in *Vimānasthāna* which deals with the methods of debate and theory development are based on the principles of *Nyāya*. The very first chapter of the treatise in the *Sūtrasthāna* elucidates the principle of the *Vaiśeṣika* school of philosophy. These concepts have been adapted to suit the purpose of medical science.

References

Alok, S.K. *Indian Systems of Medicine and Homoeopathy, State and National Profile*, Ministry of Health and Family Welfare, New Delhi, 1988.

Alvares, Claude. *Decolonising History*, Goa, The Other India Press, 1991.

Dharampal, *Indian Science and Technology in Eighteenth Century*, Academy of Gandhian Studies, Hyderabad, July 1971.

Krishnamurthy, K.H. *Wealth of Sushruta*, International Institute of Ayurveda, Coimbatore, 1991

Shankar, Darshan. *State of India's Health*, VHAI, New Delhi, 1992.

Sharma, P.V. *History of Medicine in India*, New Delhi, Indian National Science Academy.

Taylor, C.E. 'Primary health care in India: relationships with indigenous systems', in *Science and Technology in South Asia: Proceedings of the South Asia Seminar II, 1981-1982*, Philadelphia, Department of South Asia Regional Studies, 1985, pp. 77-89.

To ward off misfortunes and diseases, this household protective deity is kept hidden in a secret place. Women are forbidden to touch it and it is destroyed on the death of the head of the house. Private Collection, Belgium.

The World of Tibetan Medicine

A pilgrim circumambulates a stupa on the way to Ganden monastery.

Ancient medical manuscripts kept in their brocaded silk covers at the Mentsikhang hospital in Lhasa.

Theory and Practice of Tibetan Medicine

FERNAND MEYER

The first westerner to describe the practice of a refined medical art in the Land of Snows, albeit somewhat inadequately, was the Jesuit missionary Ippolito Desideri who lived in Tibet from 1715 to 1721. He wrote,

> *Medicine is the only profession which has qualified members, and in Thibet they are many and excellent. It is not their custom to ask the patient how he is or what is the pain, but they feel first one pulse, then the other, then both together, and then say what ails the sick man. They have not many drugs, but good medicinal herbs, either indigenous or brought from China, the Lhoba country, which I have already mentioned, Nepal or Hindustan, or shall we say Mogol. These are generally given in the form of pills or in powders, and often effect cures. The professors are well paid and generally stipulate what their fee is to be before undertaking a cure.*[1]

But it was only a century later, in 1835, that an article by Csoma de Körös, the founder of Tibetology, revealed to orientalists the existence of the *Gyushi* (rGyud-bzhi) or *Four Tantras*, the reference text used by Tibetan practitioners, along with the general outline of its contents.[2] Tibet's geographical and political isolation allowed its medical system, like the entirety of its culture, to be preserved from western influence imposed by colonial powers in the rest of Asia, and it is only in the last twenty years or so that studies and publications concerning Tibetan medicine have enjoyed a significant development and aroused the interest, worldwide, of practitioners and the general public alike.[3]

Yet this 'science of healing' *sorig* (gso-rig) or 'science of longevity', *tshering* (tshe-rig), to use its Tibetan designations, should be included among the great literary traditions of medicine, alongside those of India, China and Greece. Like these it spread beyond the borders of its vast cultural homeland, notably to Mongolia, where it was adopted from the sixteenth century onwards.

However, compared with the Indian, Chinese and Greek traditions which evolved over the centuries preceding our era, Tibetan medicine is distinguished by a relatively late appearance in the seventh century, and by a variety of external influences, particularly Indian and Chinese. It has, moreover, always coexisted with other therapeutic practices—be they popular, specialised, empirical or magico-religious—likely to offer a cure for illness, which is not clearly distinguished from the more general categories of evil and misfortune. Health and healing relates as much, if not more, to the domain of organised or popular religion, which entails the quelling of passions, the accumulation of merit, collective or individual prayers and rituals, the maintenance or restoration of harmonious relations with deities inhabiting the natural environment and so forth, as to that of medical science which more particularly concerns us here.

A THOUSAND YEARS OF HISTORY

Origins

Accounts of the emergence and development of the Tibetan 'science of healing' can be found in Tibetan texts of general history and encyclopaedias from around the fourteenth century onwards, as well as in works of medical historiography, of which the earliest prototypes seem to have appeared around the thirteenth century. The most complete form of the latter is the *Khogbug* written by the Regent Sangye Gyamtso at the end of the seventeenth century.

Certain texts of the Bön religion—a Tibetan minority religion—mention the appearance of a medical tradition in the Land of Snows as early as the time of their founder Shenrab Miwo, several centuries before our era. A Buddhist source, the biography of Yuthog the Elder to whom we shall refer later, traces the introduction of medicine back to two physicians who came from India at the time of King

Lhathothori, around the second half of the second century. However, for the most part these are legends, and reliable Tibetan historians date the beginnings of a learned medicine to the period of King Songtsen Gampo in the first half of the seventh century, after this famous monarch endowed his country with a script derived from an Indian alphabet. Until then Tibetans are reputed to have had little more than a few popular therapeutic practices, some dietary rules and a rudimentary pharmacopoeia.

When Tibet was unified for the first time under the authority of a royal dynasty, it emerged as a formidable military power and empire in Upper Asia from the seventh to ninth centuries, and its exchanges increased with the neighbouring cultures of China, India, Nepal, the oasis-towns of Central Asia, the western regions of the high plateau, and Iran. It was during these centuries that the foundations of Tibetan civilisation were laid.

The secular cultures surrounding the young kingdom became sources of inspiration. Contemporary China, under the Tang dynasty, enjoyed one of its most prosperous periods, during which Buddhism, by way of the Silk Road, combined with its existing prestigious heritage. To the south, beyond the Himalayan passes, the Tibetans encountered India, divided after the collapse of the great Gupta empire (320 to the end of the fifth century). Tibetan armies controlled the oasis towns of the Silk Road where cosmopolitan cultures flourished, influenced mainly by India, but also by China and Sassanian Iran prior to the Arab conquest of the seventh century. For the two centuries or so of the Tibetan empire, enriching contacts with neighbouring cultures brought new goods, skills and ideas. However, it was Buddhism that left the greatest imprint on all aspects of Tibetan culture. Missionaries came from India, China, and Central Asia. They spread not only the teachings of the 'Enlightened One', exegeses and a thriving cult, but also the sciences related to Buddhism. They soon came across Tibetans who, in search of knowledge, were heading in the opposite direction.

The development of medicine was particularly favoured in Tibet because of its close ties with Buddhism, according to which suffering is both the source of its initial quest, and the basis of its doctrine of salvation. In early Indian Buddhism, the Buddha was given the title of 'King of Healers' (*Bhaiṣajyarāja*), the one whose teachings are the only radical antidote to the suffering which is inherent in all existence in the cycle of endless rebirths. Subsequently, medical practice was itself incorporated into the syllabus of monastic studies. This accompanied the development, at the beginning of our era, of the Great Vehicle or Mahāyāna doctrine and its *bodhisattva* ideal. For a *bodhisattva*, a 'being devoted to enlightenment', healing the sick provides both an opportunity to cultivate the perfections of compassion and a skillful means of conversion. Since then medicine was included among the five major sciences along with the specifically Buddhist 'inner' science (*nangrig*), grammar, epistemology, arts and skills. During the same period the Buddhist pantheon was enriched with new figures possessing a specifically therapeutic function. Among these, the Buddha 'Master of Remedies' (*Bhaiṣajyaguru*) became the object of fervent worship, being introduced first to Central Asia, then to the Far East and, eventually, to Tibet.[4] The healing of the sick seems to have played a significant part in the successful propagation of Buddhism throughout Asia, which spread to the Far East alongside originally Indian medical theories and practices. It is only in Tibet that we have knowledge of any medical treatise ascribed to the Buddha himself. However, a number of sermons attributed to him, as well as several tantras, do, in part, deal with diseases and their treatments.[5]

According to Tibetan historiography, King Songtsen Gampo (first half of the seventh century AD) summoned three physicians from India, China, and Iran to his court. The collation of their knowledge is believed to have resulted in the composition of a work in Tibetan. Their names suggest that they are not historical figures but archetypes personifying distinct medical traditions. Thus, the physician named Galenos who came from 'Byzantine Lands' obviously refers to Galen, the famous Greek doctor of the second century. This anachronism nevertheless testifies to the influence of Greek medicine which probably reached the Tibetan Empire during the royal period (seventh to ninth centuries) by means of the Arab conquest of Iran. The same sources relate that Princess Wencheng, the Chinese wife of Songtsen Gampo, brought with her a medical text which was translated into Tibetan. The following century Jinchen, another Chinese princess, wife of King Me'agtsom (*regn.* 704-54), is also said to have introduced works of Chinese medicine. During the same period another physician from Iran was appointed court physician and subsequently credited with the translation of many texts. Like Galenos, he is said to have settled in Tibet where he also trained several disciples.[6] During the second half of the eighth century, translation of medical works continued under the rule of Thrisong Detsen (*regn.* 784-94) who in his turn summoned physicians from neigh-

The Root of Physiology and Pathology (TMP, PL. 2) *depicts in an elaborate arborial metaphor the three distinct roots of physiology/pathology, diagnosis and treatment, and provides an outline of the general principles of Tibetan medical science as expounded in the Gyüshi, the Four Tantras (The Tantra of Secret Instructions on the Eight Branches of the Essence of Immortality).*

Statue of Padmasambhava in the Jokhang, Lhasa.

bouring regions: from India, Kashmir, Nepal, Dolpo, China, Iran, and the Turkic regions of Central Asia. Under the patronage of this sovereign, the tantric master Padmasambhava, glorified by later tradition as a second Buddha, is believed to have received the Tibetan translation of the famous *Four Tantras* from his disciple Vairocana.[7] According to tradition, this treatise, like other medical texts, was concealed by Padmasambhava so as to be discovered later by persons predestined to propagate them. Also ascribed to the same period is a list of 'nine sages of Tibetan medicine', who founded as many teaching lineages.

Only a few rare medical documents found in the caves of Dunhuang, in the northwest of the Chinese province of Gansu, can be dated with certainty to the royal era (seventh to ninth centuries): three short texts and a medical drawing indicating the moxibustion points on the body as well as six texts concerning hippology and hippiatrics.[8]

Yet Tibetan historiography preserves long lists of titles of medical texts—some of indigenous origin, others translated from different languages—believed to have been known in Tibet at that time. Among these the *Somarādza*,[9] reputed to have been translated from Chinese, but containing Indian elements also, is the only text to have reached us, having undoubtedly undergone changes which still remain difficult to assess. The variety of foreign influences that tradition ascribes to the beginnings of Tibetan medicine, particularly Indian and Chinese, are confirmed by contemporary documents and by evidence which survives in the medical works still used today. Certain terms and the Tibetan tradition of urinalysis hint at the early influence of Greek medicine.

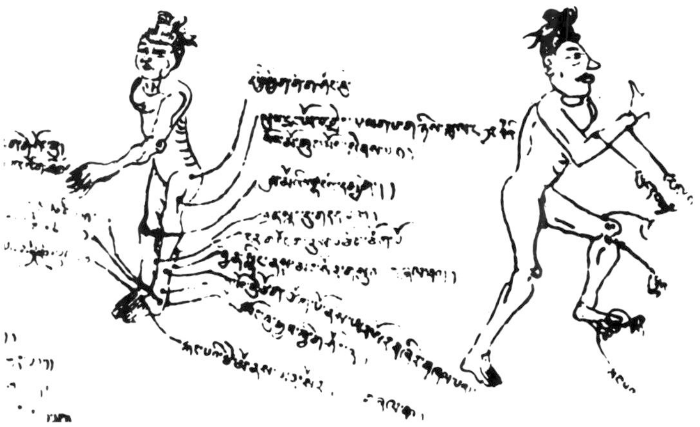

Drawing representing the locations for moxibustion points. Dunhuang, 9th-11th centuries. Bibliothéque Nationale, Paris.

Later development

The period of anarchy brought about by the fall of the Tibetan dynasty in 842 lasted for about a century and a half and was followed by a general revival. The cosmopolitan character of Tibet's cultural contacts during the royal period gave way to a predominantly Indian influence both in the religious and medical domains. The new spread of Buddhism gave birth to intense cultural and artistic activity which progressively transformed the country and shaped its future. At that time Tibet had disintegrated into many feudal polities controlled by noble families some of whom were eventually to head religious schools. Among the latter, the Sakyapa were invested with political power over Tibet under the protection of the Mongols (1244-1368). Tibet was not to be reunified until the second half of the seventeenth century, under the aegis of the Gelugpa School and the Fifth Dalai Lama.

Opposite: *Thangka of Yuthog Yontan Gonpo who receives the transmission of medical teachings from the Medicine Buddha (sMan-bla, top centre). Hayagriva and Vajrapāni are to his left and right. In the triangle, below left, are deified diseases presided over by Mahākāla, and to the right a group of protectors. Private collection, Belgium.*

During the eleventh century, several medical texts were translated from Sanskrit, and eventually included in the *Tanjur*, the Tibetan Canon comprising the exegesis of Buddhism and the treatises on sciences.[10] They include several works attributed to Nāgārjuna, a great Buddhist philosopher of the second century whose name seems to have been merged with one or several later Indian authors of medical and alchemical texts.[11] There is also the *Aṣṭāṅgahṛdaya Saṃhitā* by Vāgbhaṭa, an Indian physician of the seventh century, which is considered a fundamental reference work by both Tibetan and Ayurvedic traditions.[12] This treatise comes with a commentary often quoted by later Tibetan physicians: the *Padārthacandrikā* by Candranandana, a Kashmiri scholar of the second half of the tenth century.

Besides Ayurvedic medicine proper, Tibet also inherited, from tantric and alchemical traditions, other Indian concepts pertaining to the structure of the body, conception, physiopathology, and therapy. In this way the *Kālacakra* or Wheel of Time, the famous tantric cycle whose calendrical system was introduced to Tibet in 1027, greatly influenced not only Tibetan astrology but also its closely related science, medicine, most especially in its system of bodily channels. Likewise Tibetan pharmacopoeia came to be enriched by complex, mercury-based, mineral preparations—highly praised by Indian iatrochemistry (*rasaśāstra*) —especially after the translations from Sanskrit by Orgyenpa Rinchenpal (1230-1309).

Tibetan medical historiography attributes an important role in the development of medicine to Yuthog Yontan Gonpo the Younger. He is believed to have been born in the twelfth century, a descendant of his namesake, Yuthog the Elder, who is said to have lived in the eighth century. Their biographies evoke mystical tales of highly realised tantric masters (*mahāsiddha)*, and their similarities suggest that they might refer to a single historical figure.[13] They are associated especially with the transmission of the *Four Tantras* which became the fundamental reference work in Tibetan medicine, like the *Huangdi Neijing* in Chinese medicine and the *saṃhitās* or corpus of Suśruta and Caraka in Indian Ayurveda.

The origin and history of the *Four Tantras* remain obscure, and were the subject of heated dispute among Tibetan scholars. Some accepted it for what it claims to be: the authentic teachings of the Buddha 'Master of Remedies' (*Bhaiṣajyaguru*) translated from Sanskrit, whereas others saw it as a treatise of dubious authorship. Some even went so far as to deny the existence of a Sanskrit original and believe it to be the work of a Tibetan author—one or the other Yuthog—observing quite correctly that it contains notions foreign to India, notably those which appear to be Chinese. However the opinion that the *Four Tantras* were the authentic word of the Buddha prevailed under the political authority of the Fifth Dalai Lama and his regent Sangye Gyamtso who firmly upheld this view. They believed that the *Four Tantras* were first taught in India by the historical Buddha when he manifested as the 'Master of Remedies'. Later, in the eighth century, Vairocana is said to have translated and offered the text to his master Padmasambhava, who then concealed it in the monastery of Samye. In the second half of the eleventh century it was supposedly rediscovered by Drapa Ngönshe (1012-90),[14] and the following century it ended up in the hands of Yuthog the Younger, who completed the treatise by adapting it to the local conditions of Tibet. This would explain how it came to include non-Indian elements.

As far as modern western philology is concerned, the *Four Tantras* in its present form cannot be considered the direct translation of a Sanskrit original. It appears as the brilliant, perfectly structured and, in many regards, original work of a Tibetan author, perhaps Yuthog the Younger, who integrated the diverse foreign influences into a coherent whole. This text, which has not yet been entirely translated into a western language, is in fact a fourfold treatise composed of as many volumes, the medical teachings in each set out from a different perspective.[15]

The *Root Tantra* presents a synopsis of all the elements of this medical science in their logical relation to each other. The *Explanatory Tantra* develops the doctrine of medicine in its entirety, ranging from conceptions concerning the body—its genesis, structure, physiology and pathology—to medical ethics, including diagnosis and treatment. The *Instructional Tantra*, the longest, gives a more clinically-oriented teaching, describing the physiopathology, types, symptoms, diagnosis, and specific treatment of each disorder. The *Subsequent Tantra* focuses more particularly on the practical aspects of diagnosis and therapy.

From the twelfth century onwards the *Four Tantras* became the subject of numerous exegetical works and to this day it remains the basis of Tibetan medical practice. For centuries medical teachings were passed on by individual masters not attached to any specialised institution. They were transmitted from master to disciple or father to son in family lineages, often along with other medical and religious texts. The study and practice of medicine received no official

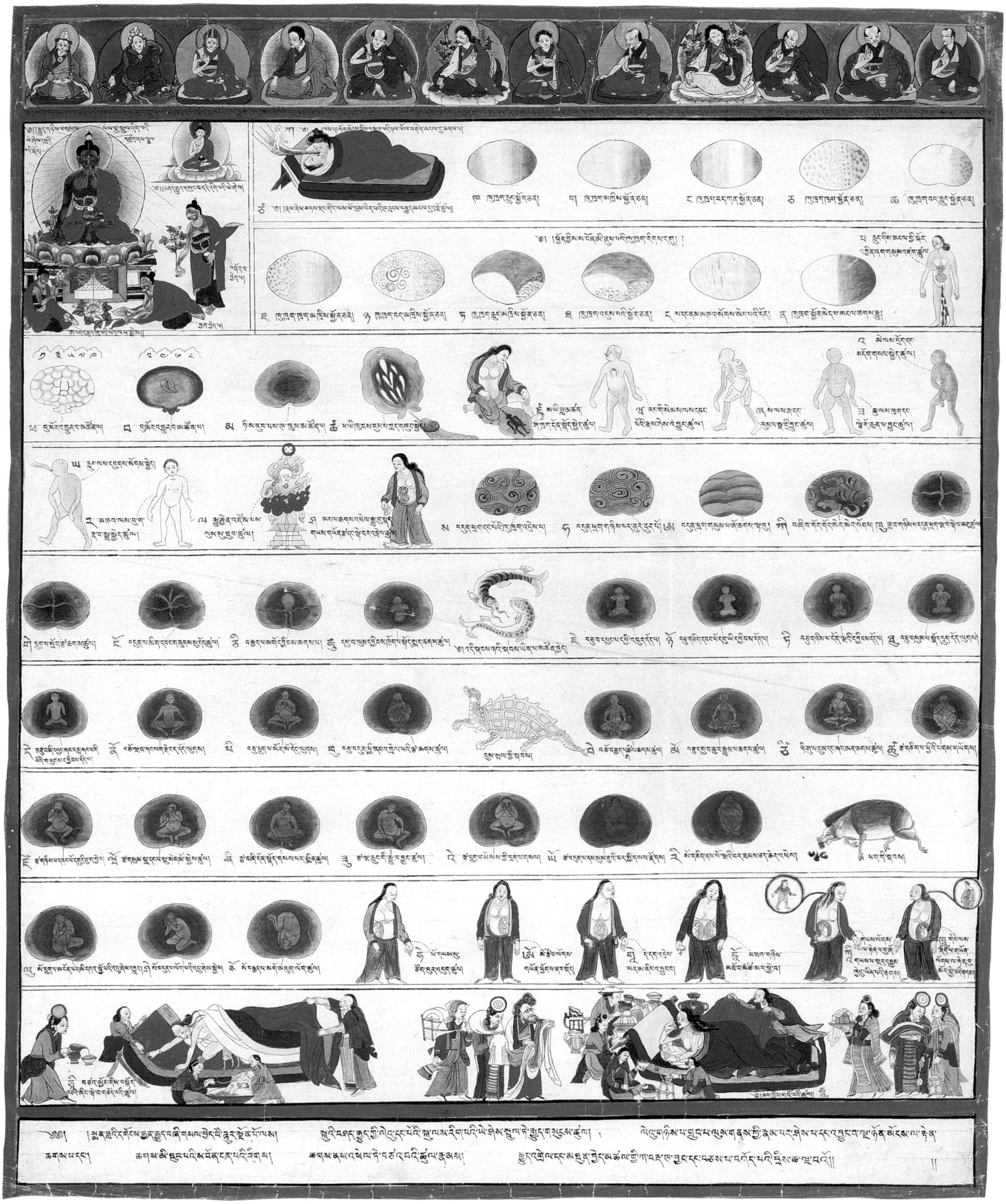

Human Embryology (TMP PL. 5) *depicts in a detailed cartoon manner the development of the embryo from the moment of conception when consciousness enters the womb, through the different stages symbolised by the fish (aquatic stage), the turtle (amphibian) and the pig (mammal), to the moment of birth and the care for the mother and baby afterwards.*

recognition or validation, whether lay or religious, which would also have required the imposition of certain standards of theoretical knowledge and technical expertise.

Tibetan medical literature grew to include a great variety of indigenous works: independent treatises, technical handbooks on diagnosis and therapy, pharmacopoeia, formularies for pharmaceutical preparations, and medical histories.[16] Despite the great value placed on the written tradition, oral commentaries and instructions continued to play a crucial role in the faithful transmission of medical theory and especially for the techniques involved in practice. The study of medicine as one of the sciences related to Buddhism could form part of a scholarly training, just like grammar or rhetoric, though it did not necessarily imply the intention or the ability to practice.

The titles of a number of texts mentioned in historical sources suggest that medical iconography, already present in ancient Tibet, endured throughout the following centuries. Thus Yuthog the Younger of the twelfth century is credited with an 'Illustration of dressings, bandages, splints and others'. Illustrations of medicinal preparations from the following century are also mentioned. The titles of several

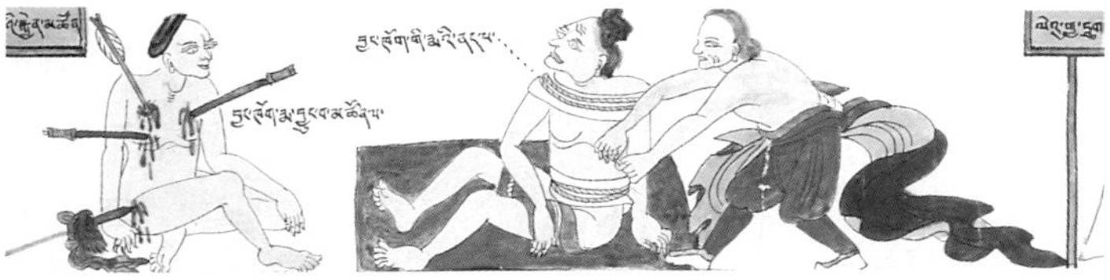

The Instructional Tantra presents curative techniques of medication and external therapy for wounds to the trunk. (TMP, PL.48)

early works contain an expression which seem to mean something like 'drawing of a corpse' *rota* (ro-bkra), and would therefore testify to the practice of autopsy in ancient times. It is also likely that the catalogues of *materia medica* were illustrated in much the same way as those known to us from the seventeenth century onwards.

After the fourteenth century, Tibetan medical tradition split into two main schools, Chang and Zur, named after their founding lineages. They differed only on minor questions such as the location of a few channels or vital points of the body, identification of certain drugs, pharmaceutical formulas, etc. Their differences also seem to reflect a degree of adaptation to different ecological and epidemiological environments: Chang originated in the northern plateaux while Zur took root in the southern valleys.

The Fifth Dalai Lama, portrait bronze, late 17th century. Boston Museum of Fine Arts.

Establishment of medical institutions

The political reunification of Tibet under the authority of the Fifth Dalai Lama in 1642, heralded a new era for medicine, as it did for Tibetan civilisation as a whole. Motivated by a keen interest in the 'science of healing', the Fifth Dalai Lama decided to promote its teaching and improve the quality of its practice. He patronised the study of medicine in his entourage and founded several specialised institutions which, however, did not meet with the success he had envisaged. In addition, the teachings of several Indian physicians living at court were translated from Sanskrit into Tibetan and added to the *Tanjur*, the collection of canonical treatises mentioned above. He also undertook a new xylographic edition of the *Four Tantras*. Yet the initiative begun by the Fifth Dalai Lama did not reach completion until after his death, and his endeavour was continued by his spiritual son and last regent, Sangye Gyamtso (1653-1705).

Whilst the *Four Tantras* were being re-edited, the young Regent realised how confusing the medical tradition had become over a number of theoretical and practical questions. This led him to study the medical texts in depth, to consult a large variety of other sources likely to provide medical information, and to seek the advice of contemporary scholars and physicians. This ambitious task undertaken alongside many other demanding literary activities, not to mention

The regent Desi Sangye Gyamtso, author of the 'Blue Beryl' medical treatise, and his main disciple Chakpa Chophel (TMP, PL. 11).

political responsibilities, culminated in a revised edition of the *Four Tantras* and the composition of a famous commentary known by the abbreviated title of *Blue Beryl* (*Vaiḍūrya ngonpo*). The concern for precision which characterises all his medical works, led the Regent to the conception and creation of a series of 79 paintings on canvas (*thangka*) illustrating the entire contents of his commentary: embryology, anatomy, physiology, *materia medica*, methods of diagnosis, therapy, etc. The numerous individual vignettes which make up each painting—amounting to around 8,000 in the whole series—are all captioned, whilst each painting bears a cartouche which situates it precisely in the series and in relation to the text. Indigenous medicinal plants were faithfully reproduced according to samples brought from different parts of the country and exotic drugs were drawn following the descriptions given by physicians from India and Nepal. To confirm the accuracy of certain anatomical descriptions in the *Four Tantras*, the Regent sent an artist to funerary sites to sketch the visceral contents of corpses which were traditionally cut up and thrown to the vultures. This type of post-mortem examination, for which there was no religious taboo, does not seem to have been uncommon in Tibet. The originality of its conception and the vast scope of its contents renders this series of paintings, known to us mainly from later copies, one of the great achievements of medical iconography.[17]

The will to codify medical theory and practice led the Regent to found in 1696 the first college specialised in medical training on the *Chagpori*, the Iron Hill, near the Potala Palace in Lhasa, which had once again become the capital of Tibet. The general administrative and academic organisation of the establishment followed that of the monastic colleges of the Gelugpa order which was headed by the Dalai Lama.

Palace of a queen on the Chagpori (Iron Hill). The central detail depicts a cave at the foot of the hill. Detail of wall painting in the Norbulingka.

Besides the fixed number of monks provided by the Gelugpa monasteries, the college admitted monks from other religious orders as well as laymen. The general rules and syllabus of the college underwent very few changes after those introduced by the Seventh Dalai Lama in the first half of the eighteenth century.

Each master was in charge of a particular group of students. First they had to study and memorise the *Four Tantras*, at least in part, along with the Regent's commentaries. Later, the students acquired practical knowledge by attending their master's consultations. They had to recite before him the passages he had explained and given them to learn by heart. Upon admission the students were expected to memorise the religious texts dedicated to the Buddha 'Master of Remedies' which were recited during the daily assemblies. The students also participated in various teachings, recitations and debates during seminars which occurred on set dates. The main aim was to pass an oral examination which consisted of reciting the first, second and fourth *Tantras* before the entire assembly. So long as a student had not passed this examination, he was obliged to perform a variety of duties for the college, such as serving tea during the assemblies, gathering fuel, collecting and processing medicinal plants, compounding medicines, and so forth. Those who failed to pass the examination in a maximum period of nine years were dismissed. Those who succeeded in passing the public examination, which took place in Lhasa's main temple during *Monlam*, the Great Prayer at new year, or during the *Tsogchö* festival the following month, obtained the degree of *Menrampa* (*Doctor es medicine*). This degree was the equivalent of that in philosophy obtained in a similar manner. Students sufficiently versed to pass an oral examination on all *Four Tantras* received the prestigious title of *Gyushi khenpo*, Professor of the *Four Tantras*.

The college's collective activities were governed by the annual calendar. For instance, the sixth month was dedicated to the 'Realisation of Medicinal Ambrosia', the longest and most complex ritual event of the year. A great variety of offerings, unprocessed drugs and medicinal preparations were arranged around a symbolic representation of the

Medical students studying texts by night (TMP PL. 77)

palace of the Buddha 'Master of Remedies'. The ambrosia produced by the continuous chanting of esoteric formulas, and whose virtues impregnated all the remedies, was supposed to collect in a skull cup placed in the centre of this arrangement. This long collective ritual was followed by a week of summer holidays during which the series of 79 paintings mentioned above was exhibited for the benefit of the students. The gathering of medicinal plants occurred at fixed times during the year and was another of the obligatory duties students were expected to carry out. During the

Appropriate seasonal conduct includes partaking of the alchemy of rejuvenation. (TMP PL. 75)

Flowers and fruits are collected in the autumn. (TMP PL. 67)

seventh month the entire college would embark on a two or three-week trip to the mountains known as 'the Great Harvest of Remedies'. It combined the gathering of the majority of drugs used in medicinal preparations and the teaching of *materia medica*. At the end, each student was tested on the names, qualities and therapeutic properties of numerous drug samples displayed before him. Towards the end of the eleventh month the new students had to clean, peel and prepare the unprocessed plants. The following month, for about a week, the drugs were ground and compounded into medicinal preparations to be used the coming year. During this time each of the college masters, administrators, and superiors would bring their own medicinal formulas, compare experiences and teach.

Sangye Gyamtso's political power and intellectual prestige caused his medical treatise to become the major reference work of a science which he had brought to classical maturity through the synthesis of former traditions, particularly those of the Chang and Zur schools. Most of the later authors were to add only minor and often redundant commentaries. During the eighteenth and nineteenth centuries, the college on the Iron Hill provided personal physicians to many religious hierarchs. Some of the masters who studied there founded other institutions modelled on that of Lhasa: in eastern Tibet at Kumbum in 1757 and at Labrang in 1784; in Beijing at the Yonghegong around 1750; and even in Mongolia and Transbaikalia. Despite this institutionalisation of medical education, Tibetan medicine continued to be transmitted unofficially by freely practising masters or within family lineages. This inevitably entailed variable levels of knowledge and practice among physicians. Thus Tibetan doctors, who often practise their trade alongside other secular or religious activities, have never formed a true socio-professional group.

In the eighteenth century medicine flourished also in eastern Tibet where, in 1727, Dilmar Geshe compiled a vast

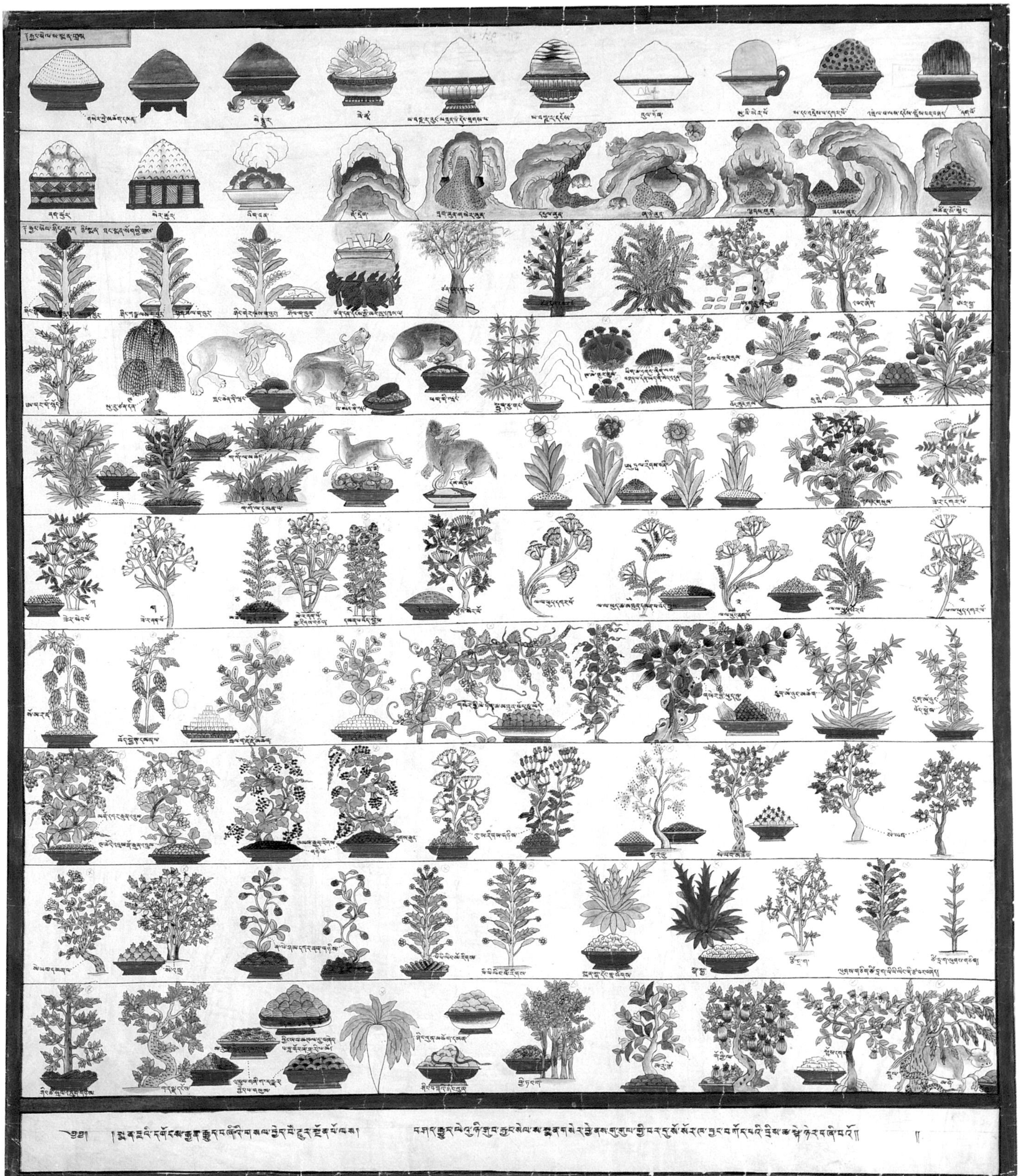

Earth, Wood, Nectarous and Plateau Medications (TMP PL. 24). *Illustrated here are over a hundred of the several thousand medicinal substances used in Tibetan medicine, here classified according to their origin from earth minerals, different woods, fragrant substances, fruits, and animal extracts.*

catalogue of *materia medica* which became a major reference work. His celebrated disciple Situ Tchöki Tchungne (1700-74) founded an important medical school, connected to Palpung monastery, which enjoyed considerable reputation throughout Kham. Due to its geographical situation the school seems to have shown a great interest in contemporary Chinese medicine.

At the end of the nineteenth century, the medical college on the Iron Hill fell into decline until the Thirteenth Dalai Lama, following the example of the Great Fifth, gave a new impetus to medical education. In 1916 he founded the *Mentsikhang,* the Institute of Medicine and Astrology, in the very centre of Lhasa, placing it under the supervision of his personal physician, Khyenrab Norbu (1883-1962). This new establishment rapidly enjoyed widespread reputation. Like the *Chagpori,* it was also open to laymen. Its teachings, however, placed a greater emphasis on practice. Khyenrab Norbu proved to be an exceptional master whose considerable influence is still remembered by most great practitioners today. His most important contribution, a vast compilation of medicinal formulas, is now used as standard reference both in Tibet and in the Tibetan community in exile.

Khyenrab Norbu (1883-1962), personal physician of the Thirteenth Dalai Lama.

Theoretical Foundations

Tibetan medical theory attempts to conceive the broad diversity of phenomena—cosmic, climatic, physiological, pathological, therapeutic—as lying within a unified rational system obeying a limited number of natural laws. Nevertheless today, as in the past, actual practice does not necessarily reflect all the subtleties or requirements of theory. This even applies to modern biomedicine, so we should not be surprised to find it in areas of the world where medicine lies outside the control of professional organisations or those central authorities which impose standards of practice.

Fire and air elements (left) lead upwards, producing emetic medications; earth and water elements (right) lead downwards, producing purgative medications. (TMP PL. 23)

The body : structure and functions

Tibetan medical theory is based on a series of philosophical presuppositions shared by all Buddhist traditions concerning the nature of the phenomenal world, the fabric of the material environment, the physical components and psychic factors which constitute the beings inhabiting it.

According to these conceptions which belong to a shared Indian background, every physical or biological substance, however subtle, is a combination of the five fundamental elements: space, wind, fire, water, and earth, each possessing an increasing number of inherent qualities. Thus, space or emptiness is defined by non-resistance alone, whereas wind possesses the additional quality of movement. Fire has both these qualities plus heat; water is further characterised by fluidity. Lastly, earth possesses all of these plus the final quality of solidity. Each element is perceived by one of the five senses with which it bears a specific affinity: respectively

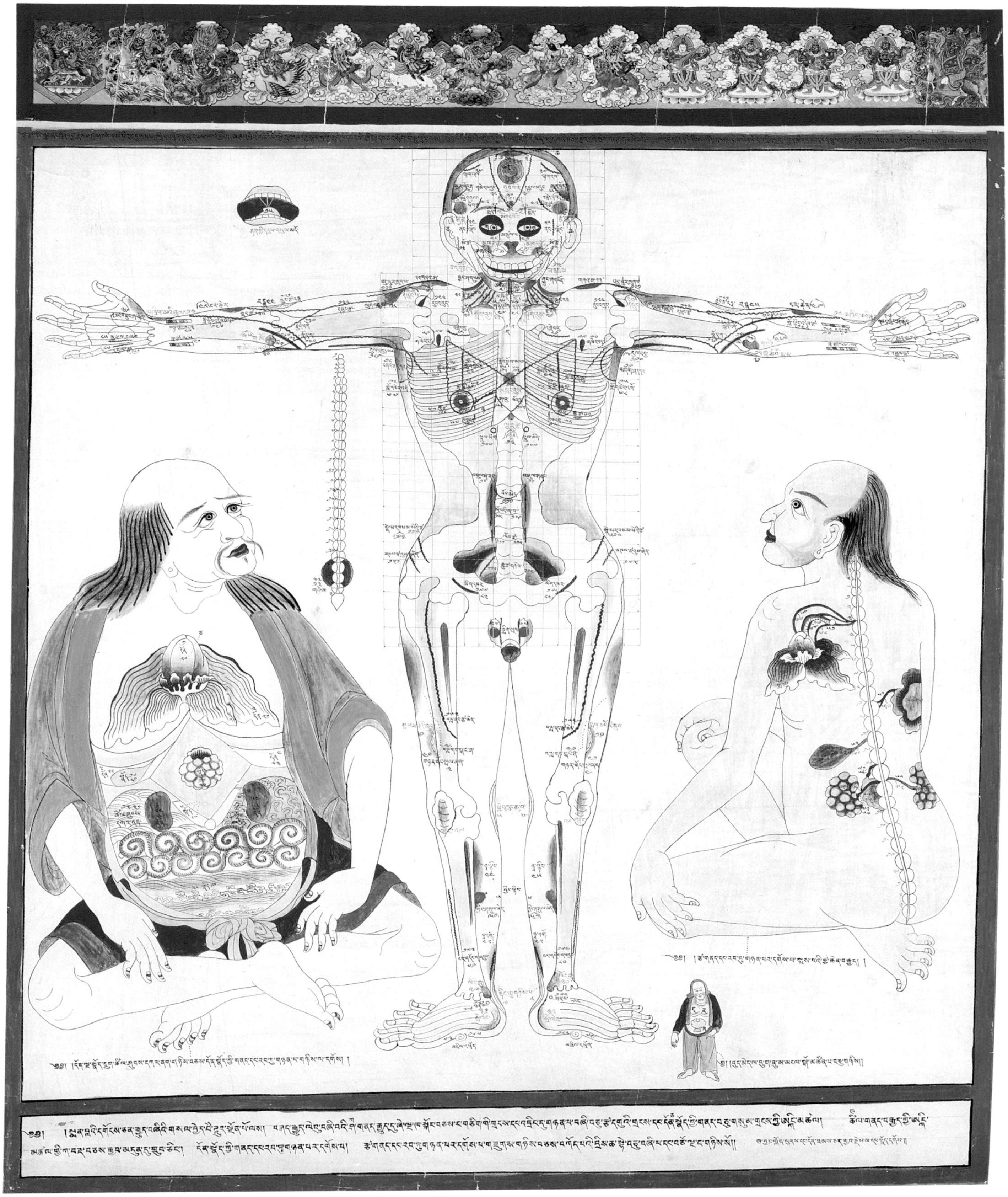

Vulnerable Points of the Human Body (TMP PL. 14). *The central skeletal figure delineates those areas in the body where external injury, for instance by weapons, is of particular danger to health, and even to life itself. The figures at either side depict the vulnerable internal organs of the human body.*

hearing, touch, sight, taste and smell. The combination, in variable proportions, of these five elements results in the infinite multitude of substances. These substances, characterised by certain perceptible qualities—hot/cold, heavy/light, etc., are said to interact according to a general law whereby the conjunction of similar perceptible qualities provokes an increase of the particular substance, and a meeting of contrary perceptible qualities leads to a decrease.

Sentient beings have no ontological reality of their own since they are but the temporary conjunction of five orders of phenomena, which are in turn subject to constant change: form, feelings, perceptions, volition, and consciousness. The body is itself a complex and varied aggregate of the five fundamental elements, which range from gross to subtle. Consciousness is the centralising principle for all sensory information and hence the seat of discursive thought. It is this stream of consciousness, blinded by passions and therefore conditioned by previous actions, whether of the body, speech or mind, which transmigrates from one existence to another when the aggregates which make up the apparent personality disintegrate at death. Life, like health and illness, involves the constant dynamic interaction of all these elements.

The entry of consciousness into the womb at the time of conception. (TMP PL.5)

An analogy of the transformation of the elements at death is the destruction of Mount Sumeru. (TMP PL.18)

The locations of two types of wind humour. (TMP PL.16)

The location of the bile and phlegm humours. (TMP PL.16)

For Tibetan medicine, as for Indian Ayurveda from which it borrowed most of its theories concerning physiology, pathology and therapeutics, the living body consists of a substratum upon which the three humoral fluids—phlegm, bile and wind—ensure the various vital functions. This bodily substratum is composed of seven types of bodily tissue: chyle produced by digestion, blood, flesh, fat, bone, marrow, reproductive fluid (sperm or menstrual blood), and of the residues generated by their metabolism: faeces, urine, sweat, teeth, hair, nails. Indeed, each tissue is the locus of a transforming process performed by each of the three humours, which replicates that of digestion. The grinding mechanical action of phlegm is followed by a melting process caused by the heating properties of bile. This produces an essence which is finally separated from its residue by the dynamic quality of wind. Thus, the seven kinds of tissue, in the above order, form part of a metabolic chain in which each produces a nutritional essence from which the next tissue is formed. Faeces and urine are obviously the residues of digestion. Bile collected in the gall bladder and sweat are viewed as the residues of blood and fat respectively; teeth, nails and hair those of bone. The notion of a metabolic chain justifies the special attention Tibetan and Ayurvedic physicians alike give to diet and digestion which give rise to chyle, the mother substance of all the other bodily tissues.

The organic functions of the humoral fluids are explained in terms of their inherent 'characteristics': phlegm is said to be cool, heavy, dull, soft, stable, and sticky; bile is unctuous, sharp, warm, light, fetid, purgative, and moistening; while wind is rough, light, cool, subtle, firm, and mobile.

According to some contemporary western and Tibetan

authors it would be misleading to translate the humours literally as wind, bile and phlegm since they are not gross material substances but metaphors expressing abstract principles or energies This opinion is misleading since the 'characteristics' attributed to the humours are evidently based on the empirical observation of biological fluids—gastric mucus, bile collected in the gall bladder and respiratory breath—even though the functions subsequently ascribed to the humours largely exceed those of their material referents.

The 'characteristics' of the humours belong to a list of perceptible qualities mentioned above which are attributed to substances in general and determined by their elementary composition. The qualities are divided into various categories of which the most important are the six tastes—sweet, acid, salty, bitter, hot and astringent—and the eight 'potencies' forming four pairs of opposites: hot/cold, heavy/light, unctuous/rough, dull/sharp. It should be noted that the humours are not directly opposed to each other in terms of their perceptible qualities, some of which are even shared by two of the three humours. This means that there may be a simultaneous excess or deficiency of two or three humours. On the other hand, the opposing 'characteristics' in the humours explain how a drug prescribed to reduce one humour might increase another, and thus create a iatrogenic imbalance. This risk is usually prevented by adding ingredients which temper the side effects of the main drug.

Among the 'characteristics' of the humours, the hot/cold pair predominates, as in many other traditional medicines throughout the world. Phlegm shares the cold nature of the moon and bile the hot nature of the sun. The position of wind in between is more ambiguous. One passage in the *Four Tantras* explains that phlegm and wind disorders are cold in nature, whereas blood and bile disorders are hot. However the same text also states that wind is neutral and therefore likely to aggravate the disorders of both bile and phlegm, just as wind spreads fire or intensifies cold. Phlegm shares the nature of water and thus performs functions of a mechanical nature: cohesion, support, lubrication, etc. Bile, associated with fire, is responsible for body heat and is involved in the metabolic processes, notably digestion which is likened to the cooking of food. Its active and hot nature opposes it to phlegm which is passive and cold. The wind humour shares the nature of wind and is at work in the physiological processes which are dynamic in nature, as well as sensory perception and psychic activity. Although wind is described in the same terms as the other humours, it enjoys a special status. Indeed, wind manifests as the vital breath and is the factor which, at the beginning of each disorder, causes the humour to overflow from its usual location. For this reason it might be said that there is no disorder which does not initially involve some kind of wind imbalance. In addition, wind is believed to play an important part in the psychophysical techniques used in yoga and meditation.

The three poisons of desire, hatred and delusion give rise to the immediate primary causes of illness, i.e. wind, bile and phlegm, subjecting them to imbalance and disturbing their natural locations. (TMP PL.19)

Each humour appears in five different forms, more or less subtle, with distinctive functions and locations in the tissues, viscera and other parts of the body.

Chyle, blood, the humours and other bodily fluids circulate through different types of interconnected channels which form a vast network. This system of bodily channels is particularly developed in Tibetan medicine and, as we have already mentioned, was strongly influenced by the psychophysical speculations of Indian tantric tradition, notably those of the *Kālacakra*, as we shall now see.

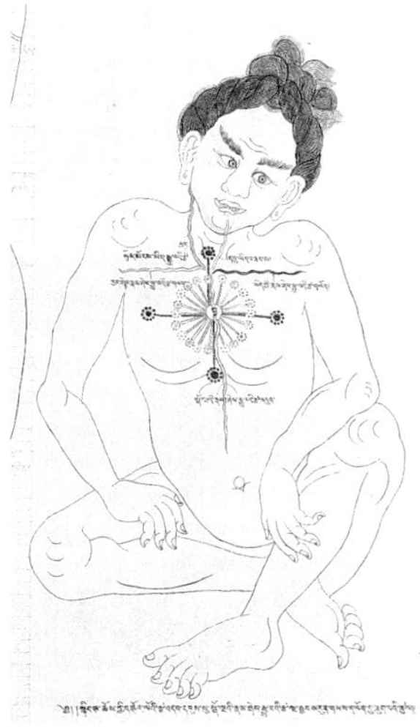

Illustration depicting how the consciousness of the five senses moves through the spokes of the heart centre (Dharmacākra) (TMP PL.10)

Cosmological and anatomical subjects of the Kālacackra Tantra, *probably based on the explanations of the Eighth Karmapa Mikyö Dorje (1507-55). 182 x 48 cm. Collection: Mimi Lipton, London. Side A (the back of this painting is illustrated on pages 126 and 127).*

Below: Tiered image of Mount Meru rising from mountains and oceans, with water, fire and wind mandalas.

Mythical geometry of the Earth illustrating the principal continent to the south of Mount Meru, the axis mundi. *At the centre is found Tibet, below to the south Bodhgaya in India where Buddha achieved Enlightenment, and above to the north the kingdom of Shambhala. The names of other countries and peoples are mentioned on the plan: Turks, Mongols, Muslim countries, India, Kashmir, Nepal and even Mecca.*

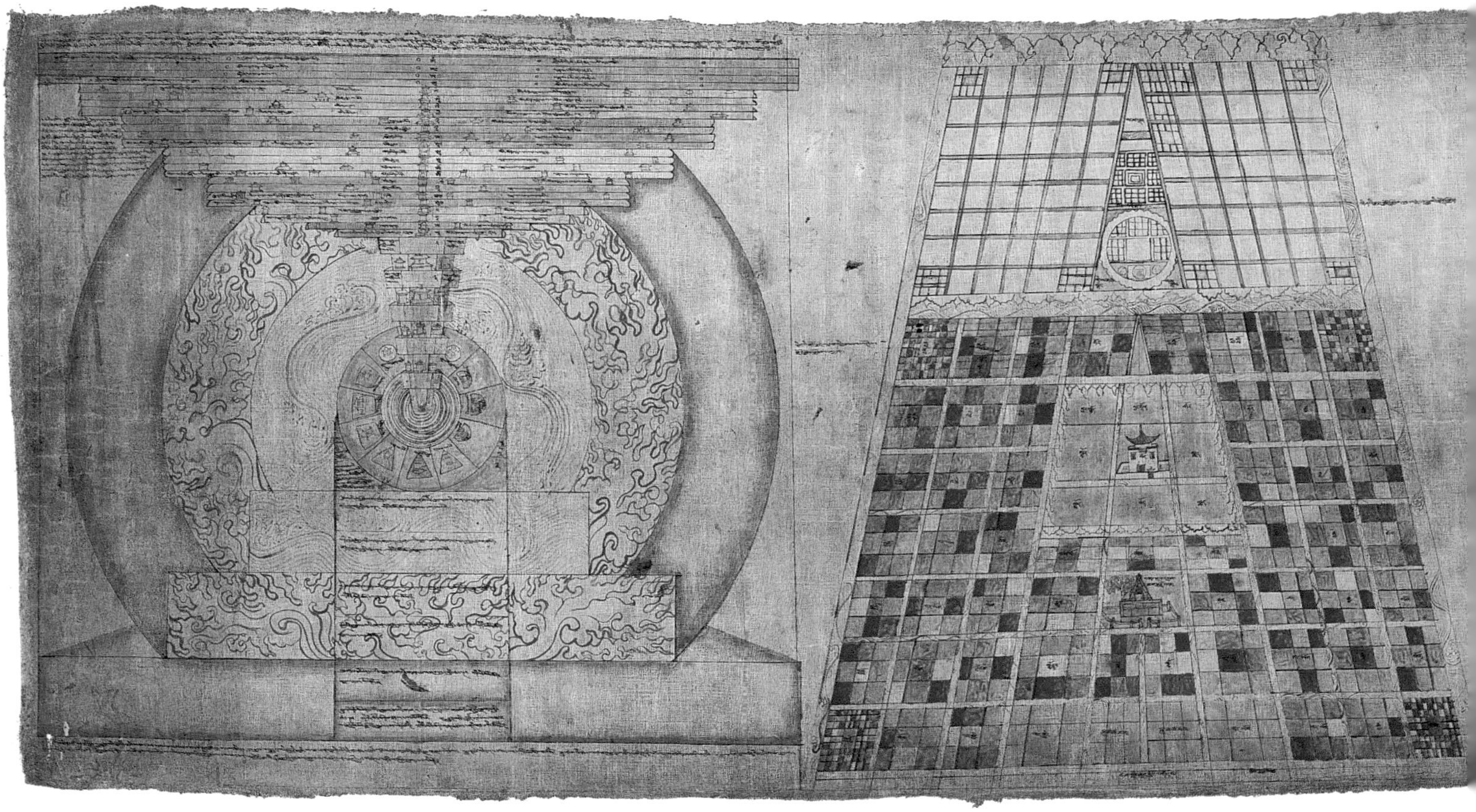

The view of the Buddhist tantras: body-mind in cosmic space and time

Since the time of early Buddhism the human body has been the subject of particular interest, albeit from two different points of view, which reflect contrasting values. On the one hand, human rebirth—with respect to the attainment of liberation from the endless cycle of transmigration—was considered the most favourable of the six types of rebirth. One had, therefore, to care for one's body so as to avoid premature death. Further, according to ideas in yoga developed in the centuries preceding our era, control over the mind, an essential factor in spiritual advancement, could be enhanced by psychophysical exercises. The body provided the precious tool for these exercises: postures and breathing techniques aimed at regulating the flow of internal 'wind', which supported the mind within a network of channels.

On the other hand, the body was also viewed as one of the five aggregates constituting the person is constituted (alongside feelings, perception, volition, and consciousness), and having no permanent ontological reality. As such, the body could not be the object of attachment and had to be belittled. Moreover, the actual experience of life made the body an ideal meditational object on impermanence and aversion, intended to draw the adept from his attachments. This is why the contemplation of corpses in funeral sites, and the visualisation of one's own body—or that of desirable women—as heaps of impure and putrescent substances, formed such an important aspect of ascetic practice.

This dual approach endured throughout Buddhism's later philosophical developments alongside a growing interest in the psychophysical techniques of yoga, especially in certain trends of Mahayana. The latter tradition adopted the view that the phenomenal world was but a projection of the mind. The ability to control the mind—by way of its more or

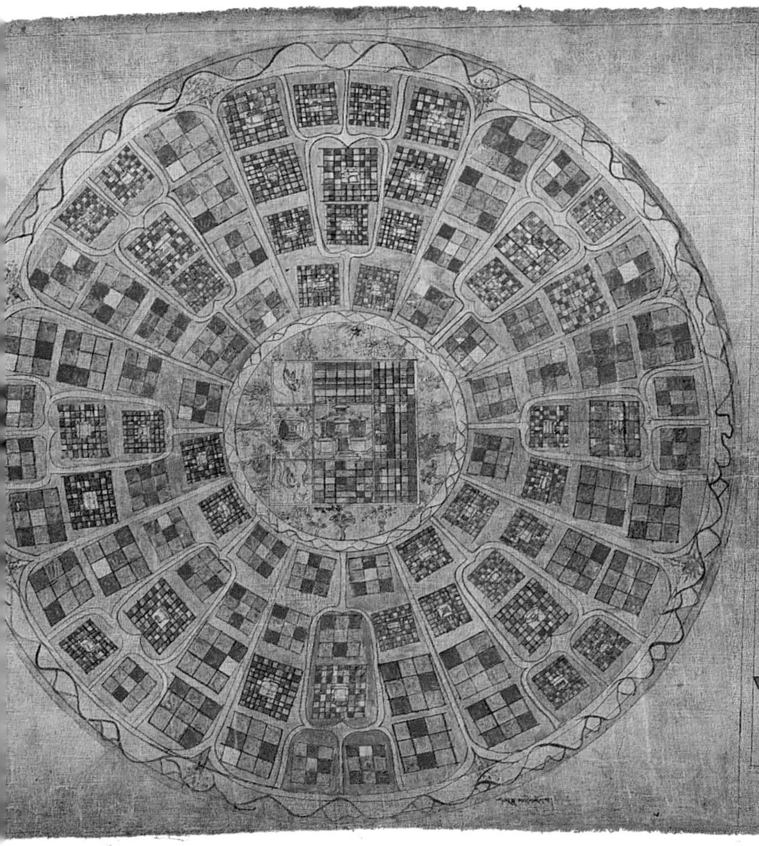

Circular plan of the city of Shambhala with nine square grids.

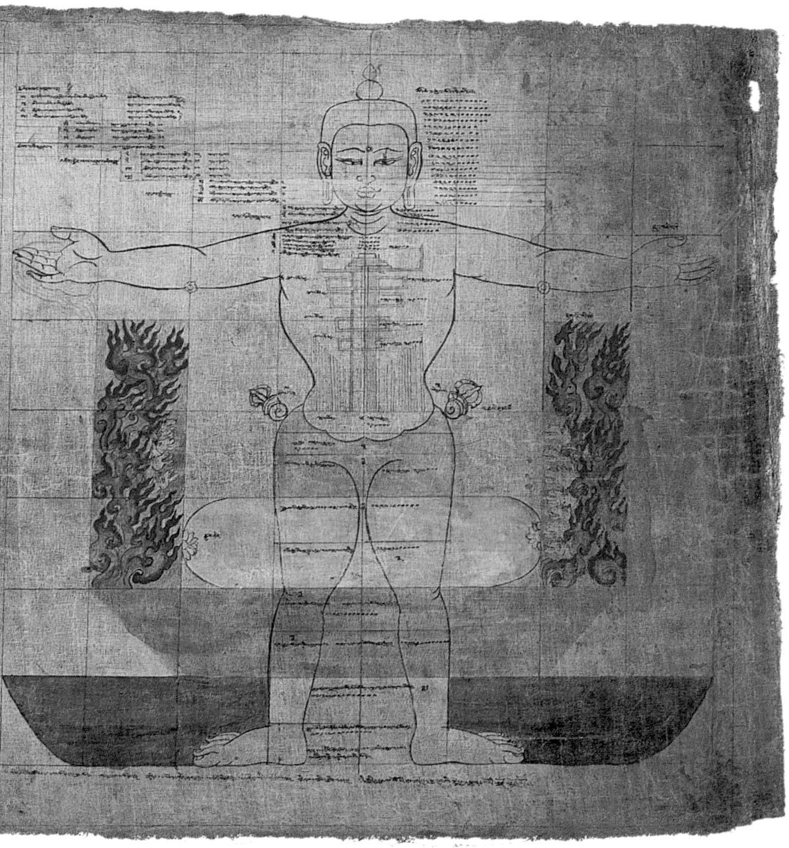

The correspondence between the human body and the cosmos.

less subtle bodily supports—would give rise to a universal power used to achieve ultimate enlightenment.

From around the fourth century onwards, Buddhist teachings were enriched with an ever-growing number of texts with an emphasis on ritual and yoga known as *tantras*. Based on the philosophical premises of Mahayana, they offered an esoteric and more rapid route to enlightenment, which the adept could even hope to attain in a single lifetime. The great efficacy of this vehicle—which was not devoid of danger and therefore required the guidance of a qualified master—relied on a series of consecrations accompanied by visualisations, and the identification with divine figures. Adepts could thereby reach the most supreme levels of consciousness, even if only transiently at first, and thus enjoy, to quote the texts, the final fruits while still on the path. The teachings of the Highest Yoga Tantras (*Anuttarayogatantra)* accord a central place to yogic practices, some of which contain sexual aspects and imagery (whether visualised or actual).

The dialectical body-mind polarity is both the means and end for the genuine transmutation induced by such practices. The body thus becomes the privileged means of rapidly attaining *siddhi* (worldly supernatural powers for vibrant health and longevity), as well as for eventual liberation, while still on the path.

The teachings of the *Kālacakratantra* (Tantra of the Wheel of Time), as illustrated on these pages, represent a culmination of Highest Yoga Tantras. The range of topics which it encompasses, render it a veritable encyclopaedia. It integrates into a remarkably sophisticated whole the universe, the course of the planets that determine its temporal cycles, the body-mind with both its gross and subtle components, and the mystic practices that utilise the body and whose composition reflects the cosmic order as well as the deity invoked and its entourage. The basic texts of the *Kālacakra-*

Anatomical and astrological subjects of the Kālacackra Tantra, *probably based on the explanations of the Eighth Karmapa Mikyö Dorje (1507-1555).* Side B *(the other side of this painting is illustrated on pages 124 and 125).* Below: *Human figure with lowered hands: some cakras are ranged along the middle axis formed by the three principal channels running parallel to the spine, others are found at twelve joints connected with the twelve constellations which indicate the lunar months.*

Human figure with hands raised: cakras of the twelve joints and that of the twelve channels converging at the navel and which correlates to the twelve signs of the zodiac.

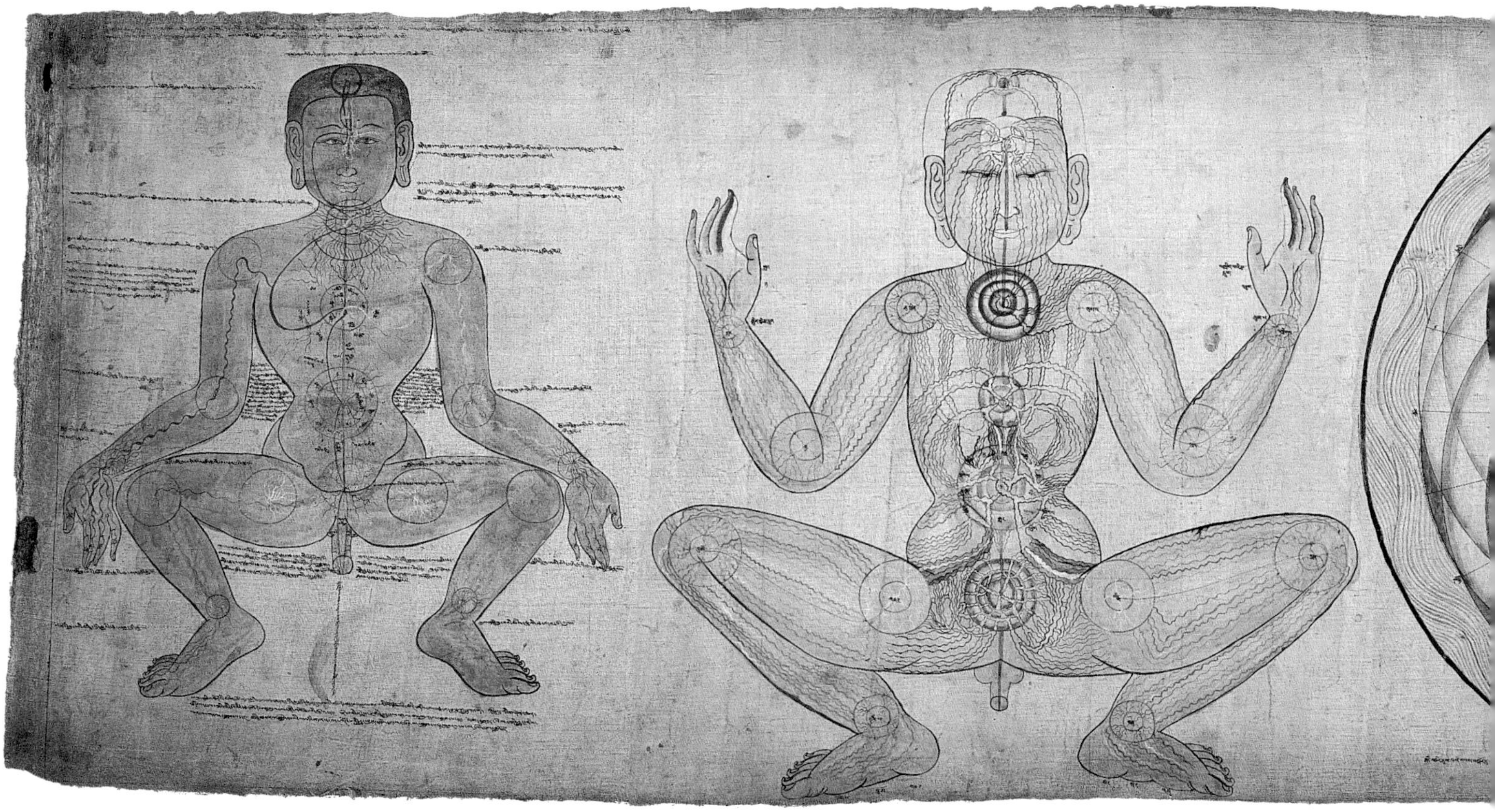

tantra, teachings ascribed to Buddha Śakyamuni in his manifestation as the *Kālacakra* deity, reached their final form in India at the beginning of the eleventh century, a short time before their introduction to Tibet where they influenced both the system of calendrical calculation and medicine.

Even though the *Kālacakratantra* is not directly concerned with medicine, it touches on many of its concerns. These include procreation and embryology, the basic components of the body and the universe, the structure of the organism, notably the network of channels through which circulate 'wind' or other biological fluids, portents of death, and various therapies including yogic practices as well as remedies and mantras (magical formulae). Different series of correspondences integrate different parts of the body and its constituents, as well as different temporal cycles. Such series include the five or six elements (earth, water, fire, wind, and space also used in medicine, plus gnosis), the five or six aggregates constituting the person (gross form, feelings, perceptions, volition, and consciousness plus gnosis), the Four Buddha Bodies, the cosmic levels, the eight or ten planets, the twelve signs of the zodiac (which also apply to 24-hour cycles), the twelve lunar months, the twenty-eight constellations (lunar mansions).

By far the most detailed descriptions of bodily structures are those relating to the channels which carry different kinds of wind or air. Their nature, whether anatomically verifiable or not, is not clearly explained in the texts. In any case, a number are evidently identified with observable anatomical pathways, such as the rectum and urethra. Three main channels run parallel to the length of the spine, from the genital area to the forehead and nostrils, by way of the crown of the head. At six points—the genitalia, navel, heart, throat, crown and forehead—the lateral channels intertwine with the median channel causing constrictions which block the

Astronomical sheme representing the universe at the centre of which is found the central mountain surrounded at the four cardinal points by the continents. The sun travels along twelve wind-cycles, moving from one track to an other at different times of the year.

Astonomical scheme showing the solar orbits at the solstice and equinox. The signs of the zodiac are placed around the these two astonomical schemes.

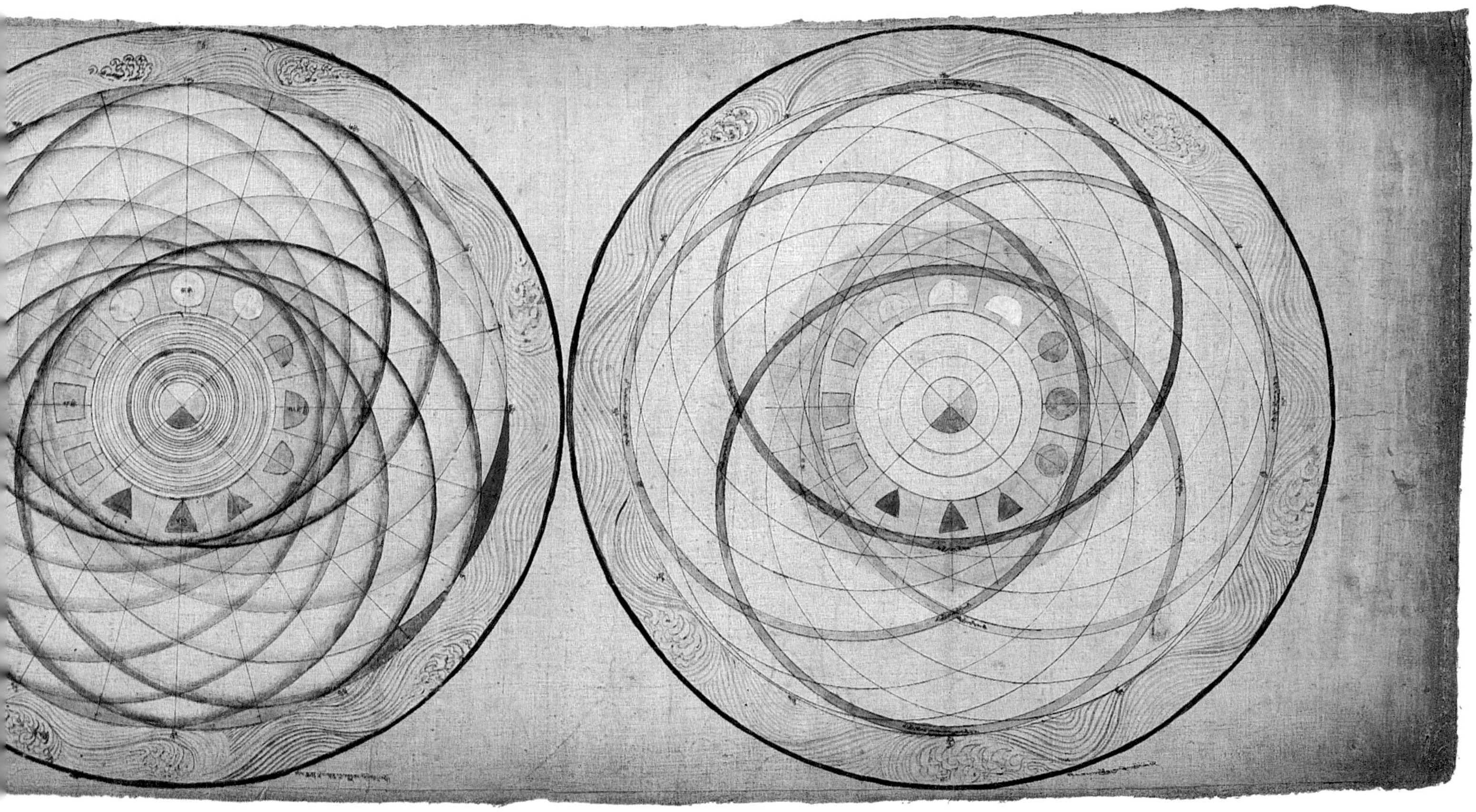

flow of vital wind and which yogic practices are meant to loosen. At these six points a variable number of channels radiate outwards, forming centres (Skt. *cakra*, 'wheel') through which 'wind' circulates. These channels subdivide into a further 72,000 channels throughout the body.

There are ten types of 'wind', five of which ensure the major functions and correspond in part to medical theory. Below the navel, the 'downwards-moving wind' travels through three main channels and expels urine to the left, faeces to the right, and sperm down the middle. Above the navel, the same channels carry 'vital wind'. Each of the eight other 'winds' spreads throughout the body from one of the eight radial channels of the heart. The most complex *cakra* is that of the navel with 6 spokes in its centre, 12 in its middle circle, and 64 in its outer circle. Here 'wind' undergoes a complex series of movements over 24-hour cycles, passing from one group of channels to another according to the signs of the zodiac. In addition, certain groups of channels are specifically related to the three humours—bile, wind, and phlegm—whose imbalances are likewise considered the basis of illness in medicine.

A number of the *cakras* are also connected with the penis and the glans and with the joints of the limbs, fingers and toes. Each of the twelve limb joints is associated with one of the twelve constellations that mark the lunar months of the Tibetan year, and is composed of thirty channels. Vital wind circulates for three days in each channel and ninety days in each joint, thereby travelling through all twelve joints over a three-year cycle. Finally, many male and female deities are associated with these different channel structures, the body thus internalising the *mandala* or mystic palace of the tantra's main deity and its entourage.

Pathology

The three humours ensure bodily functions and, so long as they are maintained in a state of balance relative to each individual constitution, they confer life and health. The state of illness is none other than the pathogenic activity of the humours when their balance is disturbed. When aggravated or disturbed, their 'characteristics' present as pathological symptoms.

Suffering is attached to a being, even when in good health, just as a shadow follows a bird, even when flying in the sky. (TMP PL.19)

Certain inadvisable conduct, such as lying on damp ground or sleeping during daytime, will cause the humours to become pathogenic and result in illness. (TMP PL.19)

Hatred is among the three poisons considered to be a remote cause of illness and which enslave beings in the endless round of rebirths. (TMP PL.19)

In Ayurveda two terms are used to express the notion we translate as humour: *dhātu* or 'constituent', when the humour is in a state of balance; and *dośa*, 'defect', when it is in a pathogenic state.

Tibetan medicine, adopting Buddhism's pessimistic view of the human condition, refers to the humours, even when they are in their normal state, either by the term *nyepa* (nyes-pa), which means 'fault', or as *né* (nad), meaning 'illness'. Hence disease is not seen as a foreign entity which contaminates the body from the outside, but rather as a potentiality inherent in the very nature of the vital principles themselves. According to the *Four Tantras, 'suffering is attached to a being even in good health, just as a shadow follows a bird, even when flying in the sky'*. Thus, by definition, the humours are not only the physiological agents responsible for health, but also the very causes of disease. They become pathogenic under the influence of a variety of immediate causes: season, environment, conduct, diet, poisons, trauma, and evil spirits. Most of these causes act on the humours by means of their identical or contrary 'properties', according to the general rule already mentioned above. For instance, an overly heavy and sweet diet, combined with an idle and sedentary way of life in an emollient natural environment, will result in the accumulation of phlegm, especially during late winter, due to the confluence of similar properties inherent in these conditions which are similar to those in phlegm. These 'properties' are not only present in material substances and phenomena, but also in mental and emotional states.

The humours are also conditioned by more remote causes of a moral character, 'the three poisons': delusion, hatred and desire. According to Buddhist teaching these passions, born of fundamental ignorance concerning the real nature of the phenomenal world, enslave beings to the endless round of rebirths. Realisation of this knowledge, attained and taught by the Buddha, delivers one from existence which is considered intrinsically painful. In certain Sanskrit texts of Mahāyāna the 'three poisons' were already associated with the three humours of Indian Ayurveda. However, it seems that only Tibetan medicine went so far as to establish a causal link between them. According to Tibetan tradition, conception occurs when the semen of the father, the menstrual blood of the mother and the conscious principle inclined towards rebirth, all merge together. During the development of the foetus, the 'three poisons'—delusion, hatred and desire—

In the rainy summer season (left), bile is accumulated, and in the winter (right), phlegm is accumulated. (TMP PL.19)

which contaminate the conscious principle, generate phlegm, bile and wind respectively.

By viewing the 'three poisons', and ultimately ignorance, as the root of the three humours and thereby of the vital processes themselves, by nature painful and precarious, Tibetan tradition has coherently integrated medical theory with the fundamental doctrine of Buddhist philosophy according to which even biological existence is conditioned by the mind.

Tibetan physiopathological theory distinguishes several stages in a humoral disturbance. Under the influence of an immediate cause a humour first gathers, accumulates, and strengthens in its normal location: wind in the bones; bile in blood and sweat; phlegm in chyle, flesh, fat, marrow, reproductive fluid, faeces and urine. This process is accompanied by a local disturbance of the flow of the channels. At this stage the symptoms are not yet clearly manifest. If the immediate cause persists or is reinforced by any other factor of a similar nature, then the accumulated humour will overflow from its location and enter the pathways of disease 'like a rising lake which breaks its dykes'. At this stage the disorder is clearly manifest on the surface of the body and in the pulses and urine. As the disturbed humour spreads along the 'six pathogenic pathways' or 'doors of disease', its gravity increases. According to the *Four Tantras*;

> *The pathogenic humour first spreads in the skin, [then] accumulates in the flesh, flows in the channels, sticks within the bones, alights on the five solid viscera [the lungs, heart, liver, spleen and kidneys], and [finally] drops into the six hollow viscera [the stomach, gall bladder, small and large intestines, bladder and the resevoir for reproductive fluid].*

The *Four Tantras* also mention five categories of 'paths of diffusion' usually associated with specific pathogenic humours: bodily tissues, metabolic residues, sensory organs, solid and hollow viscera.

	TISSUE	RESIDUE	SENSE ORGAN	SOLID ORGAN	HOLLOW ORGAN
WIND					
	bone	body hair	ears skin	heart	large intestine
BILE					
	blood	sweat	eyes	liver	small intestine gall bladder
PHLEGM					
	chyle flesh fat marrow reproductive fluid	faeces urine	nose tongue	lungs spleen kidneys	stomach bladder

Evidently, there is some contradiction between the physiopathological pattern of the 'six pathogenic pathways' and that of the 'fifteen paths of diffusion', probably owing to their different origins. The 'six pathogenic pathways' reflect an explanatory model according to which the pathogenic factor enters from the outside, and penetrates deeper and deeper into the body. This model, which is foreign to the Ayurvedic theory of humoral physiopathology, is found in ancient Chinese tradition. The classification of the viscera into five solid and six hollow organs also points to early Chinese influence.

On the other hand, the model of the 'fifteen paths of diffusion' seems to be a purely Tibetan development, combining elements from both Chinese and Indian traditions. It integrates the classical Ayurvedic locations of the three humours and their relation to the five elements and sense organs with a modified version of the Chinese correspondences between the viscera and the sense organs. The original version of the Chinese correspondences has, however, been faithfully preserved in Tibetan diagnosis.

Among the immediate causes of disease, the seasons are usually listed first and are distinctive in that they cannot be controlled. During the year each humour undergoes a period of accumulation and stimulation in conjunction with the predominating qualities of each season. The Tibetan tradition of dividing the year into six, two-month, seasons is borrowed from India, although it does not correspond precisely to the actual seasonal cycle of Tibet. The seasonal fluctuations of the humours with their periods of risk, which can be predicted according to each person's predisposition, exemplify a dynamic and cyclic conception of biological phenomena. This leads to prevention through seasonal adaptation of diet and conduct. The humours fluctuate in the same manner over a 24-hour cycle. In theory this fact should be taken into consideration during diagnosis and also in order to determine when the medicines should be taken. Moreover, the relative balance of the humours, and hence the kind of disorders likely to arise, are not only conditioned by individual temperament but also by age: phlegm is strongest during early youth, bile during adulthood, and wind during old age.

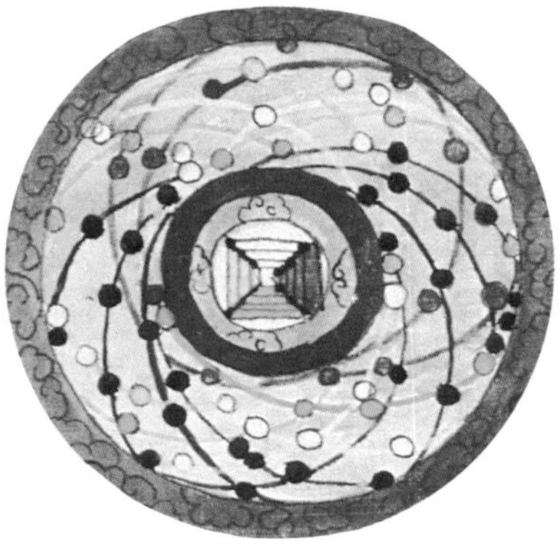

The constellation chart of the four seasons (TMP 55)

Classification of disease

From the summary given above, it is evident that Tibetan medicine conceives physiology and pathology within the framework of a single unitary theory. While more mechanistic conceptions of medicine tend to concentrate on bodily structures, this theory is founded on the notion of a subtle and ubiquitous dynamics of humoral fluids whose interaction result in a balance specific to each individual. According to this theory, disorders which are not caused by an external accident are the result of improper conduct and/or diet in relation to the environment and seasons. Knowledge of the natural laws which rule man's relationship with his environment enables one to anticipate the arising of disorders. Thus, the primary concern of Tibetan medicine should ideally be that of prevention.

In view of such theory, nosology, the classification of diseases, cannot possibly aim at reducing the infinite diversity of possible disorders to a limited number of distinct categories, as for animal or plant species. Nosology serves here merely as a guideline enabling the practitioner to direct his action in the face of the profusion of pathogenic manifestations which are not only specific to each individual but also subject to constant change. For this reason, even though the medical texts deal with a large number of nosological entities describing the characteristics and standard treatment for each of them, the doctor should always bear in mind that in reality there are as many diseases as they are persons.

The *Four Tantras* devote a large section to the various ways of classifying diseases according to different criteria: age, sex, mechanism and location of the disorder in the body, etc. For example, common diseases—or pathogenic symptoms—to which everyone is susceptible, regardless of age or sex, are divided into four groups: there are 101 disorders enumerated on the basis of their humours; 101 disorders according to the degree of excess or deficiency in their humoral balance or complexity; 101 with regard to their location in the body; and 101 distinguished by their type. This amounts to a total of 404 diseases, a number that often recurs in medical texts as a cliché expressing the range of possibilities rather than reality based on empirical observation. Although this figure does not appear in the Ayurvedic system of classification, it is not a Tibetan innovation. Indeed, several early Mahāyāna texts quote 404 as the total of the 101 ailments caused by the disturbance of each of the four elements—fire, wind, earth, and water—thus reflecting a system based on four humours, and not three as in Ayurveda.

Diagnosis

Diagnosis is defined as a process of logical inference and is illustrated, as in classical Indo-Tibetan epistemology, by the image of fire and smoke;

It is the knowledge which proceeds from the relation [between fire and smoke] which enables one to know from the rising smoke that a fire is burning on the mountain. According to this knowledge, if there is no fire, there cannot be smoke. Illness, like fire, must be identified according to its specific signs. Therefore doctors lacking methods of investigation ... do not recognise the unmistakable signs of each disorder for what they are. They are like those who seek fire in vain; even though they perceive the smoke, they mistake it for the vapours rising from a hot spring,

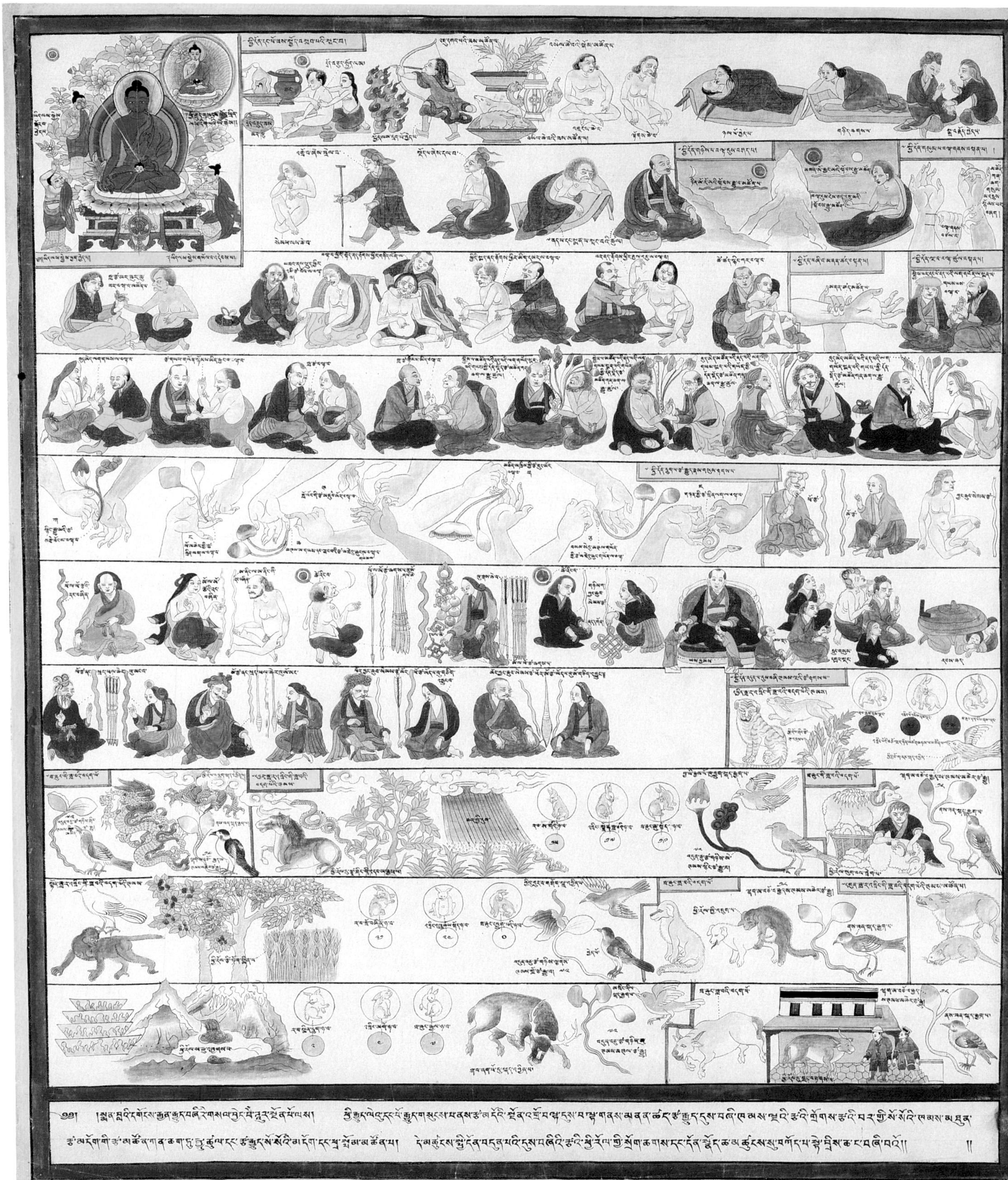

One of eight highly detailed Tibetan medical paintings concerned with pulse examination (TMP PL. 54). *This one describes the methods of preparation and conduct prior to pulse examination, the actual techniques of examination, and the variations due to place and time, such as seasonal fluctuations, lunar cycles etc.*

or hot air and therefore do not find the fire. There are others who believe that the observation of an isolated and ambiguous sign is enough to claim, "This is indeed the sign of such disease", as if one were to say during the summer, "It will certainly rain today", having merely observed a gathering of clouds without taking into account their colour, speed, etc. This is why the proper methods of investigation, the related instructions, and the ways of identifying an illness without simply relying on appearance or misleading information, are of prime importance to the physician.

Diagnostic procedures are of three types, each serving a different purpose. There are those which are aimed at identifying the illness, in other words actual diagnosis; those which involve subterfuge and ensure the doctor's credibility in the eyes of the patient and his family; and finally those which enable the physician to assess the chances of recovery and, ultimately, to decide whether or not he should accept to undertake treatment.

As far as the procedure of actual diagnosis is concerned, for the most part Tibetan tradition follows Indian Ayurveda. The identification of disease is supposed to take into account five factors: causes, initial signs, symptoms, test treatment, and the manner of inception. There are three types of diagnostic techniques, each involving a different sense organ of the practitioner. The first involves hearing as the physician inquires into the immediate causes of the disorder, namely diet and lifestyle, its symptoms and location, its progress in relation to time, environment, and into the food or remedies ingested. The perceptible qualities of these last factors, be they hot/cold, heavy/light, etc., especially their confluence, are extremely relevant in diagnosis since they affect the humours, aggravating them if they are similar or inhibiting them if they are contrary. The second diagnostic technique involves touch: by palpating the body and especially the patient's pulse the physician examines the tangible properties of the disorder: hot, cold, protruding, smooth, etc. The third technique involves sight: the physician examines the body's aspect, its form, colour, corpulence, etc., and notably the tongue and urine.

In practice however, diagnosis is based largely on pulse examination, usually preceded by a brief interrogation, which is favoured over all other techniques. In the eyes of Tibetans, the most prestigious physicians are those reputed to establish their diagnosis on pulse examination alone, without having to ask the patient a single question. The image of a physician taking a patient's pulse is as emblematic of Tibetan medicine as was that of a doctor inspecting urine for medieval European medicine. Urine observation, which is more difficult to accomplish with outpatients, is not relied upon so much, at least nowadays.

Pulse diagnosis

The physician feels the radial artery in both wrists with three fingers: the forefinger, the middle and the ring finger. The patient faces him with his forearms bent slightly upwards. The pulse under each finger indicates the condition of a body part and two viscera: the upper edge of the finger corresponds to a solid viscera and the lower edge, to a hollow viscera. In a female subject the viscera under the forefingers are inverted between right and left.

Male subject

	Right wrist		**Left wrist**	
Fore-finger	Lungs Large intestine	Upper Body	Heart Small Intestine	Fore-finger
Middle Finger	Liver Gall bladder	Middle Body	Spleen Stomach	Middle finger
Ring finger	Left kidney Bladder	Lower Body	Left kidney Reservoir for semen	Ring finger
Left hand				**Right hand**

Doctor

Pulse palpation, demonstrating how each finger of the physician examines both a hollow and a solid viscera simultaneously. (TMP PL.60)

Opposite: Doctor taking a patient's pulse at the Jokhang Temple, Lhasa.

Certain techniques and terms clearly indicate that Tibetan pulse diagnosis was derived from classical Chinese sphygmology which was developed two thousand years ago, although the location of the viscera on the fingers differs in the two traditions.

Ayurvedic literature does not mention pulse examination until the thirteenth or fourteenth century, after the Tibetans had already developed it. To date, no significant similarities revealing a direct connection between the two systems have been found. This is also true of Greco-Arab pulse diagnosis even though it was introduced to Persia when Tibetan medicine first started to develop.

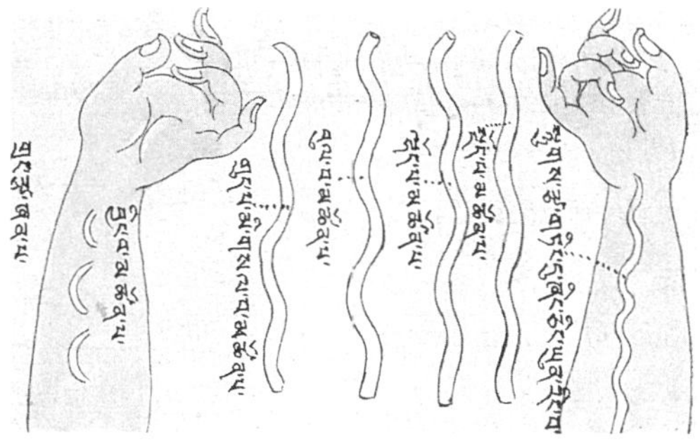

The depiction of the different types of pulses associated with 'cold' diseases. (TMP PL. 60)

Unlike its Chinese equivalent, Tibetan semiology of pulse diagnosis is not based on a limited number of fundamental aspects. Pulse description usually makes use of a rich array of simple adjectives—strong/weak, bulky/thin, sunken/protruding, etc.—but onomatopoieas and imagery are also employed. This imagery includes such expressions as 'a flag moved by wind', 'dripping water', 'jumping frog', and is especially used to describe the pulses indicative of death. Its terminology is so varied and abundant, however, that it is not always clear which sensation is being alluded to.

Among healthy persons, three types of constitutional pulses are distinguished: a 'male' pulse described as bulky and coarse, a 'female' pulse described as thin and rapid, and a *bodhicitta* or 'thought of enlightenment' pulse described as smooth, soft and long. These three pulses represent healthy temperaments in which wind, bile and phlegm predominate. As in Chinese medicine, the healthy pulse comprises five beats of the physician's respiratory cycle. Six beats or more indicates a hot disorder; four beats or less indicates a cold disorder, their intensity proportional to the number of beats. Pathological pulses are distinguished by their abnormal 'size, strength, intensity, depth, tautness, irregularities and interruptions'. Abnormal pulse indications fall into two semiological categories. The first enumerates the aspects, single or in combination, which characterise the hot or cold nature of disorders. The other describes the pulses specific to each kind of disorder starting with the pulses indicative of humoral disturbances. The finger under which these aspects are particularly clear indicates the part of the body or organ affected by the disorder. A large section of pulse diagnosis in the *Four Tantras* is devoted to divinatory techniques which seem to have fallen into disuse.

The patient's urine should be examined while it is still warm. (TMP PL. 63)

Urinalysis

Although this method is not as widely used as pulse diagnosis and is generally applied in a simplified manner, it nevertheless deserves attention. Not only is it considerably developed in the *Four Tantras,* but it also represents a unique feature of Tibetan medicine. Indeed, urinalysis as a specifically diagnostic technique is absent in Chinese medicine. In Ayurveda it is not mentioned before the eleventh century and it shares little with its Tibetan counterpart.

Ideally, the first urine in the morning should be examined, after the urines strongly modified by previous meals have been eliminated during the night. The urine, collected in a white bowl, should in theory be observed at three different intervals. First, when the urine is still warm, the colour, vapour, odour, and bubbles are examined. Then, when the odour has dispersed, the suspension and the layer which forms at the surface are observed. Finally, when the urine's aspect changes, the timing and manner of its transformation, as well as its final characteristics are analysed.

The fresh urine of a healthy person is described as slightly yellow in colour, fluid, and having 'the smell of the sheath of a ram's penis'. The vapours are of average density and duration, just as the bubbles are of average size. When the odour has faded, the sediment is of average bulk and a bluish tint pervades the urine evenly. The substance on the surface should resemble a 'pond unperturbed by winds in the summer'. Urine normally changes aspect when both vapour and odour disperse, and when the colour then turning more white or yellow.

As in pulse examination, semiology in urine diagnosis first lists all aspects pertaining to colour, odour, vapours, suspension, etc., which characterise the humours and the hot or cold nature of disorders. Then it describes at length the particularities of each specific disease. Furthermore, the upper, lower or intermediary level of suspension indicates which part of the body is affected. Urinalysis, like pulse

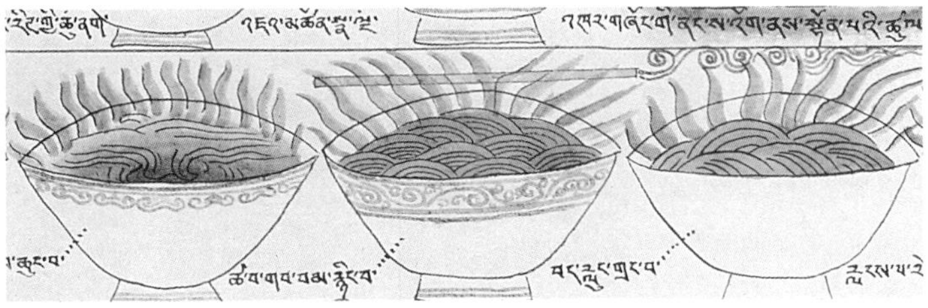

The examination of urine vapour. (TMP PL. 63)

diagnosis, also serves to identify evil spirits and is used for other divinatory purposes, but these more or less elaborate techniques are apparently no longer employed.

The overall sophistication of urinalysis as well as some of its more particular features (such as the importance given to sediment, which is compared to clouds, and its level; or to the relation of urine with blood and serum) evoke western urinalysis developed after Galen, namely by certain Byzantine authors, and eventually by the Arabs.

Thus, ideally Tibetan medical diagnosis is based on a process of rational inference which should enable the physician to identify a disorder by observing and confronting its various signs. Semiology refers mostly to spontaneous symptoms. However, some may be provoked by the physician himself, notably through treatments prescribed in order to confirm diagnosis.

Therapeutic Techniques

Treatment, which should be applied rationally according to the outcome of diagnosis, comprises four types of 'antagonists' which are always enumerated in their order of application and increasing strength: conduct, diet, medicines, and external therapy. The use of the term 'antagonist' in general demonstrates that therapies are viewed as allopathic: humours in excess are usually treated with opposing qualities.

A specific treatment obeys a set of more or less common rules which if ignored would be like shooting an arrow in the dark. Thus a disturbed humour, when it is still accumulating in its proper location, simply requires a 'pacifying' medicine. Once the humour has overflowed, it must first be gathered and ripened before it can be evacuated from its location by a treatment which should avoid disturbing the other humours in the process. The treatment should be adapted to the gravity of the disorder and to the patient's level of tolerance.

Pharmacological theory

As we have already mentioned, according to the Ayurvedic notions introduced to Tibet, every substance is the result of a particular combination of the five fundamental elements which determine its properties. These properties are in turn responsible for the chemical, biological or therapeutic effects of the substance. Hence there is no substance, when correctly prepared, which cannot be used as a remedy.

The properties of therapeutic substances are divided into several categories: tastes, potencies, post-digestive tastes, etc. The six tastes occupy a foremost position in Tibetan pharmacological theory. Each taste, alone or combined with another in an elementary drug, is directly produced by the preponderance of two elements: earth and water produce a sweet taste; fire and earth an acid taste; water and fire a salty taste; water and air a bitter taste; fire and wind a hot taste; earth and wind an astringent taste. The same classification of tastes according to the elements is found in classical Ayurveda with the exception of bitter taste which is supposedely determined by space and wind and not by water and wind.

The tastes are believed to affect the humours: sweet, acid, salty and hot tastes diminish wind; sweet, bitter and astringent diminish bile; acid, salty and hot diminish phlegm. It is implicitly understood that tastes which do not decrease a humour are likely to increase it. Here the theory differs slightly from Ayurveda which does not include 'hot' among the tastes opposing wind and recommends bitter, astringent, and hot tastes against phlegm.

Pharmacology distinguishes another category of properties called the eight 'potencies'. They form four pairs of opposites: heavy/light, unctuous/rough, cold/hot, and dull/sharp. They are directly determined by the tastes, and indirectly by the elements:

Diet and dietary restrictions (TMP PL. 22). *Shown here are the nourishing and life-sustaining cooked foods and beverages including water-sources. The lower part illustrates unwholesome foods and how to avoid food-poisoning.*

salty, astringent, sweet are increasingly heavy		
salty, acid, and sweet	"	unctuous
astringent, bitter, sweet	"	cold
bitter, astringent, sweet	"	dull
acid, hot, bitter	"	light and rough
hot, acid, salty	"	hot and sharp

Ayurveda gives a slightly different presentation of these correspondences. Apparently, there was some difficulty in associating the six tastes with the eight potencies since, in some cases, two potencies had to be grouped together. In addition, the acid taste curiously determines two opposite potencies: unctuous and rough. The potencies, like the tastes, also influence the humours: heavy and unctuous diminish wind; cool and dull diminish bile; light, rough, hot and sharp reduce phlegm.

Among the eight potencies, the hot or cold potencies of a substance are said to predominate when the hot or cold natures inherent in the following conditions coincide: the provenance of the substance, sunny or shady slope of the mountain; the timing of its collection, under the sun or under the stars; and the manner in which it was preserved. In addition to the eight potencies, there are seventeen secondary qualities which also possess therapeutic properties even though they are not referred to as much.

That certain substances do not have the biological activity one would expect with regard to their tastes is attributed to the effect of post-digestive tastes, which manifest themselves after digestion. In addition, the combination of various substances in complex medicinal preparations is likely to engender new biological effects.

Thus Indo-Tibetan pharmacological theory recognises several levels of action: tastes, potencies, post-digestive tastes of primary drugs and the combination of ingredients in a preparation. When all the levels are in harmony, the tastes appear to be active. If the potencies contradict the tastes owing to a particular combination of elements, then the action of the potencies overrides that of the tastes. Likewise, the post-digestive tastes followed by the effect of combinations will each predominate in turn if they are not supported by the preceding levels of action. This order of predominance is partly different in classical Ayurveda.

Tibetan medicinal preparations generally combine various ingredients, up to several dozen, according to an understanding that the effects of the main drugs must be tempered, corrected and oriented by the action of the secondary ingredients. Only a few decoctions are actually mono-factorial. The method of preparation is simple, their action swift and mild, and they are usually prescribed to confirm a diagnosis.

Tibetan *materia medica* is extremely rich and consists mainly of plants but also includes indigenous and imported mineral and animal products. There are several pharmacopoeias, some of them illustrated, which enumerate the names, localities, description, sub-varieties, potencies, and therapeutic indications of each drug. Dilmar Geshe's pharmacopoeia, composed in 1727, lists 2,200 drugs and their sub-varieties. However, only a 100 to 150 among these are commonly used. In indigenous literature, Tibet is often poetically described as the 'Land of Remedies'; for many centuries the vast expanses of the Himalayas and the Tibetan plateau were renowned as far as China and India for their medicinal plants. These are still exchanged for other goods at their borders. Raw drugs usually undergo various preparations, including cleaning, purification, detoxification and grinding, before they can be used in complex medicines.

Medicines

Medicines require more or less complex methods of preparation and can be divided into two main categories: those which are supposed to appease and those which are meant to evacuate the humours. The remedies defined as soothing—decoctions, pills, powders, sweet or oily pastes, medicinal butters, and ash medicines—restore the pathogenic humour to its normal location and level. The so-called evacuating remedies—purgatives, emetics, snuffs, mild or strong enemata, channel 'cleansing' medicines—expel the humour from the body.

The following passage from the *Four Tantras* clearly indicates the use of these various treatments according to progression and location:

For any disorder one must first prescribe decoctions with sharp and rapid potencies in order to ripen, gather and isolate [the humour or humours]. If this method fails then powders should be given. If these do not eliminate the root of the disorder then pills should be given. To eliminate the remaining pathogenic factors embedded in the channels, joints, skin, etc, sweet or oily pastes should be imbibed. Finally, in order to strengthen the body and clear the sense organs medicinal butters are used. Purgation expels blood, bile, etc. from the lower part of the body. Emetics expel phlegm, poisons, etc. from the upper part. Snuffs eliminate the pathogenic factors located in the head and neck.

Enema ejects the disorders of the colon and the small intestine. Finally, purgation of the channels enables one to overcome the disorder when all the preceding methods have failed.

Certain highly valued medicinal preparations, such as rejuvenation elixirs and expensive pills based on precious metals, stones and other rare substances, require ritual consecration which enhances their therapeutic action.

Blood-letting (TMP PL. 19)

External therapy

This form of therapy is destined to remove the resisting pathogenic elements after the other treatments of conduct, diet and medicine have been applied. There are two main categories: mild, in the form of compresses, fomentation, baths and embrocation; and drastic—blood-letting, cauterisation, moxibustion, and minor surgery—which should only be used as a last resort.

Minor surgery (TMP PL. 75)

Compresses, fomentation, baths and finally embrocation are recommended for complex humoral disorders in which phlegm, bile and wind predominate respectively. Blood-letting, like moxibustion, is performed on very specific points of the body and is supposed to drain the residues of hot disorders as well as 'impure blood'. Moxibustion, a Chinese importation, consists in burning cones or cylinders of dried Gerbera leaves on precise points of the body and is used to subdue cold disorders and wind imbalances. Cauterisation is applied on wounds which, along with draining abscesses, have become the main indications for minor surgery. Cataract removal, which consists in reclining the opaque crystalline lens towards the back of the eye, is no longer practised.

Administring mild enemata. (TMP PL. 68)

In contemporary Tibetan medical practice therapy consists mainly of pills and powders. Medicinal preparations have become more and more standardised. They are now often systematically prescribed for given diseases, following the example of biomedical pharmacology, rather than adapted to individual cases. For instance, the School of Medicine and Astrology in Lhasa produces 300 kinds of standard medicines which are then distributed to various regional dispensaries. The only form of external therapy commonly practised today is moxibustion.

Moxi-cauterisation. (TMP PL. 36)

Tibetan medicine spans more than a thousand years of empirical observation concerning man, the environment and its natural resources. It clearly strives to found its explanations and practice on a rational unitary theory, largely deriving from Indian Ayurveda, integrating physiology, pathology and therapy. While Tibetan medicine deserves to be

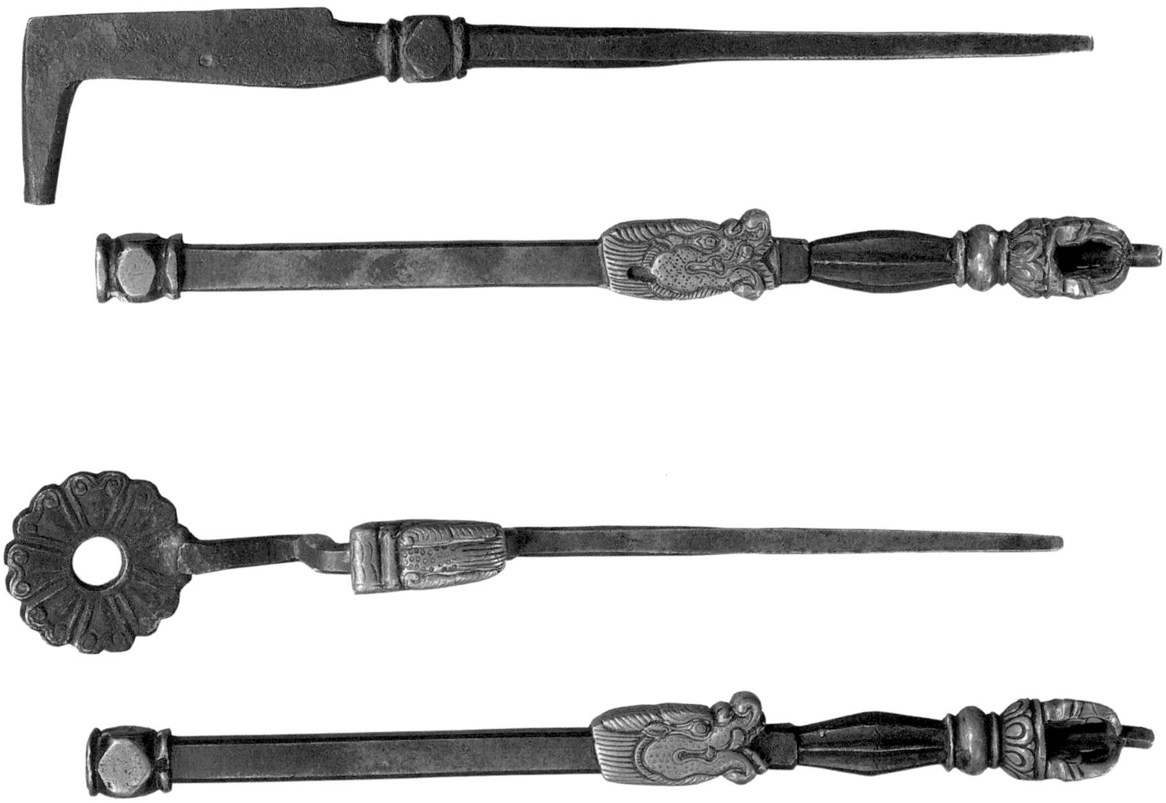

Cauterisation instruments with their separate handles. National Museum, Copenhagen.

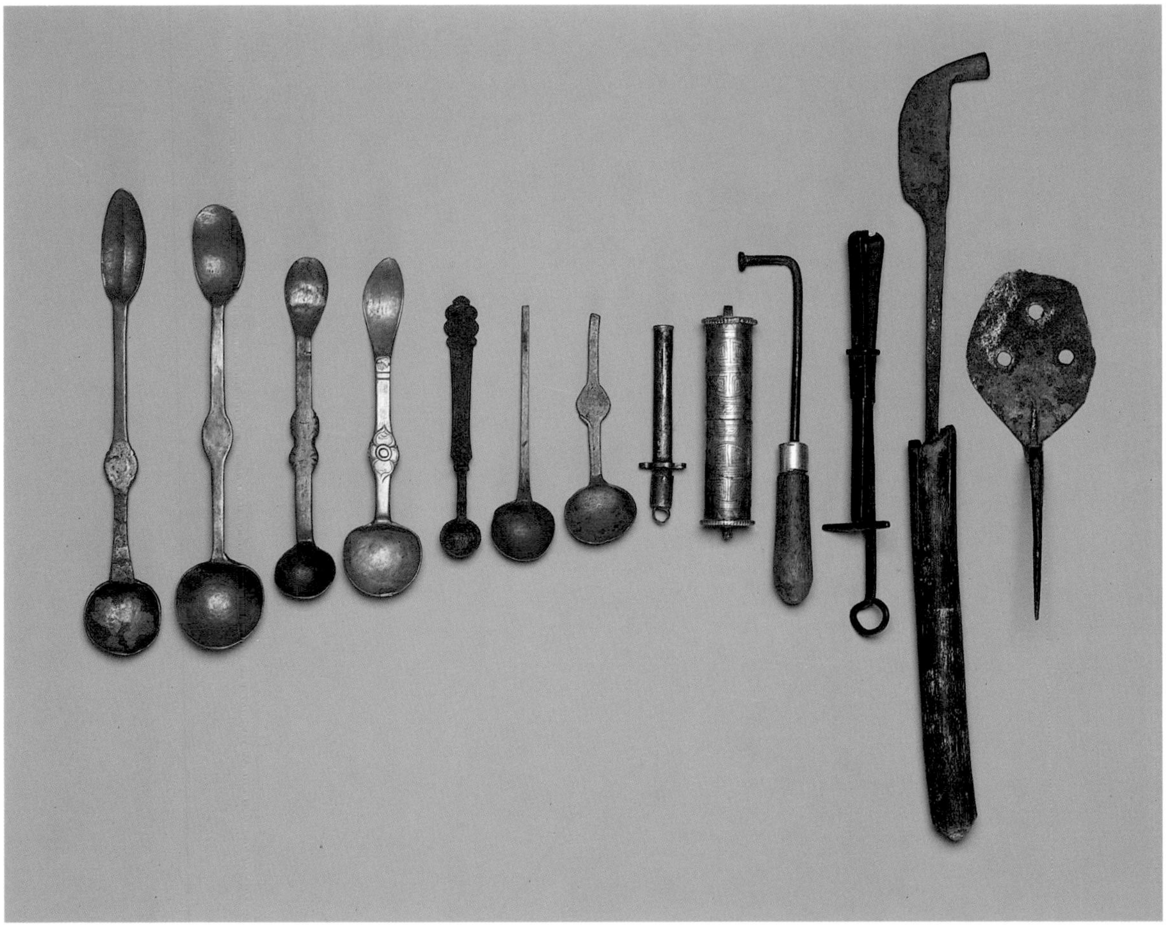

Selection of Tibetan medical implements. Heinrich Harrer Museum, Hüttenberg.

Mengyila (Sman.gyi.bla Bai.du.ry'a. od.rgy al.po), in his incarnation as a lama, is holding the same attributes as his prototype, the Medicine Buddha. An inscription on the back says: 'Sman.gyi.bla who liberates from devilish oppression such as epilepsy and other diseases...'. Around the base of his throne are placed the Eight Medicine Buddhas. Gilt bronze, South Tibet, 18th century. Private collection, Belgium.

This silver statue of a dwarfish dāka, holding a vajra and bell, is used for consecrating medicine which is inserted into the open mouth of the earth spirit and from there poured into the mouth of a sick person. The dāka or 'devourer' swallows all evil. Silver, Tibet, 17th century (?). Private collection, Belgium.

recognised for what it claims to be, a science in the broad sense of the term, this tradition is also founded on conceptions and practices which belong to the magico-religious domain: divination, demonology, esoteric formulas for healing or consecration, protective charms, rituals, etc., not to mention its philosophical and ethical links with Buddhism. Actual medical practice cannot be clearly separated from ritual or religious therapeutic procedures, even though they may not be applied together or performed by the same specialist. The religious dimensions of this 'science of healing', which go beyond those of medicine—as we conceive it—make it an integral part of a civilisation marked in all it aspects by Buddhism which, in the Land of Snows, is inseparable from daily life.

Notes

1 De Filippi 1932, pp. 186-87.
2 A. Csoma de Körös 1835.
3 For a recent and exhaustive bibliography concerning Tibetan medicine, see J. Aschoff 1995.
4 R. Birnbaum 1980
5 F. Meyer 1988
6 C. Beckwith 1979
7 This famous Tibetan translator is one of the most important religious figures in the order of the Nyingmapa, 'the ancients'. Concerning the question of his role in the transmission of the *Four Tantras*, see S. Karmay 1989.
8 See M. Lalou 1941-42, and A.-M. Blondeau 1972.
9 This text is reputed to have been first taught by the *bodhisattva* Mañjuśri on the Wudaishan mountain in China, and later reworked by the Indian Buddhist master Nāgārjuna.
10 See P. Cordier 1903
11 Translation of the Yogaśataka of Nāgārjuna, in B. Dash 1976
12 See C. Vogel 1965. German translation in L. Hilgenberg and W. Kirfel 1941.
13 For a translation of the biographies of the two Yuthog, see Rechung Rimpoche 1973.
14 This important master of the Nyingmapa religious order, believed to have been a reincarnation of Vairocana, the famous disciple of Padmasambhava, redicovered numerous 'hidden texts' and founded many religious institutions in central Tibet.
15 For examples of general descriptions, partial translations or summaries, see T. Clifford 1984; B. Dash 1994; Y. Donden Y. 1986; R.E. Emmerick 1975, 1977, 1987, 1990; E. Finckh 1988, 1992; F. Meyer 1981, 1990, 1992; Parfionovitch *et al.* 1992.
16 For a history of Tibetan medical literature, see M. Taube 1981.
17 See Parfionovitch *et al.* 1992

References

Aschoff, Jürgen C. *Tibetische Medicin / Tibetan Medicine*. Bibliography. Ulm, Fabri Verlag, 1995.

Beckwith, Christopher I. 'The Introduction of Greek Medicine into Tibet in the Seventh and Eighth Centuries', *Journal of the American Oriental Society* 99 (1979), pp. 297-313.

Birnbaum, Raoul. *The Healing Buddha*, London, Rider, 1990.

Blondeau, Anne-Marie. *Matériaux pour l'étude de l'hippologie et de l'hippiatrie tibétaines (à partir des manuscrits de Touen-houang)*, Geneva-Paris, Librairie Droz, 1972.

Body and Mind in Tibetan Medicine. An Exhibition 7 April to 31 July 1986 at the Wellcome Institute for the History of Medicine, London. Wellcome Institute for the History of Medicine, London, 1986.

Clifford, Terry. *Tibetan Buddhist Medicine and Psychiatry: The Diamond Healing*, York Beach, Maine, Samual Weiser, 1984.

Cordier, Palmyr. 'Introduction à l'étude des traités médicaux sanskrits inclus dans le Tanjur tibétain', *Bulletin de l'Ecole Française d'Extrême Orient* 3 (1903), pp. 604-29.

Csoma de Körös, A. 'Analysis of a Tibetan Medical Work', *Journal of the Asiatic Society of Bengal*, n° 37, January 1835, pp. 1-20.

Dash, Bhagwan. *Tibetan Medicine with Special Reference to Yogaśataka*. Dharamsala, Library of Tibetan Works and Archives, 1976.

— *Encyclopedia of Tibetan Medicine, being the Tibetan text of the rGyud bzhi and sanskrit restoration of Amṛta Hṛdaya Aṣṭāṅga Guhyopadeśa Tantra and expository translation in English*, vol. 1. Delhi, 1994.

De Fillipi, Filipo. *An Account of Tibet. The Travels of Ippolito Desideri of Pistoia S.J. 1712-1727*, London, George Routledge and Sons, 1932.

Donden, Yeshi. *Health Through Balance*, Ithaca, N.Y, Snow Lion Publications, 1986.

Emmerick, Ronald E. 'A Chapter from the Rgyud-bzhi'. *Asia Major* XIX, no. 2, 1975, pp. 141-62.

— 'Sources of the Rgyud-bzhi', *Zeitschrift der Deutschen Morgenländischen Gesellschaft III*, n° 2, 1977 (Supplement XIX Deutscher Orientalistentag vom 28 september bis 4 oktober 1975 in Frieburg im Breisgau).

— 'Epilepsy According to the Rgyud-bzhi', in (eds.) G. Jan Meulenbeld and D. Wujastyk, *Studies on Indian Medical History*, Groningen, Egbert Forsten, 1987, pp. 63-90.

— 'rGas-pa gso-ba', in (ed.) T. Skorupski, *Indo-Tibetan Studies*, Buddhica Britannica, Series continua II, Tring UK, The Institute of Buddhist Studies, 1990, pp. 89-99.

Finckh, Elisabeth. *Studies in Tibetan Medicine*, Ithaca, N.Y., Snow Lion,1988.

— 'Practice of Tibetan Medicine: Notes on Moxibustion (me btsa)', *Tibetan Studies, Proceedings of the 5th Seminar of the International Association of Tibetan Studies*, Naritasan Shinshoji, 1992, pp. 443-50.

Hilgenberg, Luise and Kirfel, Willibald. *Vāgbhaṭa's Aṣṭāṅghṛdayasaṃhitā*. Leiden, E.J. Brill, 1941.

Karmay, S.G. 'Vairocana and the rGyud bzhi', *Tibetan Medicine* n°12, 1989, pp. 19-31.

Lalou M. 'Texte médical tibétain'. *Journal Asiatique*, 233 (1941-42), pp. 209-11.

Meyer, Fernand. *Gso-ba rig-pa, le système médical tibétain*, Paris, C.N.R.S., 1981 (new edition 1988).

— 'Médecine et bouddhisme au Tibet', in *Le grand atlas des religions*, Paris, Encyclopedia universalis, 1988.

— 'Théorie et pratique de l'examen des pouls dans un chapitre du Rgyud-bzhi', in (ed.) T. Skorupski, 1990, pp. 209-56.

— 'La démarche diagnostique en médicine tibétaine', in (ed.) Danielle Gourevitch, *Maladie et maladies, histoire et conceptualisation*, Geneva, Librairie Droz, 1992, pp. 193-218.

Mullin, Glen. *The Practice of Kalachakra*, Ithaca NY, Snow Lion Publications, 1991.

Parfionovitch, Yuri, Gyurme Dorje, Fernand Meyer. *Tibetan Medical Paintings, Illustrations to the Blue Beryl Treatise of Sangye Gyamtso (1653-1705)*, 2 vols, London, Serindia Publications, 1992.

Rechung Rinpoche, Jampal Kunzang. *Tibetan Medicine*, Berkeley and Los Angeles, University of California Press, 1973.

Sopa, Geshe Lhundup, Jackson, R., Newman, J. *The Wheel of Time. The Kalachakra in Context*, Deer Park Books, Madison 1985, Ithaca NY, Snow Lion Publications, 1991.

Taube, Manfred. *Beiträge zur Geschichte der medizinischen Literatur Tibets*, Sankt Augustin, VGH Wissenschaftsverlag, 1981.

The Ambrosia Heart Tantra, with annotations by Dr. Yeshi Dönden, trans. Jhampa Kelsang, Dharamsala, LTWA, 1977.

Tibet und seine Medizin. 2500 jahre Heilkunst. Inssbruck, Pinguin-Verlag, 1992.

Tsarong, T.J. *Fundamentals of Tibetan Medicine according to the Rgyud-bzhi*, Tibetan Medical Center, Dharamsala 1981.

TMP: *Tibetan Medical Paintings*, see Parfionovitch, Yuri *et al.* above.

Vogel, Claus. *Vāgbhaṭa's Aṣṭāṅgahayasaṃhitā*, Abhandlungen für die Kunde des Morgenlandes XXXVII, 2. Wiesbaden, Franz Steiner Verlag, 1965.

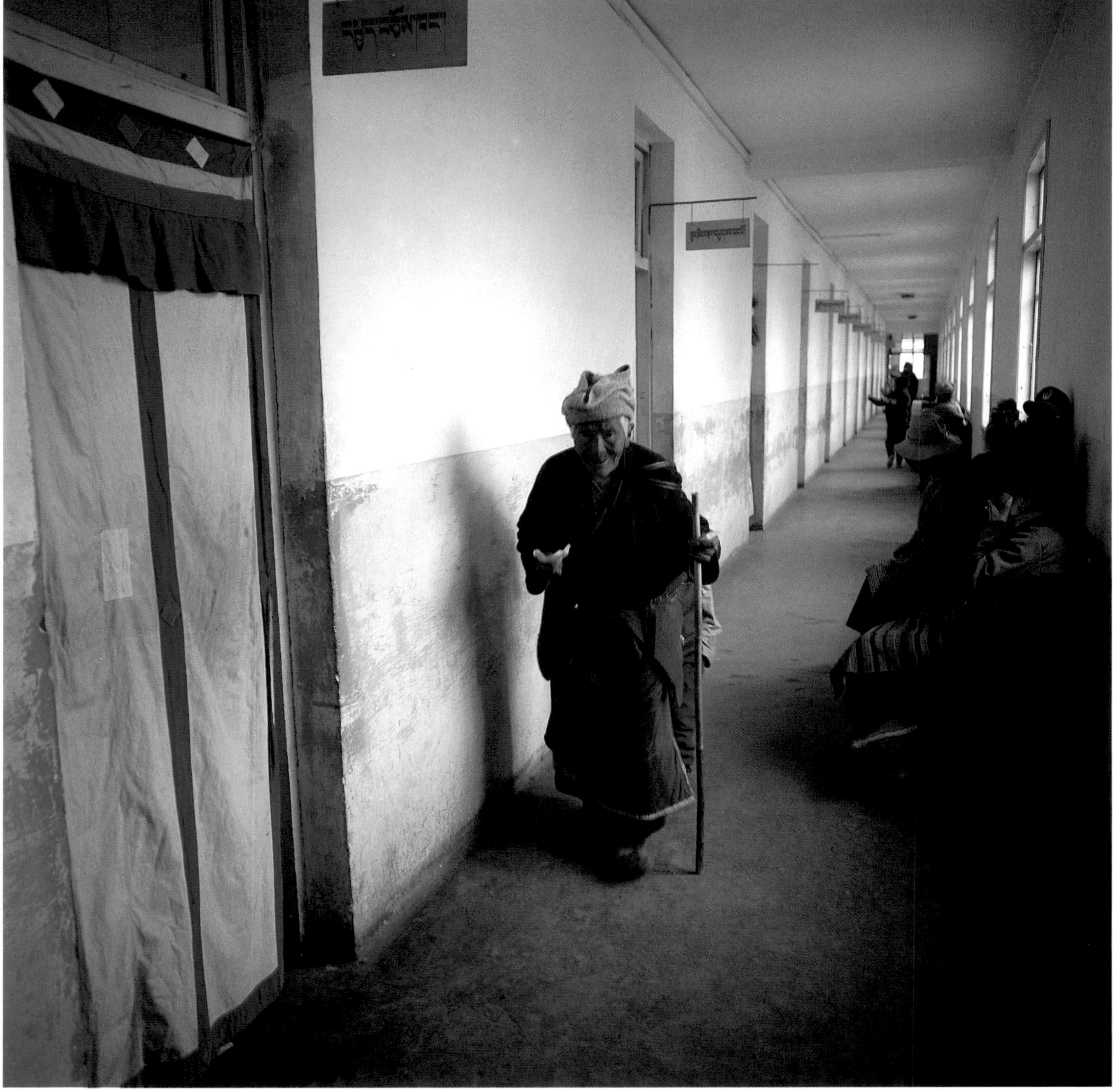

Patients attending the outpatients' department of the Mentsikhang Traditional Medical Hospital, Lhasa.

Tibetan Medicine Today

A View from outside Tibet

Fernand Meyer

The upheavals caused by the Chinese control of Tibet from 1950 onwards profoundly affected all aspects of Tibetan culture including medicine. These drastic events, along with its encounter with Western biomedicine, were to determine the future course of Tibetan medicine both in Tibet and in exile. With the escape of around 90,000 refugees—numerous scholars amongst them—who followed the Dalai Lama into exile in 1959, Tibetan medicine spread to the bordering countries of India and Nepal, and then beyond, to the West.

Peoples of Tibetan language and culture had settled in the border regions, such as Ladakh, Zangskar, highland Nepal, Sikhim and Bhutan, since ancient times, and Tibetan medicine had been practiced there in family lineages without any formal teaching institutions. In the last few years these local practitioners have tended to group themselves into professional organisations for formal training under the guidance and teaching of Tibetan refugee physicians.

As early as 1961, the Dalai Lama founded a dispensary of traditional medicine in Dharamsala (north India), the headquarters of his government-in-exile. It included a pharmaceutical unit and a small college intended to preserve Tibetan medical tradition and to provide doctors desperately needed in the refugee camps. A later addition to the centre was a hospital of fifteen beds, an innovation for Tibetan medicine. In 1967 it was further endowed with a department of Astrology, and became known as the Tibetan Medical and Astro Institute. The college grew progressively and, in 1974, the first class of fifteen students graduated. Since then the school has trained more than a hundred and fifty students. The course lasts five years and is followed by two more years of practice in the dispensaries located in refugee camps throughout India or Nepal. These dispensaries also treat the local Indian or Nepalese populations. The Tibetan Medical and Astro Institute—which boasts a research department since 1980—is now at the head of 36 branches and has built up a network of contacts throughout the world. In addition, it patronises the publication of specialised works in English and Tibetan, while the Library of Tibetan Works and Archives publishes the periodical "Tibetan Medicine".

Also within the Tibetan community in exile but on a personal initiative, Trogawa Rinpoche—a former professor of the Tibetan Medical Center from 1964 to 1967—founded the Chagpori Tibetan Medical Institute in Darjeeling (north-eastern India) in 1992. This private establishment admits both foreign and Tibetan students and offers a three year course followed by two years of practice.

In 1971, the government of Bhutan, a small independant kingdom of Tibetan culture in the eastern part of the Himalayas, established the National Research and Training Institute of Traditional Medicine. The government has included both traditional medicine and western biomedicine in its health development policy. The Institute today comprises a dispensary, hospital, pharmaceutical unit, research department on traditional pharmacopoiea, as well as a school. The school trains around twenty students and the courses last three or five years depending on the chosen degree.

Under the guidance of the Ven. Akong Tulku, the Tibetan Centre of Kagyu Samyé Ling in Scotland has set up a school of Tibetan medicine specifically for western students.

Tibetan medicine had been borrowed and adapted by the Mongols since the sixteenth century onwards. It is today undergoing a dynamic renaissance and enjoying official support, especially in the Republic of Mongolia since it recovered its independence.

Portrait of a Tibetan Doctor: Khenpo Troru Tsenam

KENNETH HOLMES

Khenpo Troru Tsenam, inspecting primula.

Khenpo Troru Tsenam is currently Directing Physician and Professor of Medicine at the Central Institute in Lhasa, and Professor at the China Advanced Buddhist Centre. He is also Editor-in-Chief of the Tibetan Medicine volumes of the *China Medical Encyclopaedia.* He has written a number of major medical textbooks and published some 200 articles on Tibetan medicine. In recent years Professor Tsenam has visited Europe, and in 1994 he taught Tibetan Medicine at the Kagyu Samye Ling Tibetan Centre in Scotland.[1] The following brief biography, condensed from his own autobiographical notes, shows how he views his life as having three main stages: that of being a Buddhist abbot and physician, imprisonment and that of a twenty-five-year endeavour to preserve traditional Tibetan medicine.

Khenpo Tsenam was born in 1928 in the Derge Kingdom of Dhokham in a place presently known as Troru commune, in Terton district of the Chamdo county of the Autonomous Region of Tibet. From 1933-43 he lived as a monk in Troru monastery where he received his first tuition and completed his training in monastic ritual. Under the guidance of the then *Khenpo* (Professor) of Troru monastery, he received general instruction in the three levels of Buddhist precepts and special training in the more profound aspects of meditation according to the Kagyu tradition, studying commentaries on the secret *yoga* practices of Naropa and on *mahāmudrā*, the highest Kagyu meditation teachings, aimed at unveiling the ultimate nature of the human mind. From other teachers he received instruction in grammar and composition as well as teachings on astrology, in both the planetary and element-related forms used in Tibet.

Having successfully completed the first phase of his education, he spent the years from 1943-46 on pilgrimage, going first to Lhasa and then to India, Bhutan and Sikkim. In 1946 he returned to eastern Tibet, staying for a few months at his home. Throughout the early period of his training his mentors recognised a tremendous potential in him and encouraged him to further his studies. One of his travelling companions, a *khenpo* of Katok monastery, a great centre of learning in eastern Tibet, insisted that he go there to complete his education.

Shortly after his return to Tibet, Troru Tsenam did go to Katok monastic university where, between 1946 and 1951, he continued his Buddhist training which now also included medicine. Here he studied elemental and planetary astrology, poetic composition and the various fields of study proper to all the traditions of Buddhism, namely *mādhyamika*, *prajñāparamitā*, *abhidharma* and *vinaya*. He received a thorough training in *vajrayāna* Buddhism, becoming well-versed in both the Nyingma and Kagyu traditions, whose theoretical teachings he mastered. He became one of very few persons entrusted with the medical science of preparing 'detoxified mercury', receiving these teachings from Tachung Lama Tsering Chopel. He thus became a physician-monk, learned in all domains, and particularly gifted in medicine.

As a young monk Khenpo Troru Tsenam showed such extraordinary aptitude for study that his teachers thought it likely that he was the reincarnation of a great scholar. This was confirmed by the Third Shertse Rinpoche who declared him to be an emanation of the early Tibetan master Butön. At Katok he received the title of '*Khenpo* of the Five Disciplines'—roughly equivalent to a professorship.

Though he was requested by several monasteries, including his home monastery of Troru, to come and lead their colleges, he was kept by Shertse Rinpoche at Katok. The 1956 troubles in eastern Tibet allowed him to return to Troru, where he took up the chair of the monastic university, becoming known as Troru Khenpo Tsenam. For three years he was responsible for the education of some thirty *tulku* and two hundred monks.

After China took control of Tibet in 1959 and particularly during the Cultural Revolution, the monasteries were closed and all religious activity ceased. Those lamas who did not flee the country were obliged to lie low, which Khenpo Tsenam also did for two years. Then, because of his former high monastic position, he was placed in a prison in the Pomi area, where he remained for ten years. Despite the tough prison conditions, Khenpo Tsenam was able to use this difficult life situation as an opportunity for development, relying on his Buddhist training. During that time, one of great threat to Tibetan culture, he tried to write down what he could of his knowledge, though the volume of literature he gradually produced was eventually discovered and destroyed. He also tried to pass on some of his medical and academic knowledge to the more gifted of his fellow inmates (some of whom were *tulku)* though this tuition had to take place in secret, at night. As Pomi was more of a labour camp than a closed prison, he had the opportunity of gathering simple herbs in the surrounding countryside to treat sick inmates. This proved invaluable.

By 1971 his immense medical knowledge and obvious value to the Tibetan community as a highly skilled doctor were recognised and appreciated by the authorities who not only released him, but apologised formally for his imprisonment. This they justified by saying they had initially thought him to be a *lama*. As he was, in fact, a doctor, and therefore of real use to the people, it was recognised that a mistake had been made which should now be rectified.

Following his release, Khenpo Tsenam continued to treat his patients in the Pomi area and the small dwelling he used as a clinic became known as Pomi hospital. There, he prepared his own medicines from local plants, minerals and animal products (though he was unable to make many of the traditional compounds as they required ingredients from elsewhere in Tibet and other countries). His renown spread.

Once the Cultural Revolution was over, China allowed Tibetans more traditional cultural expression. This period marked the beginnings of a restoration of Tibetan medicine; it was a period of intense activity for Khenpo Tsenam and those like him. He travelled, first locally to Derge, then to other former medical centres in Kham, and eventually to Lhasa, to assess the situation and make contact with other Tibetan doctors. In the Derge printing house he found the Tai Situpa's text on mercury detoxification and preparation of mercury medicines. Using this as a basis, he transmitted the secret keys of the process to suitable physicians, who acted as his apprentices in the complex alchemical processes involved. As a result, detoxified mercury was prepared in Derge, then in Chinghai, Sining and other medical centres. Once these institutions had detoxified mercurial compound as a raw material, they were able to produce medicines incorporating precious stones and precious metal—the famous *rinchen rilbu* 'precious pills'.

In 1981 Khenpo Tsenam's expertise was sought by the authorities in Lhasa. Since then he has devoted himself to the restoration of the Lhasa Astro-Medical Institute (*Mentsikhang*), which has grown from a small building with a handful of doctors to a major teaching hospital, with some 1,000 staff and students, several hundred beds and a factory for the production of Tibetan medicine.

Professor Troru Tsenam's life thus reflects the fortunes of Tibetan culture during the twentieth century. Before 1959 he held the equivalent of several chairs in Buddhist monastic universities. He currently holds two chairs within the modern Chinese academic system. He has been instrumental in the re-establishment of traditional Tibetan medicine in Tibet itself, where his life is dedicated to ensuring that as much as possible of the unique knowledge and experience that he embodies is passed on to younger generations of Tibetan doctors. He incarnates the qualities of the traditional monk-physician in the world of Tibetan medicine which for many years was stripped of its religious context and reduced to a solely materialistic science.

A View from Tibet

Khenpo Troru Tsenam

History and origins of Tibetan medicine

Tibetan medical science has its main roots in the land of Tibet itself and in the age-old experience and ingenuity of the Tibetan people who have always lived close to nature and had to rely on their own resources to survive. Over the last two millenia, the medical wisdom of other lands and civilisations have also been integrated into the indigenous system, either intentionally, or by the natural cross-fertilisations of cultures which have taken place over the ages. Three main streams have contributed to make the waters of the 'healing lake' of Tibetan medicine. These three streams are depicted on the insignia of the Central Institute, the governing body of the Lhasa Astro-Medical Institute (*Mentsikhang*). The longest stream comes from the snow mountains, representing Tibet itself. This is joined by two other streams which represent Chinese medicine and Indian Ayurvedic medicine.

The many facets of medical knowledge which together form the wealth of Tibetan medicine were all brought together in the best-known of all the Tibetan medical treatises—the *Rgyud bzhi*—or *Four Tantras*. Tibetan medicine has a recorded history of about 2,000 years, whilst the Four Tantras date back about 1,000 years. This ancient system of medical knowledge and its lineage of transmission from doctor to doctor have both been preserved throughout the vicissitudes of Tibetan history.

This tradition of medicine has been used by the people of the various kingdoms known collectively to the outside world as 'Tibet', and also by the peoples of neighbouring regions and countries: Bhutan, Nepal, Sikkim, Ladakh, Mongolia and Sinkiang. Tibet has long been renown throughout Asia as a land of medicines. Its medical tradition is a vast science with fully-elaborated notions of the bases of health and sickness, a simple but exceptionally efficient system of diagnosis and a very full range of treatments based on diet, lifestyle, medication and external treatments. Tibet's pharmacopoeia was particularly rich. The number of plants alone involved in medicine-making numbered more than 3,000. These were combined in all sorts of ways to produce medications sometimes containing 8, 15, 30 or even up to 100 different ingredients. There are also mineral and animal ingredients. Doctors obtained some of the raw materials for their medicines locally, some from other parts of Tibet, whilst yet other ingredients were imported through traders.

Traditional Tibetan medicine in its religious context: Buddhist training and the role of compassion

Nowadays Tibetan medicine is taught and practised in Tibet much as it has always been. In earlier times medicine was studied principally in monasteries, with almost every monastery having some medical activity. There were also doctors in private practice, as well as clinics sponsored by the local aristocracy. The transmission of medical knowledge was carried out through apprenticeship and family tradition.

The monasteries in Tibet, like those of Europe in the Middle Ages, were major centres of learning and of medical study and practice. They served as bases from which monk-physicians would tour surrounding areas. The religious aspect of Tibetan medicine was a vital one: the whole science of medicine was presented as teachings given by the Buddha, through his emanation as the Healing Buddha. The collecting of medicinal plants, their preparation and administration were all accompanied by prayer and performed as a religious act. When medicines could not help the patient, specific religious healing ceremonies were performed. Besides providing this spiritual context to healing, monasteries were important seats of medical study and knowledge was seen as a key part of an overall education in the nature of the human condition, which needs to be understood in its entirety in the Buddhist quest for a complete wisdom. Medicine forms the second of the five main fields of Buddhist study.

Besides functioning as an efficient diagnostic system with a rich pharmacopoeia, Tibetan medicine is also a vocation based upon a rigorous moral code and altruistic approach. Throughout the centuries, the ethical code of the doctor was that of the *bodhisattva*, a person inspired by the Buddhist motivation to free all beings from suffering. There is a wealth of teaching on this in Mahāyāna Buddhism, which explains how to keep one's mind in a frame of altruistic purity and how to live in a way which aspires to perfect one's generosity, self-control, forbearance, diligence, meditation and wisdom. It is with all that in mind that medicine was practised. It is one of the finest and most satisfying professions, as it genuinely alleviates suffering.

The word compassion evokes many qualities of the *bodhisattva*, and the role of compassion in the healing art is a vital one. Compassion, as traditionally understood in Tibet, involves a skilful refinement of the human mind. In the case of medicine, compassion is not a fixed attitude of the doctor's mind, rooted subjectively in abstract notions of love, but a clarity of awareness and a quality of openness and sensitivity on the part of the healing physician concerning what is objectively happening in the patient. This is why compassion is described as being 'inseparable from wisdom'. It means being as fully aware as possible of what is taking place in the body and mind of the patient being treated, not just at present but over all sorts of timescales.

Tsimi Tundor, a physician at his practice near Sera monastery.

Principles of Tibetan medicine: the five elements, three humours, and causes of illness

One obvious aspect of the wisdom involved in the diagnostic phase is the ability to detect the humoral imbalance which is the cause of the symptoms which the patient is presenting. The humours are three fundamental sets of systems within the body's functioning. When a person is healthy they all work together in harmony. But when one or more of the humours is either deficient, over-active or upsetting the others, there will be ill-health. This is why the humours are called *nyes pa* in Tibetan, meaning 'ills'.

The humours themselves are manifestations of the interplay of the elements. To understand the flux of the elements in a patient's body at any given time, one needs to be aware of the nature of the elements where the patient lives and works, the play of the elements due to the changes of the seasons and times of day, and the power of the elements in the patient's diet. Everything is a manifestation of these prime elements: earth, water, fire, wind and space (or alternatively, wood, fire, earth, metal and water).

The elements exist on many different levels and their manifestations vary in a complex way according to the level. Earth is the material quality of things, their matter, weight, hardness, resistance etc., which—in the case of the human body—means the flesh and bones etc. Water is really the power of bonding between the various aspects of matter, between particles etc., and also therefore the fluid, lubricating quality. In the body this is the fluids and the overall cohesion between the physical constituents. Fire is the development, the transmutation, the coming to maturity, of matter. In the body it is its physical heat of digestion and so forth. Wind is the dynamic aspect, movement, flow, represented in the body by all the circulations of oxygen, the flow of blood in the veins and arteries, the impulses in the nervous system, the lymphatic system etc. Space is the dimensioning that allows the other elements to fulfill their functions; in the human body it is the hollow spaces and the orifices.

The elements within the body are in constant interplay with those outside it, as it relates to its environment. The body-environment dialogue occurs through the ingestion of nutrients such as oxygen, food and drink, through the impulses received through the senses, and through the way the person reacts in response to other people and the world around. Nutrients are themselves composed of the elements, as is the world—of trees, rocks, sun, sky and so forth experienced by the senses—and other people.

Medicines, which are concentrates of the powers of the elements, are administered to correct what goes wrong in this body-world dialogue. Besides the taking of medications, diet and behaviour are considered important factors in redressing the elemental balance. As everything has some elemental characteristics, anything could be used as a medicine. In practice, whatever resources are available are brought into play to bring the imbalanced elements in the patient's body back into harmony. Deficiency in one or another of the elements can be compensated for by a diet or an environment rich in that element. Likewise, excess of one or another of the elements can be corrected by reducing the power of that element in the diet, environment or behaviour.

The rare herbs of Tibet are not sufficient in quantity to heal many millions of people. It is certain that, as time goes by, the teachings of Tibetan medicine on how to use diet and a controlled personal behaviour and environment to cure oneself will come more to the fore. Many ancient scriptures predicted that that would be the case and said, furthermore, that the extraordinary healing power of a physician's compassionate mind and of healing prayers and meditations would become very important in future centuries.

Besides the more short term elemental and humoral causes of the ailment—due to the diet, lifestyle and the specific behaviour of the person—there are also the psychosomatic triggers of illness which, according to the traditional teachings of medicine, exist on three levels: remote cause, long-term cause and proximate cause. These are, respectively: the degree of lack of contact between the person and the innate purity of their mind; the powerful tendencies to strong emotions such as craving or anger in the more distant past, including past lives; and, finally, the factor of more recent emotional patterning.

The above description affords just a glimpse of the complexity of the composite phenomenon which is a human being, from the Tibetan medical point of view. In actual medical practice, sometimes mind and body are quite distinct from one another. Sometimes they are indistinguishable, and very often they are powerfully interconnected.

Besides the psychosomatic triggers of illness and short-term elemental factors, there are also longer-term physical considerations related to the proper functioning of the metabolism, particularly in terms of the intake of nutrients and the elimination of wastes.

Tibetan medicine discusses metabolism in terms of a sevenfold cycle. It is almost as though the prime nutrients—the food we eat, liquids we drink, air we breathe—go through seven 'reincarnations' within the body to produce the very substance of life, the glow of health. These are seven major steps of transformation, each of which produces by-products and wastes which need to be eliminated. All the major organs and bodily systems are involved in this complex and subtle process of refinement. When there is some malfunctioning in this constant process of refinement, there is a potential cause for illness; the longer and more serious the malfunctioning, the more serious the consequences can be. In fact, it is remarkable how many illnesses have their root in one of the major steps in the metabolic cycle, namely digestion and, indirectly therefore, diet. Digestion is one of the earlier stages in the sevenfold process and a lack of suitable nutrition at this stage will have its repercussions throughout all the later stages. Needless to say, Tibetan medicine aims to detect the long-term deficiencies or excesses in the overall metabolic picture and to correct them as much as is possible, given the circumstances of the patient.

It is said that diagnosis is achieved through three channels of investigation. The first, using sensitivity of touch, uses palpation of the pulse to attune the physician's perception to the various workings of the patient's bodily systems and to the functioning of the major organs. Like the fine training of a musician's ear, this is a subtle art developed over years of experience. The second uses visual observation and is particularly applied in urinalysis and observation of the tongue. These first two also include astrological considerations. The third method of diagnosis is questioning, which can be straightforward questioning about symptoms or quite clever questioning that will dig out a hidden truth.

The compassionate task of the doctor is to arrive at an accurate appreciation of what is truly ailing the patient by taking into account all of the above factors. Without compassion—which is the sensitivity the physician has for what is taking place in the patient—there will only be an awareness of the symptoms related to the immediate physical condition of the patient. Sometimes this is enough, as when a patient is merely suffering from a cold, a minor food poisoning and the like. In such cases a straightforward diagnosis will lead to a simple treatment or sometimes no treatment at all, and the patient recovers. However the main task of Tibetan medicine is to bring the whole psycho-physical unity of the patient back into true health. Without clear awareness of all the long- and short-term factors involved, and a truly compassionate motivation, what a doctor can achieve in this domain is relatively limited.

The role of the doctor in providing overall support and not just medicine for the patient—the one who is suffering—has been much stressed in traditional Tibetan medical texts, and in earlier times this was given its due emphasis in daily medical practice. More recently, since doctors in Tibet did not receive a full *bodhisattva* training and medicine was viewed, in a more materialistic light, as a job among others with a government salary, this has receded into the background. Fortunately it is now being restored, thanks to the relative liberty to follow the *bodhisattva* training and the drive to restore traditional Tibetan medicine in all its fullness.

The understanding of what true health really means is very profound. The main long-term factor in determining a person's well-being or health, is the purity or impurity, maturity or immaturity of mind. It is a question of how 'well' a human being feels in relation to what is happening in his or her life; how well they can cope with situations, including physical health itself. The enlightened feel physical and mental felicity no matter what is happening around them or within them. This point—that health is as much in the mind as in the body—is quite a subtle one but one which also needs to be taken into consideration. One is not simply treating a specific problem in the body, but the body as part of a body and mind combination which is suffering. Although in daily medical practice the physician is not assuming responsibility for the spiritual or psychological progress of the patient, some understanding of this longer-term spiritual and emotional dimension is needed for there to be a wise analysis of an ailment, especially where hard-to-treat, deep-rooted, or chronic ailments are concerned. Besides these considerations of mind's effect upon the body, there is also serious mental sickness itself—a whole branch of Tibetan medicine.

In Tibetan medicine the commonplace and longer-term psychosomatic triggers of illness are discussed under three groups known as the 'three poisons': *desire*, covering all sorts of human feelings from those of greed through to sexual passion; *anger*, ranging from frustration to real hate; and *ignorance*, ranging from thick mental torpor through to ignorance of the innate purity of mind. Each of these have many subcategories and there are many states of mind, such as jealousy, which contain elements of two—or even all three—main groups.

In the long term, a predominance of desire, attachments, frustrated longings etc., will create an imbalance in the physical system known as 'wind' (*rlung*) humour. Wind is the dynamic quality within the various physical systems. When the wind humour is in harmony, digestion, the nervous system, blood flow etc., are all working fluidly. A long-term predominance of anger will create imbalance in the 'bile' (*mkhris pa*) humour. This does not just mean the physical bile or gall bladder. It refers to the production of heat and energy in the body, especially through the ingestion and transformation of nourishment. A long-term predominance of ignorance will create imbalance in the 'phlegm' (*bad kan*) humour. This particularly concerns the fluid balances in the body and what we might describe generally as its coolness.

Recent history and the revival of Tibetan medicine

Whilst the widespread application of this healing science by dedicated physicians was the status quo in Tibet for more than a thousand years, during the Cultural Revolution the Tibetan medical system suffered great damage and, with only one or two exceptions, the great centres of medical learning were destroyed. Moreover, the medicine practised by individual doctors in rural areas almost came to an end too. One of the few institutions which survived was the Lhasa Astro-Medical Institute, the *Mentsikhang*.

The indigenous Tibetan medical system suffered because it was viewed by the communist regime of the time as being based entirely on superstition—an invention of the lamas—and not a real medical science. It was not until after the 3rd National Assembly that there was the beginning of a restoration of some Tibetan cultural activities. Since then there has been a steady revival of Tibetan medicine, sometimes through the initiative of government bodies or of local authorities and, more recently, with the support of international charities.[1] This process is not simply a question of restoring what was there previously but of reviving Tibetan medicine in a way which responds intelligently to contemporary needs.

Traditional Tibetan medicine seems to have become acceptable to the governing Chinese authorities through its sheer efficacy. Being relatively cheaper to implement than more modern treatments requiring expensive machinery and facilities, its cost is another important factor.

Doctors who qualify in state-recognised medical schools become state employees with a wage. There are five levels of medical qualification. The lowest involves a traditional theo-

Pulse taking at the Mentsikhang in Lhasa.

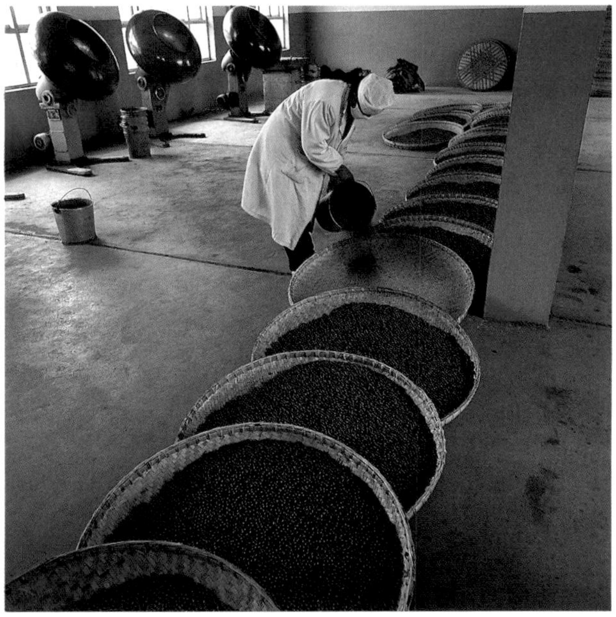

The drying of medicinal pills at a drug factory in Lhasa.

retical training over three years followed by some years of practical work alongside established doctors in hospitals or clinics. This leads to the title 'doctor' but not a university medical degree. The second level requires a longer training within a university context, and leads to the award of a medical degree. The remaining three levels are attained through numbers of years of practice and experience, teaching, research, and papers published.

The re-establishment of Tibetan medicine has been achieved through the growth of medical centres-cum-teaching hospitals in large towns. As the doctors trained in these centres take their practice out to the nomads and remote rural areas, it is likely that, as in the old days, they will take on apprentices who will commence their learning in the field rather than in the classroom.

Thus the revival has resulted in a significant and organised growth of medical schools. Some hospitals and medical centres have been established in places where there were none previously, and certain institutions have been restored far beyond their previous capacity. The Lhasa Astro-Medical Centre, for instance, has been significantly developed and its present form and capacity—in terms of number of doctors, beds, machines, buildings and allocation of funds—is much greater than before. Its dispensary, college and pharmaceutical unit were considerably enlarged, and in 1985 a hospital of 150 beds was opened. There is a staff of almost 1,000, and a major medicine-producing factory. In 1986 around 202,000 patients were treated and 7,500 kg of medicines produced.

The Lhasa Astro-Medical Centre now forms part of the Central Institute, an academic body in which I have just taken up a major directing role. Since this year (1995), the Institute not only has full university status within the overall Chinese system but also acts as the umbrella organisation for medical colleges both in the Autonomous Region and beyond it, in Yunnan, Aba and so forth. It will now receive the brightest students from those establishments and offer them degree and postgraduate training possibilities, as well as some parallel training in modern medicine. The main medical training offered by the Institute is a five-year degree course followed by by two years of practice.

Large astro-medical centres have also been founded in Shigatse, Chamdo, Nagchu, Soka, Nyitri, and other towns. These have provided hospitals, doctors, medicines, and regional healthcare centres where there were none before. Other astro-medical centres have been restored in major towns such as Derge, Payul, Dartsedo and some in the Chinghai province.

At present Tibetan medical science and education is going through a period of great development. The revival of Tibetan medicine is also attested by the great number of publications: new editions of ancient works, handbooks, pharmacopoieas. In all the centres, Tibetan medicine is taught according to the tradition. Modern scientific methods and machines are also used, and there is an attempt to see how modern ways can be combined with ancient wisdom. This is an ambitious, though necessary, task which has to be tackled

The new Mentsikhang (Astro-Medical Centre) at Lhasa is the tall building to the left, and in the background stands the Potala.

sooner or later. It is being approached in a pragmatic and open-minded way and should, if handled intelligently, move both medical systems further towards the joint overall goal of eradicating and preventing disease.

A Tibetan doctor who has successfully diagnosed a tumour will be happy to have an x-ray or other information which shows its exact size and effect on the organs around it. In the past, the strength of Tibetan medicine derived from the fact that it absorbed and integrated useful elements from other medical systems; remember the analogy of the three rivers. Now it seems quite likely that traditional Tibetan herbal and mineral remedies will, in many cases, be able to provide more effective and less intrusive solutions than present-day surgery or modern chemical medicines. Tibetan preparations for removing kidney stones and gallstones have impressed modern Chinese scientists by their efficacy. Besides these remedies to ailments, Tibetan diagnostic techniques are of great interest to modern investigators. Whereas modern diagnosis requires more and more expensive machinery, requiring patients to go to the hospitals where they are located, Tibetan diagnosis uses refined human sensitivity as its 'machine', offering a diagnosis which is therefore cheaper and mobile. I have not made much mention of the very important topics of pulse, urinalysis and so forth, as I understand these to be fairly well documented. Another area of great promise is that of Tibetan medicines based on detoxified mercury.

Traditionally, not all doctors were able to manufacture mercury-based compounds. The preparation of the basic ingredient of detoxified mercury required much time, money and manpower. Hence it was only produced in the very large monasteries or at the request of extremely rich sponsors. The knowledge of how to produce detoxified mercury is kept secret. It is an oral tradition handed down from one master-physician to another. Although a part of the technique has been committed to writing, certain key steps are purposefully omitted in order to keep this knowledge tightly controlled and free from abuse.

This knowledge was almost completely lost. The actual practice had not been carried out for a long time and the first revival was performed by myself and Dr Tenzin Chodrak. After the initial revival, it was manufactured by me in Pomi, before I took up the post at the Lhasa Astro-Medical Centre. Since then I have transmitted the know-how to many people—students and colleagues—and the continuity of this rare and important aspect of Tibetan medicine has been preserved for posterity. I have since manufactured this important medicine in Derge, Chinghai, Yushu, Chamdo and many other places. Having made the mercury, I then proceeded to revive production of the various complex precious-substance medications based on mercury, gold, gemstones and other rare substances. This has proved very successful, to such an extent that now there are many doctors all over Tibet well-trained in the production of these vital medicines and there is no longer fear of losing this knowledge forever.

The process for producing detoxified mercury in Tibetan medicine is not quite the same as that of Ayurveda. It does not come from the Vedic tradition but from the revelation of Urgyenpa, the great *siddha* and Kagyu master. The process currently used also differs slightly from that discussed in the *Four Tantras*.[2] Tibetans have always had considerable alchemical knowledge and understood how to transform one thing into another. The mercury process itself involves some hundred people working constantly for about a month. As a result of these transformations, the mercury—at first highly poisonous, shiny, mobile, like liquid metal—becomes medicinal, matt black, immobile and solid. It becomes the king of antidotes for all types of poisoning.

Detoxified mercury is a complex compound the making of which involves mercury, gold, silver, copper, and various sorts of iron. Hundreds of grams of gold are needed. During the process of transformation and detoxification, the gold—a noble and immutable metal—becomes oxidisable i.e. it burns. Before it is fired in a kiln, the gold is beaten and boiled in special ways and treated with various natural chemicals over a period of several days. The end product is a gold powder which can be burnt. There is an old Tibetan saying, *'Don't worry if the gold falls in the fire—it can never burn but will, on the contrary, improve'*. However, the detoxified gold compound *does* burn, and once burnt it becomes black. When we have prepared gold in the Lhasa Astro-medical Centre, we have at times burnt up to 3lbs of gold in these processes.

The preparation of the gold catalyst in the mercury preparation is quite complicated and takes many days. Thus when one takes into account the preparation of all the other metals and minerals it is not surprising that the whole process takes a month of non-stop activity. As mercury detoxification involves many people and resources, it was a rare event. Many secret techniques are preserved through an oral tradition for making powerful and special medicines. They involve wondrous phenomena such as those mentioned above or indeed the powdering of diamond to make it blend with other substances in medicinal preparations.

Nowadays many people are involved in the practice of Tibetan medicine in Tibet itself and medical equipment and many medicines are available. Much money and foresight have gone into redeveloping the Tibetan Medical Institute in Lhasa. Yet there is still much to do before the fullness of Tibetan medicine is well-established for centuries to come. This will involve, among other things, gathering the necessary rare ingredients to make many traditional medicines which have not been made for some decades now and which present-day doctors do not know how to prepare.

Much skill, knowledge and experience goes into the preparation of Tibetan medicines. Medicines prepared in Tibet are often regarded as more effective than the same remedies prepared in other Himalayan countries. There are many reasons why this might be so. First there is the land itself: its geography, climate and altitude are quite unique. A religious person might say that centuries of widespread and profound religious practice imbibed the hills and valleys with something special too. The location of specific plants and how they are collected are also significant.

Over the millenia, we have come to know the best places to collect each herb and it is very important that this knowledge be preserved and that the environment in which they grow remain unpolluted. Each area, as well as a specific location within each area, has its floral speciality and the plants there have a particular potency. One needs to know exactly when to pick the plant not only in terms of its life cycle but also in terms of astrology and time of day. Traditional explanations even indicate who should pick the plant and how it should be gathered. Following these directions properly produces a very different raw material. Once the finest raw materials have been gathered, these need to be processed and combined to make the various medicines. Not only does this need to be done properly, from a technical point of view, but, according to the medical tradition, with prayer and in the proper state of compassionate mind.

If, in the West, a plant has been found to have medicinal

value, its active ingredient is analysed and then produced synthetically. In Tibet, we believe that there is more in a plant than just a chemical active ingredient; there is a fragile elemental energy that can also be harnessed. Perhaps modern research, which finds ever more subtle chemicals and processes, will one day confirm this. Furthermore, rather than treating one symptom with one antidote, we aim to treat the whole body. Therefore we use medicines with many ingredients, administering different complex compounds in the morning, afternoon and evening because the bodily energies change through the day.

At the Lhasa Medical Institute traditional Tibetan medical literature, Tibetan astological literature, as well as grammar, language and composition, Chinese language, English language, politics and other related subjects, are studied. The Tibetan medical system and literature have always emphasised the purity of motivation and conduct of doctors and—as the quality of the physician's mind determines the quality of the medical treatment itself—it is essential that there be enough training and instruction given on these topics. In the past, the *bodhisattva* attitude was nurtured by studying the classical Buddhist scriptures about the *bodhisattva* path (*Ratnāvalī, Bodhicaryāvatāra* etc), which are gradually being reintroduced.

Besides the restoration of the traditional medicines and medical ethic, various techniques and implements used in more ancient times are also being revived. Unlike the type of operations one sees in the West, where the body is opened up on a large scale, Tibetan surgery was minimally invasive, used mainly to remove tumours from different organs and parts of the body. At one point these techniques formed part of Tibetan medical practice but now are almost forgotten. We hope to regain the know-how of these old wisdoms and to reintroduce those which may be of use today.

Looking beyond Tibet, it is evident that there are many new diseases in the world, such as cancer and AIDS. As a result of greater contact with the outside world there are also new diseases in Tibet itself. There are plans to establish a research wing to investigate such diseases at the Institute. Through research and an enthusiastic re-establishment of Tibetan medicine, we hope to be able to contribute to the effort of combatting some of these maladies. The healing art is one of the finest sciences a human being can apply himself to, and I am convinced that the traditional wisdom and the exceptional possibilities offered by Tibetan medicine will have something to contribute to the medical understanding of the coming millenium.

Notes

1 Samye Ling hosted the first teaching session of the Tara-Rokpa Tibetan Medical College, set up by the Rokpa Trust (Scotland) in conjunction with the Central Institute (Lhasa). Khenpo Tsenam officially opened the College and supervised the first month of instruction. Also teaching were Dr Sonam Chime, Assistant Professor at the Lhasa *Mentsikhang*, and Dr Thubten Phuntsog, Assistant Professor at the University of Nationalities in Beijing.

2 Rokpa is an international charity deeply committed to the revitalisation of Tibetan medicine in Tibet. It is working in conjunction with local authorities to put more doctors in remote areas. So far, eleven medical colleges, providing primary and secondary education and traditional medical training to 310 students, have been set up, with a view to providing country doctors and to giving priority and career opportunity to bright young girls.

3 The technique was given to Khedrup Orgyenpa, by Vajrayogini, in the land of Orgyen. He taught it to Karmapa Rangjung Dorje, who taught it to Sonam Zangpo, who was the grandfather of Sungkar Nyamme Dorje and it became the Tsurpu tradition. During the time of the Fifth Dalai Lama it was made by Dharam Nyammo. Later Situ Choji Jungnas made it in Derge. Other famous lamas of more recent times, in the last century, such as Kongtrul Lodro Taye, Jamyang Chentse Wangpo, Mipham Rinpoche and so forth maintained the tradition, many of them having a strong link with Derge.

Medical charm (fu) from the Yushujing, 'Canon of the Jade Pivot', a manual of rituals of the Quanzhen (Complete Realisation) school of Taoism.

Inner courtyard of a Taoist temple. After a visit to the temple's many shrines, including that of Shennong, the medicine god, taoists complete their worship at the central incense burner.

名醫華佗
壽亭侯關羽
一勇斎國芳画

where it comes from. His *Jingui Yaolüe Fang* (Summarised Prescriptions from the Golden Case), containing recipes, is a famous text as well.

A later practitioner is Ge Hong (third-fourth century), actually a Taoist alchemist whose writings (*Baopuzi*, also his pseudonym) contain interesting details about the Taoist medicine of the time.[11] Like other alchemists he contributed to the further development of a systematised pharmacology. The third century also witnessed the appearance of books on herbal medicine, such as the *Shen Nong Bencaojing* (Classic of Roots and Herbs of Shen Nong). The Chinese herbal medicine tradition and literature on pharmacology (Chinese medicinal recipes contain not only herbal but also animal and mineral ingredients) reached its climax many centuries later, during the Ming dynasty (1368-1644).

A sophisticated text on acupuncture is the *(Huangdi) Jiayijing* (Essential Classic of the Yellow Emperor), written by Huang Fumi in the third century, a text describing acupunture, but also rephrasing theories of (mostly) *Neijing* origin. Later physicians and scholars wrote commentaries on it and used it as a basis for their own works. Diagnosis was a topic in the most ancient classics, though pulse diagnosis in particular is discussed in detail in the *Maijing* (Classic on *Mai* [these are important roads of circulation of fluid-like substances in the body, but also the pulse where these circulations can be measured]), written by Wang Shuhe in the fourth century. Wang mentions 24 types of pulse.

Like Ge Hong, the Taoist physician and writer Tao Hongjing (fifth century), was an alchemist, but his contributions to the general medical tradition were essentially pharmacological. His works also contain notes on the cultivation of life (*yangsheng*, how to keep one's health through certain ways of living), a favourite Taoist theme.

Taoists and others of this period, and also those of the Sui-Tang era (seventh to tenth century), were influenced by the ascendency of Buddhism and its contributions to Chinese medicine. Chinese and Tibetan Buddhist scriptures dealing with medicinal recipes and the descriptions of certain therapeutic exercises affected one of the great Taoist physicians of this period, Sun Simiao (581-*c.* 682). His most famous writings are the *Qian Jin Yao Fang* (Essential Recipes Worth a Thousand Gold Pieces) and *Qian Jin Yi Fang* (Additional Recipes Worth a Thousand Gold Pieces), an expansion of the former written several decades later.[12] Both works contain recipes for various diseases prescribed by the *yaowang* (King of Medicine), Sun's honourary name. He also distinguishes between general diseases and the problems of children and women, writes about acupuncture and exercise, and the cultivation of life. It is a comprehensive book on preserving and restoring health, and one of the most influential books on Chinese medicine.

A classic on the origin of diseases, written in the seventh century by Chao Yuanfang, is the *Chaoshi Bingyuan* (The Origin of Diseases according to Mr. Chao), also known as *Zhubing Yuan Hou Lun* (Treatise on the Phenomena of the Origin of Diseases).

In Song and Yuan times (tenth-fourteenth century), the study of *xue* became predominant. *Xue* are the holes or apertures—so-called acu[puncture] points—and sensitive places on and in the body that are treated in various ways to influence *qi* circulation. During the Song dynasty physicians created and used a model known as the 'bronze man' (*tongren*), a bronze mannequin showing the *xue* then known. Written descriptions of the bronze man also appear at this time. The Song period is also known for developments in anatomical research based on the dissection of corpses.

Li Shizhen (1518-93) of the Ming dynasty wrote his *Bencao Gangmu* (Outlines of Roots and Herbs Studies) as a true encyclopaedia of *materia medica*, discussing the characteristics of medicinal ingredients. His methods of examining *mai* also became popular with physicians of later times.

The early Qing dynasty (1644-1911) saw further developments in medicine and culture, but the later Qing did more to impede cultural creativity than to encourage it. The year 1822 is crucial. The Imperial Medical College (Taiyi Yuan) prohibited most therapeutic techniques that required the patient to undress because this was considered highly indecent, even for medical purposes.[13] However, medical work—especially popular medicine—did not suffer too badly and more medical texts were written, mainly commentaries on, and expansions of, older texts. In the meantime Taoist medical concepts reached a climax through the development of internal alchemy, a technique or method requiring from the practitioner the utmost use of body and mind. This became the supreme Taoist exercise, which led to new physiological and psychological insights. Fundamentally, the practice of inner alchemy was based on the creation of a stable, healthy

Opposite: Hua To, the legendary Chinese surgeon, operates on the wounded arm of the war hero Huan Keng who is playing chess to distract his attention from the pain. Japanese colour print. Wellcome Institute, London.

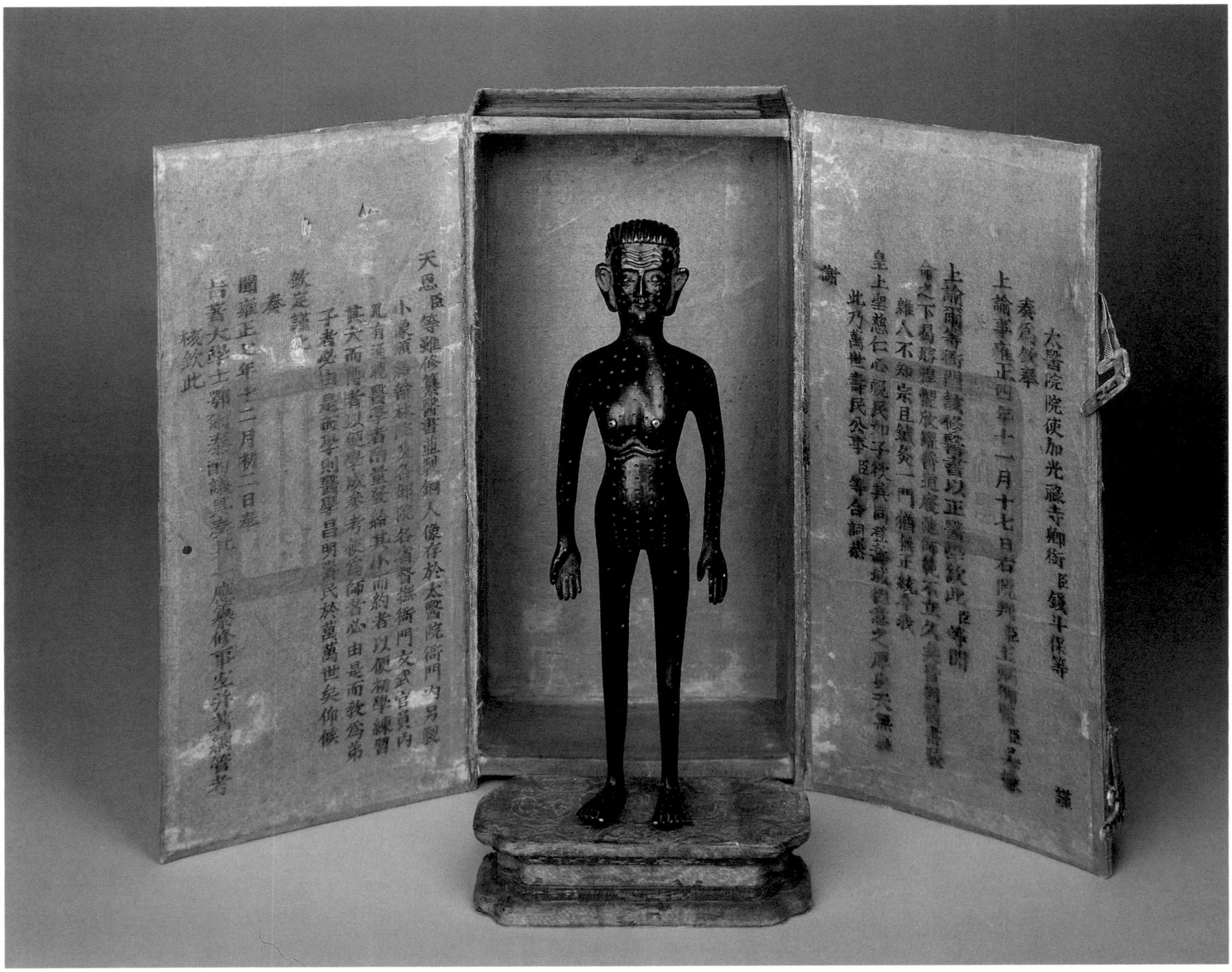

Bronze acupuncture figure, 26.2 cms. high, in a box disguised as a book, covered with imperial yellow silk. The box has four inscriptions, all containing the imperial seal mark of emperor Yung Cheng (Yongzheng), r.1723-1735. One of the inscriptions on the outside of the cover reads: 'Made under the command of the Imperial Ministry of Medicine at Kung Lu temple by Chien Tue Pao (Artisan) an accurate model for acupuncture and pressure points to assist research. By order of the Emperor Yung Cheng, 17th November 4th year (1726).'

Part of the inscription on the inside reads as follows. 'We have also made other models for the Academy and other centers of learning, for the offices of the Provincial Governors and Ministers of the Imperial Court who have knowledge of medicine ... for beginners to practice with so that more people can know how to use acupuncture and to educate students.' Collection: John Barnett, UK.

condition and in this way its preliminary exercises were suitable for *yangsheng*, a whole way of living. These ideas spread widely, first among Taoists who could read the many reference works of Taoist literature, but by the end of the Qing such information reached other Chinese intellectuals.[14]

The twentieth century is characterised by the promotion and expansion of Western medicine in China, a phenomenon that evolved out of earlier contacts with Westerners (mainly medical missionaries), the efforts of foreign governments in the nineteenth century, and especially proselytisation by Christian organisations. Fortunately, Chinese medicine has survived, even if its modern, official version is Western in philosophical approach.

The Taoist view of the body in medical practice: the internal world

Traditional Chinese views of the body, whatever their origin, were influenced by the Taoist concept of bodily functions and its ideas about the internal world of the human body.[15] Basically, Taoists view the body as a small world, a country or even a model of the universe (*tiandi*). Like any other country the internal landscape (*neijing*) is governed by a ruler (*zhi*, to govern),[16] called *junzhu* in the *Neijing*. Government is a serious business, so the ruler is assisted by officials and ministers who also keep assistants in their service. It is understood that if this country is to prosper, these ministers should facilitate each other's work and harmonise their multilateral relations lest the whole country should suffer from their misconduct.

Transport and communication in this internal world are based on a well-developed system of watercourses, originating from several sources and flowing towards the four seas. There are twelve main arteries, just like the twelve main rivers of ancient China, and they are filled with a water-like substance called *qi*. The internal realm is full of things that appear in the macrocosm: stars, mountains, woods, lakes, waterfalls, animals, human beings. When all these are in harmony and the country is well-governed, the human body enjoys perfect health. This condition is referred to as *zheng* (upright, correct). Unfortunately, it is hard to keep the body in good shape and frequently its functioning is chaotic and uncoordinated. Instead of being 'upright' the body is 'on a slant' (*xie*). External influences create internal reactions that interfere with the normal processes of government, though these external factors do not necessarily bring about disease. In fact, they can often be beneficial. They are represented as natural phenomena—wind, heat, cold—and these forces produce the same kinds of results within the human body as they do outside it.

In Taoist religion it is believed that the body is inhabited by spirits (*shen*), which live in the body's important areas and take care of its different functions.[17] Certain circumstances, such as dreaming, allow the *shen* to leave the body temporarily and communicate with the celestial spirit world. Some Taoist rituals and medical practices (e.g. *fu*-writing)[18] are concerned with appeasing the *shen*, thus harmonising the

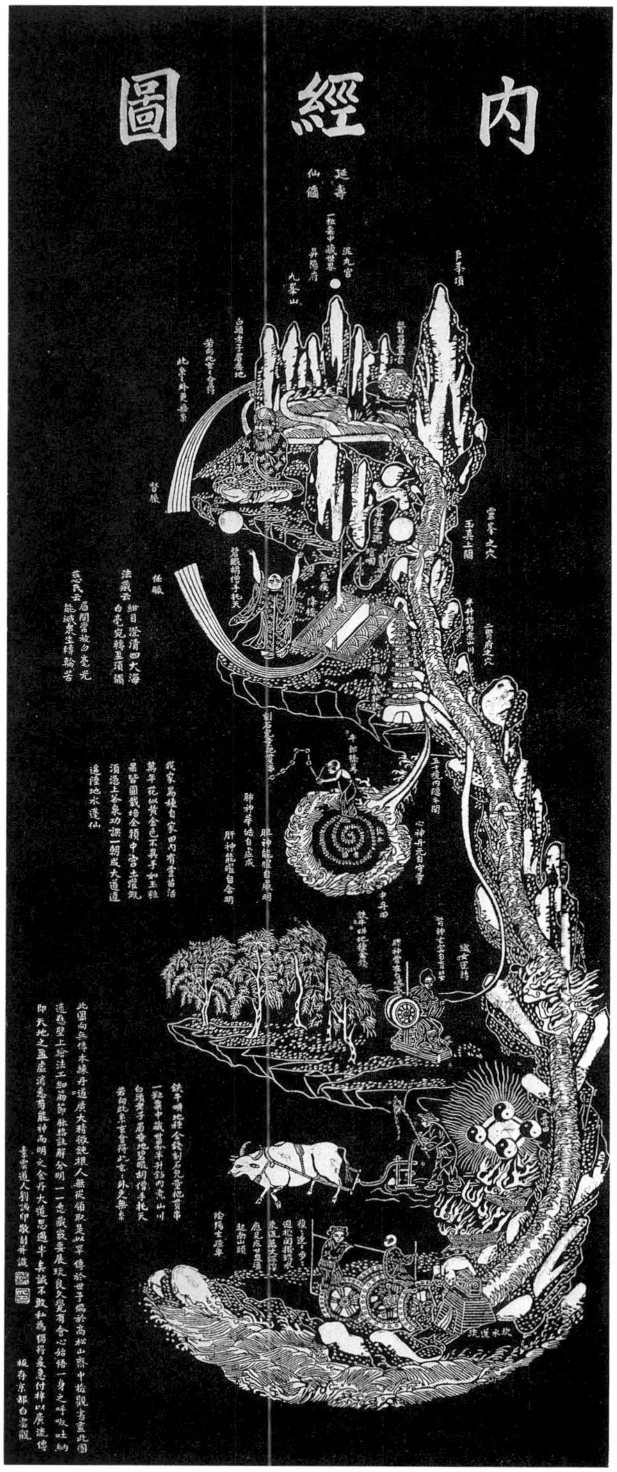

Neijing Tu, *stone rubbing from the Baigunguan Temple, Beijing. The inner landscape, reflecting the ancient Taoist medico-philosophical concept of the human body as a microcosm: stars depicted as the herd-boy (in Aquila); a woman spinning (Vega in Lyra); an old man symbolising the Lord of the Inner World; a forest representing gan, one of the fundamental bodily functions; a mountain ridge representing the spine. Specifically Taoist alchemical symbols include: the lower field of cinnabar (dantian) as a revolving circle of taiji (yin-yang) symbols, radiating heat, and as a field being ploughed to cultivate the herb of immortality. Collection Dan Vercammen, Belgium.*

body. After death—which is itself the defeat of *zhengqi* (correct functioning of the body)—the spirits discard the body and take up their positions in the celestial hierarchy. According to popular belief, family members of the deceased should honour his spirit and do all that is necessary to allow the *shen* to find a good position. Appropriate treatment of *shen* always took place when treating a patient, even if the practitioner was not a Taoist. Ancient medical works usually contained notes on where and when to locate *shen* in the body, so that they would not be hurt by treating the wrong place at the wrong time.[19]

Medical treatment aims at preventing problems or restoring a normal situation and it tries to make the patient recover completely, though eventually, people—like any other part of the macrocosm—must die. Taoists, however, say there exist ways of escaping this end. Whilst traditional medicine does not include treatments that defy death, Taoist 'alchemists' study ways of prolonging life beyond normal limits so that man can live 'as long as heaven and earth'. In this way man becomes *dao* (the way) and *dao* becomes man. This is achieved by taking in 'medicine' (*yao*), be it the external kind, consisting of minerals, metals or herbs (*waiyao*, external medicine), or the internal kind (*neiyao*) developed inside the human body through special exercises, and without the help of *waiyao*. These sophisticated practices are reputed to change man's genetic material, and might even cure genetic diseases.[20] For many Taoists this remains the supreme training, attainable by the few, leading to 'long-life without death' (*changsheng busi*). In fact, this leads not to immortality, but to a delivery from the world of creation and destruction. It is like turning things upside down or going the wrong way, which is itself the way of *dao*.[21]

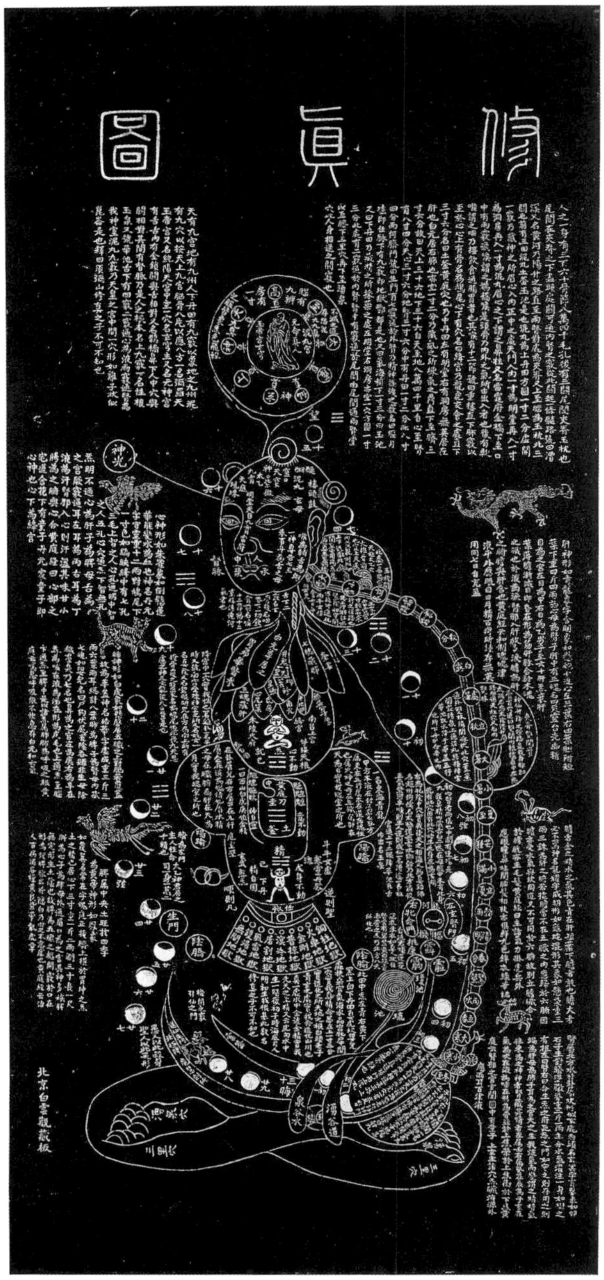

Xiuzhen Tu, *stone rubbing from the Baigunguan Temple, Beijing. The Development of Truth. The inner universe is represented in alchemical symbolism: the blue-green dragon (ginglong), symbol of Yang-qi; the white tiger (baihu), symbol of yingi; the vessel (ding) for exchanging their essences; the carts drawn by a goat, a deer and a bull, symbols of the use of yi (mental power), by which jing (essence) is transported along the backbone to the brain. The cyclical evolution of the years is shown as changing yin-yang circles, explaining the effect of concentration and transportation of qi. Alchemical practice leads to the development of an embryo, called 'true man' (zhenren), that will arise from the head (of the human being above) to become one with Dao. Collection Dan Vercammen, Belgium*

The ruler and his assistants

In China, the view of the body as a country or microcosm of the universe is essentially Taoist. The *Neijing* contains a chapter on the governing of this country.[22] Within the book different concepts of the body are integrated, so that we find ancient Taoist (i.e. functional) ideas in one chapter, and newer, more exact, descriptions of the dimensions and weight of 'organs' in another. Neither approach is 'scientific', yet both were attempts at identifying substances, functions, feelings and experiences connected with the whole body and mind in a way that was of practical use to the people for whom this work was written. Its confusing and paradoxical concepts, which present problems to a Western scientific mind, were and still are of use to the Chinese physician. What cannot be explained clearly by means of one theory may well be 'logical' from another point of view. If we take this into consideration, the text has its own validity—it looks for answers and provides different opinions for the reader to digest and select.[23]

Following on from the view that the body can be seen as a country, the *Neijing* tells us that the Supreme Lord of this state is called *xin*, often translated as 'heart-mind', but referring equally to 'centre', which is the most important and centralised function in the human body. He is concerned with *shen*, the spirits, and is one of twelve state officials. The other eleven officials are listed below:

fei ('lungs'): an official concerned with internal connections and instructions, taking care of adjusting conditions;
gan ('liver'): a military official who makes decisions and plans;
dan ('gallbladder'): a justice official, responsible for verdicts;
chanzhong or *tanzhong* (altar at the centre of the body): directs the official messengers and is capable of making one feel joyous. In the medical tradition this term does not usually appear as one of the ministers; *chanzhong* is described elsewhere in the *Neijing* (*Lingshu*, chapter 35) as being the wall to the palace of the Supreme Lord, *xin*;
pi-wei ('spleen-stomach'): two officials who control the barns for storage of cereals (food), thus making us taste things;
dachang ('large intestine'): a transport official, transformation (of food) is what pertains to his office;
xiaochang ('small intestine'): an official whose office receives any excess, and who makes sure that the transformed matter (food being digested) can leave the body;
shen ('kidneys'): the 'enforcer' and 'activator', he forces the body to do things, stores its power and controls mental and physical capacities;
sanjiao ('the three burners'): responsible for opening sluices and concerned with watercourses;
pangguang ('bladder'): an official concerned with water regions, where fluids are stored and transformed.

It is stated explicitly in this chapter of the *Neijing* that the ruler should be enlightened or illuminated (*ming*) lest the country and its officials fall into disorder. Otherwise, the roads connecting different parts of the body may become blocked, which is harmful to man's health.

At first glance, this description of the internal world may seem partly clear (some of the Chinese 'organs' are comparable to Western notions of organs) and partly obscure (e.g. the explanation of *sanjiao*).[24] Any confusion actually derives from not understanding the Chinese point of view. When examining ancient Chinese concepts of the body we should not think of 'organs', but rather of phenomena we know from the world around us. Indeed, most people are at a loss when confronted with their own body and its power, but know a great deal about the outside world.

Taoists affirm that it is not necessary to look for *dao* in external places, for it is right here, right now, within us. Understanding *dao* therefore means understanding that with which we are continually confronted: our own body. Perhaps early Taoists chose to make the workings of the body more readily comprehensible by using images from the familiar outside world.[25]

The officials of the inner world are also seen as storage-places (*zang-fu*). *Zang* and *fu* have different functions; *zang* are reservoirs, used to store what is of capital importance to the functioning of body and mind, and *fu* are temporary storage-places or palaces that hold waste material until it can be transported, transformed, and ultimately expelled from the body through the orifices (*qiao*), the 'holes' (*xue*) and the pores (*maokong*). As storage-places, *zang* and *fu* can be measured. Both the *Neijing* and the *Nanjing* mention their size and weight.[26] For instance, the *Lingshu* (chapter 32) describes *wei* ('stomach') as measuring one *chi* and five *cun* in circumference, two *chi* and six *cun* in length, having a diametre of five *cun* and a capacity of three *dou* and five *sheng*.[27] Its position is horizontal and it is bent in shape.

Change and movement are the essence of the universe, and so it is for the human body. Therefore, *zang* and *fu* perform their duties mainly through their main watercourses (*jing*). These are the channels through which *qi* flows and they are interconnected directly and indirectly through smaller channels, called *luo*, that diverge into even smaller vessels, called *sun*. Still other main channels are called *mai* (arteries or vessels), located in the body's most important parts, like the spinal column or the waist, through which *qi* and *xue* (blood-fluids) are circulated. In fact, the *qi*-roads, like *jing*, are not to be seen as anatomical parts of the body but as the correct, fastest 'ways' of connecting different places in the body. The Chinese therapist should make himself familiar with the exact location of *xue*, holes or apertures through which the flow of *qi* may be influenced, so as to become acquainted with the *qi*-roads, since these are nothing more than the normal connections between *xue*. Traditionally, the names and locations of these points on the human body would be memorised by learning rhymes or songs which incorporated all the names, and by observing drawings or studying the 'bronze man' (*tongren*).[28] Modern methods include studying the locations of *xue* on the basis of Western-style anatomical charts and accurate models. All *xue* bear names that refer to their place in the inner world or their shape (e.g. *xue* '*quchi*', curved pond or pond in a bend, located at the bend of the elbow) or the function they fulfill within the microcosm (e.g. *qihai*, the 'sea of *qi*', a point under the umbilicus functioning as a reservoir of *qi*).

The fundamental idea behind this systematic knowledge of crucial areas of the body is that there is a continual movement of 'something' (Taoists sometimes refer to *qi* as *wu*, 'thingy') inside and outside the body, which should be observed and understood. This 'moving thing' has its natural direction and rhythm. Each and every part of the body is reached by this omnipresent *qi*, but it is more active and more concentrated in one part or another according to a naturally regulated pattern determined by the rhythm of the universe. Whenever man acts contrary to his own rhythm and the universal rhythm, he is liable to contract diseases because his natural immunity system (*weiqi*, protective *qi*) and nourishing system (*yingqi*, nourishing *qi*) have diminished 'fuel'. The *qi* has become blocked somewhere in its circulation.

Since the whole body is interconnected and there is a pattern to these connections, an irregular situation can be dealt with through knowledge of the body's important spots and their interrelationships. It may be more efficient to treat not the affected area, but some of the connected parts in order to create a new balance in the body. The *qi* should be distributed properly over the entire body, increasing the amount of activity in some places and reducing agitation in others. There are appropriate therapies for all cases, and these are described in ancient and modern medical handbooks. It should be clear that the importance of *qi* and what it represents—movement, change and their opposites—are essential to the Chinese (Taoist) medical perception of the body.

The principles of change, *yin* and *yang*

Chinese philosophers have always concerned themselves with understanding changes in the universe, some to control those changes and others to create stability.[29] In the world of medicine changes occur all the time and understanding such fluctuations can mean the difference between life and death.

'The Inner world' or the order of 'Later Heaven' (Bagua: the 8 trigrams). Yin and Yang, combine in one circle (taiji), become fourfold (heaven, earth, sun and moon) and produce by their interaction the eight trigrams or eight natural phenomena (heaven, lake, fire, thunder, wind, water, mountain, earth). These symbols are used in philosophy, medicine, geomancy, fortune telling and many other branches of Chinese culture. They represent the symbols of constant change. Collection Mark De Fraeye, Belgium.

Many a Westerner possesses a copy of the *Yijing* (I Ching, or Book of Changes) in translation and uses it at leisure to find answers to puzzling questions.[30] In China, too, this ancient book was frequently consulted by diviners and common folk alike to solve the mysteries of life. For philosophers, however, it was a source of wisdom and the key to understanding universal changes. Neo-Confucianists, like the influential Zhu Xi (1130-1200) and his predecessor Zhou Dunyi (1012-73), commented on and interpreted the *Yijing* and its Confucian commentaries, thus preparing the way for what was to become China's orthodox philosophy.

There exists a far less known but equally important Taoist collection of commentaries and explanations on the use of the *Zhouyi*, the *Zhouyi Can Tong Qi*, one of the most important classics of Chinese alchemy.[31] It contributed to the development of Taoist medicine and expanded the field of pharmacology. The *Yijing* reduces the complex manifestations of change to the simple observation that any change is created by the interplay of two 'forces', *yin* and *yang*. The written characters *yin* and *yang* show their fundamental meaning; they are the two faces of a single mountain, one face bright and sunny (*yang*), the other cloudy and dark (*yin*). The amount of light shining on the mountain changes continually, and the sunny side will become darker after some time, when the darker side brightens.

The ubiquity of change in the universe means that everything, once simpified, can be explained through the *yin-yang* theory. One only has to replace the words *yin* and *yang* with other words that express the same principle of two opposing yet united aspects of an entity. What is warm, positive, hard, active and male belongs to *yang*, what is cold, negative, soft, passive and female to *yin*. *Yang* and *yin* must be understood as neutral words, without any intention of discrimination.

The *Yijing* expresses *yin-yang* by means of lines (*yao*), a full line being *yang*, a broken line being *yin*. When these lines combine and interfere with one another different combinations of lines result. These combinations, called *gua*, are translated as 'trigrams' when they consist of three lines, and 'hexagrams' when they consist of six. Anything in the universe, including man, can be drawn as a combination of these lines. Both Confucian and Taoist commentaries refer to the human body when commenting on the meaning of *gua*.[32]

The *yin-yang*-theory and the *gua* are used extensively in ancient Chinese medicine as a means to describe the human constitution, to grasp the origin of diseases and their evolution, and to guide the practitioner in his treatment. For example, the upper part of the body is seen as more *yang* than the lower part, the top of the head (the warmest part of the body) being supreme *yang*. The front of the body is more *yin* than the back. The exterior (skin, muscles) is seen as more *yang* than the interior (organs). Located in the front of the body, the chest is more *yin* than the buttocks, but at the same time the buttocks are more *yin* than the chest because they are closer to the feet (the utmost *yin* in the vertical alignment of the body). The *zang*, being hollow, permanent storage-places, are considered *yin* because their operations have an inward (*yin*) direction when compared to the *fu*, solid, temporary storage-places with outwardly-directed (*yang*) operations. Because *zang* have a *yin* function and *fu* operate in a *yang* way, they may be viewed as complementary pairs—a *zang* has no use without its *fu*.

Relativity is essential in understanding the *yin-yang* theory because nothing is forever *yin* or *yang*; something can be more *yang* in a certain situation, under certain conditions, at a certain time, but it is likely to change into its opposite when conditions alter. There is no absolute certainty, no absolute truth. There is only change, and nothing except *dao* can escape being changed. This relative conception of *yin* and *yang* can also be applied to the genesis of disease. Whenever *yin-yang* proportions are not as they should be, the body falls into disorder. Order can be restored by adapting the *yin-yang* proportions to the situation at hand. If, for instance, *xin* ('heart-mind') is the main source of malfunctioning, the root cause may be deficient *yin* and excessive *yang*, too much heat and not enough cooling. Restoration of the original balance becomes the goal. Herbal medicine, massage, acupuncture or other therapies can then be used to accomplish this. Cooling herbs that mainly influence *xin* might be used. In practice other *zang-fu* will be affected too, so steps must be taken to harmonise the entire interrelated complex.

This is the basic philosophical explanation of the origin and treatment of diseases, though other concepts also played an important role in the Chinese view of the universe.[33]

Wuxing (five agents)

The Naturalist School of philosophy, also known as the Yin-Yang School, evolved from naturalist, even shamanistic, practices. Zhou Yan (third century BC) is the school's most famous representative. The Naturalist School developed the *yin-yang* theory and also viewed relationships between worldly phenomena as dependent upon five ever-changing 'ingredients'. These five were called *wuxing* (five agents), the essence of a complex system of correspondences that govern the universe, five essential components which constitute evolution in its different phases.[34] Wood, fire, earth, metal and water (*mu, huo, tu, jin, shui*) are intertwined within two basic relationships. One is a productive relationship (*xiangsheng*), whereby one agent helps to create another. The other is a controlling relationship (*xiangke*), whereby one agent limits the impact of another (see drawing overleaf).

Any relationship between elements of the universe can be seen as a *wuxing* relationship, allowing for a systematic categorisation of things and their interactions (the table indicates how different sets of relations can be integrated in this system).

As can be observed, the *zang* and *fu* are compatible with the *xing*. Using this system, the Chinese physician was able

wuxing (five agents)	five colours	five *qi*	five phases in evolution	five periods (seasons)	five directions	five *zang*	five *fu*	five officials	five tastes	five essential substances	five tempers (dispositions)
mu wood	dark bluish green	wind	come into existence	spring	east	*gan*	*dan*	eyes	sour	sinews	anger
huo fire	reddish brown	heat	grow	summer	south	*xin*	*xiao-chang*	tongue	bitter	vessels	joy
tu earth	yellow gold	dampness	transform	prolonged	centre	*pi*	*wei*	mouth	sweet	muscles	think-toil
jin metal	white	dryness	harvest	autumn	west	*fei*	*dachang*	nose	spicy	body hair	sadness
shui water	black	cold	store	winter	north	*shen*	*pang guang*	ears	salty	bones	fear

Wuxing Chart

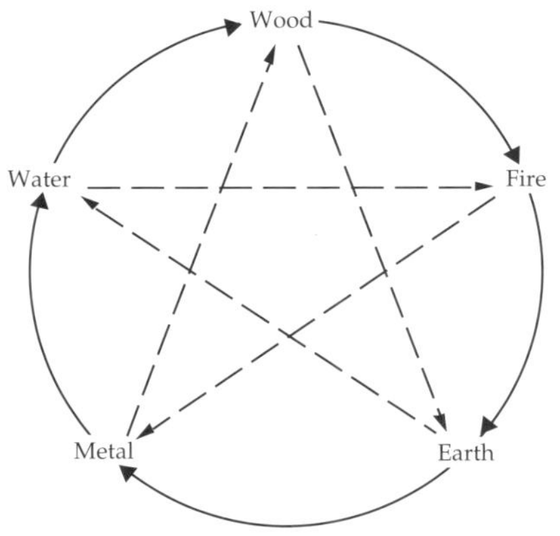

The Five Agents: Relations between agents
——— production
- - - - - - - - - control

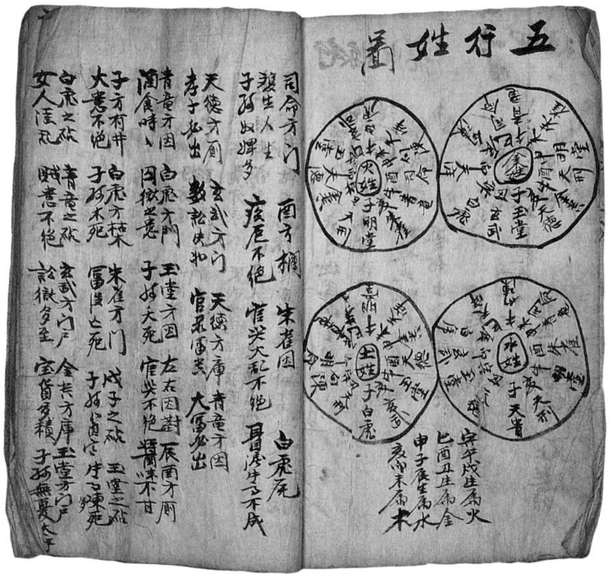

Page from the manual of a Korean shaman, describing the Wuxing correlation with diseases. In many Far Eastern communities, the shaman is often the first to be consulted on the cause of an illness. Collection Mark De Fraeye, Belgium.

to notice causative and consecutive evolutions in the body.

For example, when *gan* ('liver', corresponding to wood) is in bad condition, the first place affected is *xin* because the former helps in the creation of the latter's action. On the other hand, *pi* ('spleen', corresponding to earth) might become too strong because *gan* is losing its influence on it.

Wuxing is not a rigid, dogmatic theory, but rather a way to better understand how things work. The example given above leaves room for interpretation. *Xin* is the 'producer' of *pi*, so when *xin* is weakened by a weakening *gan*, *pi* may also be weakened through *xin* instead of becoming stronger as in our supposition.

Practice shows and teaches the likely outcome, but the practitioner, aware of these equivocal relations, will try to prevent further developments involving the *zang-fu* which are directly related. Therapy is therefore also based on stimulating or inhibiting certain reactions caused by these *wuxing* correspondences.

Qi and other concepts

The word most used and abused in Chinese medicine is *qi*. It is translated as 'energy', 'vital power', or 'inner power', though none of these translations adequately grasp its actual meaning. Several scholars have suggested that *qi* be left untranslated.[35]

The written character representing *qi* in its ancient form shows water transforming into vapour and means 'clouds of vapour'. In practice, *qi* has many meanings. For instance, when a Chinese talks about breathing he uses the word *qi* to express 'breath'. When talking about the weather, he says *tianqi* (heavenly *qi*, natural *qi*). When a person's body shows signs of weakness, a physician confirms that the person's *qi* is malfunctioning. One can hardly assume that all this is merely vapour at work. *Qi* is complex in nature, highly changeable and—like vapour—it suddenly appears, only to disappear again the next moment or undergo a protean alteration. Its characteristics are manifold. *Qi* is that which can change and cause change at the same time; that which can sometimes be seen and sometimes not.

The *Yunji Qiqian* claims that *qi* works within everything in the universe, and is also *dao*.[36] Our perception of it is limited; we can only notice some of its consequences and know little of its origin or constitution. Sinologists like Porkert have noted that *qi* can be compared to electricity, and in fact *dianqi* (lightning-*qi*) is the Chinese word for electricity.[37]

Chinese philosophers found the term *qi* handy for labelling things inexplicable and illogical. For Taoists and physicians it formed the essence of existence and the understanding of cosmic evolution. We already know that *yin* and *yang* were used to explain all changes, but they are nothing more than *qi* itself, namely *yinqi* and *yangqi*. In other words, the theory of *qi* can be combined with other theories of change, the main preoccupation for Chinese philosophers.

Relations between the *wuxing* (five agents) are determined by *qi*. Different phenomena caused by, or involving, *qi* are described as different manifestations of *qi*, and prefixes are added to differentiate these multiple manifestations. Chinese medicine frequently uses the following words associated with *qi*:

yuanqi: original or source *qi*, the source of all other manifestations of *qi* in the human body; refers to the original condition at a person's conception;

zhengqi: *zheng* means 'straight', 'correct', 'upright'; it is used for the correct functioning of the body; when a person is healthy, he is said to have strong *zhengqi*; throughout a person's life his *zhengqi* is fighting its opposite, *xieqi*, which represents many (mainly external) influences that may cause disease;

xieqi: the opposite of *zhengqi*; *xieqi*, when too strong, causes illness;

zhenqi: real or true *qi*; refers to *qi* that truly works as it should and is thus comparable with *zhengqi*; *zhen* is a Taoist term, used for when one, through practice, becomes different from the common man, this state of realisation means that one is devoid of the corruptions typical of an ordinary life;

zongqi: ancestral *qi*, referring to the *qi* one receives from parents and ancestors at conception;[38]

zangfuzhiqi: the *qi* of *zang* and *fu* determines the action of *qi* when it is storing or transforming and expelling things through the *zang-fu*; this *qi* is first received by *wei* ('stomach'), one of the six *fu*, which indicates that it is transformed out of food and drink;

jingluozhiqi: when *qi* moves about in its 'watercourses' it is named *jingluozhiqi*; the *qi* of these roads is said to always return to the *zang* called *fei* ('lungs'), which transports it to the skin and hair on the body (as they depend on *fei*);

shuiguzhiqi: the *qi* of water (*shui*) and cereals (*gu*), due to its nature, is fundamentally a transformation of food and drink, which generally enters the body through the mouth and arrives in the *wei*, which is the official responsible for the imperial storehouses;

weiqi: protective *qi* defends the body, circulates continuously towards the extremities and the skin outside of the *mai* (vessels) and originates from food in the *wei*; as such it is *zhuo* (muddy, dirty) *qi*, composed of what is not stored or used to nourish the body;

yingqi: *qi* that nourishes the body; it is *qing* (clear and clean) *qi* that keeps moving about inside the *mai*.

Other manifestations of *qi* are also mentioned in medical classics, such as the *Neijing*, and frequently relied upon in practice. The causes of diseases discussed below can be categorised as *qi*: *hanqi* (cold *qi*), *fengqi* (wind *qi*) and others. They have the same characteristics as other *qi*, are always changing and can hardly be defined.

One other 'type' of *qi* brings us back to Taoist ideas about health. A text in the *Yunji Qiqian*, called *Yuanqi Lun* (Treatise on Primary Qi),[39] refers to *yuanqi* (primary *qi*), the source of all *qi*. In the body it is the *qi* moving in the *zang* called *shen* ('kidneys'), as well as the root of all *zang* and *fu* and of the twelve *jing* (meridians), the gate of breathing and the source of the *sanjiao* (three burners). The purpose of *yuanqi* in the body is to guard against *xieqi* (slanted *qi*), which should not enter the body. If *yuanqi* acts as it should, *xieqi* cannot enter the body to wreak its destruction.

Yuanqi is in fact *yiqi*, the one, single and unified *qi*, and can be called *dao*. The goal and role of *yuanqi* is to keep the body united, so that it becomes strong enough in itself to repel all evil influences. This fundamental Taoist principle helps us understand why Chinese physicians and philosophers pay so much attention to *prevention* of illness; if we keep our body in shape we do not need medicine.

Certain practices and exercises can actualise this condition and are used to 'guard unity' (*shouyi*), a unified state that leads to the circulation of *qi* without hindrance and the proper cultivation of life.

Other concepts are important in relation to *qi* and appear often in medical and philosophical texts; these are *jing, shen, xue* and *jinye*.

Jing (essence) is considered to be the origin of the body, or that which is needed and essential to make anything what it is. Part of the written character for *jing* means rice, and its basic meaning is 'the best part of rice'.[40] The best part of anything is its *jing*. For Taoists and their medical tradition there is 'former-nature *jing*' (*xiantianzhijing*), which stands for the essence of man (fertile secretions from male and female sexual glands), and 'later-nature-*jing*' (*houtianzhijing*), the essence of that which is taken in by breathing, eating and drinking. Without this *jing* the body would not exist, nor could it make *qi* (*qi* is the transformation of *jing*). In Taoist alchemy the art of transforming *jing* into *qi* is fundamental to the success of the entire alchemical process. To keep one's health, it is essential to guard one's *jing*. Thus it can be understood that the sexual life of the patient is an interesting source of information for the physician. When too much *jing* is lost, it cannot be replaced and the body is depleted of its essential source. Many famous physicians, such as Sun Simiao,[41] commented on sexual activity and its influence on man's condition.

Qi, as a transformation of *jing*, can itself be transformed or refined into *shen* (spirit). *Shen* is in fact a transformation of food and drink, elements that were first transformed into essential *qi* (*jingqi*). It is of the utmost importance to store *shen*, because when it is able to leave the body at will, the body dies. In Taoist religion, keeping the *shen* spirits at ease and preventing them from doing harm is paramount, a task performed by Taoist masters during rituals for the local people. The master commands and controls these spirits which are in fact forces and functions of the human body. Indeed the term *shen* refers to all kinds of mental action but should not be separated from organic actions. What Western psychologists call 'consciousness' and 'sub-consciousness' pertains to *shen* (e.g. being 'unconscious' is a state when *shen* has left the body).

When treating a patient, a physician might consult an instrument to measure time and space (*tuisuanpan*, 'cyclic evolution of the microcosm and macrocosm') in order to find the *shen*'s exact location, for if he inserts a needle incorrectly, at a place where the spirit is residing, he may risk killing the patient instead of curing him. The *shen* circulates constantly throughout the body and is more active in certain areas at certain moments of time; its movements is related to the activity of sun, moon and stars. This relation to the cosmos is logical since man is but a small model of the macrocosm, and it is expressed in an ancient drawing, the Illustration of Developing Trueness (*Xiuzhen Tu*).[42] Taoist philosophy and medicine demand mastering the secrets of time and space.

Body fluids are regarded as essential in Chinese medicine and *qi* itself might be viewed as a transformed fluid. Another important fluid is *xue*, usually translated as blood. It is closely related to *qi* and stored in the *gan* ('liver'). The essence of food and drink changes inside the body and links up with other fluids (*jinye*) to form *xue*, which is distributed throughout the body and may then be named *yingqi* (nourishing *qi*). We can thus assume that it is this *xue* that nourishes the body. The main roads for this nourishing essence are *mai* (vessels), but what do these *mai* represent?

The term *mai* has different meanings throughout the medical classics. Since *xue* runs through them, they are regarded as the *fu* (lodgings, palaces) of these fluids. In this context, *mai* resemble blood-vessels and should be open and able to communicate in order to let the *xue* and *qi* flow. There are eight large *mai* (of which four are single and four are double) comparable to the other large roads in the body, the *jing*, which are twelve in number. The primary *mai* is *dumai* (controlling vessel), situated in the spine and functioning as a communicating vessel between the abdominal region (the area of water) and the head (site of the brain, *nao*, the area of fire).[43] In drawings of the internal microcosm it can be discerned as a river flowing through mountain chains (the backbone), and in medical text illustrations it is drawn as

Compasses (above: Chinese, below: Japanese) intended for geomantic and astrological calculations, and also used for medical purposes, especially to identify locations and circumstances with the healthiest aspects. In China they are called fengshui, in Japan jishaku. Early 19th century, collected between 1823 and 1829 by Philipp Franz von Siebold, 19th century, National Museum of Ethnology, Leiden.

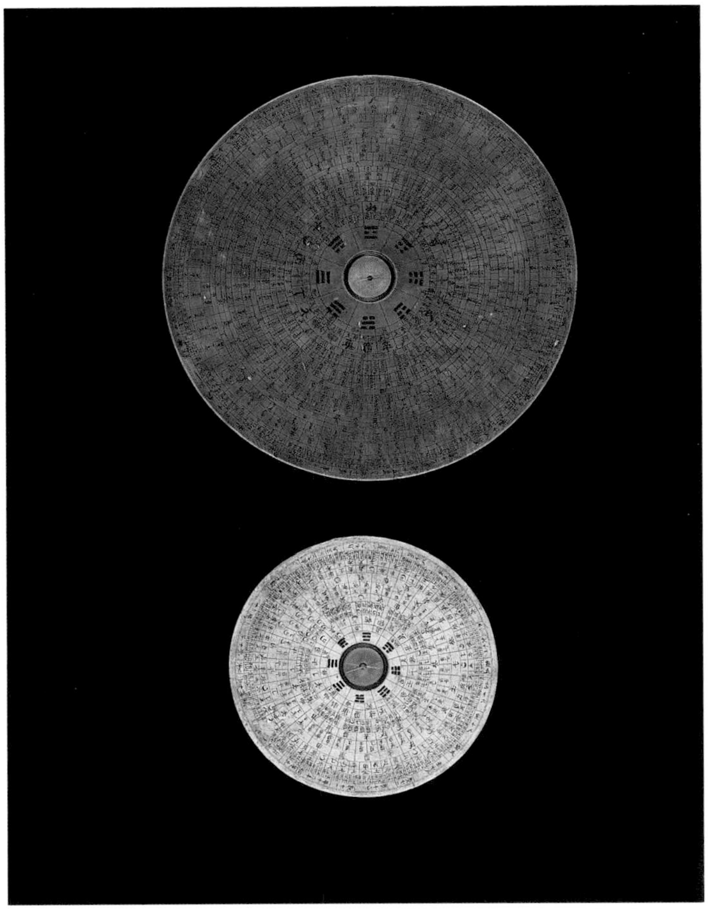

Below: *Set of 33 Chinese surgical instruments in their folding leather case. 19th century (?). Science Museum, London.*

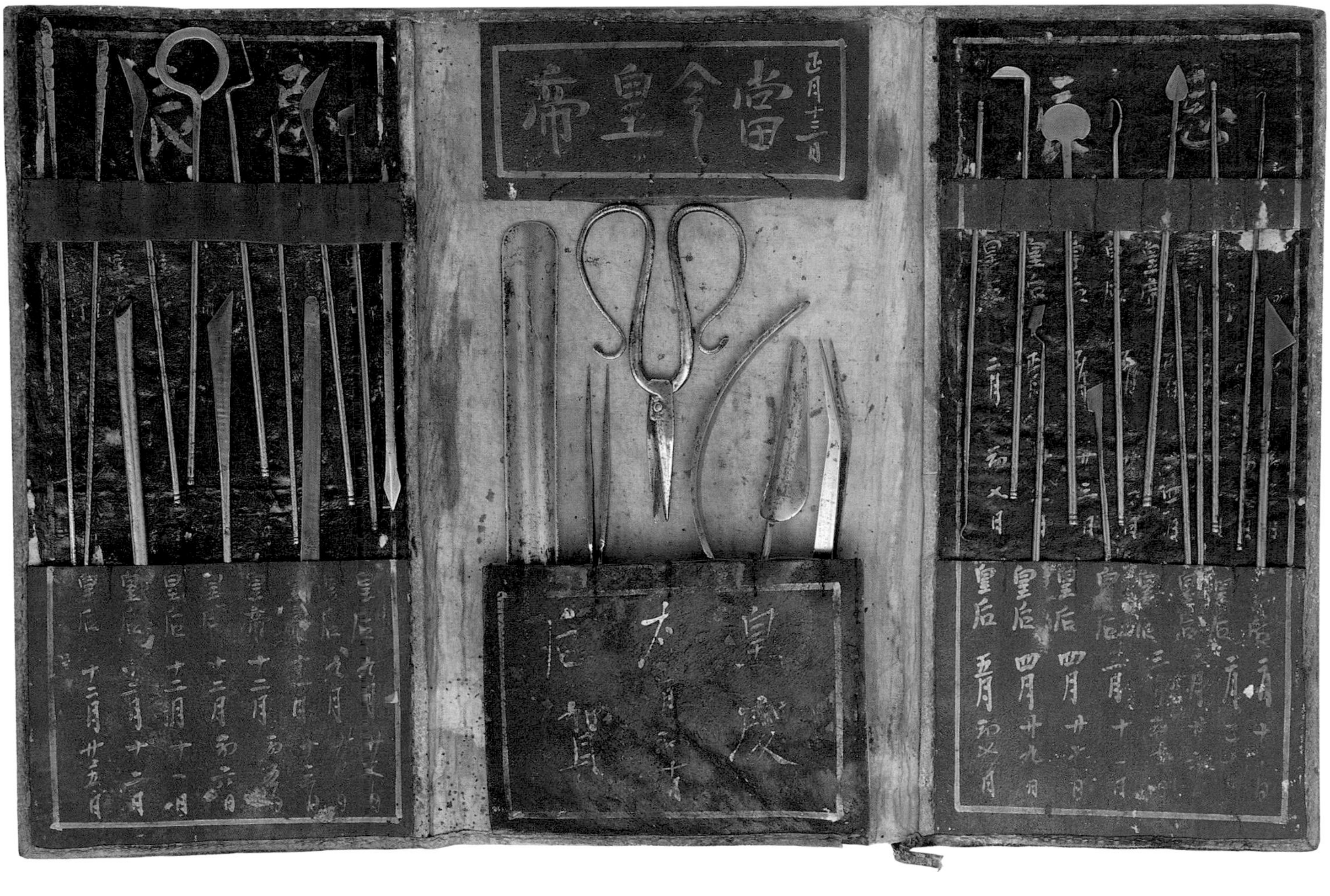

running directly through the backbone and brain. When seen as a river it meets three 'passes' (*guan*) on its way. These are narrow, difficult places, where *qi* and *xue* can hardly pass. Ordinary men, therefore, lose control over their body when growing older because less *qi* reaches the upper part of *dumai*. Taoists and physicians have ways to open *qi*-tracts again, so that everything can be restored to order.

Forming a link with *dumai* is *renmai* (functioning vessel), which can be seen as running centrally through the front of the body. Connecting these two makes the body work well and leads to the expulsion of all disease, since the opening of *dumai* will gradually open all *mai* (*Xing Ming Gui Zhi, yuan*).[44]

The term *jinye* is used for different kinds of fluids, usually five, whose storage-place is the *fu pangguang* ('bladder'). These fluids are necessary elements in the process of making *xue* and each fluid has its own function.

Chinese physicians are concerned with how the body functions, not absolute definitions, because they know everything changes and cannot be restricted to the boundaries of definition. They therefore prefer to observe changes and in this respect the medical classics have much to offer, since they mostly discuss actions and reactions inside and outside the body that may lead to disease, and they also try to propose the most accurate treatments. Other 'anatomical'

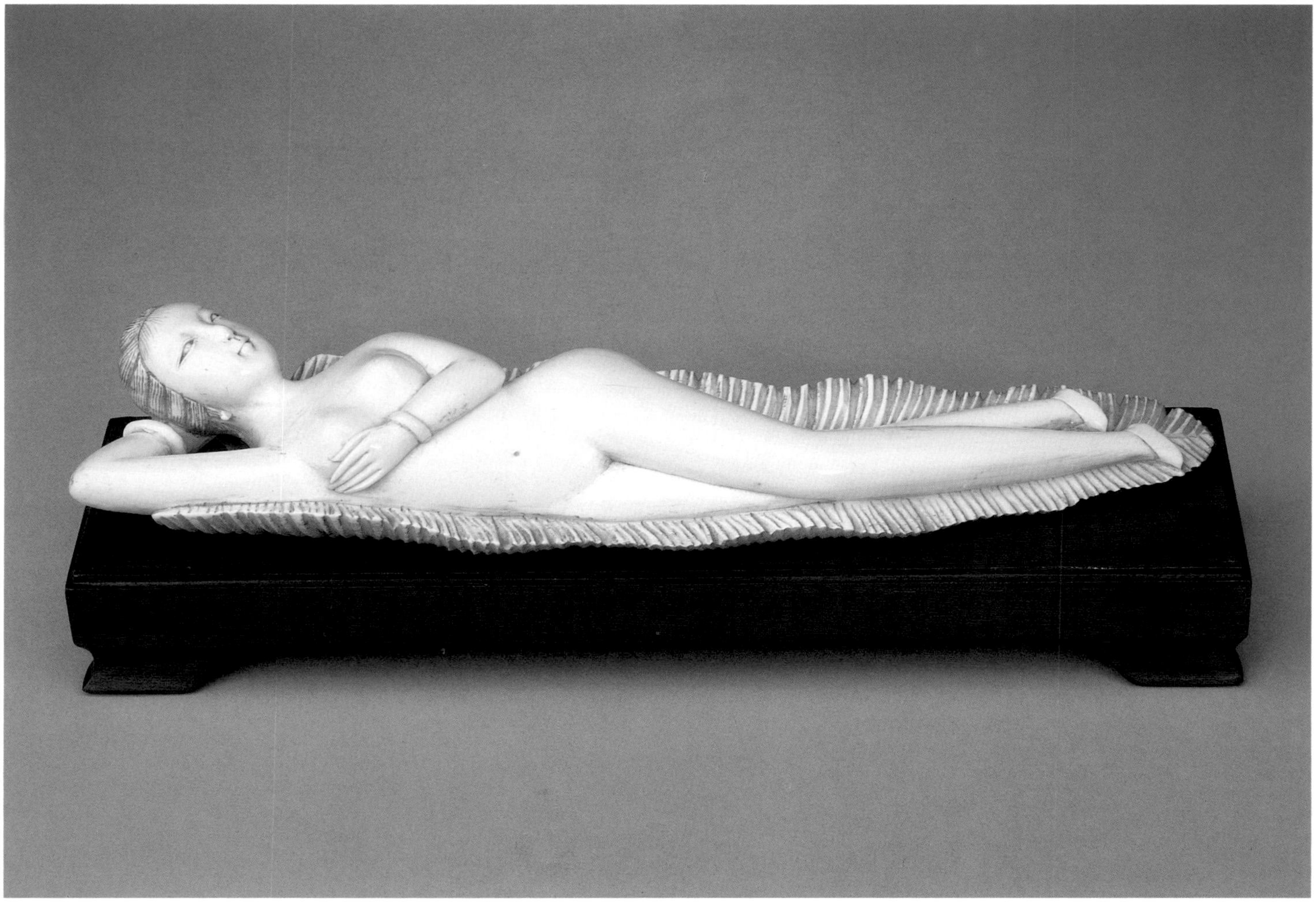

Female diagnostic figure in ivory on which the patient could point to the precise spot of her malady. In this way the doctor did not have to actually observe or touch the lady. China, 19th century. Private collection, Belgium.

and 'physiological' terminology exists in Chinese medical texts, but little appears in the earlier canons. Such terminology becomes clearer in the Qing period (1644-1911, see *Shenjiu Jinglun, juan 1*, for an extensive list of body parts, *xue* and *jing*-meridians).[45]

Causes of Disease

Disease means disharmony in the body and the English word 'dis-ease' is a perfect translation for the Taoist idea of illness. For a Taoist, one becomes ill through lack of 'rest' (*jing*). The *Daodejing* (*Tao Te Ching*) describes the condition of *jing* as 'returning to the roots' and 'renewing life'.[46] Taoists consider it necessary to prevent illness through exercise, and different Taoist schools use different kinds of exercise. For them, a person's life does not depend on God or Heaven, but largely on the person himself. Therefore, if one wants to enjoy a long and healthy life, one should not wear out the body or destabilise one's *jing*, the essential material of survival, and one's mind should remain quiet. Exercises should lead to this condition, otherwise they are worthless. The condition everyone needs is called *yuanqi* (primary *qi*) the guarding of 'oneness' and the flow of *qi* without hindrance. As Wordsworth observes, *Why all this toil and trouble? ... Let Nature be your teacher. ... Spontaneous wisdom breathed by health*, and this is also what the Taoists tell us.

Ziran (spontaneity) and *wuwei* (purposeless action) are the methods that belong to *dao*. They mean getting rid of attachment to persons and things, and not suffering from living in a world where detachment is hard to find. This way is difficult for a common man, who prefers attachments and therefore suffers and frequently falls ill.

To cope with these problems, Taoists and other physicians developed another 'way', which still retains the characteristics of *ziran* and *wuwei*. The main aim of medicine is to prevent and if curing is necessary, it will be done by natural means directed at strengthening the patient's own capacities of curing himself. Becoming addicted to medicine is to be avoided at all costs.

Yin and *yang* are the source of all change and should be followed by man, lest he become ill. They are the basis of creation, and so they are also creators of disharmony. Diagnosing disease is only possible if one understands *yin-yang* and any malfunctioning can be explained in *yin-yang* terminology (including associated terms such as hot-cold, wet-dry). When a person is ill, his condition changes continually and the physician adapts his diagnosis to the changing phenomena, so even the nomenclature of disease is fluid. Only after the introduction of Western medicine did Western-style definitions and names of diseases appear in China, and even today what we call 'disease' is often seen as a symptomatic condition by the Chinese physician and not as the real illness, which continues to be expressed in changeable terminology.[47]

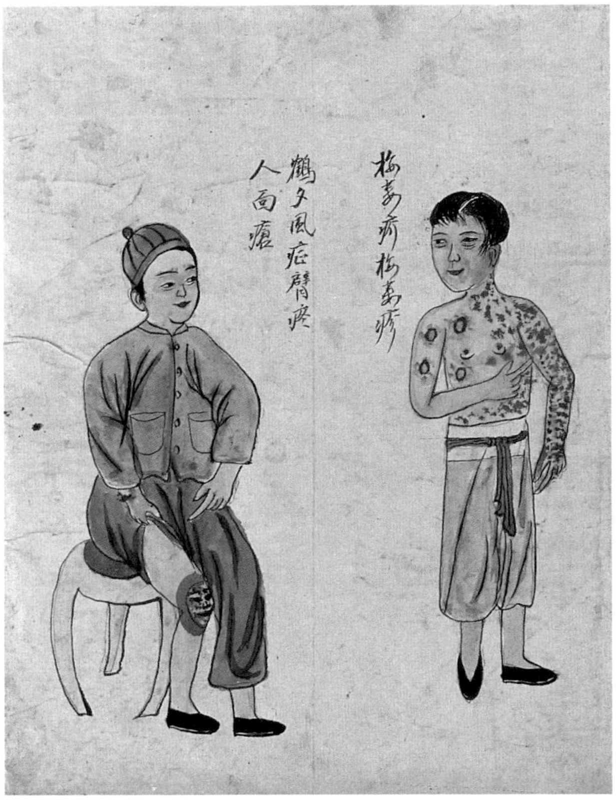

Skin diseases are frequently depicted in Chinese medical manuscripts. One, known as 'the human face' is shown here on the patient's leg. Wellcome Institute, London.

An influential classic on the origin of disease is the *Chaoshi Bing Yuan* (Origin of Diseases according to Mr Chao). This work, dating from AD 610 and ascribed to the official Chao Yuanfang (sixth-seventh century), lists many symptomatic phenomena that appear when disharmony in the body occurs. These phenomena are described by referring to the parts of the body they affect, the way they are affected, and by determining the cause. Chinese traditional medicine uses a terminology alien to Western medical terminology, because its philosophy has different concepts and causes of disease. The Chinese way of looking at illness, however, is quite accessible to the person suffering; it helps to make the patient realise for himself what is wrong and how he is involved in the process of illness and cure. Following a

圖 瘡 臁

臁瘡生兩腿脛之裏外廉骨

腳氣瘡生膝之下足之上腿脛胖腫出黃水結黃痂左右同

Two illustrations from the I-tsung chiu-chien, 'The Golden Mirror of Medicine', a compendium of medical works edited by Wu Chien and first published in 1742. The figure holding the fan may show symptoms of beriberi disease (right), while the man above shows skin ulcers on his leg. Wellcome Institute, London.

detailed discussion of terminology, we consider how the Chinese physician carries out his diagnosis. As source material on this from ancient times is limited, we will restrict ourselves to the contemporary context and comment on possible changes through the ages.

Liuyin: external causes with internal reactions

Chinese cosmic perceptions assume that man is influenced by the macrocosm. Taoist observations show that climate, sun and moon, stars, mountains and all other things on earth have a profound influence on human beings. Increasing control over these forces, which reduces the body's automatic, unconscious reactions to them, is of paramount importance. '*My fate does not depend on Heaven (or Nature), it depends on me*', a Taoist assures.[48] One can learn how to use these external influences to ameliorate the condition of one's body, consciously, instead of being used or abused by them, as most people are. It takes years, even a lifetime of study, to learn the *dao*.

In general Chinese medicine it is accepted that climate strongly influences the human condition. Other influencing elements, like stars and moon, have long been forgotten or degraded to the realms of superstition. Ancient classics of medicine all contain references to the macrocosmic aspects of disease, but we will restrict ourselves to the *liuyin* (six excesses). The word *yin* actually means 'too much rain causing overflow for too long a time'.

The *liuyin* can be seen as *liuqi*, six manifestations of *qi*. When these six *qi* appear and are not excessive or lacking in strength, all is well and stable. The world cannot do without them, nor can human beings. Unfortunately these *qi* do not always behave well. When this happens, harmony is lost and people who have little protective *qi* fall ill because they are unable to cope with the abnormal, changing circumstances.

The *liuyin* are: *feng* (wind), *shu* (heat), *huo* (fire), *zao* (dryness), *han* (cold) and *shi* (humidity). Together they create atmospheric and climatic changes and as such they are absolutely necessary. The human body is supposed to react to these external changes by adapting its own microclimate to them. Philosophically speaking, this is an extrapolation of the theory of *sancai* (three powers) which takes man to be a medium between heaven and earth, combining their *qi* within his body (*Suwen*, chapter 25). The body may absorb some of these *qi* and can even create its own wind, fire, etc. (see table of correlations for *zang* and *fu* involved in this creative process). This process should lead to a more harmonious inner climate, and that which is not needed will be expelled. If the process fails we can say the *liuqi* are becoming *liuyin*. The relations between each of them and their respective correlative agents must then be used to restore order. For example, *feng* is related to *gan* (the *zang* of wood); when the body's fire (*huo*) is excessive, it may be influenced by too strong a *feng* condition since *feng* helps in producing *huo*. This can be dealt with by increasing the amount of *han*, which means stimulating the water-region of the body (*shenpangguang*).

Feng is considered to be the main evil factor, the beginning of all diseases. In fact it is *yangqi*, and shows all characteristics of it; it is highly active (it can move swiftly in and out the body) and changes continually. A disease caused by wind will often lead to fever, rapid and uncontrollable changes and other pathogenic conditions (it sees other *qi* as its host). Of all pathogenic causes, *feng* is the most feared.

Shu behaves like heat striking the earth in summer; it causes the body to become hot and overheated and should lead to sweating if the body responds in a correct way. The highest degree of heat in the body is called *huo*, fire. Like the previous two *qi*, it is a *yang* factor. *Han* (cold) is *yin* in nature; it has similar effects in the body as cold, ice and snow have in the outer world. It can restrict movement and even cause immobility of body fluids. *Shi*, humidity, and *zao*, dryness, can manifest themselves in *yin* or *yang* conditions. They are each other's opposite, but are of the same nature. They serve primarily to make the body climate more humid or dry, and are pathogenic if they cause significant disharmony.

Liuyin are interactive. They create, help and restrict each other, and the physician tries to exploit their relationships to improve his patient's health. He may also advise his patient to move to a different place with a different climate.

Qiqing: emotional and psychological actions in the body

Not only external factors are capable of making one ill. The main source may be the internal actions of the body, which are always connected with what is called psychology in the West. All *zang* and *fu* harbour so-called *qing* (emotions, also called *zhi*, mental, psychological and emotional conditions; see table of correlations), and are influenced in their functioning by their own and other emotions. As with the *liuyin*, these emotions (*qiqing*, seven emotions) are normal phenomena. The body needs them to function correctly. When, for instance, something sad happens, one should feel sad. A problem arises when the *qiqing* become excessive or fail to appear at the right time. To translate Chinese *qiqing* terminology is misleading, since in the West we immediately attach positive or negative connotations to these terms. In the ancient Chinese philosopher's mind they were considered neutral, with the capacity of becoming harmful or beneficial.

The seven *qing* are: *xi* (joy), *nu* (anger), *you* (concern), *si* (deliberation), *bei* (sadness), *kong* (fear) and *jing* (fright). They pertain to the sphere of *xin*, Supreme Ruler of the body, but are connected with the ministers (*zang-fu*). A *zang* or *fu* in bad condition will immediately cause damage to the connected emotion and may also damage the emotions of related functions. But the opposite—emotions damaging *zang* and *fu*—happens as well, and it may be more serious, because this means *xin* is losing its grip.

The damage caused by the seven *qing* to the body's health is described in several chapters of medical classics (e.g. *Neijing, Suwen*, chapter 5). Taoists see the loss of a condition of *jing* (rest, quietness) as the source of destruction, and the recovery of *jing* as the exit to longevity (*Daodejing*, chapter 16). Over-excitation of one's *xin* is therefore of no use, and even noxious. The *Daodejing* (chapter 4) states that governing a country (which, in the first place, means governing one's own body) is a matter of emptying one's mind and its emotional-psychological world (*xin*) and filling one's belly, the region of vitality. *Zhuangzi* (chapter 4) advocates the 'fasting of *xin*', by which is meant detachment, not becoming entangled and thus consumed by one's wishes, desires and emotions. The Taoist physician pays much attention to the restoration of *jing* in his patient's *xin*.

Other pathogenic causes

Other causes of health problems are in fact mostly normal life conditions (with the exception of accidents and animal attacks) that create trouble when one is not careful. Eating, drinking, sleeping, working and sex are considered normal activities which should cause few problems. But as we all know, many of man's difficulties are in fact connected with these ordinary life conditions. The way we eat and the amount of food consumed should be adjusted to our circumstances. What we drink and how much are crucial issues in the development of some health problems. Whether we sleep enough or too much may prove fundamental to regaining health and balance. Too much work and too much tension will produce malfunctioning in the body. For some people lack of sex makes them feel miserable; for others having sex in certain ways can lead to serious diseases. Whatever we do, if we do it under conditions that are harmful or exaggerated, it may make us ill. Adjusting the conditions of our life can be enough to cure the illness or prevent it from developing further. Chinese medical literature is full of recommendations on how to eat, rest, have sex and work. For instance, physicians such as Sun Simiao (see above), wrote that sex needed to be adjusted to a person's age and capacities. Many Taoist texts discuss diets to keep healthy or cure ailments (e.g. *Yunji Qiqian*).[49] Less has been written about other causes of health problems—accidents, poisoning, animal bites. Some measures to treat these problems do occur in literature and have been passed on in practice.[50] Much stress is laid upon preventing daily life practices from becoming a source of disease. Many texts touch upon exercises of body and mind in order to teach how to control one's health. *Yangsheng*, the poetic name for exercises that 'nourish life', is part of the daily activities of many Chinese and though not everyone is fully successful, these practices show that the Chinese realise good health is based on taking one's fate in one's own hands. We will deal with exercising when discussing therapy.

Diagnosis

A Chinese physician seeks to gain as much information from his patient as possible and uses several methods to achieve this goal. The descriptions below are based on modern practice in Chinese hospitals and my own and my teachers' clinical experience. Examining the patient is as crucial in Chinese medicine as in other traditions. In modern Chinese hospitals this is done in an examination room, after which the physician refers him to another physician for treatment.

The four basic methods of examination (*sizhen*, four observations) are: looking at the patient (*wangzhen*), examination by listening, smelling and tasting (*wenzhen*), examination by interrogation (*wenzhen*), and examination by touching (*qiezhen*).

Observing the patient

When looking at a patient a Chinese physician may notice many things. He first observes the body as a whole; some diseases clearly show in the way a person moves and looks. The shape of the body (small, large, fat, thin) may give important information. The posture of the patient may indicate some problem (e.g. deviation of the backbone). Facial colour can tell a Chinese doctor quite a lot about the internal

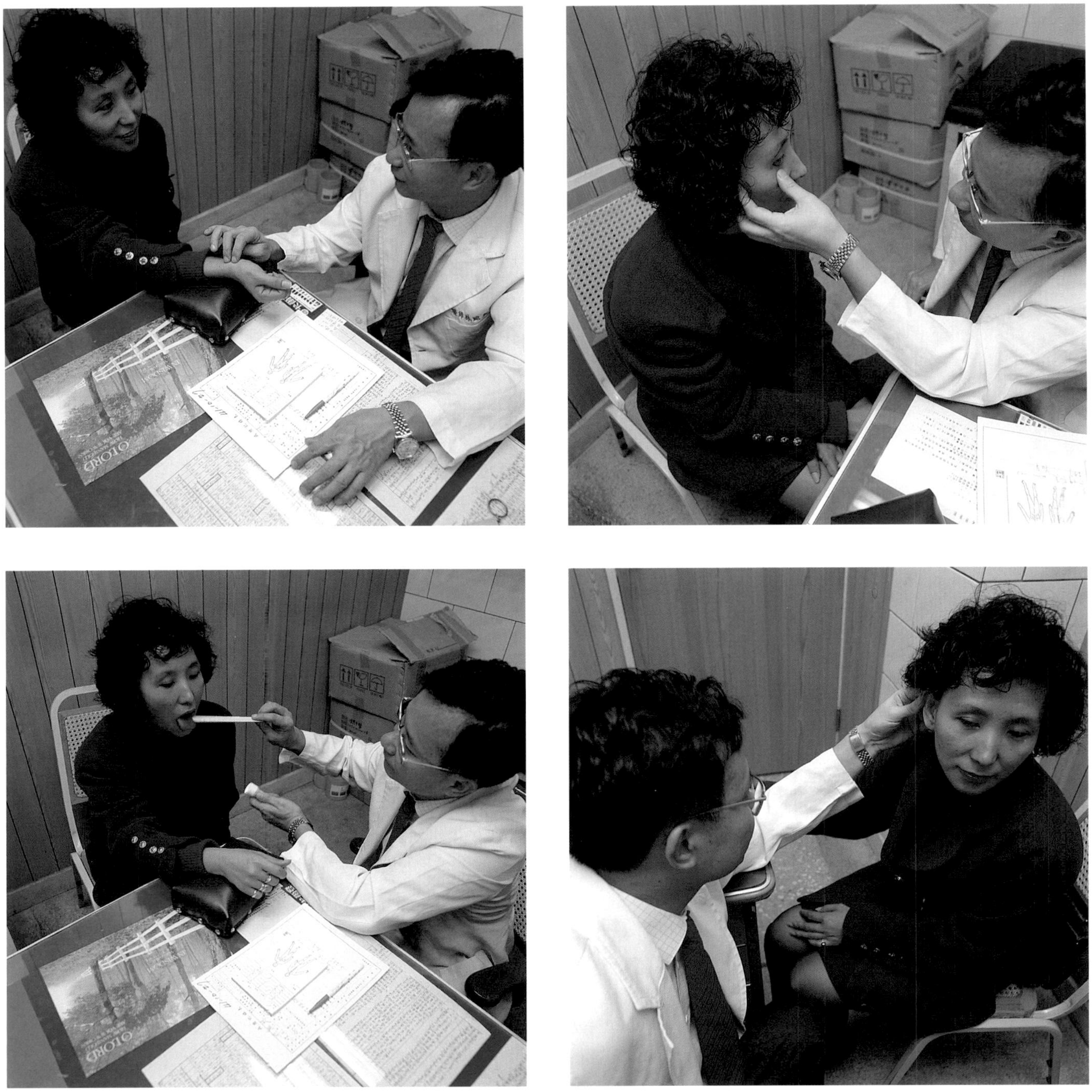

Dr. Lin Jaung Gong diagnosing a patient at his clinic in Taipei. After having observed the patient's general condition, the physician feels the pulse—a highly sophisticated diagnostic technique requiring much skill. It involves counting beat frequency and feeling for several different pulses at three levels of the radial artery. Inspection of the eyes and the tongue reveals much about the patient's health. The ears, hands and other parts of the body may give additional indications, depending on the complaints of the sick person. Listening, smelling, sometimes even tasting are part of the doctor's diagnostic techniques.

condition of the person in front of him. The colour of other parts of the body also tells a story (e.g. bruises). How does the patient behave? Is he disturbed, quiet or aggressive? Can he think normally, does what he says make sense? These issues should become clear after a short period with the patient.

The physician will then take a closer look at certain parts of the body. He observes the position of the head and looks for any external signs of illness. Then he examines different parts of the head (forehead, nose, ears), and the hair (colour, loss of hair). He looks at the eyes (shape, colour of the pupil, white of the eye), lips and mouth (inside and outside), teeth and gums (condition of teeth, colour of gums), throat, skin (spots, rash) and lines of the hands. All these parts of the body, apart from local problems, can reveal the condition and the connectedness to internal functions (see table of correlations).

Chinese medicine probably attaches more importance to the tongue than to any other part of the head. The different sections of the tongue relate to different parts of the body: the root of the tongue reflects the situation of the abdominal cavity and lower back, the middle of the tongue corresponds to the stomach area, the tip of the tongue is related to the head and thoracic cavity. A change of shape or colour indicates an internal change and a serious internal problem is noticeable as a constant abnormal shape or colour of the tongue. The tongue's surface and colour indicate the origin of the problem and help to define whether it is superficial or serious. Too much white on the surface, for instance, may reflect too much cold in the body; not enough white (a red tongue) appears when there is too much heat inside.

Listening and smelling

The Chinese word *wen* means both listening and smelling. Some problems can be heard first, before they can be seen (if they can be seen at all). The physician listens to the patient's voice (a soft voice may indicate loss of strength); he also listens to his patient's breathing and coughing. Traditionally, Taoists distinguish several types of breathing of which some are considered ordinary, others pathologic, and still others attainable only after a long period of practising breathing exercises.[51] The way someone breathes reveals information about the respiratory system, but also other functions. Heavy breathing may be a symptom of heart problems and may also be the result of digestive problems causing the respiratory organs to suffer from increased pressure. Other sounds, like sighing and yawning, can be interpreted in a similar way.

While listening to the breathing a doctor will also notice how the breath smells. Different smells are correlated with different kinds of functional disorders (see 'five tastes' and their respective functions in the table of correlations). A physician will try to identify what causes this smell and relate it to the associations of the 'five tastes' (*wei*, meaning both smell and taste).

Interrogation

Asking questions helps to locate where the illness originates and how the person got it in the first place. The physician takes into account that his patient may be deliberately or involuntarily misleading him. Many people have no idea how their body works and do not notice its signals and warnings. Therefore, the answers a patient gives should be considered carefully and tested by other forms of examination. Many symptoms may be felt and thus be clear to the patient, but as they are not visible or do not manifest themselves externally, they may escape the physician's attention.

The patient will be asked if he feels cold or hot. This may lead to the conclusion that he is running a fever, but since heat and cold are important pathogenic factors, the doctor may deduce something more as well. Does the patient sweat or is he unable to sweat? Being able to sweat and the amount of sweat one produces are both important factors in determining the condition of the body fluids.

People clearly feel pain and are willing to talk about it. The Chinese physician will ask his patient where the pain manifests itself and what kind of pain he is suffering from. There are different words for different kinds of pain and finding out about the exact nature of the pain can be of great help in deciding whether the problem is superficial or not and whether it is caused by fullness (*shi*), which causes sharp pain, or its opposite, emptiness (*xu*), which results in a lack of pain. The area affected by the pain tells what function(s) are being attacked by *xieqi*, and the nature of this *xieqi*. To be able to work out the internal connections of pains, the physician must be completely familiar with the *jing*, *luo* and *mai* running through the body.

As all living creatures need food and drink, questions about appetite and problems with the digestive system are crucial. The amount of food consumed, the likes and dislikes of certain kinds of food, the degree of thirstiness, the types and quantity of liquids taken, are all matters of concern because they tell the physician a great deal about the digestive, respiratory and urinary systems. Too much or too little food and drink will influence stool and urine. The amount of both *bian* ('convenience', meaning stool and urine), and their frequency, are the first things to ask about. Their shape, colour and smell are next. If the patient does not know about odour and colour, of necessity the doctor will have to find out for himself (in ancient days he sometimes had to taste them).

Many people sleep badly. This is related to daytime habits, especially eating habits that can disrupt or influence sleep. Women and children have their own illnesses and these are analysed through questions too. A woman's menstrual periods, their frequency and circumstances are of extreme importance, because they originate in a body part that is considered to be the storage place of vitality. Any disorder there will influence the functioning of the entire body, especially the brain and heart, masters of the body.

Palpation

Examination by touching the patient's body is not as obvious as it sounds. It used to be indecent to touch the body of a person of a different sex; the only part of the body that could be felt was the pulse. This contributed to the development of a sophisticated system of feeling and interpreting the pulse, and raised pulse diagnosis to the most esteemed position among diagnostic techniques. Skill in pulse diagnosis is still highly praised, though nowadays examining other parts of the body by touch is more or less acceptable.

The Chinese physician will touch certain parts of the body if this helps to clarify the picture of a disease. He is not restricted to touching and pressing painful or affected areas but may also press on some of the important *xue* (holes) or even follow the tracks of the *jing* (meridians). Taoist tradition often concentrates on pressing the backbone area, the fingers and toes, but others may prefer to feel the belly or the face. In any case, if some body parts are definitely affected they can be examined by touching and feeling. This results in reactions from the patient, who can feel different levels of pain, and in the physician experiencing all kinds of sensations when touching or pressing (heat or cold, roughness or softness, swelling or lack of elasticity, etc.).

The ultimate technique of pulse diagnosis appears in several classics, such as the *Maijing* (third-fourth century), that discuss basic methods and multiple details when explaining this complicated art. It demands a lot from the practitioner; he must be able to distinguish extremely subtle changes of pressure in the three parts of the pulse at three depths, he must also be able to relate these to pathogenic factors. Learning pulse diagnosis takes many years of experience and even this does not guarantee absolute accuracy.

Chiropodist inspecting the leg of his patient. Watercolour by Zhou Pei Qun, (Chinese Trades and Professions) early 19th century. Wellcome Institute, London.

First there is the frequency of the beats to be counted. Traditionally this is not done with the help of a clock or watch, but by relating it to the rhythm of breathing. Age and constitution play an important role in determining whether someone's rhythm is appropriate. Then the pulse, when palpated, will feel different from one place or depth to another. The classics of pulse diagnosis give analyses of these phenomena and describe or draw them in detail. The *Maijing*, for instance, lists and discusses twenty-four types of pulse sensations. Each of these sensations is related to the corresponding part and functions of the body, and also indicates the source of the problem (dampness, emptiness, fullness, heat etc.). The terminology of pulse sensations tries to express the phenomenon as clearly as possible, therefore the descriptions used talk of superficial, string-like, slippery, slow, empty and full pulses.

When examining the patient's body became prohibited in the late Qing period (nineteenth century), reading the pulse became almost the sole diagnostic technique available to the Chinese physician. It is still the king of diagnostic techniques in modern Chinese medicine.

Peculiar methods

Some medical practices in China could easily be dubbed quackery in the West, and many irregular or unorthodox types of treatment and diagnoses are often considered worthless or misleading. The Chinese attitude towards other kinds of medicine is quite different, however. For example, if an aspect of Western, Indian or Tibetan medicine works, it will be eagerly accepted. This accounts for the success of Western medicine in China; it is accepted for its effects, though it will never replace Chinese medicine but rather coexist and partially blend with it.

In ancient times medicine was a part of religion and religious people used unusual methods of diagnosis. Taoist and Buddhist therapy and diagnosis, even today, require a good physician to develop his mental and bodily capacities to the utmost. After long and intensive practice all senses are well-trained instruments that gather subtle impressions which an untrained person could never feel. The relaxed and clear mind that results from the *jing*-condition of 'quietness' becomes a means to absorb all these impressions and combine them into one clear image. This image may be revealed in several kinds of internal experience. Taoists often mention 'internal visualisation' (*neishi, neiguan*), which means that one visualises the internal condition of one's body. For medical purposes this can also be done with someone else's body, whereby the physician visualises the inner workings of his patient. His body becomes one with his patient's body for a moment, providing the physician with visual images (*guan bing*, visualising disease) or other perceptions (*ting bing*, 'listening to' disease). Some Chinese doctors use only these diagnostic methods; others combine them with the various other techniques described above. The official policy is to discourage these methods, but they still survive, albeit in clandestine ways. In fact, they are relics of the most ancient cultural and religious heritage of China.

Symptomatic phenomena: the eightfold network

Symptomatic phenomena are distinguished by eight main concepts that form an interwoven network to guide the practitioner in his analysis. These eight factors can be reduced to the two basic elements of change, *yin* and *yang*. In changing circumstances, the two may be called by different names, so it is possible to distinguish *biao* (superficial, on the surface) from *li* (fundamental, internal), *han* (cold) from *re* (hot), and *xu* (empty, powerless) from *shi* (full, over-powerful). The underlying theory is still the *yin-yang* relationship.

When deciding how to treat someone it is important to distinguish whether the symptoms are more *yang* or more *yin* in nature, since this will alter the therapy. In general, different conditions appear in different parts and functions of the body. Some *zang* may show a *xu* (powerless) function, whereas their corresponding *fu* are *shi* (full of power). The lack of power in some functions may be caused by an extreme *han* (cold) development in these parts of the body, thereby shifting too much *re* (heat) to other parts. It is often the case that one kind of pathogenic factor is only causing superficial damage (*biao*), whereas, at the same time, other factors are disrupting internal functions in a severe way, a *li* condition. A mostly *yang* condition rules the body when, for instance, heat (*shu*) and wind (*feng*) are at work. Cold (*han*) causes a *yin* tendency. One should always keep in mind that *yin* cannot exist without *yang* and therefore may be caused by it. Cold at its climax may well turn into heat, and in this way result in a *yang* condition.

To explore the fundamental source of a disease the physician should not only understand the present situation, but also the causes of that situation. The elements of the eightfold network can only be distinguished by using the techniques of diagnosis described. The network itself serves to categorise and analyse the information obtained by these diagnoses.

Analysis by reference to *zang* and *fu*

The parts and functions of the body, seen in Chinese medicine as *zang-fu* and their tracts of action (*jing-luo*), usually show distinctive features. Traditional Chinese medicine links the action in the organs with actions elsewhere in the body. The tracts along which these actions occur in regular patterns are called *jing-luo*, the 'meridians', or 'collaterals'. The doctor tries to find out the effect of pathogenic factors on the respective *zang* and *fu* and must discern differences between them. The relationships between these functions (see table of correlations) provide a guide for identifying these differences and seeing how one influences the other.

Several diagnostic techniques help to locate the disorder. Pulse diagnosis can differentiate between the *zang* and *fu*, and looking at the patient's tongue and face improves the accuracy of the observation. When it becomes clear that certain functions and places are more affected than others, the physician will work out how this came to happen by referring to the interrelations of *zang* and *fu*. He knows that a troublesome *zang* causes its *fu* to react. It is crucial then to treat both. He also takes into account that the productive and controlling relationships between *zang* and *fu* are liable to create expanding disorder in other parts of the body. As we have seen before, the workings of the body create change in body fluids. The defensive and nourishing capacities of *qi*, its sources and actions, and *xue* (blood-fluid) should be checked by examining the *zang* and *fu* involved in the process of *qi* and *xue* production. A complete investigation presents the physician with a clear picture of where the disease originated and where it will lead if unchecked. It will determine his course of action in fighting the *xieqi* and strengthening the *zhengqi*.[52]

Taijiquan is practised in public parks all over China, such as in Beijing (above) and Shanghai (below).

Chinese Therapy & Therapeutic Techniques

Preserving health and preventing disease are far better than curing, says the *Neijing*. Herbal medicine and other practices of prevention, whether used externally or internally, have always been popular in China, to prolong life or prevent premature aging. Centuries of concentration on these goals have endowed Chinese medicine with innumerable exercises and herbal preparations.[53] Before discussing these and other aspects of Chinese therapeutics, we will consider the general principles and traditional practices common to all types of Chinese therapy that guide the physician.

General principles

The first principle is to prevent disease and its development. Practising therapeutic and preventive exercises, like *qigong* or *taijiquan*, is one possibility.[54] Physicians often advise their patients to take up some form of traditional exercise, to keep in shape, to recover from health problems or to prevent these from continuing or recurring. There are also pills and medicines for regaining vitality.

If a patient already suffers from a disease, the physician puts a few golden rules into practice. First he looks for the origin of the disease, using the diagnostic techniques described above. This principle appears in the *Neijing* and in practice it may be applied in several ways. When, for instance, a disease is caused by *han* (cold) it can be treated by using what is called an 'upright' treatment, *zhengzhi* or counter-acting treatment (*nizhi*). This means treating the cold by heat (*re*), perhaps by taking in herbs that heat the affected functions of the body. Sometimes the symptoms of the illness will display the opposite characteristics of the cause; a problem caused by cold is likely to make the patient run a fever.

In this case the physician may still use herbs that heat, although from the outside it seems that the person is suffering from a heat problem. Treating in this way is called 'reverse' treatment (*fanzhi*), or co-acting treatment (*congzhi*). The disease mostly has external symptoms caused by internal disharmony. If these symptoms are a nuisance to the patient or if they stand in the way of accurate treatment of the root of the disease, the physician can treat these external phenomena first, otherwise he should confront the source first. In general, however, it is often easier, faster and more satisfactory to both patient and doctor to deal with the external symptoms before going to the origin. In modern practice the fundamental cause is often neglected in favour of 'symptomatic' treatment, because it brings about rapid, if temporary, relief. The circumstances of Chinese society—too many people, too few physicians, too little time and space for thorough treatment—have caused a shift towards this way of dealing with disease, though it is a fundamental deviation from Chinese medical philosophy.

We have seen that good health may be described by using *qi* terminology; a body that functions well is strong in *zhengqi* (upright or correct *qi*), whereas an unhealthy body has a weak *zhengqi* and suffers from strong *xieqi* (slanted or incorrect *qi*). Therapy always aims at weakening the influence of *xieqi* and strengthening *zhengqi*. Therefore, Chinese physicians have developed a range of methods that make *qi* move.

Qi can be made to move in different directions, i.e. the reactions of bodily functions created by treatment may differ according to the technique used. It is possible to cause the removal of certain waste material (e.g. cold, heat, wind) by applying massage, acupuncture or herbs. The process that brings about outward movement is called *xie* (draining). If the physician wants to ameliorate the *zhengqi* condition, he uses techniques that are likely to induce a better distribution of nutritive material in the body. In this case he tries to improve *bu* (supply). Quite often both will be applied at the same time. In fact, they are the *yin-yang* of therapy; if applying *bu*, there is always *xie*, but less than when applying *xie* as the main method, which limits *bu*. The diagnosis helps the doctor decide what he should do. If, for instance, his patient is too weak to react quickly to *xie* treatment, he will probably try to strengthen the capacities of the patient's body to resist pathogenic causes. An accurate diagnosis of course leads to quicker and better results.

Change is the central focus of Chinese philosophy. So it is in Chinese medicine and therapy too, which is subject to three facets of change that have to do with the circumstances of treatment. One facet of change has to do with the way therapy is applied. Curing is about helping people, and as no two persons are alike, their illnesses also differ, even if—from a Western medical point of view—they show similar symptoms. The Chinese physician treats patients with seemingly similar problems in a different way if his diagnosis of the problem's origin reveals fundamental differences. Some people need less treatment, some need 'softer' treatment, some need higher concentrations of herbs.

The second aspect subject to change is time, a crucial factor in Chinese medicine. If one is familiar with the rhythm of change in the human body, it is possible to find out the best moment for treatment. Sophisticated theory and complex methods of calculation exist for the physician who wants to adapt his therapy to the changing circumstances inside the body, though in practice it is hardly feasible to treat patients at the optimum moment.

Another use of time is more likely to be put in practice. Since Chinese medicine stresses the influence of climate and weather on health, some diseases will be cured more easily under favourable conditions that change with time. In short, treatment is harmonised with weather. When, for example, the patient is suffering from a heat condition, the physician will prescribe fewer cooling herbs (or other cooling means) if the outside temperature is lower. Different seasons and climates create different kinds of illness (wet and cold weather cause more muscle, bone and joint problems).

The third influence of change on cure relates to place. Different places show different health problems and a close relationship exists between place and climate. If the place the patient lives in has a strong influence on his health, it may also limit the effect of treatment. In some cases the person must move or alter his environment or place of work to be cured. In former times, place was a factor in limiting the types of herbs and medicines a physician could acquire. Now, modern transport and medical companies assure a supply of *materia medica* all over China.

The 'eight methods of therapy'

Traditionally, there are eight fundamental methods for curing patients and each type of health problem requires an appropriate treatment. The long history of Chinese medical experience has made it possible to arrive at an effective system of cure that provides solutions to different problems. The eight methods that form the basis of any technique of therapy (acupuncture, massage, herbology, etc.), and a brief introduction to their use, are listed below:

han (sweating): making the patient sweat; this method is used when there is superficial damage, mostly caused by external circumstances;

tu (vomiting): making the patient vomit; used for instance when the person has been poisoned or when food is not being digested;

xia (lowering): lowering matter inside the human body by creating downward (outward) movement; used for instance when there is constipation;

he (harmonising): regulating or adjusting one bodily function to the other; for instance when the upper part of the digestive system is not in harmony with the lower part;

wen (warming): making the temperature in certain parts of the body rise; used when cold is the cause of disease;

qing (purifying): clearing heat and purifying the body; applied mainly when heat is the source of illness;

xiao (dispelling): eliminating or dispersing the causes of disease; used for elimination of blockages on the 'roads' of *qi*, or of other blocked body fluids and material;

bu (supplying): improving the conditions of *qi*, *xue* (blood-fluid) and all functions of the body; accelerating the recovery of someone by giving him more strength.

Due to the complex nature of some diseases it may prove necessary to combine several of the methods listed above.

Acupuncture

Acupuncture, the best known Chinese therapeutic technique, was popular in ancient times, forbidden in 1822, and rediscovered this century. Acupunture (*zhenfa*, needle technique) is a way of influencing bodily functions by inserting needles in the *xue* (acu[puncture]-points in Western literature). The physician must be acquainted with the exact location of the *xue* lest he insert the needle incorrectly, which might cause damage instead of cure.

Patient undergoing acupuncture therapy at the hospital of China Academy of Traditional Chinese Medicine Hospital in Beijing.

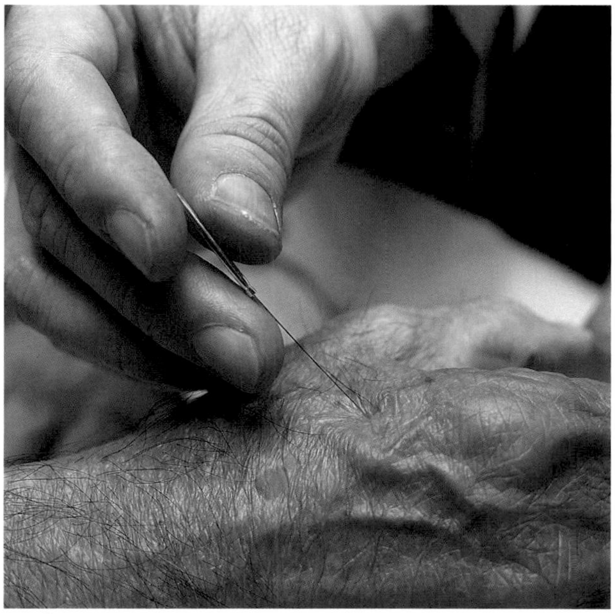

A village doctor treating a peasant with moxibustion. Detail from a reproduction of a painting by Li Tang of the Sung Dynasty. Taipei National Palace Museum, Taiwan.

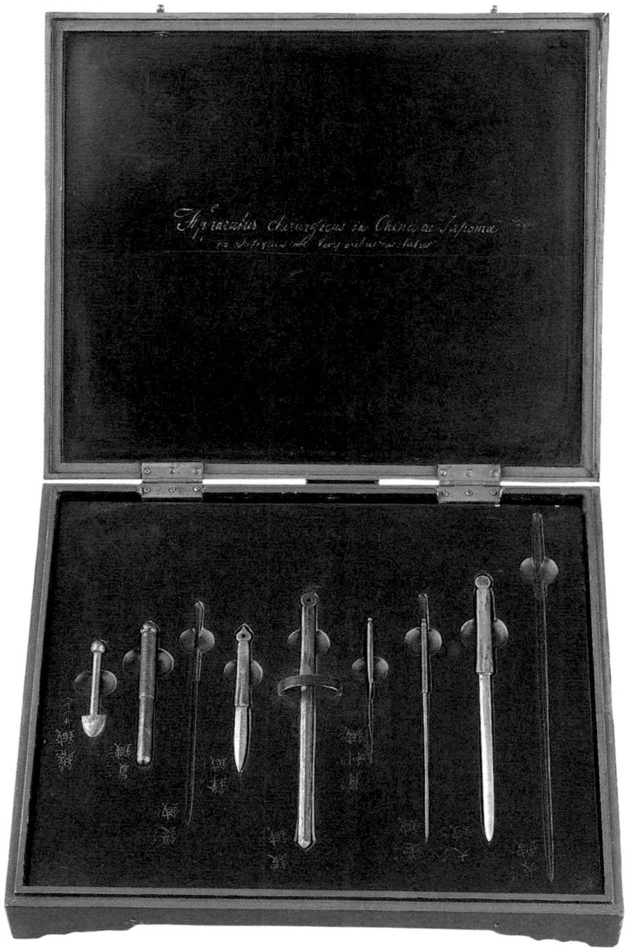

Set of medical instruments with inscription: 'Apparatus Chirurgicus in China ac Japonia'. Japan, early 19th century, collected c. 1825 by Philipp Franz von Siebold. National Museum of Ethnology, Leiden.

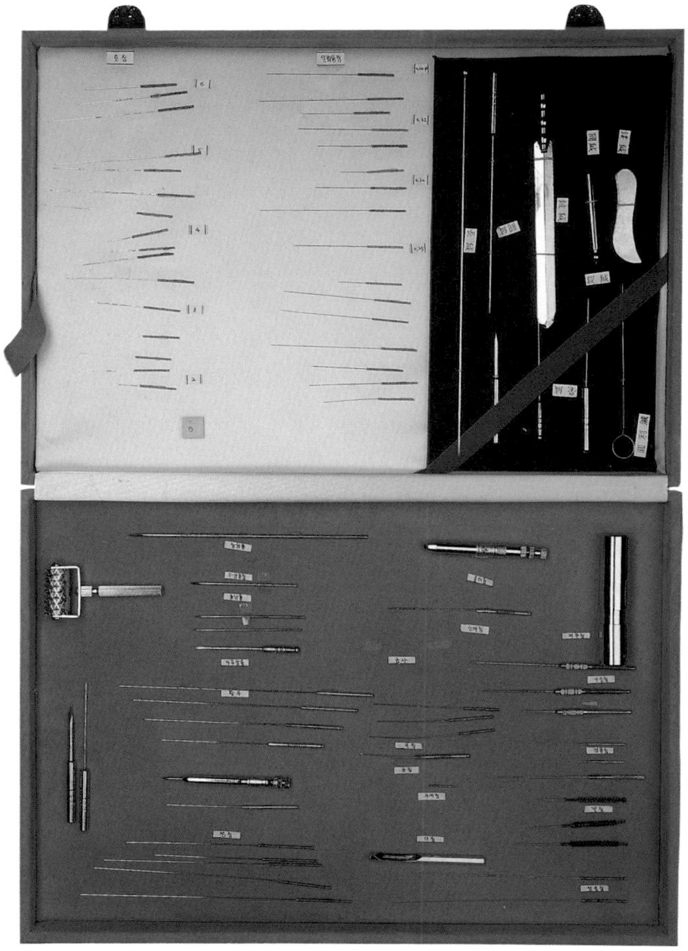

Modern acupuncture set from Korea. Collection: Mark De Fraeye, Belgium

此症乃痰飲停滯胸膈賊風串入腦戶偏正頭風發來連牽邊皮肉疼痛或手足沉冷久而不治變為癱患亦分陰陽針之或針力未到故不効也此症宜先針風池

偏正頭風

絲竹
風池
合谷
三里

The treatment of cataract by acupuncture, from Shen-Shih yao-han compiled by Fu Jen-jü, a compendium of opthalmology first published in 1644. Wellcome Institute, London.

足少陰腎經 左右五十四穴

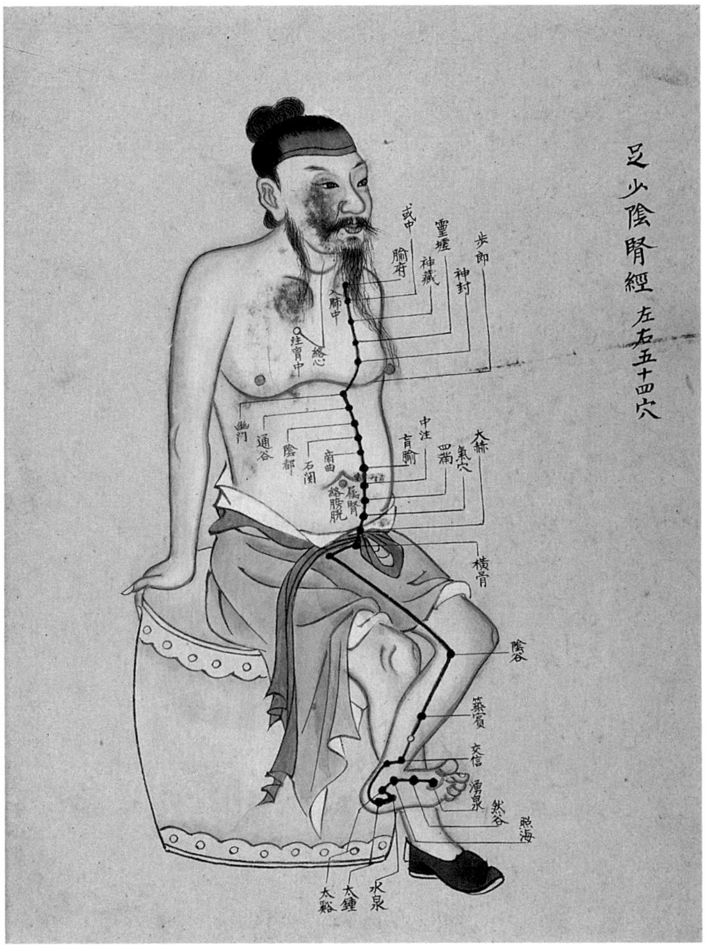

Right: Watercolour of a seated man, showing the shen or kidney-meridian and its acupuncture points. Wellcome Institute, London.

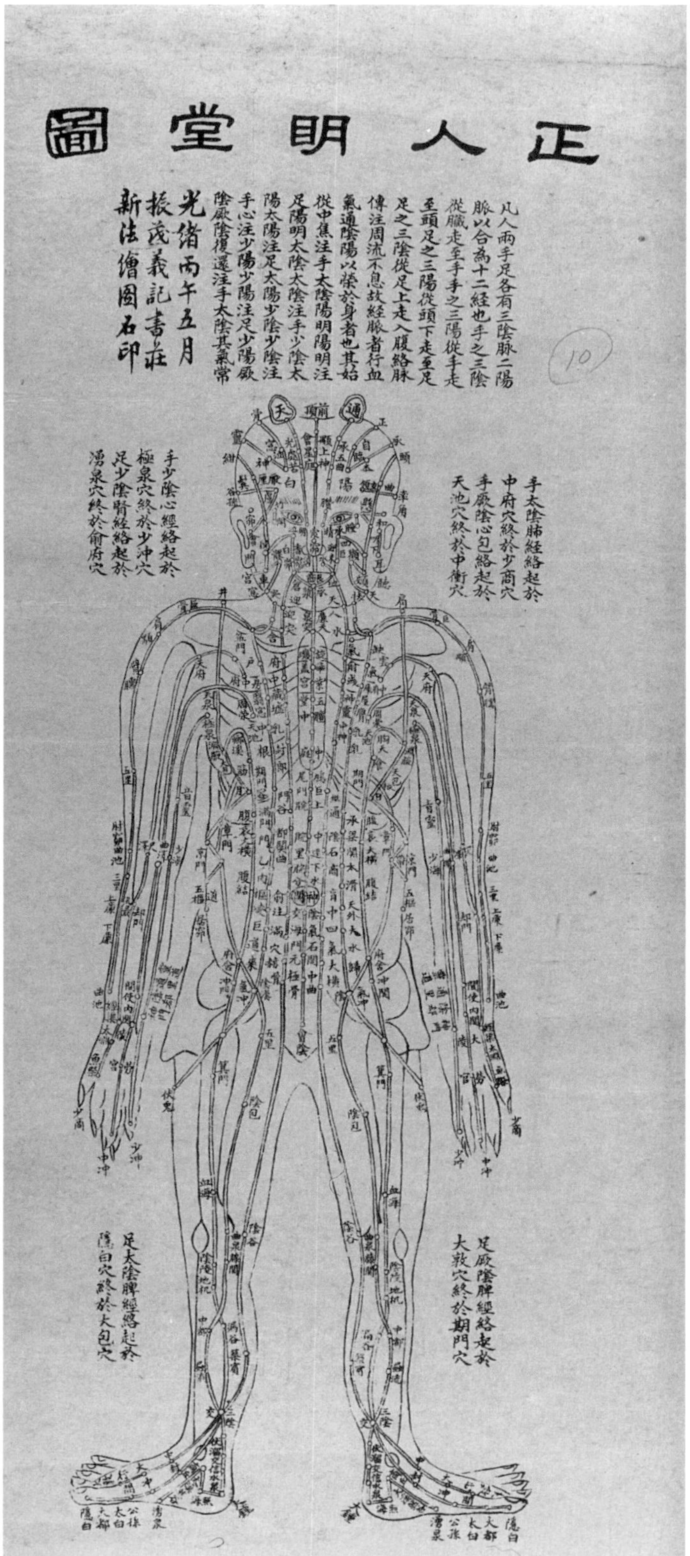

Four acupuncture charts printed by imperial decree in 1906 from old blocks. The charts are probably based on the so-called bronze man (tongren) of the Song Dynasty. Above: Anterior view, showing the jingluo (meridians and collaterals) of the human body. The text provides general information on the classification of the jingluo. Wellcome Institute, London.

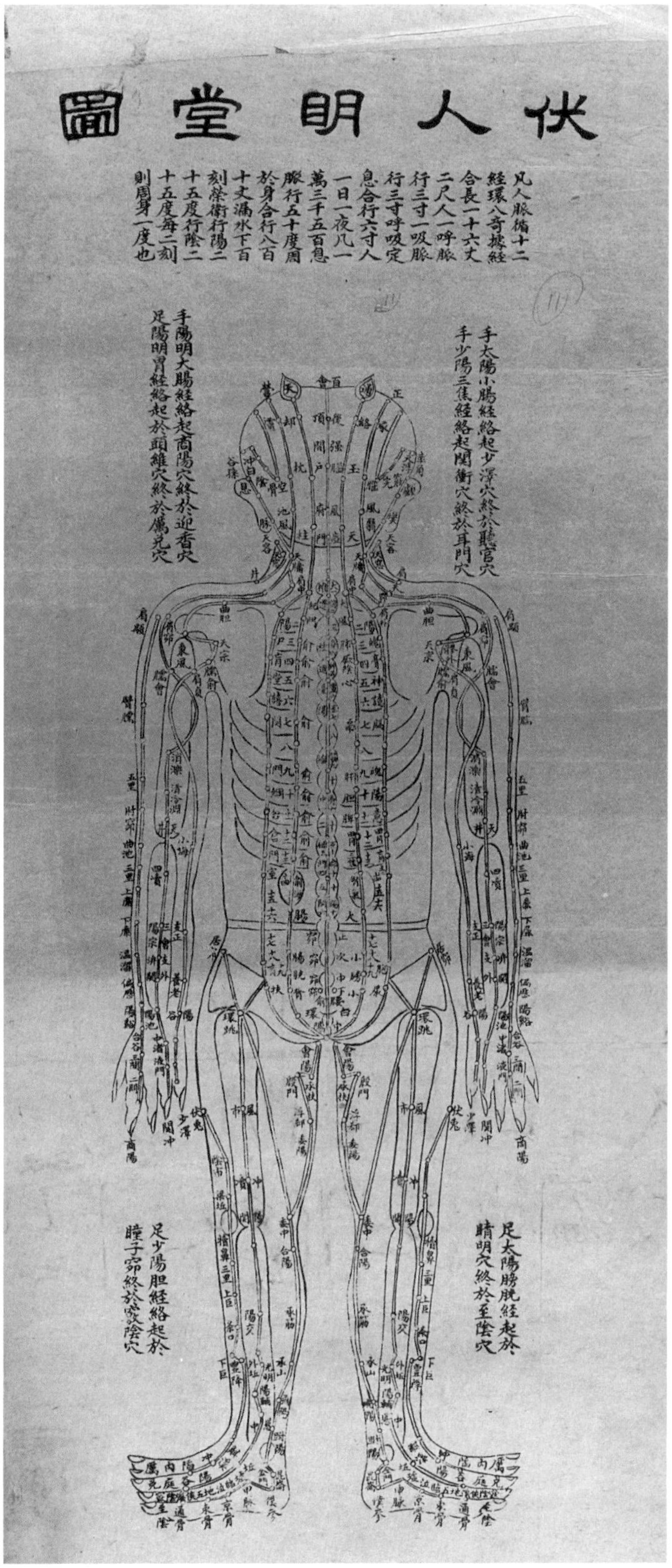

Posterior view: This diagram also shows the backbone which harbours the main mai or vessel, the controlling vessel (dumai).

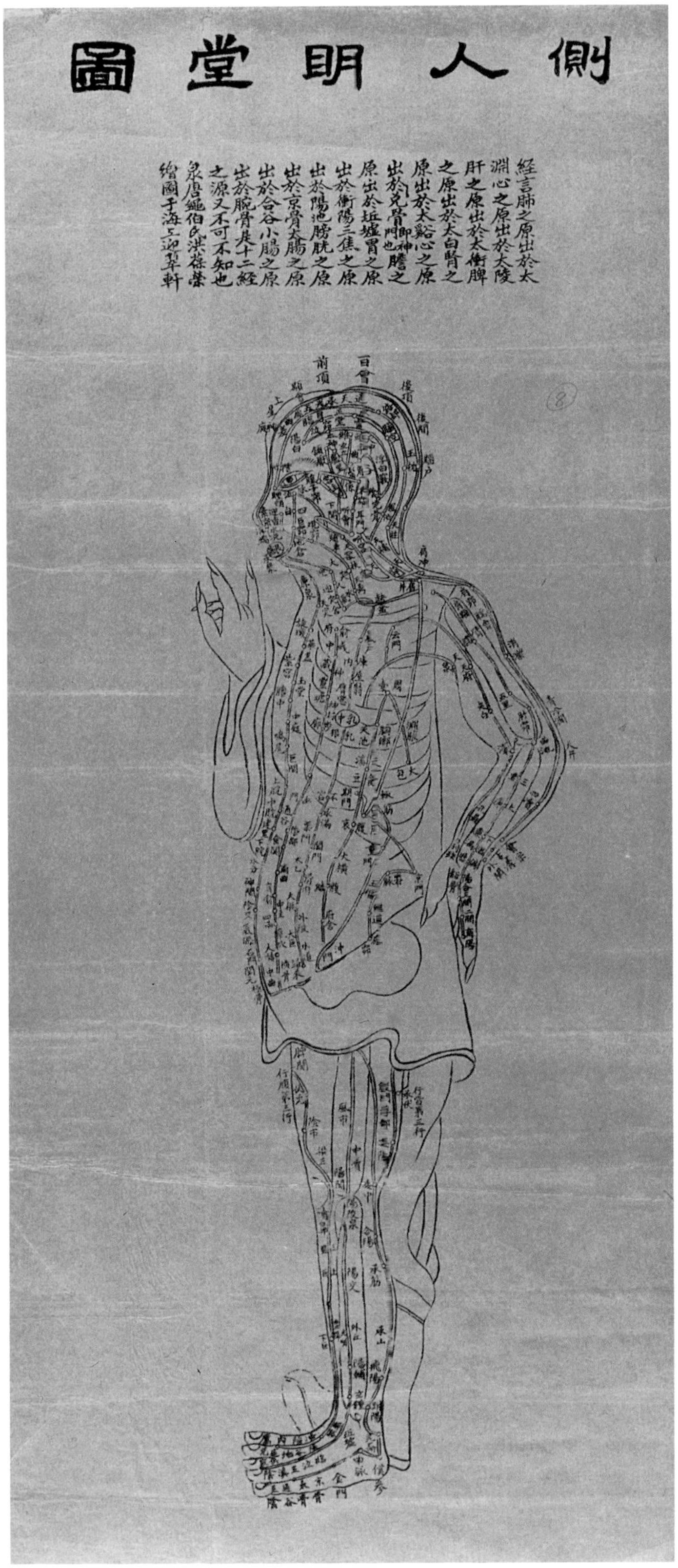

Side view: The text describes the origin of the zang and fu.

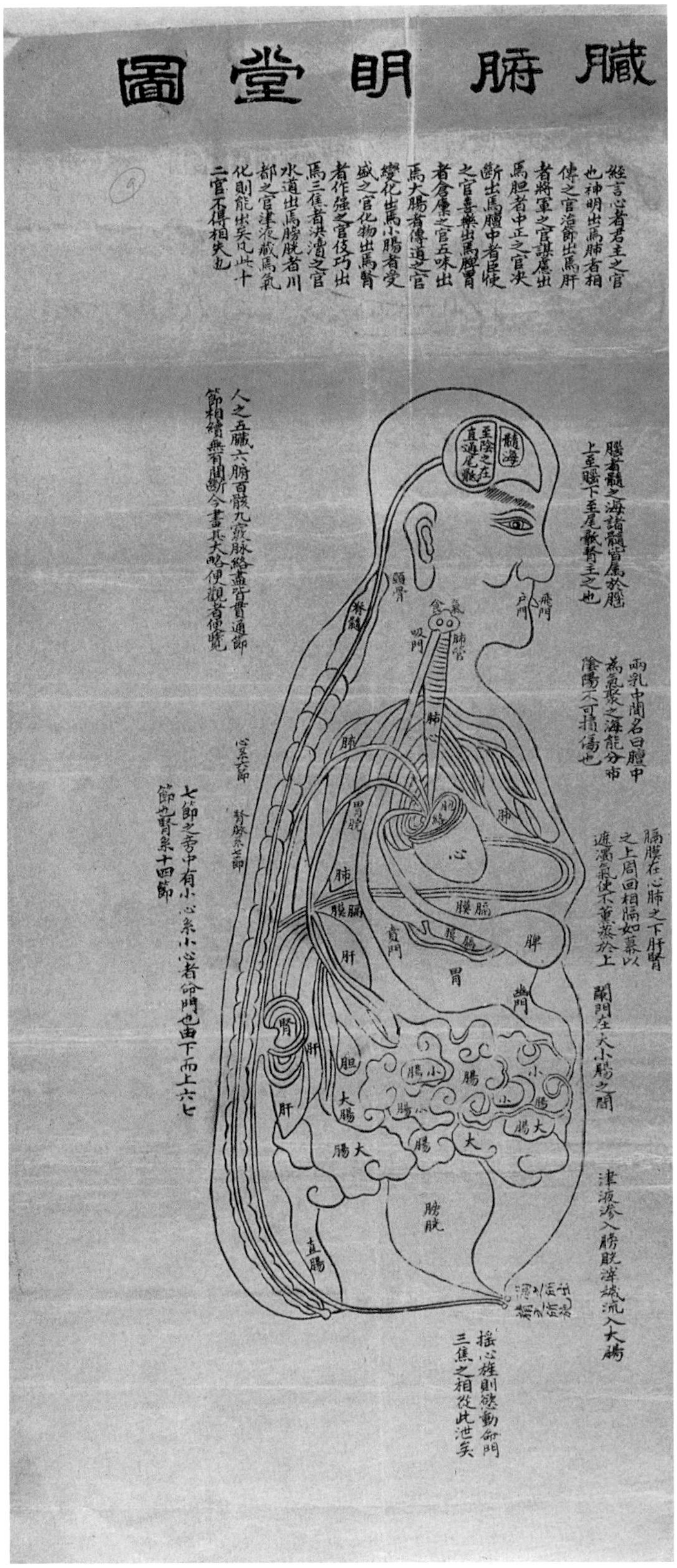

Anatomical scheme of zang and fu, viewed as internal organs. The text at the top cites the linglan midian chapter of the Neijing, where the zang and fu are described as officials in the inner landscape. Both concepts zang and fu were already in existence when the Neijing was compiled (c. 200 BC).

At an early stage, acupuncture used nine different needles (*jiuzhen*, nine needles), though today many more are used in daily clinical practice. The modern needles are made of stainless steel, while ancient needles were made of bone, stone or metal, often gold or silver.[55] In most cases, several needles are inserted in different *xue* and the needles may differ in length and thickness. The smaller ones measure less than one inch, the largest needles measure about one foot. They can be inserted perpendicularly or slanting, most commonly at angles of 45° or 15°. The speed of insertion may differ, the depth will be adapted to the condition and shape of the patient, and once the needle is inside the body it may be turned, pulled, made to shake, or influenced in other ways (by heating, transporting the physician's *qi* through the needle, etc.). The needle will then be used as a means to effect one or more of the methods described previously.

Some places of the body are not treated with acupuncture. The *Neijing* contains warnings against inserting needles in these places (for a Western appreciation of these prohibitions see *Celestial Lancets*).[56] Often acupuncture is combined with moxibustion, which tends to reinforce its effects. Frequently, parts of the body are regarded as 'special acupuncture zones'. The ears, for instance, are used in acupuncture as 'small bodies', where all bodily functions can be influenced, each part of the ear corresponding to a part, or function, of the entire body; this is called *erzhen*, ear-acupuncture or auriculotherapy.[57]

Since the 1930s, electro-acupuncture has come into existence and is increasingly popular with Chinese physicians, being less tiring and less time-consuming than the manual method. In electro-accupuncture treatment, therapeutic reactions in the patient's body are caused by needles connected to an apparatus that supplies electric power. Acupuncture was the first therapeutic technique of Chinese medicine to reach the West and other parts of the world and its influence is still spreading. The therapeutic value and results of acupuncture treatment have been tested both in China and in Western research institutes, affirming its growing and universal acceptance.

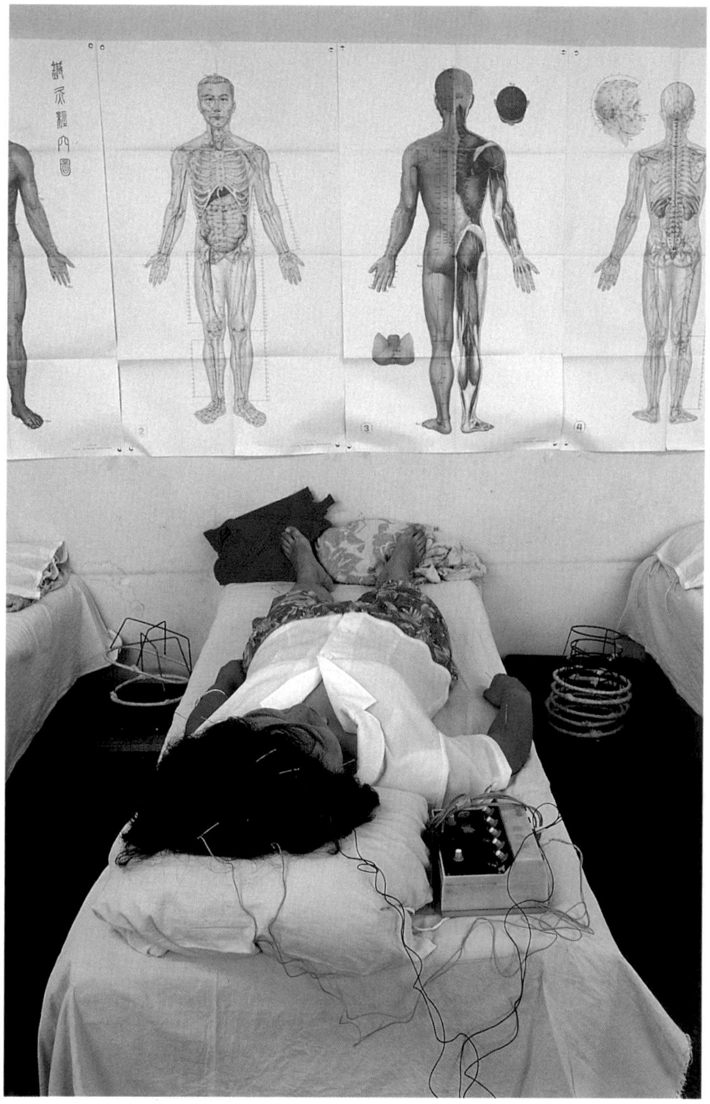

Electro-acupuncture (above) at the Academy of Traditional Chinese Medicine, Beijing, and (below) with computerised imagery at the China Medical College of Taiching, Taiwan.

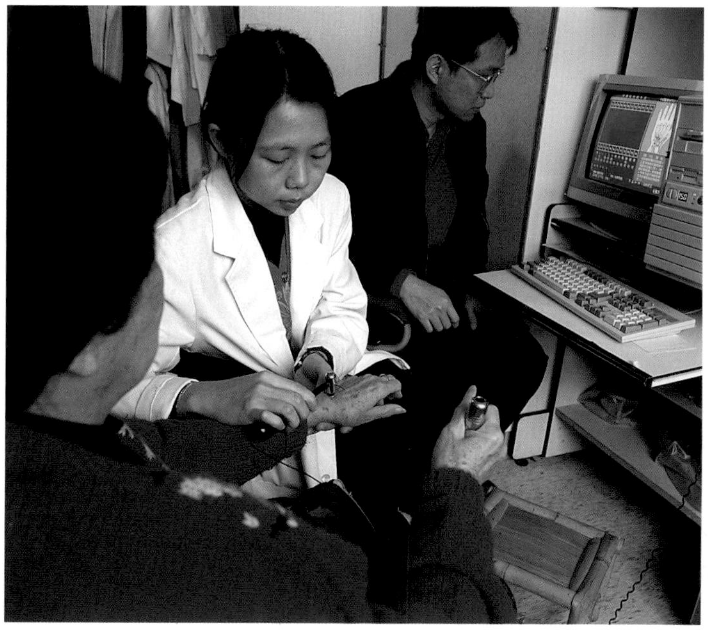

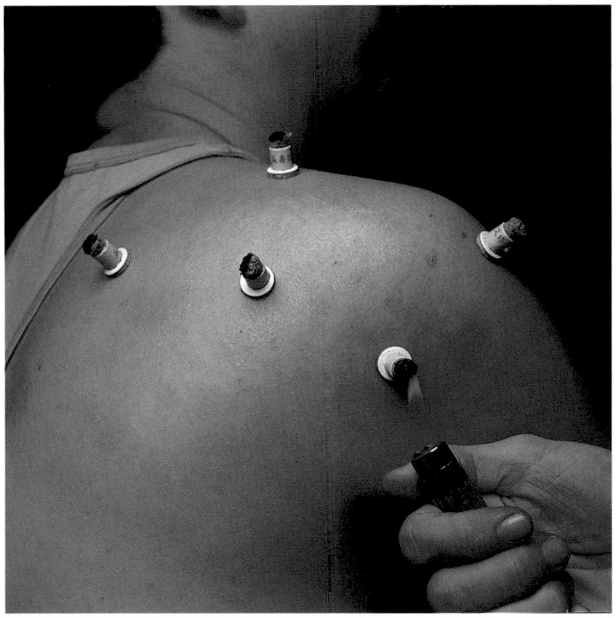

Igniting moxibustion cones at Dr Lin Jaung Gong's clinic in Taipei.

Moxibustion

The Chinese word *zhenjiu* (acupuncture and moxibustion) implies that the two techniques are almost inseparable; they combine well and are mutually supporting. Where acupuncture fails, moxibustion (*jiufa*) may be helpful.

Moxibustion is the burning of *Artemisia vulgaris* (moxa in Western literature; Ch. *ai*). It used to be collected, dried and prepared by the physician himself, but nowadays it is readily available in medical stores. Moxa is particularly effective when the patient is suffering from cold and dampness. The herb is thought to be pure *yang* in nature and therefore suitable for warming. One method of treatment consists of igniting the cylindrical moxa-stick, which consists of pressed *artemisia* leaves mixed with other herbs and rolled in thin paper, and moving it at a short distance from the skin along the track of the *jing* (meridians). The burning stick can also be held over the *xue* (holes) to cause heat to enter the body at these spots. Skimming the surface of the skin with the stick is also possible.

Frequently cones of moxa are prepared. These are rolled out of moxa taken from the stick, and measure up to one inch in height. They can be used directly on the skin, indirectly with an insulating layer, or they can be stuck on top of an inserted acupuncture needle. Moxa used directly on the skin will leave a scar after treatment, and this inflammation will help extract *xieqi* out of the body. More often, moxa is insulated from the skin by layers of other herbs, such as ginger slices, or salt. The insulator serves to produce an extra effect; ginger, for instance, is known to release warmth which influences the digestive function.

A moxa cone on top of a needle allows the heat and curative effect of the burning *artemisia* to be conducted through the needle into the body, without leaving a scar. Some parts of the body (like the face) are not to be treated with direct moxibustion. At certain times some *xue* must not be treated with moxa, because *qi (shen)* may be too heavily concentrated there. People suffering from heat are usually excluded from moxa treatment.

Moxibustion is widely used in China and was once even more common, which explains the existence of sophisticated literature on the subject, such as the Qing-dynasty *Shenjiu Jinglun*.[58] Regular moxa treatment is believed to be helpful in preventing disease.

Using the body to cure: massage and *qigong*

Therapy may include such techniques as massage, chiropractic, *qigong* and exercise. These form a vast field of study and demonstrate that the ancient culture of China was extremely developed in its array of curative and preventative methods. In the techniques described, the physician uses his own body to help his patients.

Chinese massage consists of external and internal aspects. The effects of the massage not only influence the condition of the skin and muscles, but are also directed at bones and joints and, most importantly, at the *qi*, *xue* (blood-fluid) and other internal parts and functions. It uses techniques that would be called chiropractic in the West. All parts of the body can be treated and almost every part of the physician's body can be used to treat patients. Self-massage is a form of therapy as well.

Different systems of massage exist: *tuina* (pushing and grasping), *anmo* (pressing and rubbing), *dianxue* (touching holes), and others. Quite often one system combines all these techniques. Eight fundamental techniques exist, from which all other methods derive: *tui* (pushing), *na* (grasping), *an* (pressing or pushing downwards), *mo* (rubbing), *gun* (rolling like waves), *qian* (pulling), *da* (beating), and *dong* (moving). Some techniques are practised using one hand, some use two hands, some are performed with the feet, and some use other parts of the body. Sometimes a massage-medium is employed. This may be a herbal preparation, perhaps made from scallions, vegetable oil or milk. It is also common to use massage-aids, like sticks or rollers. When using this kind of

Two stone reliefs representing qigong stances. The Taoist physician Hua Tuo is reputed to have based qigong exercises on the movements of animals (wuqinxi: the game of five animals). Above a relief showing the monkey's movements, below, the bear's.

therapeutic technique for curing the effects of accidents (such as fractures) other instruments or aids can be of help: ropes to pull legs and arms, boards to support a broken part and, especially in former times, a large construction resembling a gallows to hang people by their arms, feet or head. More than one person may be required to stretch or lift heavy individuals, but mostly the physician works alone. The therapeutic results expected from these massage techniques range from the relief of pains caused by muscle problems to the curing of cancer. Most techniques are not dangerous and can be combined with other types of therapy.

The past decades have seen an incredible growth of *qigong*-therapy. *Qigong*, the skill of directing and controlling *qi*, has a long history and, even if the name is relatively recent, it has always been in use in China, albeit under different guises.[59] A Western scientist might view *qiqong* as quackery, but the rapid development of *qigong* therapy in China is based on its spectacular clinical results and is supported by scientific research in China, Japan and even the USA. *Qigong* includes methods somewhat similar to hypnosis, psychotherapy, trance, laying of hands and magnetism. The physician primarily uses concentration and relaxation in his body to make his own *qi* flow in the direction he desires. He can transport it outside his own body to make it enter the patient's body, transmitting the *qi* directly or by touching the person. Chinese scientists have discovered that when this is done, magnetic and bio-electrical reactions occur, as well as hormonal and molecular changes. The greatest changes seem to occur within body cells.

Vast amounts of written material have been published on experiments and therapeutic practices in China. These publications report the many medical successes of *qigong*, even for intractable health problems like cancer, on its own or in combination with Chinese and Western therapies. The unusual nature and mysterious origin of this therapy does attract quacks who fake techniques to mislead people and earn money. But serious practitioners willingly have their capacities and therapeutic results examined by China's most distinguished medical research institutes, like the Academy of Traditional Chinese Medicine. Chinese scientists believe *qigong* to be the medicine of the future.

Qigong is also the practice of exercises. Indeed, to become an expert the physician must undergo a long period of intensive body and mind training. Only when one reaches the higher levels of *qigong* can one teach others. Every respectable hospital employs one or more physicians able to teach their patients health exercises, be they for rehabilitation or as a way to prevent further development of diseases.

Preparing medicinal compounds in the 'Lerentang' Yao Dian traditional pharmacy in Kaifeng.

Pharmacist of the Qianyi Yachang Pharmaceutical Company, Nakung, Penghu (Pescadores Island).

Herbs and other medicines

Chinese pharmacology is an ancient science. Influenced by Taoist practitioners of *waidan* (external or experimental alchemy) and encouraged by Taoists and Buddhists investigating natural ways of improving health, it developed into an extremely rich medical system, though its basic principles remained simple. This led to a vast literature on the subject, with encyclopaedic works, such as the *Bencao Gangmu*, but also with many 'family' handbooks full of recipes.

The ingredients used in Chinese medical recipes range from herbs to minerals and animal components. Within these boundaries there is almost nothing that is not suitable for use as medicine. Chinese *materia medica* are classified according to their medicinal nature (*yaoxing*) and taste (*weidao*). Their nature can be cold (*han*), hot (*re*), warm (*wen*) or cool (*liang*). These attributes are called the *qi* of the medicine, and so they can be seen as the four *qi* (*siqi*). Some medicines do not fit into one of these four categories; these are called medicines of neutral nature (*pingxing yao*). The taste and smell of the medicines allow them to be classified according to five other categories: sour (*suan*), bitter (*ku*), sweet (*gan*), pungent (*xin*) and salty (*xian*). Beside these there are also tasteless (*dan*) and astringent (*se*) medicines. Each and every taste or nature influences the basic causes of disease (cold, heat, etc.) and in this way creates a change of condition. Furthermore, their taste makes them harmonise with certain body functions (see table of correlations), and through the relationships of the 'five agents' (*wuxing*), they may affect these functions directly or indirectly.

When preparing medicinal recipes, it is important to take account of the compatibility (or incompatibility) of different medicines, of the volume used (it should fit the conditions of the disease and the patient), of the way it will be used (orally or externally) and of certain restrictions, prohibitions or contra- indications. Traditionally, medicine was prescribed for and bought by the patient, so that he received highly individualised prescriptions. This also meant that he prepared the medicine (dried herbs, animal parts, minerals, etc.) by frying (*chao*), roasting (*pao*), broiling (*zhi*, roasting by means of a liquid, including vinegar, honey, alcohol, etc.) and stewing (*wei*, wrapped in wet paper or wet bread, stewing until the outer material becomes dark). In past decades many manufactured medicines have been produced. These provide an easy, yet less individualised, and therefore often less effective, alternative for the traditionally home-prepared recipes.

Philosophy, Princeton, 1963; and Fung, Yu-lan (transl. D. Bodde), *A History of Chinese Philosophy*, 2 vols, Princeton, 1953.

30 Many translations of the *Yijing* are available. One of the most popular is the RichardWilhelm German translation, translated into English by Cary F. Baines as, *I Ching or Book of Changes*, London, 1951.

31 On alchemy in China see Needham 1974, vol. 5, parts 1-2, section 33.

32 See Baines, *op. cit.*, p. 274.

33 General theory of Chinese medicine may be found in several Western books. See for instance T.J. Kaptchuk, *Chinese Medicine, The Web that has no Weaver*, London, 1983.

34 On this system see Unschuld, *Nanching, The Classic of Difficult Issues*, 1986, Prolegomena.

35 See, for instance, Unschuld, *op. cit.*, who discusses *qi* and other terminology in his Prolegomena (especially pp. 5-6).

36 The *Yunji Qiqian* is a compilation of Taoist texts dating from the Song period (960-1279). The text *Fuqi Taixi Jue* (Formula of Absorbing Qi and Embryonic Breathing) says: '*Jing (essence) is qi. Qi is dao*', (p. 341a). Throughout this article we have used the one-volume publication of the *Yunji Qiqian* published in Beijing in 1988.

37 See Porkert 1974, pp. 166-96, where he discusses several usages of *qi* in Chinese literature.

38 In modern Chinese medicine, and in Western works based on this tradition (like Kaptchuk's *Chinese Medicine*), it is erroneously assumed of *zongqi* that, '*its main function is to aid and regulate the rhythmic movement of respiration and heartbeat, and so it is intimately connected with the Lungs and Heart*' (Kaptchuk 1983, p. 39).

39 This text can be found on pp. 306-14 of the *Yunji Qiqian* edition mentioned above.

40 See the ancient dictionary *Shuo Wen Da Zidian*, *juan* 5.

41 See chapter 2.

42 See C. Despeux 1994.

43 The brain (*nao*) is mentioned in the *Neijing* as a kind of *zang* (storage-place). *Suwen*, chapter 11.

44 The *Xing Ming Gui Zhi* dates from 1669, and belongs to the *Quanzhen* (Complete Realisation) tradition of Taoism. It is a text discussing the successive stages of 'internal alchemy' (*neidan*) and as such reflects the strong (Tibetan) Buddhist influence on Taoist practices.

45 The *Shenjiu Jinglun* (see above) also contains drawings of the *jing-mai* (meridians and vessels) system.

46 *Daodejing*, Chapter 16.

47 See also Y. Liu 1988, vol. 1, p. 18.

48 *Yuanqi Lun*, p. 309c.

49 For a translation of certain texts from the *Yunji Qiqian*, see H. Maspero 1971. He also deals with more ancient texts on diets (pp. 365-73).

50 See 'The World's Earliest Works on Forensic Medicine', in *Ancient China's Technology and Science*, pp. 377-82.

51 Maspero, *op. cit.*, contains translations of several texts on breathing exercises.

52 Kaptchuk 1983, chapters 5-8, discusses the theory and practice of diagnosis in a simplified way.

53 'Herbal' medicine is the most used type of medicine in China, but animal and mineral ingredients are also prescribed and mixed with herbs.

54 See Maspero, *op. cit.*; Despeux 1981; Vercammen 1991a and 1991b.

55 On acupuncture, see G.D. Lu and Needham 1980.

56 G.D. Lu and Needham *op. cit.*, pp. 302-18.

57 See, for example, K. Chen and Y. Cui 1991.

58 See above. This book not only informs the reader about how to use moxa, but also contains chapters on how to grow, prepare and store it, as well as chapters on Chinese 'anatomy' and 'physiology'.

59 There are many publications on different types of *qigong* in China. Some of these types remain true to their ancient name and their practitioners prefer not to be called '*qigong*-masters'. This is especially the case with Taoist practitioners.

60 See Jingwei Li's article 'Surgery in Ancient China' in *Ancient China's Technology and Science*, Beijing, 1986, pp. 369-76.

61 J. Li, *ibid*.

62 Many Taoist books and texts deal with this subject and the Taoist way of living. The *Yunji Qiqian*, for instance, abounds with mostly short texts on *yangsheng*. For translations, see Maspero 1971.

63 There are several reasons why this will never become popular literature; most texts are esoteric, written in complex characters and often quite expensive.

64 Some (Western and other) dances may even be included. There has been an explosion of *qigong* courses and publications and many 'secrets' are revealed by real or so-called experts. Much abuse exists.

65 One of the commonest mantras in China is the Tibetan Buddhist *om mani padme hum*. Also popular is a system of pronouncing six simple sounds, combined with body movements and breathing. This is called *liuqi jue* (six *qi* formula) and is of ancient Buddho-Taoist origin.

References

Chinese sources are mentioned in the text. I have consulted different editions of these sources when writing this article; as this text was written for a general public, I only list the titles, not the different editions; general works are listed as in the Western bibliography.

Chinese Sources

Chaoshi Bing Yuan

Huangdi Neijing Suwen

Huangdi Neijing Lingshu

Kong, Jianmin, *Zhongguo Yixue Shigang*, Beijing, 1989

Li Shizhen, *Bencao Gangmu*

Nanjing

Shen Nong Bencao Jing

Sun, Simiao, *Qianjin Yao Fang*

Sun, Simiao, *Qianjin Yi Fang*

Wang, Shuhe, *Maijing*

Wu, Yiding, *Shen Jiu Jinglun*

Xing Ming Gui Zhi

Yunji Qiqian

Zhenjiu Jiayijing

Western Sources

Chan, Wing-tsit (translation & compilation). *A Source Book in Chinese Philosophy*, Princeton N.J., 1963.

Chen, Ken and Cui, Yongqiang. *Handbook to Chinese Auricular Therapy*, Beijing, 1991.

Cheng, Xinnong (ed.). *Chinese Acupuncture and Moxibustion*, Beijing, 1990.

Davies, Walford (ed.). *William Wordsworth, Selected Poems*, London, 1990.

Despeux, Catherine. *Taiji quan: Art Martial, technique de longue Vie*, Paris, 1981.

___ *Prescriptions d'acupuncture valant mille onces d'or*, Paris, 1987.

___ *Taoïsme et Corps Humain*, Paris, 1994.

Geng, Junying *et al. Medicinal Herbs*, Beijing, 1991.

Henderson, Gail E. and Cohen, Myron S. *The Chinese Hospital, A Socialist*

Work Unit, New Haven and London, 1984
Hillier, S.M. and Jewell, J.A. *Health Care and Traditional Medicine in China 1800-1982*, London, 1983
Huard, Pierre and Wong, Ming. *La Médecine des Chinois*, Paris, 1967.
Institute of the History of Natural Sciences, Chinese Academy of Sciences, *Ancient China's Technology and Science*, Beijing, 1987
Jia, Lihui and Jia, Zhaoxiang. *Pointing Therapy - A Chinese Traditional Therapeutic Skill*, Jinan, 1990.
Jiao, Guorui, Qigong. *Essentials for Health Promotion*, Beijing, 1990.
Kaptchuk, Ted J. *Chinese Medicine, The Web that has no Weaver*, London, 1983.
Liu, Yanchi. *The Essential Book of Traditional Chinese Medicine*, 2 vols, New York, 1988.
Lu, Gwei-Djen and Needham, Joseph. *Celestial Lancets, A History and Rationale of Acupuncture and Moxa*, Cambridge, 1980.
Lu, Henry C. *A Complete Translation of The Yellow Emperor's Classic of Internal Medicine and the Difficult Classic*, 5 vols, Vancouver, 1978.
Lu, K'uan Yü. *Taoist Yoga, Alchemy and Immortality*, London, 1970.
Luo, Xiwen. *Treatise on Febrile Diseases Caused by Cold with 500 Cases*, Beijing, 1993.
Maspero, Henri. *Le Taoïsme et les religions chinoises*, Paris, 1971.
Needham, Joseph. *Science and Civilization in China*, Cambridge, vols I-V, 1956-1980.
Porkert, Manfred. *The Theoretical Foundations of Chinese Medicine*, Cambridge Mass., 1974.
Porkert, Manfred, with Dr. Ullman, Christian. *Chinese Medicine*, New York, 1988.
Schipper, Kristofer. *The Taoist Body*, published in several languages.
Sun, Chengnan (ed.). *Chinese Massage Therapy*, Jinan, 1990.
Unschuld, Paul U. *Medicine in China: A History of Ideas*, Berkeley/Los Angeles/London, 1985.
___ *Nanching, The Classic of Difficult Issues*, Berkeley and Los Angeles Ca. and London, 1986.
Veith, Ilza. *The Yellow Emperor's Classic of Internal Medicine*, University of California Press, 1972 (1949).
Vercammen, Dan. *Qigong*, Antwerp, 1991a.
___ *The History of Taijiquan*, Antwerp, 1991b.
Waley, Arthur. *The Way and its Power*, London, 1934.
Ware, James R. (transl. & ed.) *Alchemy, Medicine & Religion in the China of* AD *320, The Nei P'ien of Ko Hung*, New York, 1981.
Watson, Burton, *The Complete Works of Chuangtzu*, New York & London, 1968.
Zhang, Enqin (editor-in-chief), *A Practical English-Chinese Library of Traditional Chinese Medicine*, Shanghai, 1990 (12 vols, presenting a comprehensive work on Modern Chinese Medicine).

Mock fight with fans, performed as physical exercise on the quayside, Shanghai.

Traditional Medicine in China Today

Cai Jing-Feng

In the course of Chinese history, traditional Chinese medicine has rooted itself deeply in the life and traditions of the country and contributed to the well-being of the people. Before 1949, there existed a government policy to suppress traditional medicine and replace it with Western medicine. Traditional medical practices did indeed go into decline and the whole system of support and functioning of traditional Chinese medicine (TCM) became weakened. Even with this policy, though, TCM did survive and proved that its depth and strength in the life of China could not be eradicated.

After 1949, China's new administrators adopted a policy in favour of TCM, with the aim of giving equal significance to Western medicine and traditional Chinese medicine. The Ministry of Public Health was established in November 1949 and five years later a full, independent, Department of Traditional Medicine was set up within this ministry, headed by an experienced traditional medical doctor. The personnel of the department came mostly from TCM backgrounds. Similar institutions were established at provincial or even prefectural levels to manage TCM affairs.

Though TCM suffered setbacks during certain periods, in general it has grown and developed steadily over the years. In both urban and rural areas it plays an equal role to Western medicine. Today at the village level, nearly 90% of rural communities have a health station of some sort that is responsible for all health care issues of the villagers, including treatment and prevention, vaccination programmes, inoculations, family planning and childbirth. Simple illnesses such as the common cold, bronchitis and superficial injuries are treated at the local level with TCM and Western remedies. Only more complicated cases are referred to the county hospital for further treatment or hospitalisation.

Policies to support traditional Chinese medicine

In China, Western-oriented physicians were always concentrated in large and medium-sized cities. The vast countryside, where 80% of China's 1.3 billion people live, has had to satisfy its needs of medical access with traditionally trained physicians. This situation led to a new policy that differed greatly from the health care vision of the old, pre-revolutionary society. Its main points are summarised below.

The development of traditional Chinese medicine was protected and encouraged. An early step was the study of TCM by physicians trained in Western medicine. In the latter half of 1955, the first group of Western-trained doctors—all with years of clinical experience—arrived to learn about, study and assess TCM. The success of this early programme led to the creation of similar training classes throughout the country, from part-time courses to full six-month and two-year enrolments.

The China Academy of Traditional Chinese Medicine, the highest research institution for TCM, was established in December 1955. People of high academic standing were summoned to carry out scientific research and clinical study with the aim of pushing forward the development of TCM. Later, similar institutions were established at all provincial and municipal levels.

Medical colleges for traditional Chinese medicine were also established. The first four medical colleges were set up in 1956 in the cities of Beijing, Shanghai, Guangzhou and Chengdu. Colleges in the provincial capitals came later. For example, one in Yunnan Province was founded in 1960, and one in Shanxi Province in 1989. Along with the colleges, this system allowed and encouraged veteran practitioners of traditional medicine—physicians and masters of Chinese *materia medica*—to take on apprentices. This kind of relationship has been a tradition in China for thousands of years and remains full of potential for the healing arts.

The first hospitals of traditional Chinese medicine were established in the early 1950s. Traditional Chinese medicine hospitals with sophisticated modern instruments and equipment initially sprang up in large cities and later in smaller centres. Departments of TCM were also set up in hospitals of Western medicine. Pre-existing clinics were sometimes combined into a larger one to create the embryonic form of a TCM hospital. The aim of such hospitals and departments is to train medical students in TCM, to offer a clinical basis for practising TCM, and nurture clinical science.

The social status of traditional Chinese medicine and its physicians has been upgraded. Relevant government departments were required to receive officials and administrators with TCM backgrounds. TCM personnel at hospitals and offices were given the same rights and privileges as physicians with training in Western medicine. Traditional doctors were authorised to prescribe common Western remedies and issue certificates of diagnosis and death. TCM was gradually involved in the system of free medical insurance for reimbursement of patients' expenses.

Equal rights were granted to both traditional Chinese medicine and Western medicine at all medical institutions, including clinical, teaching and research units. This has manifested itself in several areas: equality of manpower, funding, resources, and research opportunities.

All practitioners of traditional Chinese medicine have been encouraged to learn modern science, especially medical science, to raise their academic level, and to share a common language with contemporary scientists. Traditional theory has thus become more fully intelligible in scientific terms.

The time-honoured healing system of TCM has not only survived the trials of time, but also developed tremendously to play a fundamental role in the health care of the Chinese people in rural and urban areas. The ongoing formulation of TCM policy is based on the analysis of social conditions, the needs of the people and the disparity between rural and urban regions. This has necessitated the participation of social activists, health officials, politicians, sociologists, demographers, and medical personnel: doctors, researchers and health educators.

The Chinese government holds that TCM should not be treated merely as an alternative to biomedicine. In selecting a therapy for a certain disease, it should not be taken for granted that the first choice be given to biomedicine. Instead, when TCM yields the same effects as Western medicine, the priority must be given to the one that is more convenient, economical and readily accessible.

Under the government's preferential treatment, the steady development of TCM can be seen clearly in the figures below (rearranged after Chinese Health Statistical Digest, 1991).

		1949	1991
Number of physicians	Western	3,800	1,065,200
	TCM	27,600	362,600
	Total	31,400	1,427,800
Number of hospital beds	Western	84,400	836,360
	TCM	220	188,200*
	Total	84,620	1,024,560

*beds below county level not included

Development of TCM and integrated medicine

In China today there is a clear effort to realise and create a medical infrastructure going beyond a simple reliance upon two divided systems, TCM and Western medicine. There exists, in fact, a three-tiered medical system comprising traditional medicine, biomedicine, and integrated medicine.

In urban areas, where Western and traditional medical facilities may be equally accessible, those who fall ill have tended to visit Western clinics or hospitals first. Middle-aged and elderly people, however, do not necessarily follow this trend. A certain proportion pay their first visit to traditional doctors because they trust and have more faith in these 'indigenous' healers who apply readily acceptable folk terms to explain medical problems.

The health-seeking behaviour of urban people also depends to a great extent on the type of disease present. For acute organic ailments, they most often seek Western physicians and treatment. However, many chronic and functional disorders (e.g. neurasthenia, vitiligo, functional uterine bleeding, chronic gastroenteritis, chronic colitis, sexual, and other problems) that last for months or even years, lead them to seek traditional doctors. Western doctors customarily refer patients with retractable chronic illnesses to traditional doctors after they fail to cure the problem. Still, it is unfair to draw the conclusion that TCM cures only chronic and functional disorders. Many acute diseases, including infectious dysentry, encephalitis, pneumonia and influenza, can be cured by TCM. When TCM and Western medicine are equally effective, the patient would generally request the traditional one because it is cheaper.

In rural areas, most village doctors apply a dual set of therapeutic methods, including simple patent medicines, both Western and traditional, minor surgery, acupuncture and moxibustion, massage and injections. Village doctors can no longer be easily classified as solely traditionally-oriented or Western-oriented. The term 'integrated doctor' is perhaps more suitable.

Nowadays many city and county hospitals employ a consulting system in which Western and traditional doctors take part in discussing a patient's diagnosis and therapeutic schedule, especially in complicated and refractory cases.

Claims and methodology of traditional Chinese medicine

Frequently reports come in alleging that traditional Chinese doctors have cured various types of malignant tumours. Some even claim a cure rate or recovery rate of 90% or higher, and most claim verification by modern biomedicine, including biopsies, laboratory and x-ray examinations, before and after treatment.

A recent example is that of a doctor in Zhejiang Province, who treated a 56-year-old police officer with carcinoma of the rectum. He had undergone three surgical operations to the abdomen, but was still not rid of the cancer. After ten months of treatment with traditional Chinese medicine, the tumour had disappeared when checked by biomedical methods. It was reported that the doctor treated 170 cases of late-stage cancer with medicines containing heavy dosages of Chinese caterpillar fungus, ginseng and roots of membranous milk vetch (*China Daily*, Nov. 2, 1994). Among the cancers he treated were cancers of the oesophagus, breast, alimentary canal and lungs. The patients who recovered each received the honour and title of 'anti-cancer star'. In Beijing, scores of such 'stars' were recently organised as an itinerant group to proclaim their victory over death. No doubt their experiences have raised the courage of other cancer patients, and the phenomena of such cures is reinforced by the stream of papers that now appear regularly in medical journals on TCM cures of cancer.

Unfortunately, up to now no conclusions can be drawn from these many cases. Traditional Chinese medicine emphasises flexibility and the adaptation of general principles in treatment, and it is questionable whether experiences are repeatable. Nevertheless, it seems conceivable that TCM is effective in strengthening the immune system, improving resistance, and raising patients' quality of life. TCM certainly helps cancer patients who receive radio and chemotherapy by enabling them to see the therapy through to its conclusion. Such combined measures fall under the category of integrated medicine.

Rural medicine

People are interested in the fate of China's 'barefoot doctors'. The term itself appeared during the period of the Cultural Revolution. It was widely used to describe the primary medical workers, or health cadres, who came from the peasantry, in rural areas, and who in fact first appeared shortly after the founding of the People's Republic. In the 1950s, a large number of young villagers underwent short training courses of three to six months to become rural doctors; some even studied for one or two years. These doctors, though only at a basic level, had close and intimate ties with the rural masses and could satisfy their fundamental health care needs.

'Bare-foot doctor' astride a galloping horse. Chinese title: pao ma song yi, 'a race by horse to bring medicines'. China, Guangdong, Shiwan Glazed stone ware. National Museum of Ethnology, Leiden.

After the Cultural Revolution (1966-76), the 'barefoot doctors' disappeared; it seems they came and went with the turbulent times. It should not be concluded that they were of no practical significance; they played an important part in rural health care during that period.

Doctors and paramedics continued to live and practise throughout the rural and remote parts of China. Nowadays they are known as 'village doctors'. The style of work, the long history of traditional medicine, folk remedies, and use of special medical terms, made them invaluable in helping the rural people, bringing primary health care and alleviating the worst health problems. Those doctors and medical personnel who evolved out of the 'barefoot doctors' in time needed to accommodate to the changing conditions in society, both in their livelihood and level of training.

Today, most village doctors are financially self-supporting. Their reputation and practice demand that they steadily upgrade their knowledge and continue to meet the requirements of patients. The 1992 National Symposium of Directors of Bureaux of Public Health and Presidents of Hospitals Above the County Level strongly suggested that village doctors of the 1990s go to special training schools or county health schools for training courses of over three years. Many village doctors have achieved such qualifications.

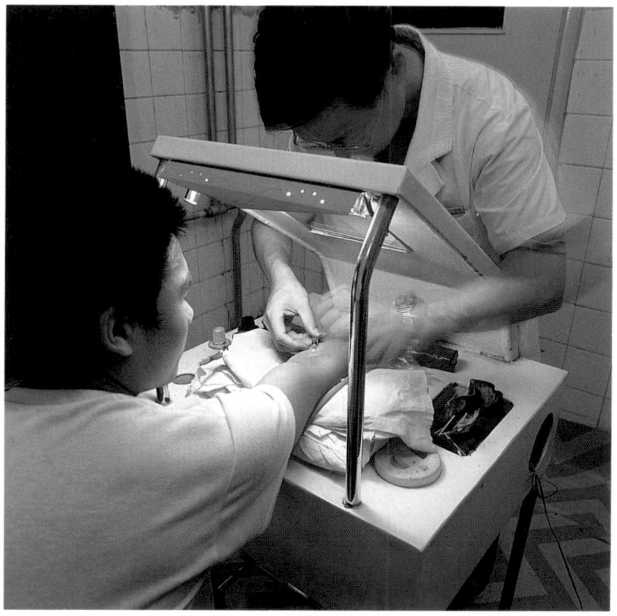

Treatment with radiocative material at the Beijing Military Hospital, Department of Nuclear Medicine.

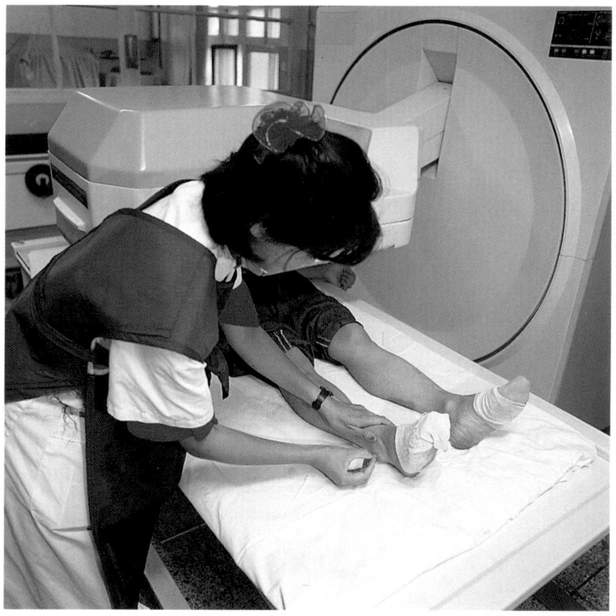

Accomplishments

The integration of TCM and Western medicine, once called 'confluence of medicine', became a government policy after 1949. The aim of integration is to create a new medical sector by drawing on the strong points of both traditions. This approach is especially beneficial when disorders, particularly refractory ones, cannot be solved satisfactorily by either system alone. To date, integrated medicine has done well with such diseases as acute abdominal problems (e.g. biliary stones, urinary stones, ectopic pregnancy), some cancers, complex bone fractures and chronic functional diseases (e.g. chronic atrophic gastritis, protracted viral hepatitis).

Physicians from this sector have created a variety of approaches for the integration of both systems. In the beginning, they adopted simple measures. Traditional recipes and techniques such as acupuncture, moxibustion, massage and decoctions were combined with simple Western remedies: aspirin, eye and nose drops, penicillin injections, sulphonamides, vermicides, mercurochrome, gentian violet, and others. Later, systematic and scientific measures and projects were set up for the observation of therapeutic results. Integrated medicine has approached and clarified some traditional theoretical problems (e.g. *yin-yang* principles, one satisfactory conclusion has been to show that kidney *yin* and *yang* deficiencies are related to hypofunction of the pituitary-adreno-cortico axis). It has also looked at the intrinsic nature of visceral disorders, including blood stasis, kidney asthenia, spleen asthenia and the underlying pathophysiology. The synthesis of TCM and biomedicine has yielded some satisfactory results. Diseases such as bronchial asthma, lupus erythematous, coronary atherosclerosis, neurasthenia, functional uterine bleeding and gestosis—all separate entities within biomedicine, with different pathologic and pathogenic mechanisms—are seen by TCM as having a single pathological background, that is, deficiencies of kidney function. By treating the diseases with the same therapeutic principles, even the same recipes, TCM treatment yielded satisfactory results for all the above diseases. This shows that TCM theory and practice are well grounded and involve obscure scientific principles that need further interpretation with the help of modern biomedicine. Integrated medicine, a major element of China's healthcare policy, holds great promise for the development of modern medicine.

Medicine of the minorities

China is a republic of many nationalities, with 55 minority groups comprising about 6% of the population. The overwhelming majority (94%) belongs to the Han (Chinese) nationality. Even so, minority medicine is an integral part of traditional Chinese medicine; each minority group has its own medical experience and history with special local features. Some systems of medicine have preserved intact a rich heritage that is widely used in health care and treatment of the local people in far-flung areas. Among these, Uighur and Tibetan medicine are worthy of mention.

Tibetan medicine is a tripartite tradition with indigenous medicine at its core, supplemented by long contacts with Ayurvedic and traditional Chinese medicine. Chinese people value Tibetan medicine and medicaments. A popular outpatient clinic has been established in Beijing where not only Tibetans but other nationalities seek assistance from Tibetan doctors.

The Uighur nationality of China's westernmost Xinjiang region has a strong medical tradition that combines Islamic (Unani) medicine with Ayurvedic and traditional Chinese medicines. There are also people of the Kazakh, Tajik, Uzbek, Hui and Mongol nationalities in that region.

The Hui, or Muslim, people are found all over China, though they are most heavily concentrated in the north and west. The arrival of Arabs in the seventh century, and the spread of Chinese Muslims—especially during the thousand years since the Song Dynasty (960-1279)—is a complex and fascinating story. Their early medicine was based on the Islamic experience. A book entitled *Hui Hui Yao Fang* (Prescriptions of the Hui Nationality) survives with much of the text in Arabic. Some scholars say it is identical in parts to the Canon of Avicenna, the classic of Arab medicine.

To date, most diseases can be treated, controlled and prevented at the village level, where village physicians are active applying both simple biomedical methods and traditional measures simultaneously. Complicated cases are referred to the county level where, again, doctors might use approaches derived from either system, depending on facilities, costs and resources of the patients. Statistics from the Ministry of Public Health show that 70% of villagers have illnesses treated at village clinics by village physicians, 20% at township health centres, and 5% in county hospitals.

In China, as elsewhere in the world, people look forward to a unified medical system, a true cosmopolitan medicine, drawing the strong points from all existing medical systems, weighing the merits and advantages, which are universally accepted. Integration and intelligent choices are the key. This process may take generations to accomplish. In any case, it is clear that traditional Chinese medicine will live on and coexist with biomedicine for a long time to come.

Preparing herb samples for distillation in a laboratory at the Brion Research Institute of Taiwan, Taipei.

Traditional Medicine In Taiwan

CHEN BIN-CHERN

Taiwan has long had cultural associations with mainland China. Many Chinese immigrants to Taiwan were involved in the medical field and brought with them their traditional ideas and medicines, which led to the spread of traditional Chinese medicine throughout Taiwan, probably no later than the Ming dynasty. According to the *History of Taiwan*, during the Yung-Lin period (1647-61), a Dr Shen Kuan-Wun from Chekiang province was the first to undertake Chinese medical training and clinical practice in Taiwan. Many followed. The traditional Chinese medical system and medical institutions developed rapidly.

In 1897, two years after Taiwan came under Japanese control, a survey put the number of doctors practising Chinese herbal medicine at 1,070. By 1945, when Japan surrendered, the number of doctors qualified to practise traditional Chinese medicine had fallen dramatically. Japan's hostile policy towards traditional medicine had a devastating effect on traditional Chinese medicine in Taiwan.

After 1949, the development of traditional Chinese medicine slowed down, though in the early 1970s there was a resurgence of interest in traditional medicines, natural therapies, and herbal drugs in Taiwan as elsewhere in the world.

Education and training

The Taiwan Department of Health places great emphasis on the continuing education of those already working in the field of Chinese medicine.

In 1958, the China Medical College was established as a private college, its aims: 'to develop Chinese medical sciences, catch up with modern Western medical sciences, and to combine Chinese and Western medical sciences in order to establish a new system of medical science'. In 1966, the Department of Chinese Medicine was created, The seven-year baccalaureate course is the only one of its kind. For the first five years students take courses in both Chinese and Western medical sciences. The Chinese medicine component is compulsory. The holidays of the fourth and fifth years (eight months in total) are spent either in the China Medical College Affiliated Hospital, or other recognised hospitals or clinics. In the final two years students gain clinical experience in teaching hospitals. Qualified students receive a degree in Chinese Medicine , and can take exams to allow them to practise both Chinese and Western medicine. Graduates can use both Western and Chinese medical techniques, thus helping to establish a new system that combines both forms of medicine.

In 1984, the Post-baccalaureate Department of Chinese Medicine was set up to encourage students to undertake academic research in traditional Chinese medicine. A five-year course was introduced. Teaching staff are Masters of Western and Chinese Medicine from the department's graduate school. Professors of medical colleges, along with visiting scholars and physicians from Hong Kong, teach the basic curricula in Western medicine. The Chinese Medical Research Institute offers a suitable environment for post-baccalaureates to pursue advanced studies. Students must take part in a Chinese medicine probation during the fourth semester, and a Chinese medical clinical probation in the fifth. Those who pass all exams are awarded the degree of Bachelor of Medicine.

The Graduate School of Chinese Medicine was established in 1975, in order 'to combine ancient, current, domestic and foreign medical knowledge, to train teachers of Chinese medicine, and to develop Chinese medicine in general'. The two- year Masters course includes such subjects as the history of Chinese medicine, Chinese medical treatment, acupuncture and moxibustion. The three-year doctoral course, established since 1989, is open to holders of a masters degree in Chinese medicine and aims at integrating Chinese and Western medicine. The graduate school is re-editing many Chinese medical texts, such as the *Nanjing*, the *Shan Han Lun* and others.

Official texts for the Chinese medicine curricula have been compiled by the China Medical College. The Chinese Medical Institute has edited and published many medical texts and re-examined some of the early sources. In 1981, the Department of Health put forward a plan to review ancient Chinese medical texts. It engaged a number of experts to compile a Chinese Medical Science Dictionary and Medicine Index. The dictionary was divided into ten sections: internal medicine, gynaecology, paediatrics, surgery, traumatology-orthopaedics, ophthalmology, acupuncture and moxibustion, ENT, and massage therapy.

The China Medical College is the main teaching centre of Chinese medicine, though other shorter courses in Chinese medicine and laboratory courses are offered at many medical and pharmaceutical departments. The Graduate School of Pharmacy offers special courses in pharmacology.

Between 1950 and 1960, the qualifying examination for Doctor of Chinese Medicine was held four times, and since 1977 it has been held annually. Those who pass must undertake eighteen months of clinical training at a designated hospital before a licence to practice is awarded.

The qualifying examination is open to graduates of the Department of Chinese Medicine, the Post-baccalaureate Department of Chinese Medicine, or the China Medical College Department of Medicine, who have completed the necessary credits in Chinese medicine. Chinese doctors living overseas may also apply, if they can show that they have been operating a Chinese medical clinic for a specified period, and that they have achieved an outstanding reputation in a country other than their own.

The examination in Chinese medicine is held to determine the qualification of government employees, and is open to anyone over the age of twenty-two with a specific interest in Chinese medicine. The competitive examination in Chinese medicine is held for those who have qualifications, or who have already passed the qualifying examination in Chinese medicine. Those who pass the qualifying examination, or the special competitive examination, are awarded licences to practise Chinese medicine.

The rapid development of modern technology and medical knowledge have brought calls for the modernisation of Chinese medicine, an improvement in standards, an updating of medical knowledge, and the merging of Chinese and Western medicine. The Department of Health with the China Medical College and the Chinese Cultural University have set up various training courses to improve the clinical and medical skills of traditional Chinese doctors.

The Development and Education Centre of the China Medical College established three staff improvement courses: an advanced course in modern medicine for traditional Chinese doctors, a course in acupuncture and moxibustion research, and a course in traditional medicine for pharmacists. The Development and Education Centre of the Taipei Medical College also established a traditional medicine course for pharmacists.

Administration of traditional medicine

The Department of Health administers traditional Chinese medicine in Taiwan through a number of different institutions including the Chinese Medicine and Drug Committee (in charge of the administration of public affairs and the research and development of Chinese medicines and pharmacology); the Military Medical Branch (which cooperates with the Department of Health and Planning to improve and develop the skills of the staff of the Chinese Military Medical and Drug Branches); and the Military Medicine Branch (which is legally responsible for the control of medical and pharmaceutical firms, and oversees the administration of enrolements and applications for the importation and/or production of Chinese drugs). The National Laboratories of Food and Drugs, which oversees and manages the analysis and testing of Chinese herbs in Taiwan, examines the sample preparations from manufacturers, inspects local hygiene, supervises the quality of herbs sold on the market, and answers consumers' questions. An examination-scale for herbs has been set up which acts as a reference for the quality control of traditional Chinese drug producers. Besides the Department of Health, the cities of Kaoshung and Taipei and local public health offices manage the local administrative affairs of Chinese medicine.

Chinese medicine and therapy

Those who choose to be treated with Chinese medicine need to attend a hospital or clinic of Chinese medicine, or the department of Chinese medicine of a Western hospital. Doctors of Chinese medicine identify symptoms by using the four methods of diagnosis: inspection, listening and smelling, inquiry, and palpation. Herbal therapies, acupuncture, moxibustion, and other therapeutic techniques are used for treatment. Those practitioners who have also received Western training can use x-rays and some biochemical procedures to supplement their diagnostic practices. However more general practice of Western medicine is strictly reserved for doctors of Western medicine.

The Chinese medical insurance system

The Government Employees Insurance System and the Labourers Insurance System were started over thirty years ago. In 1973, it was decided that Chinese medicine should be included. Chinese medical services were limited to simple bone fractures and dislocations. In 1983, it was decided that insurance should be extended to include internal Chinese medicine, gynaecology, acupuncture and moxibustion, and this was initially implemented by eight hospitals. In 1988, the government of Taiwan agreed to allow a number of hospitals to start governmental insurance in Chinese medicine. The Chinese medical hospitals government insurance policy was opened to the public in 1990.

Chinese and local Taiwanese herbal medicine

Although some medicinal herbs are produced in Taiwan, the majority are imported from mainland China, and some from Korea and the USA. As traditional decoction methods are no longer cost-effective, concentrated Chinese herbs are now mainly used. The government is making every effort to standardise the quality and quantity of these concentrated Chinese herbs. The import and use of rare animal products (such as rhinoceros horns and tiger bones) for pharmaceutical purposes is prohibited.

Since 1979, the Department of Health has required that prescriptions of Chinese medicine be accompanied by the original text. Excellent prescriptions can be found in the *Yi Zong Jin Jain*, *Yi Fang Ji Jie*, *Ben Tsao Gang Mu*, and the Chinese Herbal Medical Dictionary. Any variations in composition from the original formulas need to be explained. By 1984, Chinese herbs had to undergo a basic stability test and approval of registration became dependent on the analytical results of such tests.

For thirty years, the Chinese medical and pharmaceutical concerns have conducted research on the many medicinal plants grown in Taiwan. The nomenclature and active components of Chinese herbs are also being widely researched, thus enriching the content of Chinese herbal medicine. The aim of this project is to reduce Taiwanese dependence on imported Chinese herbal materials, and to promote effective research into the medicinal plants of Taiwan.

Integration of Chinese and Western medicine

Doctors of both Chinese and Western medicine have the same task of protecting people from disease, and it is imperative that they learn to cooperate with, and complement, each other. However, Western medicine has made great progress in recent years and, in Taiwan, the quality of service offered by Western medical doctors (who have excellent medical training, modern equipment and advanced research methods) far outweighs that of Chinese herbal doctors.

The current health administration of the Taiwanese government has not, to date, set up an independent institution of Chinese medicine. Although the council for traditional Chinese medicine and herbs under the Department of Health has the power to manage the affairs of traditional Chinese medicine, its personnel and finances are insufficient to revive the situation of traditional Chinese medicine in Taiwan.

If it is to compete with, and be accepted by, the Western medical community, Chinese medicine must modernise, improve research methods, and conduct scientific investigations. The Chinese medical practices of acupuncture and moxibustion are well known in the West, yet they are still not accepted as viable therapies by many in the mainstream of Western medicine. The use of Chinese herbal preparations often suffers the same fate. We hope that by improving development and research methods, modernising, redefining and promoting the fundamental theories of Chinese medicine, it will be possible to demonstrate that—in Taiwan at least—a new form of medicine that actively incorporates both Chinese and Western medical practices is possible.

In recent years the integration of Chinese and Western medicine has been actively promoted in Taiwan, and many research centres and combined courses have been set up to this end. The Chinese Cultural Renaissance Bureau, supported by many other organisations, established a commission to undertake a cooperative study of Chinese and Western medicines. The China Medical College's second hospital set up a Committee of Integrated Chinese and Western Medicine. It has studied many illnesses including asthma, allergic rhinitis, rheumatoid arthritis, hypertension, cerebrovascular accidents (strokes), and hepatitis. The Doctors' Union of Taiwan also set up a special research team to look into cases of cerebrovascular accidents in Taipei and Taichung. In an attempt to systematise disease names, the Taiwan Bureau of Food and Drugs Control established a compendium of Chinese medicine with cross-referenced tables of Chinese and Western disease nomenclature.

Developments in Chinese medicine

Chinese medicine has made great progress in Taiwan, with breakthroughs in areas such as internal medicine, surgery, gynaecology, paediatrics, orthopaedics, acupuncture and moxibustion. The treatment of tumours, hepatitis and renal diseases has also improved.

Regarding internal medicine, Chinese and Western medicine are both employed in the identification of pathogenesis and the causes of disease. As well as Chinese drugs, acumoxa is used as secondary therapy. Systematic research is being carried out into treatment with Chinese drugs and therapy, and into the selection of Chinese drugs and formulas. Besides traditional identification and treatment, Western diagnosis and treatment are also used, and dual treatment with Chinese and Western drugs is being researched. Chinese medicine in Taiwan has performed well, not only in discussions of pathogenesis and the causes of disease, but also in scientific research into clinical therapy.

In the department of traumatology there is an emphasis on manual therapy as well as drug treatment. Treatment is divided into the three stages of stasis and oedema formation, bone knitting, and bone callus formation. The most important orthopaedic drugs are those used to relieve swelling and pain, regulate the muscles, reduce blood stasis and promote the formation of bone callus. Acumoxa therapy is also used in orthopaedics.

Acumoxa research, which began early on, has been supported by the Government of Taiwan, the National Science Council, and the Department of Health. In 1972, the National Science Council, the Taiwan Veterans General Hospital, Taiwan Tri-Service General Hospital, National Taiwan University Medical School, National Defence Medical Centre, and other associations, organised an Acumoxa Research Conference. Here it was decided to set up an Acumoxa Research Unit which was to use traditional acumoxa as a foundation, together with the techniques and theories of modern medicine, to observe the clinical effects of acumoxa on the treatment of diseases, its use in analgesia and anaesthesia, as well as to study associated physiological and biochemical reactions so as to find its mechanism of action. Foreign experts and scholars were invited to review and evaluate the research. In 1975, the first symposium on acumoxa was held.

In 1978, the Department of Health formed the acumoxa study group, and in 1979 the second symposium took place with the participation of the Department of Health and the China Medical College. Whilst earlier studies of acumoxa were oriented towards clinical treatment, a move towards more basic theories now took place. The symposium opened an important page in the medical history of Taiwan.

In 1982, the Department of Health and the China Medical College held the first National Acumoxa Research Meeting in Taipei, with the participation of over 1,000 experts. The meeting proposed unifying academic theories and concepts, thereby enabling scholars to communicate, and Chinese and Western medicine to interact with each other.

In 1981, the China Medical College and the Life Science Research Centre of the National Science Council, held a seminar on 'Acupuncture, moxibustion and cauterisation research and clinical application'. Subjects included pain relief, meridian and acupoints research, immunology, and clinical diagnosis.

The government has supported research into acupuncture and moxibustion by providing manpower, materials, and financial resources. Organisations for studying acupuncture and moxibustion were established at the General Veterans Hospital, the National Taiwan University Hospital, and the China Medical College Hospital. In recent years, this research has successfully promoted the integration of traditional Chinese medicine with Western medicine thereby extending the theories of traditional Chinese medicine, and contributing to the development of a new medical system.

New forms of acupuncture and moxibustion therapies have been developed such as, disposable needles, portable acumoxa machines for home use and a fully computerised acumoxa bed and acupuncture machine. In a recent study Dr Ha compared acupuncture and moxibustion with the He-Ne laser on pain thresholds. This study is the result of introducing Western medical techniques into the field of Chinese medicine. It is now possible to replace acupuncture needles with a laser beam, which is both painless and safe.

In recent years research into acupuncture and moxibustion has progressed only in individual hospitals or research units, and has therefore been difficult to coordinate. Taiwan is undergoing a surge in the scientific research of Chinese medicine. There are some ten centres involved in acumoxa research. The adoption of Chinese and modern medical diagnostic practises and double blind tests to treat patients with acumoxa and drug therapy, makes it possible to compile statistical data. These results can be used as an indication of the standard of development of acupuncture and moxibustion, and of clinical research in Taiwan.

Further education courses for doctors practising acupuncture and moxibustion are held at the extension centre of Taiwan's China Medical College. Classes in acupuncture and moxibustion were introduced after the State of California (USA) expressed concern about doctors adding acupuncture and moxibustion to their licences. They now have to complete 30 hours of professional education in Taiwan. Acupuncture and moxibustion are listed as required subjects for students of Western and Chinese medicine at the China Medical College (Western medicine department students must learn four grades of acupuncture and moxibustion, students of the Chinese medical departments must learn eight). Other public and private medical colleges list acupuncture and moxibustion as optional courses, and there are also acupuncture and moxibustion associations and student associations in each public and private college.

As cancer is one of the ten leading causes of death in Taiwan, cancer research has been given a high priority. Since 1976, the National Cancer Institute of the National Science Council has underwritten a medical research project on the application of Chinese medicine in the treatment of cancer. A variety of projects are included. As part of research into Chinese anti-tumour medicines, 147 kinds of Chinese medicine were selected for trials. The researchers of the National Cancer Institute established an experimental model that could be effectively applied to the treatment of cancer with Chinese herbs. A study into the effective anti-tumour composition of Chinese medicine includes research into the inhibition of cancer cells, enhancement of the immune system, the use of Chinese medicine to induce cell differentiation, etc. Research into anti-cancer compound formulas in Chinese medicine has focused on enhancing immune systems with traditional Chinese supplementary formulas, and also more common clinical formulas.

Clinical identification and treatment, coordinated with acumoxatherapy, can help to relieve cancer patients to a certain degree. Many effective formulas for cancerous tumours are being collected. The treatment of cancer will be enriched through the use of Chinese medicine.

Top: The herbarium documentary centre of the Brion Research Institute of Taiwan, Taipei.

Middle: Preparing patients' prescriptions of crude herbs in the pharmacy of the China Medical College Hospital in Taichung.

Below: Drugstores in the Far East are often spacious supermarkets such as this one in Taipei.

Rice fields in the mountains near Hao Binh, north-west Vietnam.

Traditional Medicine in Vietnam

NGUYEN VAN THANG

A characteristically Vietnamese medicine

As a country of Indochina, Vietnam has seen a mixture of many different cultures and civilisations. It has a tropical climate, hot and humid weather with a monsoon season. This climate has produced a lush and abundant florae diversity with approximately 10,000 plant species from north to south.

The origins of Vietnamese traditional medicine probably date back thousands of years. It is a combination of a number of different therapies and uses a multitude of wild and domestic plants whose leaves, flowers, fruits, root barks and sap have curative properties. Other therapies include acupuncture and moxibustion, lancing, scarification, and cupping, to treat a multitude of diseases.

This traditional medicine is principally composed of two elements. The first, popular medicine (usually referred to as 'Southern medicine'), dates back to time immemorial and makes use of a multitude of disparate recipes handed down from generation to generation. The second, the medicine of scholars (popularly referred to as 'Northern medicine'), was introduced mainly from China, and is based on the principles of ancient oriental cosmogony.

Vietnamese traditional medicine comprised an important part of the official health system of Vietnam, and it developed alongside and together with modern medicine, from which it derives scientific foundations and to which it brings centuries of experience.

The revaluation of traditional medicine has provided many convenient solutions to the immediate problems of our country. We hope that in the future traditional and modern medicine can combine to bring about the foundation of a characteristically Vietnamese medicine that is not only scientific, but also national and popular.

A brief history of Vietnamese traditional medicine

The traditional medicine of Vietnam can be dated back to the period of the Hung kings (2,879-250 BC). From the time early man first began to live in communities in our territory, a traditional medicine began to take shape. Through a system of trial and error and experiences drawn from the gathering of food, the early inhabitants learnt to identify plants with medicinal properties that could be used for the prevention and treatment of diseases. They also developed various techniques such as inhalation, hot compress application, moxibustion, lancing and blood-letting, acupuncture, massage and digipressure, bone-setting, and the application of compresses soaked in medicines, to solve disease problems which occurred in living and working activities.

Everyday life experiences relating to nutrition, clothing and housing were taken into consideration and these, together with an understanding and knowledge of the natural world, astronomy and bio-meteorology, have contributed to the development of a national traditional medicine.

A number of practices from this early period highlight the therapeutic effects of diet. During the period of the Hung kings, starch was discovered in the stem of the bang tree and the tro fruit. Palm trees were found to contain a nutritious substance that was eaten to avoid starvation. Ginger was eaten with breads, fish and trionychid turtles, to reduce the fishy odour and to facilitate digestion. These practices led to the habit of using ginger, onions and garlic not only as condiments but also to prevent disease.

The practice of making square glutinous rice cakes (filled with green bean paste and pork fat), glutinous rice dumplings, cooking sticky rice with *Momordica cochinchinensis* seeds at New Year and other festive occasions, and the daily drinking of green tea and *Eugerna operculata roxis* decoctions, all have their origins in the therapeutic, nutritional and preventative status of foods.

The practice of betel-chewing began in the eleventh century. Betel (areca nut and lime) is chewed to warm the body, freshen the breath, and to prevent the penetration of harmful energy through the naso-buccal pathway. A lacquer made from sticklac, *Galla Sinensis* and pomegranate roots, was applied to the teeth to prevent loosening. People in mountainous areas ate Job's grass and drank Galingale water as a malarial preventative.

By the third century BC the techniques of alcohol distillation (promoting strength and enabling the preparation of medicines) were mastered. Under the Thuc dynasty (257-179 BC) the practice of applying poisonous substances to the tips of copper arrows was introduced. In the second century BC many medicinal plants were discovered.[1]

From 179 BC to AD 938 Vietnam was under Chinese feudal control. A number of Chinese practitioners came to Vietnam to act as doctors for the Chinese lords. During this time a large number of Vietnamese drugs were exported to China, and some of these (e.g. *Coix lachryma jobi L.* and *Quisqualis Indica L.*) were selected and described in Chinese herbal manuscripts, with references to the utilisation of the plants as practised by our people. A number of the tropical plants of Vietnam were also introduced into China (these included water rice, summer rice, sweet potato and sugar cane).

Since that time these two forms of medicine Vietnamese and Chinese—have been intermingled. This exchange of ideas and experiences brought about the integration of our traditional medicine with the Chinese, which in turn led to the formation of a Vietnamese national traditional medicine.

A strong national traditional medicine began to develop during the independent Ngo dynasty, AD 938, and continued under the Dinh and Le dynasties. The establishment, under the Ly dynasty (1011-1223), of the Royal Physicians' Service to oversee the king's health, brought about the extension of medicine to the whole country. However the people were still strongly influenced by myth and superstition, and treatment by magic was still common in many areas. In 1136, King Ly Thanh Tong was treated for insanity with Soapberry baths and incantations at the Gian Thuy Pagoda (Nam Ha Province) by the bonze Nguyen Ming Khong.

Medicine developed significantly during the Tran Dynasty (1224-1399) with the founding of the Institute of Royal Physicians, and in 1261 the practice of recruiting through examination was established. The Institute also organised the gathering of wild herbs in the An Tu Mountains. The Military Health service also cultivated medicinal plants for their own use in Vanan Duoc Son (Hung Tao Commune, Chi Linh district, Hai Duong province). In 1306, King Tran Du Tong distributed drugs to the population to control epidemics, and organised the cultivation for sale of onions and garlic along the banks of the To Lich River (Hanoi Capital).

The bonze Tue Tinh founded curative institutions for the population in pagodas belonging to Son Nam province (Giao Thuy District) and Hai Duong province. He also launched the movement towards the cultivation of medicinal plants by families, in temples and pagodas, so as to ensure a readily available supply of drugs. Since then the professional herbal drug plantations in Nghia Trai (Van Lam district, Hai Huy province) and Dai Yen commune (Hanoi), have prospered. The bonze Tue Tinh became popularly known as 'the god of Southern medicine'. Tue Tinh also wrote a number of medical books including the *Nam duoc than hieu* (Miraculous Effects of Southern Medicines), which was compiled from manuscripts listing 499 Vietnamese drugs and 10 other specialised works that contained 3,932 Vietnamese prescriptions, and the *Thap tam phuong gia gaim* (The Thirteen Medical Remedies and their Variations), with dissertations in rhythmic prose on the pharmacological properties of plants.

Under the Ho dynasty (1400-6) acupuncture was developed. Nguyen Dai Nang handed down the book *Cham cuu tiep hieu dien la*, for the treatment of 130 kinds of diseases with 140 acupuncture points, 13 of which were his own creation.

The Le dynasty (1428-1788) laid down a policy for the development of medicinal plants and medicines. The Academy of Royal Physicians in the court had a Department of Medical training, with medical schools in the provinces. The Military Health Service had practitioners among the defence troops and, since 1666, its own medical health institute. The eighteenth century also saw the creation of the Royal Institute of Medicine for Elephant Troops.

The *Hong Duc* code had specific regulations regarding social hygiene. Poisoning was severely punished, abortion was forbidden, and under-age marriages were discouraged.

There are a number of specialised works dealing with traditional medicine from this period. These include, *Nguyen Truc* (1429) on paediatrics and massage, *Chu Doan Van* (1461) on epidemics, *Hoang Don Hoa* (1574) on military medicine and veterinary medicine, and *Le Duc Vong* in the eighteenth century on ophthalmology. One of the most detailed collections is the *Hai Thuong y tong tam linh* (Treatise on Medical Knowledge by Hai Thuong), which is a veritable encyclopaedia of traditional Oriental medicine, and was written by the great and famous physician Lan Ong Le Hun Trac (1720-91). It comprises fundamental theory, medical ethics, medical education, hygiene and the prevention of disease, methods for maintaining and prolonging life, nutrition, the pathology of internal, surgical, gynaecological and paediatric diseases, pharmacological empirical recipes, and case reports. Lan Ong has bequeathed to us the therapeutic orientations according to the clinical picture of Vietnam.

The other great physicians of the Le dynasty, Tay Son dynasty, and Nguyen Dynasty, are: Trinh Dinh Nguan, Tran Ngo Khiem, Nguyen Hoanh, Nguyen Quang Luong, Le Trai Nhu, and Nguyen Dinh Chieu.

Some characteristics of Vietnamese traditional medicine

The Chinese domination of Vietnam lasted for over 1,000 years. Its influence on the cultural and medical traditions of Vietnam can be clearly seen in, for example, the classical distinction between *Thuoc nam,* 'Southern medicine', and *Thuoc bac*, 'Northern or Chinese Medicine'. Both were practised and gradually combined to give rise to a medical science that is now identifiably Vietnamese.

The most characteristic aspects of 'Northern medicine' were its complete system which worked on the basis of the principles of ancient Chinese cosmogony, and the use it made of Chinese therapeutic agents prepared according to formulas handed down through classical Chinese writings.

Chinese medicine as practised by Vietnamese physicians in a Vietnamese environment has, through the centuries, been modified slowly but surely to suit the physical, physiological and pathological characteristics of the Vietnamese people. The hot and humid tropical climate of Vietnam is very different to that of northern China.

'Southern medicine', on the other hand, is wholly indigenous to Vietnam. It derives from popular practices and dates back to time immemorial. Although it lacked a perfect theoretical system, it did contain a vast range of internal and external therapeutic treatments, and a set of methods for small scale surgery using a host of remedies handed down from generation to generation. The predominant ingredients were leaves, flowers, fruits, barks and woods.[2]

'Southern medicine' was practised long before the introduction of 'Northern medicine'. It continued to develop alongside the latter, separately and in conjunction with it. 'Southern medicine' was regarded as an invaluable heritage. Its use in association with 'Northern medicine' was advocated and, eventually, a Vietnamese traditional medicine that contained both elements was practised.

Dr. Nguyen Van Le works in the La Bac tribal area. His living room serves as a practice, pharmacy and dispensary.

Villager from the Zao tribe in her hut at To Ly, north-west Vietnam.

Tue Tinh, 'the god of Southern medicine', and Hai Thuong Lan Ong Le Hun Trac, 'the great master of traditional medicine'

Tue Tinh, 'the god of Southern medicine', was regarded as the greatest forerunner of traditional national medicine studying Chinese classical medicine critically and applying it creatively. He tried to adapt it to Vietnamese conditions, being aware that the human body adapts to the environment and that geographical and climatic conditions have a concrete bearing on man's physiology.

His own experiences had shown him that while some medicines worked effectively on the Northern (Chinese) people, they had a contrary effect on the Southern (Vietnamese). Chinese practice stated, for example, that ginger and cinnamon gave a feeling of pleasant warmth. Tue Tinh took the tropical climate of Vietnam into consideration and prescribed smaller quantities of so called 'calorific' ingredients for the treatment of the Vietnamese. He made a special point of making up prescriptions adapted to the characteristics of Vietnamese tropical pathology. For colds, influenza and fevers that were allegedly caused by heat and humidity, he made a *hoa giai*, literally 'reconciling remedy', composed on the one hand of agents to soothe 'heat' (such as *Dolichos hirsuta*, *Gardenia florida*, *Bambusa*, *Gypsam* and *Hodgsonia macrocarpa*), and on the other hand pungent therapeutic agents against 'humidity', (such as *Zingiber officinale*, *Allium fistulosum*, *Perilla frustescens*, *Pericarpinar*, *Citris deliciosae*, *Cyperus rotundus*, *Atractylis lanca* and *Strychnos ignatii*). This remedy had the double effect of lowering the body temperature by means of the sudorific and antithermic elements, while regulating the functioning of the organism by active stomachic and tonic ingredients.

The axiom for every Vietnamese physician remains 'Vietnamese remedies to treat Vietnamese people'. Tue Tinh's work deeply influenced subsequent generations of practitioners, particularly the eminent, eighteenth century, representative of national medicine, Hai Thuong Lan Ong.

Hai Thuong Lan Ong Le hun Trac (1720-91) is the great master of traditional Vietnamese medicine. His major work, the collection *Hai Thuong y tong tam linh* (Treatise on Medical Knowledge by Hai Thuong), is a true encyclopaedia of Oriental traditional medicine as regards both theory and practice. In this work he touched upon all the major aspects of Vietnamese traditional medicine.

Deontology was given a prominent position at the beginning of the treatise. The fundamental theories of Eastern medical treatments were explained clearly and in a critical spirit. The great master dealt with medicine, pharmacy, semiology and diagnostics (there is a meticulously written chapter on the art of feeling the pulse), internal and external pathologies, obstetrics, gynaecology, paediatrics, meteorology as applied to medicine (or the theory of 'five movements' and 'six energies'), preventive hygiene and physical education, methods for maintaining and prolonging life, and nutrition, amongst others.

In his work he recorded thousands of popular prescriptions and medicines developed by the great masters, together with detailed descriptions of various ailments where he displayed a propensity for subtle observation. He was scrupulous and thorough in recording clinical observations of typical cases he had treated, whether successfully or not. He also noted the lessons he had learnt from them for his own and his colleagues' benefit in the books *Y duong an tap* and *Y am an tap* (Clinical Observations—Positive and Negative Experiences).

While studying Chinese medicine, he constantly held that the medicine practised in Vietnam must take into account the special features of the Vietnamese, as well as the climate and the medical resources of Vietnam. In book XI, *Ngoai cam thong tri* (Current Treatment of Diseases of External Origins), he makes a point of drawing the attention of Vietnamese practitioners to the differences between the hot climate of Vietnam and the cold climate of northern China, and to the different pathological aspects of weather-induced ailments in the two countries. He doubted the existence of the classical *thuong han* in Vietnam—a high fever following a heavy cold described by the renowned Zhang Zhongjing; Lan Ong insisted that there was a much milder form in Vietnam called *cam ham* or simple cold, and that this should not be confused with *thuong han*. He strongly advised against slavishly applying therapeutic formulas prescribed by Chinese great masters to cases of simple colds. In particular he warned against using medications based on *Ephedra* and *Cinnamonim* which were highly recommended in China for their 'heat-conveying' properties, but were inappropriate for Vietnamese bodies in a Vietnamese climate. He advocated the use of other medicines based on less potent 'heat-conveying' agents such as perilla, onion and ginger.[3]

Lan ong's writings indicate a highly independent mind, especially the *Dao lun du van* (A Guide to the Comprehension of Medical Doctrines), book VII of his medical treatise. In it he took ancient authors to task over outstanding problems, explaining points that were vague in classical medical reasoning. Lan Ong made constant, conscious references to the national, cultural and medical heritage .

In books XXI and XXII of his medical treatise, *Bach gia tran tang* (Collected Prized Prescriptions), and the *Hanh giam tran nhu* (Simple Remedies), he recorded a large number of popular prescriptions that he had himself tried and found successful. Book X, entitled *Linh nam ban thao* (Vietnamese Herbarium) and written in doggerel in the national language described 722 species of Vietnamese medicinal herbs and gave their different names and properties; most of these species were selected from those studied by Tue Tinh in his *Nam duoc than hieu* (Miraculous Effects of Southern Medicine, vol. I). Others were gathered by Lan Ong and recorded in vol. II. As an addendum to the poems, a nomenclature of 140 medicinal plants with their Chinese and Vietnamese names was drawn up. The total of 962 Vietnamese therapeutic agents thus classified has not been improved on to this day.

Traditional and modern medicine in health policy

Vietnam's health policy is to give priority to prophylaxis (prevention) while boosting therapeutics, and to bring about the systematic combination of modern and traditional medicine with regard to both therapy and prophylaxis.

In a message sent to a Health Cadres' National Conference in February 1955, President Ho Chi Minh suggested that medical cadres should,

> *build up our own medicine based on the principles of it being scientific, national and popular .... Our ancestors had rich experience in treating diseases by utilising both Southern remedies and those of the North. To widen the scope of our medical activity, it is necessary for you to study the means of harmonising eastern with western remedies.*

The following passages all deal with the heritage of traditional medicine, and the combination of traditional and modern medicine to build and improve Vietnamese medi-

Top: Sellers of crude herbs are concentrated around a few streets in the centre of Hanoi.
Middle: Tiger bone powder and seahorse, details from a showcase in a local pharmacy.
Below: Chopping dried medicinal roots in the National Institute for Traditional Medicine, Hanoi.

cine. A resolution of The Third Party Congress (1960) talks of,

> ... *combining traditional and modern medicines in all fields: prophylaxis, therapeutics, pharmacy, cadre training and scientific research.*

The use of traditional medicine and its *materia medica* is encouraged,

> *We must encourage the growing of medical plants and the rearing of animals which provide materia medica.* (Instruction 210 TTG, 6th December 1966)

> *From the results obtained by eastern medicine in prophylaxis and therapeutics, we must draw lessons about the basic principles of the medicine and using our scientific knowledge, go further in examining its theory, correcting what is in error, and raising its levels. We must pay particular attention to popular experience, to recipes handed down from generation to generation, and to remedies used by ethnic minorities.* (Instruction 21, CP 12th December 1967)

As a result of the policy of studying Oriental medicine and combining Oriental and modern medicine, the Institute of Oriental Medicine was founded in 1957, and the Institute of Materia Medica in 1961. Chairs of Oriental medicine were established in health schools. Oriental pharmaceutical factories, stations of *materia medica*, state-run farms or cooperatives dealing with the cultivation of medicinal plants, and medicinal plant gardens in communes were set up. Provincial or city Oriental medicine hospitals, people-funded Oriental medicine infirmaries, and departments of Oriental medicine in Western (or modern medicine) hospitals were also established, along with 1,000 Oriental medicine and pharmacy cooperatives and 3,000 commune health stations using traditional medicine. The Ministry of Health has a department of traditional medicine and a commission to combine Oriental with Modern medicine. In 1957, the Association of Vietnamese Traditional Medicine was founded, and in 1968, the Association of Vietnamese Acupuncture. The Institute of Traditional Medicine and Pharmacy of Ho Chi Mihn City was founded in 1975, and the Institute of Acupuncture in 1979.

From the central to the provincial level, many short and long term amelioration courses for traditional practitioners and Western health workers were started. We have about 10,000 practitioners of traditional medicine. Thousands of secondary physicians, doctors and pharmacists have attended a six-month course on traditional medicine, and over 1,000 doctors have specialised in Oriental medicine.[4]

Some 550 books on Vietnamese traditional medicine have been collected, and a number of Chinese medical texts have also been translated and published. Knowledge of the experiences of traditional practitioners, as well as those scattered among the general population, has also contributed to the promotion of traditional medicine. The number of people benefiting from the combination of traditional and modern medical treatment is increasing rapidly.

Opposite: Acupressure is a highly developed therapeutic technique in Vietnam which many Western chiropractors come to study. Dr. L.Y. Hoang Khac Don at work in the Institute of Acupuncture of Vietnam, Hanoi.

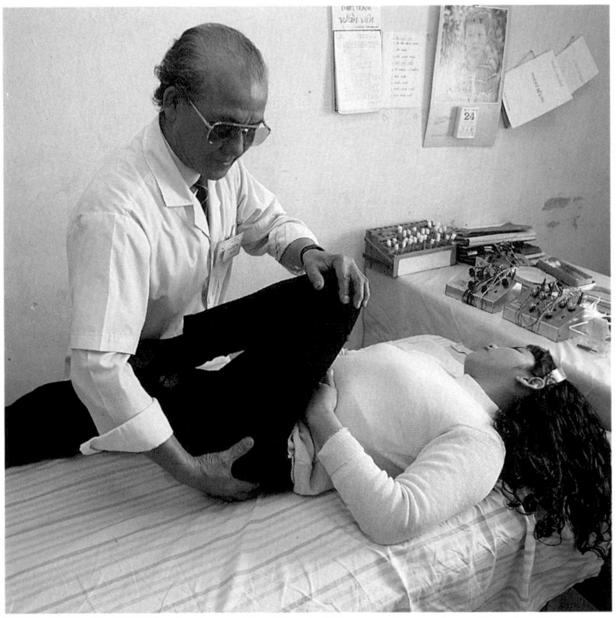

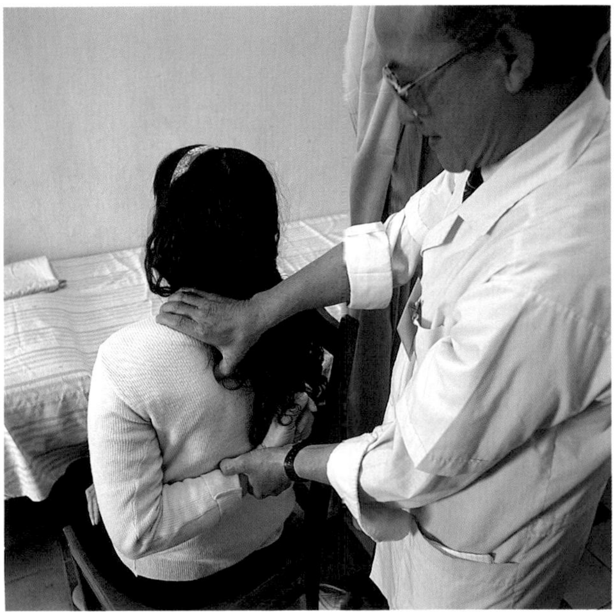

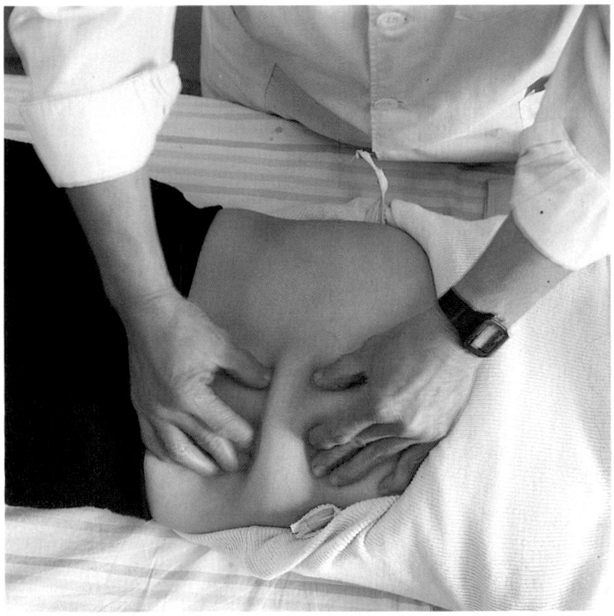

Notes

1 These included longam, litchi, mandarins, Acorus Calamus L., Puerzaria Thorsoni Benth, Alpinia Oxyphykla Mig, and Quisqualis Indica L.

2 Besides using drugs of plant origin, traditional Vietnamese medicine also makes use of the very rich fauna, as well as a number of mineral substances. The prescriptions for drugs of animal origin are derived either from family recipes handed down over the generations, or from particular ethnic groups, or from ancient medical texts. The medical substances of animal origin include both invertebrates and vertebrates. Among the former the *Mulberry bombyx* or silkworm contains many therapeutic agents. Caterpillars treated with *botrytis* and dried on quick lime are administered to children with convulsions. They are also used as an aphrodisiac. *Bombyx* excrement is an ingredient found in antirheumatic and antihaemorragic prescriptions. In traditional Vietnamese medicine the vertebrates are believed to produce better drugs than the invertebrates. Small animals are generally used whole. Often only the smaller part of larger animals are used: the skin, horns, bones, gall bladder, flesh, placenta. A bone jelly known as *cao* can be made of the bones of animals such as tigers, bears, leopards, mountain goats, macaques, etc.

3 The people of Vietnam have long treated influenza, colds, headaches and fevers with an original and often effective method which dates back to time immemorial: 'The bath of sweet-smelling steams' or *xong*. The recipe may vary from region to region, but the basic formula remains unchanged and includes the leaves of the lemon tree, grapefruit tree, bamboo, *artemisia*, *ocimum Sanctum Linn*, *Perilla Ocymoides Linn*, and *Elshotzis crista wilel*. The leaves are put into a pot, covered with water, and boiled. The patient then sits with the pot under a blanket and inhales the fumes. The steam and odorous substances cause sweating (this method can only be used in cases of sweatless influenza, fevers and headaches) and lowers the patient's temperature. The headache abates and the patient is relieved of his symptoms. Some hospitals today use sweating rooms.

4 In his work *Towards a New Medicine*, Dr Pham Bau of the Vietnamese Institute of Traditional Medicine has offered some opinions on the integration of traditional Oriental medicine with modern medicine to build a new Vietnamese medicine. In 1969, Dr Pham Bau introduced the 'hepato-biliary' theory based on the relationship between *zang-fu* (internal organs) and the 'channels-collaterals' according to traditional medicine, and the physiological function of the liver and gall bladder, according to modern medicine. It is possible to view the 'hepato-biliary' system as having a decisive role in the fundamental activities of man: digestion and excretion, nutrition and protection of the organism, sexuality and sexual development, nervous and mental activities, and waking and sleeping psychology. In the meridian system, the hepatic meridian represents 'blood' and the gall bladder meridian represents 'vital energy'. For the viscera and bowels (*zang-fu*), the hepato-biliary system constitutes the main organ generating blood, vital energy, and ensuring the nutrition of the organism. The eleven viscera and bowels depend on the hepato-biliary system which is the centre for the control of the basic physiological processes, anabolism, catabolism, growth, sexuality, development, mental activities and sleep. The waking and sleeping process, especially, have a great significance on health, work efficiency and longevity.

Medicinal herbs and plants grow in profusion in Korea. Sorokto, South Korea.

Traditional Medicine in Korea

Kim Jung Jae

The theory of medical science that originated in China was gradually systematised, and it spread to Korea and Japan where it developed as the main current of medical science in a long historical process which preceded the introduction of Western medicine. In those days cultural exchanges were limited, and Oriental medicine developed largely within the limits of the individual countries involved. Even so, Korean civilisation was highly influenced by its proximity to China.

Evidence indicates that medical books and techniques flowed from old China into Korea in the era of the Koguryô Dynasty (AD 100-668). Since then, both nations seem to have promoted a more intimate cultural exchange in the medical sciences. The medical history of Korea in the Koryô (918-1392) and Yi (1392-1910) dynasties, shows that the Koreans did not simply imitate Chinese medical science, but actively sought to establish a medical system that incorporated their own native medicines and traditions. The historical evidence is found in the medical books and prints of the time.

In the Paekche Dynasty (316-663), Korean medicine was influenced by Indian medical science by way of Buddhism. During the Koryô Dynasty famous medical classics such as the *Chejun iphyo pang* (Effective Prescriptions for Saving People), and the *Hyangyak kugûp pang* (First Aid Prescriptions in the Native Drugs), were published in Korea. In the age of King Sejong (1419-50 early Yi dynasty), the 85-volume *Hyangyak chipsông pang* (Compilation of Native Prescriptions), and the *Uibang yuch 'wi (Classified Collection of Medical Prescriptions)* were edited and incorporated into a medicinal policy for relieving the nation. Moreover the 25-volume *Tongûi pogam,* (Precious Mirror of Eastern Medicine, 1631), compiled by the noted royal physician Hô Chun in the period of King Sônjo (1568-1608), on the basis of fourteen years of research on the medical classics of China and Korea, made a great contribution to the development of Korean medicine.

After the publication of the *Tongûi pogam* in 1613, medical classics such as the *Kyôngak chônsô (Jingue quansha,* 1624*)* and the *Uijong kûmgam (Yizong jinjian,* 1742*)* were published in China. In Korea many famous medical books were also issued, such as the *Chejung sinp 'yôn,* the *ûijong sonik* and the *Pangyak happy'yôn*. However in Korea the general opinion is that on the clinical side these books are not superior to the *Tongûi pogam*. Even though more than 360 years have passed since Hô Chun died, his meritorious achievement remains alive among Korean medical students.

Prior to the introduction of Western medicine into Korea, all diseases and health problems were treated with traditional Oriental medicine. In recent times, however, this long-established system of medicine was overwhelmed by the rapid spread of Western medicine and culture, and went into decline. To a greater or lesser degree, this was a common phenomenon in many countries of Asia. From 1910 to 1945, Korea was also under the control of Japan, and its national Oriental medical system was virtually obliterated. At one time even politicians tried to eradicate Oriental medicine, insisting on its worthlessness. Some Western medical practitioners still look askance at it.

However, thanks to Koreans' attachment to their national medical therapy and the efforts of their medical practitioners, Oriental medicine was able to maintain, though only barely, its traditional existence. The national liberation of August 15, 1945, brought with it a period of renewed interest in, and restoration of, traditional therapies. Oriental medicine is now undergoing a period of development. It has been newly constructed on the firm foundation of its compatibility with Western medicine. Its theory and practice have become the object of worldwide interest and research, attracting the attention of the medical world.

The approach of Oriental medicine

Many scholars have made comparative studies of Oriental and Western medicines, and have analysed and examined the characteristics of the various systems, some of which are outlined below. We should attempt to understand the respective merits and features of the different aspects of both medicines, and to exploit them in a cooperative fashion for a joint contribution to human health.

In comparison with the merits of Western medicine which are minute and analytic, the characteristics of Oriental medicine are to examine and diagnose the function of the human body synthetically. In Oriental medicine, the viscera and bowels are at the centre of the human body, and each part of the body and the mental activities are observed in an organisational correlation. The essence of a disease is seen as an imbalance of the constitution. Therapeutic measures aim to foster the physiological faculty of a natural cure of the human body, thus making the bodily harmony of *ûm* (*yin*) and *yang* a main object. Oriental medicine is therefore referred to as a medical science of balance.

The analytical methods of Western medicine have achieved great effects in the fields of immunology and surgery through the examination of bacteria and the application of chemotherapeutical drugs. According to the synthetic approach of Oriental medicine, a living creature is a unified organism of mind and body that cannot be completely analysed; the analytical method does not account for everything.

Internal and external causes

Western medicine has developed largely around the treatment of diseases which have external causes, such as those caused by bacteria or external wounds. Oriental medicine, however, takes a serious view of the internal causes. These include the functional imbalance of viscera and excesses of the 'seven sentiments' (joy, anger, sorrow, fear, love, hate, and lust). In the pathology of Oriental medicine external causes such as *yukûm oegam* (six causes of external infection: wind, cold, heat, humidity, dryness, and fire), or epidemics, are also taken into account. Yet even diseases with external causes are thought to be influenced by internal causes. Thus, even if communicable germs are present in the body, a good constitution of strong anti-bacteria may not become infected. The existence of many healthy carriers indicates that external causes are not the decisive factor of a disease; whether or not one becomes ill is dependent upon the condition of one's constitution or internal causes.

Harmonisation with nature

Oriental medical science stems from the theory of harmony with nature; the human body can be viewed as a microcosm corresponding to the macrocosm. The existence and development of living things is directly or indirectly affected by objective circumstances and the human body is no exception. Accordingly, there are inseparable relations between the human body and the natural world. Hence, Oriental medicine does not attempt to either counter or conquer nature, but rather strives for harmony with it.

The meditative spirit of Buddhism and Taoism continues to have a great influence on many Koreans. Kounsa Buddhist temple.

The *Hwangdje naegyông* (*Huangdi Neijing*, The Yellow Emperor's Medical Classic) mentions that each part of the human body is a contracted cosmos equivalent to the macrocosm. Following this theory, the Chinese physician Son-Jin-In also maintained that the human body and all other life phenomena operate in accordance with the principle of universal changes.

The human body depends on the operation of the natural world and, like other living beings, it adapts to the natural laws of birth, growth, gathering, and storage, in accordance with the four seasons. Thus in the treatment of disease one of the principal characteristics of Oriental medicine is that it mainly uses natural herbal medicines, and that it soothes the circulation of energy and blood in the meridian connections.

In Western medicine the effective ingredients are extracted artificially from the source of drugs. Whilst such drugs often produce an immediate effect, some drugs and medical treatments also cause serious side-effects or diseases. In comparison with Western medicine, Oriental medicine is deemed to be more natural, as the selection and organisation of the drug ingredients produces a harmonious effect. As the medical value is developed gradually, damage due to long term dosage rarely occurs.

Organ and function

Western medicine, based mainly on anatomy and histology, views the pathological change of organs as the main object of treatment, and it is excellent in treating diseases of the organs and takes surgery as its representative example. Oriental medicine, however, views functional change of the human body as the principal object. The fundamental aim of treatment is to restore the organisational function of viscera-bowels and limbs-body to a normal condition. Hence Oriental medicine may be described as functional pathology.

Reflecting on some of the above features, Oriental and Western medicines inevitably show contrasting characteristics and discrepancies in the fields and methods of diagnosis and treatment. The objective of the medical treatment has therefore to be precisely defined. Neither system should monopolise the medical field.

Those diseases which are caused by germs or conditions requiring operations or surgical treatment, must rely on Western medical techniques. Internal illnesses or semi-healthy situations could become the main object of Oriental medical treatment. Moreover, in many cases, nutrition therapy as applied in Oriental medicine has proved to have a rapid and remarkable effect for expediting the functional recovery of patients who have been operated on.

Schools of Oriental medicine in Korea

Oriental medicine has long followed the essence of the classics such as the *Hwangje naegyông*, *Si Nong ponch'o-gyông* (*Shen Nong Bencaojing*, The Classic on Medicinal Herbs), and *nan'gyông* (*Nanjing*, The Classic on Medical Problems of the *naegyông)*, and it has developed in accordance with the times by supplementing academic theory and clinical practice. It ultimately became divided into several schools.

Sanghannon (*Shang Han Lun,* The Book on Typhoid) with *Kûmgwe yorak* (The Book on General Diseases, *Jinguei yaolüe*) written by Zhang Zhongjing of the Han Dynasty of China, (second to third century), is the first to fulfill the system of scientific theory. It is still used as an important clinical book and is one of the main medical classics. Some considered it the canon of clinical medicine, just as *Hwangje naegyông* is the canon of theoretical medicine. The school that adheres to the prescriptions printed in this book is known as 'The School of Classical Prescriptions'. This school is more prevalent in Japan.

In China, while developing over many generations after Zhang Zhongjing, Oriental medicine was divided into several schools. The Song and Yuan Dynasties, between the twelfth and thirteenth centuries, were especially productive. The four noted schools of this time were: 'The Cooling School' of Liu Wansu, 'The School of Stomach Invigoration' of Li Dongyuan, 'The Attacking Down School' of Zhang Zhihe and 'The School of ûm Nutrition' of Zhu Danxi. These four physicians, in advocating their respective theories and treatments, obtained remarkable remedial effects in accordance with geographical and environmental conditions. Although none of them has universal validity, nevertheless there is still a tendency to adhere narrow-mindedly to the opinion of a single school.

The modern medical science of the Ming and Qing dynasties of China was influenced by the four physicians mentioned above. It utilised free prescriptions regardless of 'The School of Classical Prescriptions' and it became known as 'The Post-Classical School'. The school that compromised between the classical and the post-classical schools is known as 'The Compromise School'.

The general current of Korean medical treatment neither clings to Zhang Zhongjing's classical school, nor does it lean upon the four schools of the Song and Yuan dynasties.

The *Tongûi pogam* widely quoted and investigated such Chinese medical classics as the *Hwangje naegyông*, the *Sin Nong ponch'o-gyông*, the *maekkyu-ong* (The Book on Pulse), the *Sanghannon,* and the other noted medical classics from the Tang, Song, Yuan and Ming dynasties to the Qing dynasty. Furthermore it systematically explains the essence and origins of Oriental medicine by thoroughly consulting the records of successive generations of Korean physicians. This book has generalised, from the orthodox Oriental medicine standpoint, the results of medical experiences accumulated in a long historical process without inclining toward any school or theory. Since the substance of medical science must also be constantly selected and developed in the light of historical changes and according to actual conditions prevailing, a permanent and immutable science cannot be expected.

Korean medicine pays great attention to the original classics, yet to understand them the fundamental theory must be placed against the historical background of the medical literature and their contents should not be accepted unconditionally. For example, over time one finds remarkable changes and differences in diseases (in smallpox and typhoid, for example). Although the types of diseases have changed over time, the main current in the clinical field of Korean medicine is still based on the *Dong-eui-bo-gam*. Therefore it is characteristic of Korean Oriental medicine to have succeeded and developed on this basis.

In Korea there is a special school known as 'The School of Four-Phenomenon Medicine', *Sasang ûihak*. It was advocated by Yi Chema (pen-name: Tong Mu, 1837-99) in the nineteenth century by means of clinical practices in his medical book *Tongûi suse powôn* (The Four-Phenomenon Medical Book). This theory—which originated in Korea—enabled Oriental medicine to develop in a new direction. The many clinicians who follow this theory form the 'Four-Phenomenon Sectional Society'. The theory states that when man is born he is gifted with an innate physical constitution that is classified into four unchangeable types: *Tae Yang* (greater *yang*), *So Yang* (lesser *yang*), *Tae ûm* (greater *ûm*) and *So ûm* (lesser *ûm*). The regimen, dosage and acupuncture for the prevention and treatment of disease should be applied differently in accordance with the different characteristics of these constitutional types in order to maintain the balance of their respective physical constitutions.

There is a 'theory of five-type men' in the chapter by Tong-cheon in the *Hwangje naegyông*, and another theory of constitutional classification is mentioned in the chapter of ûm-yang, 'Twenty-five Men' in the same book. However, Yi Chema's 'Four-Phenomenon Medicine Theory' has greater significance as he gives a more detailed account of the theory and clinical practice behind the curing of a disease.

Clinical practice of Korean medicine

Treatment with Korean medicine is classified into treatment by drugs and treatment with acupuncture and moxibustion. *To'in*, a form of physical therapy similar to gymnastics, as well as massage and digi-pressure therapy may broadly be included in the range of Oriental medicine treatments.

The outstanding virtues of acupuncture have recently attracted the attention of Western countries and the interest of many people. It is well known that widespread and remarkable developments have been made in this field, including acupuncture anaesthesia. Yet, acupuncture is no more than a part of Oriental medicine, and it should be remembered that medical therapy (treatment by drugs) predominates in Oriental medicine.

The drugs used in Oriental medicine are natural substances, such as the roots and barks of plants, nuts and berries, and in some cases animals and minerals, and are mainly used in accordance with the medicinal nature of *sagi omi*, 'Four Energies and Five Tastes', rise and fall, float and sink. They achieve a remedial result without hardly any of the side-effects caused by chemicals. It should also be noted that most of the principal and side dishes of our daily meals contain medicinal herbs.

According to the *Ponch'o kangmok* (A List of Medicinal Herbs), a typical pharmacopoeia of 1892, and the *Chinese Medicinal Dictionary*, recently compiled by the *Kang-So* Modern Medical Institution in China, there are 4,773 vegetal drugs, 740 animal drugs, 82 mineral drugs, and 172 manufactured drugs. These are classified into 5,767 types. Nowadays, however, the medicinal needs of clinical therapy in Korea are met with several hundred herbs or combinations of them. Medical therapy is divided into eight categories: *han* (sweating), *to* (vomiting), *ha* (purging), *hwa* (harmonising), *on* (heating), *so* (dispersing), *chông* (clearing) and *po* (nutrition). These categories are applied to the various symptoms of a disease.

A drug is seldom prepared from a single herb, and prescriptions are generally composed according to the principles of drug-preparation. There are also the categories of *kun* (lord), *sin* (minister), *chwa* (assistant), and *Sa* (servant), in the preparation of drugs, as well as the principle of *Ch'iljông hapwa* (union and harmony of seven sentiments), which concerns the different variations and prohibitions of drug combinations.

In accordance with the theory that there is laxity and emergency in the treatment and large and small prescriptions, the preparation of drugs is classified into seven groups: *tae* (large), *so* (small), *wan* (laxity), *kûp* (emergency), *ki* (odd), *u* (even) and *pok* (complex). Sô Chijae and Chin Kanggi classified the ingredients of drugs into ten types: *sôn* (spreading), *tong* (piercing), *po* (nutrition), *sôl* (leakage), *kyông* (light), *chung* (heavy), *hwal* (smooth), *sap* (astringent), *cho* (dry) and *yun* (moist). In accordance with the rule of treatment, Chang Kyôngak classified it into eight formations: *po* (nutrition), *hwa* (harmony), *kong* (attract), *san* (dispersion), *han* (cool), *yôl* (heat), *ko* (solidity), and *in* (cause).

In modern Korean medicine, drugs are usually classified as: *poyangje* (a drug for aiding nutrition or an eutrophic), *palpyoje* (a drug for disclosing the outer skin or diaphoretic), *choedoje* (a drug for expediting or an emetic), *kongnije* (a drug for attacking inside or a purgative). This classification depends on the effects of the drugs, and takes the *Uibang-chiphae* (A Collection of Comments on Medical Prescriptions) of Wang Ang into consideration.

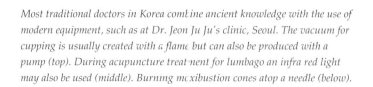

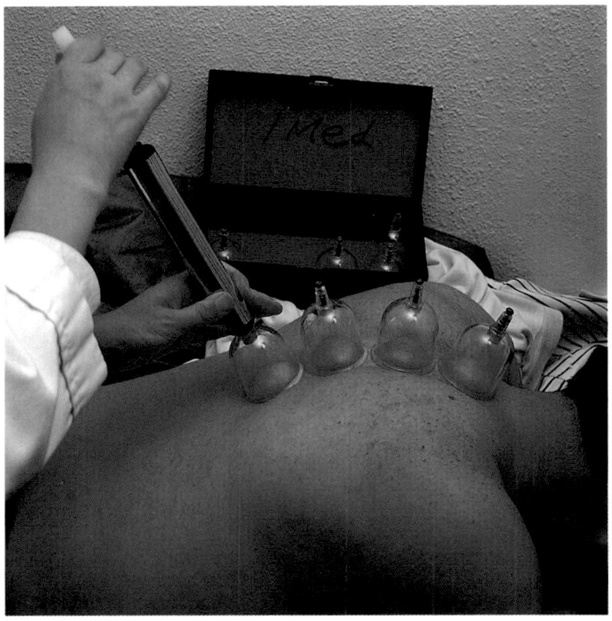

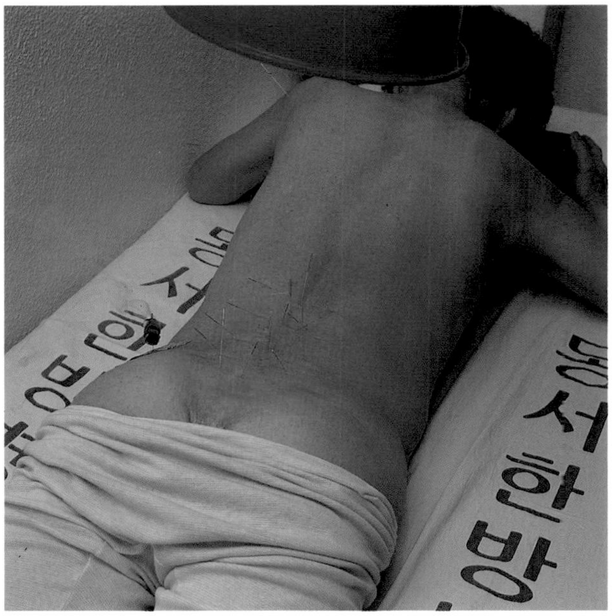

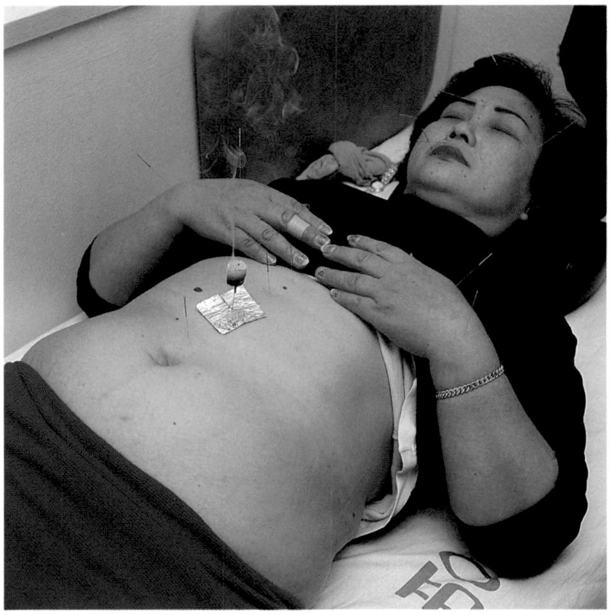

Most traditional doctors in Korea combine ancient knowledge with the use of modern equipment, such as at Dr. Jeon Ju Ju's clinic, Seoul. The vacuum for cupping is usually created with a flame but can also be produced with a pump (top). During acupuncture treatment for lumbago an infra red light may also be used (middle). Burning moxibustion cones atop a needle (below).

In clinical medical therapy, I have made it a rule to adopt the prescriptions listed in the *Tongûi pogam* by Hô Chun. Listed in this book are about 4,000 prescriptions for nearly 1,300 symptoms. Numerous prescriptions are also found in the *Sanghannon* and other medical books. In spite of this, beginners have difficulty in selecting prescriptions, and on many occasions they search for secret prescriptions.

I sometimes receive inquiries from fellow physicians to disclose any secret prescription I may have in view of my comparatively wide experience. Frankly speaking, however, I do not believe that there is a place for secret prescriptions in the orthodox diagnosis and treatment of Oriental medicine. Knowledge must be widely spread and accessible to the public. If there are any secret prescriptions in Oriental medicine they must be the remnants of folk remedies. However proud one may be of private prescriptions, they can not surpass those of orthodox scholars. In order to select and adapt a prescription, physicians should not be dazzled by secret recipes or mysterious measures that rely on chance. Instead, they should make every effort to study in order to properly dispense drugs by being familiar with the pharmacology, and the identification of diseases by means of the four diagnoses on the basis of the orthodox principles of Oriental medicine. All prescriptions form a basis for the preparation of drugs, which must be prepared in accordance with such material situations as changes in symptoms, the weakness or strength of an individual's physical constitution, age, the condition of the environment, and climate.

As to treatment by acupuncture and moxibustion, I have seldom applied the method of moxibustion but I have almost always given acupuncture treatment together with drugs.

It has been verified that acupuncture displays a rapid efficacy on pain, stitch, anaesthesia, bruise, stagnant blood and sudden illness due to the bad circulation of energy and blood. Its range of application is very wide and it plays an important part in Oriental medicine. It is not, however, applicable to all diseases.

When applying acupuncture to patients, the first consideration is that the user must be well versed in meridian theory and have a perfect knowledge of the circulatory system of meridian vessels. Secondly, the user must know about the 365 acupuncture points (meridian points) in the human body, and practise acupuncture according to the principles of the manual arts.

Yi Chun (pen-name: Nam P'ung), author of the *Introduction to Medical Science*, once said that even if a point is missed, a meridian must not be, indicating that great importance must be attached to the meridians. In clinical treatment, I have obtained good results by utilising 66 acupuncture points of *ûm* and *yang* meridians in accordance with a rule of acupuncture points on one meridian.

The immediate effects of acupuncture treatment may explain the tendency of most practitioners to use many acupuncture points at a time. Our elders recommended a minimum of one, and a maximum of four, points. Excessive acupuncture may cause waste or dispersal of energy and blood, from which a better efficacy will not result. Clinical experience also suggests that a better method of acupuncture is to select and apply the acupuncture points exactly in accordance with the meridian related to the organ which causes the disease.

Treatment and education in Oriental medicine

In Korea, diagnosis and treatment is rooted in a respect for tradition and reflects the people's preference and trust. After national liberation a medical code was constituted and proclaimed for the first time and, in 1952, the 'Oriental Medical Doctor System' of our traditional culture was legalised. Consequently the dual natures of Oriental and Western medicines was adopted into the medical system.

At present, thousands of licensed Oriental medical doctors who have passed the national examination are engaged in the frontier fields of national health and educational research at institutions together with Western doctors and dentists all over the country.

Acupuncturists, moxacauterisers, and bone-setters who were issued licenses prior to the introduction of the medical code are still entitled to practise. At present, there are no more than 200 registered acupuncturists and moxacauterisers in Korea. No new licences will be issued under the present medical code. Some acupuncture-moxibustion practitioners are planning to establish a System of Acupuncturist and Moxacauteriser, in order to separate acupuncture and moxibustion from the system of Oriental medical treatment. But this will be difficult under the existing medical system as, at present, Oriental medical doctors are entirely responsible for diagnosis and treatment. Even in pharmaceutical law there is a system of licensed herb dealers engaged in the sale of herbs. They mix and sell medicinal herbs to the public according to the prescriptions in the existing Oriental medical books or those issued by Oriental medical doctors. There are about 3,000 legal herb dealers all over the country.

Korean ginseng (Panax ginseng) is world famous as a panacea and for its stimulating and revitalising effects. Ginseng plantation (top left) and flowering ginseng plants (top right) in Kanghwado. A ginseng wholesaler (bottom left) and stuffed ginseng chicken in broth, a favourite and healthy dish in Korea (bottom right).

However, since new licences are also reserved, the Oriental medical doctor's role in this system of medical treatment is now increasing.

Physical therapies such as *Do-in*, massage and digi-pressure are also very important. Professional massage licences are, however, only issued to blind men. Physical therapists belong to the category of medical technicians and take charge of this ever growing field.

The Korean medical system is strictly classified into general medicine (Western medicine) and Chinese medicine (Oriental medicine). Therefore, Oriental medical treatments such as the use of Oriental medicinal herbs, acupuncture, moxibustion and digi-pressure are practised only by Oriental medical doctors. If a doctor of Western medicine wishes to use Oriental medical treatments, he must obtain a Bachelor degree in Oriental Medicine from an Oriental Medical College, and pass the Oriental Medical Doctors Examination, to obtain a license to practise.

Thus Oriental and Western medical treatments are allowed to cooperate with, but not to infringe upon each other's medical realm directly. In this the Korean medical system differs from that of China, or Japan. In other words it contains a political intention of devising the balanced development of Oriental and Western medicines by protecting and fostering the professional field in order to fully exploit the characteristics of Oriental medicine, in turn contributing to the independent development of Oriental medical science and treatments.

I should like to explain briefly the educational system of Oriental medicine in Korea. The college education of Oriental medicine began in Korea about thirty years ago. The genesis of the present school (The Kyung Hee University) was the Dong Yang Academy, founded in 1948. It suffered much during the Korean War in 1950, and was reorganised a number of times into the Seoul Oriental Medical College, the Oriental Medicinal College, and so on. In 1963, it was reorganised and raised to the status of Oriental Medical School, and a regular six-year course (two years preparatory and four years regular) was started. A graduate school was established in the department of Oriental medicine in 1968, offering Masters courses in Oriental medicine. In 1973, the doctor's degree course was established. At present the Oriental Medical School has about 500 students and 50 professors.

Due to the increasing demand for Oriental medical doctors, an Oriental Medical College was established in Won Kwang University in 1972. In 1979, an Oriental Medical Department was founded at the branch college of Dongguk University in Kyungju City, and in 1981, Taegu Oriental Medical College was established. Thus there are now four Oriental medical colleges in Korea that contribute to the research and progress of Oriental medicine and the scientific development of its education and treatment.

The present curriculum of Kyung Hee University is divided into two parts. In the two-year preparatory course, the liberal arts are mainly taught. The subjects included in the first and second years of the regular course are: anatomy, histology, physiology and biochemistry of Western medicine, and the fundamental subjects of Oriental medicine such as the principles of Oriental medicine, phenomenal theory of viscera and bowels, meridian theory, physiology, pathology and herbology etc. In the third and fourth years the stress is placed on clinical subjects and training.

The school, founded thirty years ago, was a pioneer in the college education of and research into Oriental medicine and, because it was such a new and unexplored field isolated from international exchanges of scholarship and information, it had to learn by trial and error. Every effort has been made to achieve modernisation and educational rationalisation. The professors have translated difficult classics into easy modern styles and filled in deficient parts to compile new college books.

The efforts to raise the educational and research functions and status of the University Oriental Hospital are producing encouraging results. We have obtained a series of good results in the preparation of herbal drugs and the development of medical appliances for diagnosis and treatment.

In Korea there are three authorised corporative research institutions of the Oriental Medical Institution: the Juridical Foundation, the Chehan Oriental Medical Academy and the Oriental and Western Medical Research Centre attached to the university. There are also about ten corporative medical facilities such as Moon Sung Oriental Medical Hospital on Medical Corporation. Several circles for academic research have also been organised.

The course of Oriental medicine

Despite the brisk progress of Western medicine, the use of and belief in traditional Oriental medicine continues to grow. It is certain that both Oriental and Western medicines will contribute to the advancement of medicine—their common goal—by developing the characteristics of both medicines on a cooperative foundation in bilateral coexistence.

Above: Dividing cut herbs into portions, Maeng Hwa Sup Haniuwan, Seoul.
Below: Storing medicinal stocks of cut herbs, sliced horns, etc., Taegu.

Above: Beds of medicinal plants at a herb farm in central Korea.
Below: Medicinal plant garden at Kwangnûng.

The recent worldwide acupuncture boom, has seen an expansion in research and international academic exchanges. An international academic exchange and cooperative research system to cover the whole of Oriental medical science, including acupuncture and medical therapy based on Oriental medical theory, is needed.

Acupuncture has already spread to a number of Euro-American countries and has achieved good results. As far as the whole of Oriental medicine is concerned, however, China, Korea and Japan, with their long tradition of Oriental medicine, will have to play a leading role in its development and progress. These three nations could easily act in concert with one another in this field. They share common features and possess the advantage of comparatively easy cultural exchanges and communications. They also have a long history of research into Oriental medicine.

When presupposing the international unification of Oriental medicine, technical terms and disease names need to be standardised. We should have a common meaning or concept of what a word signifies in the modernisation of a word based on original classics. Furthermore, international cooperation is required for the standardisation of medicinal herbs. A trial draft on this matter is currently being made in Korea, but an international system of herbal medicine needs to be established as soon as possible. We have to concentrate our research and endeavours on establishing an objective scientific system of the theory and clinical treatment of Oriental medicine. Finally, the international exchange of new treatment experience and scientific research has to be promoted. The domestic case report system of Oriental medicine also leaves something to be desired. Therefore, reforms in the reporting of these matter must be devised, on both the national and international levels.

Cooperation of Oriental and Western medicine

As the ultimate goal of all medical science is to cure patients, promote health and longevity, Oriental and Western medical systems must be regarded impartially in the broad view of medical science. Both medical systems, with their contrasting characteristics, have to develop their strong points which will hasten the creation of a third medical science. The first step ought to be the close cooperation between Oriental and Western medicines.

At one time a section of the Western medical field in Korea proposed the unification of Oriental and Western medicines; this was not supported, however, as it was feared that Oriental medicine would lose its independence by becoming integrated with, and absorbed into, Western medicine. Under the existing circumstances in Korea, Oriental and Western medicines are placed into a dualistic coexistent system. The cooperation of Oriental and Western medicines is not a reckless integration or unification but a contribution to the advancement of medicine through mutual cooperation on the basis of a full understanding of each system's traditional features. In order to achieve this, we have to fully utilise many established products of Western medicine and, in some cases, apply the combined treatment of Oriental and Western medicines.

It is a logical conclusion that when the merits of both medical systems—analytic and scientific Western medicine, and holistic Oriental medicine which gives primacy to controlling function—are properly applied to clinical treatment, remarkable results will be produced. Therefore, while acknowledging the co-operation and tie-up of Oriental and Western medicines to be an important problem, presented by the demands of the present generation, the physicians and scholars of both medicines who believe in its necessity and validity, must play a leading role in the resolution and progress of this problem.

Of the university's fourteen colleges, one is a Medical College majoring in Oriental medicine, whilst another Medical College majors in Western medicine. Favourable conditions thus exist for a comparative study of Oriental and Western medicines. Moreover, three educational hospitals attached to these colleges are found in the same building. So the foundations of maximum co-operation of Oriental and Western medicines have already been laid. Moreover, the Oriental-Western Medical Research Institution attached to our university, plays a bridging role. It promotes research activities, and obtains good results from the combined treatment research of Oriental and Western medical teams.

Medicine chest, 'yak-chung', for storing herbs, with 77 small and 3 large drawers. The front of each drawer bears a general name for the stored herb in Chinese characters, as well as a more detailed description on the drawers' inside side panels. c.1880. Collection: Mark De Fraeye, Belgium.

Bronze pitcher for boiling medicine 'chu do'. Silla period, 9th century. This pitcher with tiger-shaped legs was discovered in a royal tomb. Han-Dok Medico-Pharma Museum, Korea.

Bronze pitcher with handle used for dispensing liquid medicine. Koryô period, 11th century. Han-Dok Medico-Pharma Museum, Korea.

Celadon pitcher for decocting medicinal herbs. Chosôn period, 13-14th century. Han-Dok Medico-Pharma Museum, Korea.

Celadon mortar for medicinal preparations. Koryô period, 13th century. Han-Dok Medico-Pharma Museum, Korea.

Medicine chest of the traditional Korean 'pillow' type. The character in mother of pearl inlay translates as to 'to promote health'. Chosôn period, 18th century. Han-Dok Medico-Pharma Museum, Korea.

Advertisement for a proprietary remedy for intestinal problems, 'Wakyogan'. Coloured woodblock print, anonymous. Japan, c.1870. National Museum of Ethnology, Leiden, Holland.

A Brief History of Medicine in Traditional Japan

INEKE VAN PUT

Earliest native medical practices

However little is known about native Japanese medicine, therapy was based on three main elements—exorcism, purification (bathing), and herbal therapy. A story from the *Kojiki* (Record of Ancient Matters) narrates the healing of the white rabbit of Inaba according to these three elements.[1] It tells us how the deity Opo-namudi-no-kami prescribed the following cure for the white rabbit of Inaba who lost his fur to the crocodiles:

> *Go quickly to this river-mouth and wash your body with its water. Then take the pollen of the kama grass of the river-mouth,*[2] *sprinkle it around, and roll on it. If you do this your skin will certainly heal as before.*[3]

The first element, exorcism, was practised by medicine men or magic healers; the Shintō deity (*kami*) Opo-namudi-no-kami is the archetype of the ancient shamanistic practitioners.[4] According to the *Nihon Shoki* (Chronicles of Japan),[5] this deity 'determined the method of healing diseases'. In primitive Shintō, purity was one of the most important concepts; the notion of disease was connected to the notion of pollution. Illness, like natural disasters, physical disfigurements or plagues, was listed as *tsumi* (sin or evil) because its sight 'caused both *kami* and men to feel unpleasant'.[6] It was inflicted on man by neglected *kami* or vengeful spirits taking possession of their victims. Thus the most obvious cure for disease was exorcism and this was carried out either by a shaman who wards off the evil spirits, or by all kinds of purification rites (*harai*).[7]

Since physical uncleanness could itself be the cause of divine wrath, communal purification rites as well as personal bathing and hygiene were even more important as prevention against evil spirits than as treatment. The importance of prevention was further highlighted by the fact that disease and constant contact with it was tabooed, and could potentially lead to public ostracism of an entire family.[8] It is not surprising that out of these early superstitions and aesthetic interpretations of illness an entire culture centered around bathing arose, so typical for Japan that B.H. Chamberlain described it as, 'one of the few original items of Japanese civilisation that does not have its roots in China'[9]. Outings to thermal springs for curing, but also for the mere pleasure of bathing, are still very popular today and their healing effect has been described since ancient times in many legends of the indigenous Ainu people.

Concerning the use and variety of herbs no earlier source is available than the *Kojiki*, which was compiled in 712. Numerous items were listed in this work including: *kuzu* (arrowroot), *shiōsai* (Chinese colza), *suzuki* (pampas grass), *kaba* (birch), *momo* (peach), *kashi* (oak), *hiiragi* (holly), etc.[10] Though it cannot be accepted as an entirely reliable source, every plant listed is native to Japan and only the method of application may have been modified after contact with Chinese medicine. Among ingested drugs, *sake* was the main remedy.[11]

Introduction of Chinese medicine

From the fifth century AD Chinese medicine trickled in mostly through Korean physicians invited by the Japanese imperial court. As early as the year 459, a Korean physician from Koguryö named Te Lai[11] established a medical tradition known by the name of *Naniwa no kusushi* (Medical Practitioners of Naniwa).[13] Not until one to two centuries later, however, was Chinese medicine known as a complete science, and did it become an object of study. The first medical works from abroad, including texts on *materia medica* and acupuncture and moxibustion diagrams, were brought by the Chinese physician Zhi Cong from the kingdom of Wu around 562.[14] The first classes in Chinese medicine are said to have been given in 602 by the Korean Kwal-lük[15] from

Kudara, on the demand of Empress Suiko (*regn.* 592-628).

During the reign of Empress Suiko, the Japanese court also started to send envoys to China (589-618), and again from 630 on to Tang China (618-907). These envoys were originally of a diplomatic nature, but soon they became channels through which Chinese learning, science, and religion entered Japan, largely through the books brought back by scholars on these missions. Precisely when each book arrived is not known, but it has generally been accepted that major Chinese classics on medical theory, acupuncture, moxibustion, sphygmology and pharmacology were introduced through these envoys.[16]

Having studied medicine in China for about fifteen years, two Buddhist monks, Enichi and Fukuin, returned to Japan in 623 and started to promote the systematic adoption of Chinese medicine; up until that time it had been introduced only piecemeal and irregularly. However, the realisation of this goal could only begin after the founding of the government's Institute of Medicine.[17]

In 701 and in 718 two codes, the *Taihō Ritsuryō* and the *Yōrō Ritsuryō* were compiled and established the so-called *ritsuryō* political structure.[18] One of the aims of this system was to further propagate and utilise learning and science; this eventually led to the establishment of an academic system patterned after the Tang dynasty model. Three different institutes were founded in the capital: a University (*Daigakuryō*), an Institute of Divination (*Onmyōryō*), and an Institute of Medicine (*Ten'yakuryō*).

The Institute of Medicine was under the authority of the Imperial Household Ministry and took care of medical administration as well as education. The Medical administrators supervised the choice of physicians employed at the court, and their practice of medicine. The educational programme for physicians was divided into five courses: medicine (subdivided into internal medicine; surgery; pediatrics; and eye, mouth, ear and teeth medicine), acupuncture (including moxibustion), massage (including bone-setting), exorcist incantations, and herb cultivation. All courses took between three to seven years of study each, depending on the specialisation.[19] Applications could be made by members of the aristocracy only, and preferably those who belonged to medical families; women were accepted and educated in midwifery, nursing and acupuncture.[20] After the establishment of the schools in the capital, from 703 smaller versions followed in every province, combining the courses of Confucian studies and medicine. These institutes were known as *Kokugaku* or Provincial Colleges.

However important they were for the adoption of Chinese medicine, the services of these medical institutes were restricted to the higher aristocracy and did not entail an improvement of medical care on a broader level. Medical care for the poor was largely dependent on the private initiatives of Buddhist temples often aided by devout aristocrats; in 723 a pharmacy and an asylum for the poor, the sick and the orphaned were established at the Kōfukuji, clan temple of the Fujiwara family. Again Empress Kōmyō (701-60) established a dispensary supplying free medicine to the needy in 730. Those and other similar facilities continued to exist up until the tenth century.[21]

The first contact with systematised sciences and medicine was quite difficult for the Japanese who were still not literate at that time.[22] Even after they adopted the Chinese writing system, their understanding of the imported books came with difficulty. Moreover, rather than concentrating on the theories underlying the newly imported sciences, Japanese doctors blindly adopted their practical applications. As a result, when the Japanese started to write their own works on medicine, they were basically uncritical compilations of extant Chinese classics. The earliest known work written in Japan, *Yakkei-Taiso* (Outline of Materia Medica), was a short manual on *materia medica* written by Wake no Hiroyo during the Enryaku period (782-806).

A more elaborate work on the same subject was the *Honzō Wamyō* (Japanese names of drugs) written in 918. It described 1,025 different drugs relying mainly on the *Xin Xiu Ben Cao* (Newly Revised Materia Medica) by Su Jing in 659, China's first pharmacopoeia; the *Xin Xiu Ben Cao* was made obligatory for the study of *materia medica* in 787 by the Institute of Medicine. The *Honzō Wamyō*'s appearance is an early indication of the continual attention given to *materia medica* throughout the history of Japanese medicine. The main reason for this was the fact that many Chinese drugs were not available in Japan and so the need to fill this lack gave rise to the study of *materia medica* and research on possible alternatives.

Originally Japanese is the *Daidō ruijûhō* (Classified Prescriptions Collected in the Daidō Era) written in 808 by Abe no Manao and Izumo no Hirosada. This work contains old recipes from family and temple chronicles as well as prescriptions of famous physicians. Its compilation was ordered by Emperor Heizei who feared that native medical practices would be lost.[23]

Another major work and the oldest extant document on medicine in its original form, is the *Ishinpō* (Prescriptions at the Heart of Medicine) by Tanba no Yasuyori in 982. This book mainly lists quotations from over 100 major Chinese works. Written in thirty chapters it is the first complete survey on medicine.[24] Due to its varied and complex background however, it proved too extensive for everyday use, and in 1081 Yasuyori's great-grandson compiled a collection of emergency treatments excerpted from it.[25]

Decline and recovery of Chinese medicine

By the time the *Ishinpō* was written, Japan had already started to put drastic limits on foreign contact. Feudalism and isolationism had gradually taken hold, and the last envoy had come back in 894. The *ritsuryō* system stopped being effective and consequently the Institute of Medicine lost much of its influence on the level of administration as well as education. At court, medical practices were dominated by superstition, exorcism and prayer, as depicted in such famous novels as the *Tale of Genji* and the *Pillow Book*. Medical education was mainly in the hands of the Wake and Tanba families who taught the knowledge accumulated by former generations.

However, the general decline of the sciences and isolationist policy occurred at the same time as the flourishing of Buddhism which continued to develop its relations with the continent. Along with works on religious matters, Buddhist priests—who were about the only ones to get court permission to go abroad—also brought new books on medicine which gradually incited a new interest in improving Japanese medicine. On his travel from China, Eisai (1141-1215), founder of the Rinzai Sect,[26] introduced tea to Japan and wrote about its healing and strengthening qualities in *Kissa Yōjōki* (Guide to Good Health through Tea Drinking). Towards the end of the Kamakura period (1185-1392), and before the reopening of the trade relations with China in 1401, Buddhist sects started to dispatch monks for the sole purpose of studying medicine in China. Evidence indicating the coming age of renewed interest, development, and specialisation in Chinese medical science was the compilation of the *Ton'ishō* (Selected Medical Cures) by the priest Kajiwara Shōsen (1266-1337). Not only did he cover Chinese medicine from the Sui period to the Tang dynasty, the work itself was written in mixed character and *kana* style so as to make it accessible to a broader public. Furthemore there was the establishment of an ophthalmological school by the monk Majima 'Seigan' (Brighteye) Shigetsune (d. 1379), and the compilation of a medical encyclopaedia by the Zen priest Yûrin. His *Fukudenhō* (Prescriptions Gathered for [Buddha's] Blessing), compiled about 1368, was also based on Chinese works, but utilised an original classification of diseases in terms of cause, symptoms, diagnosis, prognosis and therapy, much like modern approaches.

In addition to the new influx of scientific knowledge from abroad, civil wars at the end of the Muromachi period (1392-1568) greatly contributed to the further development of medicine. Because of the wars, there arose a demand for 'combat medicine', and this eventually led to the development of surgery.[27] Medical practice spread from the capital since many physicians lost their jobs with the defeat of their masters, and then started wandering the country to earn a living. Furthermore, facing the scarcity or financial unavailability of certain herbs and drugs, these physicians were obliged to use substitute products found readily in Japan, and to return to some of the native practices of folk medicine.

The establishment of Chinese medicine as a Japanese discipline

Finally, as the assimilation of Chinese medicine adapted to the needs and circumstances of the Japanese, *kanpo* (Chinese method) or Japanised Chinese medicine, took shape. Typical for *kanpo*—as distinct from continental medicine—was and still is its use of fewer and more easily obtainable ingredients, as well as application in smaller doses. Uniquely Japanese is the practice of measuring abdominal palpation in addition to regular pulse palpation when evaluating the patient's physical and psychic condition according to the 'four methods'.[28]

The tradition on which *kanpo* schools today are based goes back to the sixteenth and seventeenth centuries, and more specifically to the establishment of two major schools. The founder of the first school *Goseihōha* (the Latter-day School of Medicine) was Tashiro Sanki who stayed in Ming China for eleven years to study Li and Zhu medicine, also called Yuan medicine after the Yuan era (1279-1368). In contrast to their predecessors from the Jin period (1126-1234), Liu Wansu and Zhang Congzheng, Li Ai and Zhu Zhenheng opposed the use of strong drugs and advocated prevention—in Zhu's case by sometimes using mild drugs—claiming that external pathological agents can enter the body only when it is weak. However, it was Tashiro's student Manase Dōsan (1507-94) who made Yuan medicine clear to several hundred students. He taught them in his own private academy, the *Keitekiin*, in order to maintain his principles of simplicity and practicality in medicine which he incorporated in the textbook, the *Keitekishû* (Collected Orientations, 1574). In the 1650s advocates of the newly introduced Liu and Zhang theories (which were actually older) raised criticism against Yuan medicine, but this school never gained substantial strength.

Of more importance was the classicist school (*kohōha*), which would finally overrule the Li-Zhu tradition. The Li-Zhu tradition is followed by only a small minority of *kanpo* schools today. What they attacked was not so much the classics such as the *Neijing* and the *Shang Lun* upon which the Li-Zhu and Liu-Zhang schools based themselves, but rather their interpretation. Instead they sought to reaffirm the primacy of the classics (and especially the *Shang Lun*)[29] by returning to the simplicity of early Chinese medicine and 'creating a new and more empirical approach to therapy which was unprecedented in China'.[30] Besides the empirical approach that in the eighteenth century led to the first human dissection by Yamawaki Tōyō (1705-62), the classicist school was also concerned with the search for the origins of disease. Much debated and attacked even among fellow classicist physicians was Yoshimasu Tōdō's (1702-73) theory that all diseases come from the same poison. To expel the poison many laxatives, emetics and sudorifics were used; influences from the Shintō belief system are apparent.[31] The theory itself might seem naive today but Yoshimasu's approach is in fact closer to contemporary Western pathology than are the humoral pathologies of traditional Chinese medicine.

Iberian 'southern barbarian' medicine

In 1549, the first missionary, Franciscus Xaverius, arrived at Kagoshima with two Portuguese Jesuits, two servants and three Japanese he met on Malacca, thus opening Japan to the coming influx of Western culture and science. In addition to the teachings of the Bible, the Jesuits and later on the Dominicans and Franciscans too, also made use of Western learning and medicine seeing in these a means for spreading Catholicism. For the common people who were denied access to medical services the arrival of these *nanbanjin* (southern barbarians) meant some relief in this time of war among feudal principalities. The introduction of 'cosmopolitan medicine' by making medical care accessible to the common people, was the main accomplishment on the level of medicine in this first wave of Western influence.

Luis de Almeida (1525-1583), a Portuguese merchant who entered the Society as irmão (brother), was a pioneer in cosmopolitan medicine. He was disgusted by the increasing practice of *mabiki* ('thinning out seedlings', i.e. getting rid of unwanted children by means of abortion, infanticide or exposure) among the poor, and opened a home for foundlings in 1556. Supported by Ōtomo Yoshishige, lord of Bungo, he expanded it at the end of the same year with a hospital for sufferers from leprosy and syphilis and a pharmacy supplying herbs from Macao.[32] The Society however changed its attitude and prohibited further involvement in medical practices. The result was that Almeida left the hospital he opened only one year earlier. The Jesuits did not exactly cease supplying medical care completely, but mainly restricted it to *samurai* and nobles, leaving the poor, the lepers and those suffering from venereal diseases, to their Japanese helpers or their Spanish colleagues, the Franciscans and Dominicans.

However by the end of the sixteenth century, pressure against Christianity grew, ending in the expulsion of all Spanish and Portuguese and the complete closure of the country to foreigners in 1639. With the banishment of the 'southern barbarians', Iberian medicine was gradually replaced by its Dutch counterpart.

Dutch 'red-hair' medicine

During the period of national isolation that lasted until 1854, only the Dutch (and Chinese) were allowed to continue their trade under very strict conditions. Dejima, an artificial island just off the coast of Nagasaki, was appointed to the Dutch as the only place where they could stay and trade. This island thus became the only place through which Western knowledge infiltrated into Japan.

At the Dutch trading post there were always one or two physicians to serve the needs of the director and his employees, in all amounting to some sixty physicians by the time the last one was dispatched in 1850. The greatest contribution of these Dutch and sometimes German physicians to Japanese medicine consisted in introducing Western anatomy and surgical techniques.

Because only the government interpreters had direct access to Western medicine brought by the Dutch, they were the first to found surgical schools and publish books on the subject. One such interpreter was Narabayashi Chinzan (1643-1711) who wrote *Kōi geka sōden* (Orthodox Tradition of Red [-hair] Surgery), one of the most unusual works on Western medicine of the Edo period (1603-1868). Though some claim it to be a retranslation of Ambroise Paré's work on surgery, it is probably a mixture of what he learned from the Dutch physicians at Dejima and parts of Paré's book.

During this first century of Dutch-Japanese relations the work of the Dutch physician Willem ten Rhijne (1647-1700), who wrote about acupuncture and moxibustion in his *Dissertatio de arthride: accedit mantissa schematica: de acupunctura et orationes tres* (London, 1683), introduced these oriental techniques to Europe for the first time.

In 1740 even the Japanese government showed an interest in Dutch studies and commissioned Aoki Kon'yō and Noro Genjō to study Dutch. The most important result of the official study of Dutch learning appeared in 1774 in the form of *Kaitai Shinsho* (A New Treatise on Anatomy) by Maeno Ryōtaku and Sugita Genpaku among others. Enthusiastic about the striking resemblance between the relation of organs in the dissected bodies of criminals and what appeared in the charts of a Dutch translation of Johan Adam Kulmus' *Anatomische Tabellen* (Danzig, 1722) they promptly began the translation.[33] After this the number of translations increased precipitously and so did experimental work in medicine.

Most practitioners who contributed to major developments in medicine were educated in both Dutch and Chinese medicine, thus founding what might be called the eclectic Dutch-Chinese school of medicine. At the beginning of the eighteenth century Fuseya Soteki (1747-1811) discovered that urine is not produced in the intestine, as the Chinese claimed, but in the kidneys. His discovery was actually earlier than William Beaumont's who came to the same conclusion only in 1842. In *Oranda Iwa* (Medical Tales from Holland, written in 1803 and printed in 1805) Fuseya described his experiment and its results.

After endless experimentation, Hanaoka Seishû (1760-1835) invented a drug for general anaesthesia, which he called *mafutsutō*. The name came from a legendary Chinese doctor who was said to have used it to perform major surgical operations. With this drug, composed of *Datura alba*, *Aconitum spp.*, *Angelica dahurica*, *Angelica decursiva* and *Ligusticum wallachii*,[34] in 1805 Hanaoka succeeded in removing a breast cancer under general anaesthesia.[35] In the West, where general anaesthesia was not discovered until 1846, similar operations were still impossible.

Notwithstanding these major discoveries that originated from the eclectic Dutch-Chinese school, the conceptual foundations between both traditions were so different that the combination finally turned out to be impossible. The practice of 'pure' Western medicine was initiated by Von Siebold, a German physician who during his first stay in Japan (1823-29) introduced direct clinical instruction.

Now, 150 years later, cosmopolitan or Western medicine is state-supported and it dominates the Japanese medical system. However, this does not mean that the Western scientific approach has replaced all superstitious and religious thinking in medicine. Even today many Shintō and Buddhist temples sell talismans and amulets, and shamanistic practitioners still offer their services in warding off diseases. A nationwide survey of 1950 showed that at that time about 50% of the Japanese still believed in the effect of magic against disease.[36] *Kanpo* is the second most employed medical system, and it is offered by private clinics. Its traditional healing methods include acupuncture, moxibustion, massage and herbal therapy, all of which underwent adaptation and development, sometimes leading to specifically Japanese methods such as *shiatsu*, a massage technique using some principles from the martial arts.

Generally speaking *kanpo* refers to the entire system brought from China to Japan, but nowadays the term is often used when referring to its application of herbal therapy in particular.

'Hashika yōjō no kokoroe'. Dietary advice for patients with measles. 'It is good to take dried radishes, carrots, red adzuki beans, etc. Some items that should not be taken are: chicken, shellfish, fish, fried bean curd, sake, vinegar and rice cakes. These kinds of food can sometimes be fatal'. Ukiyo-e woodcut print by Kunimasa, 1885. Naito Museum of Pharmaceutical Science and Industry, Gifu.

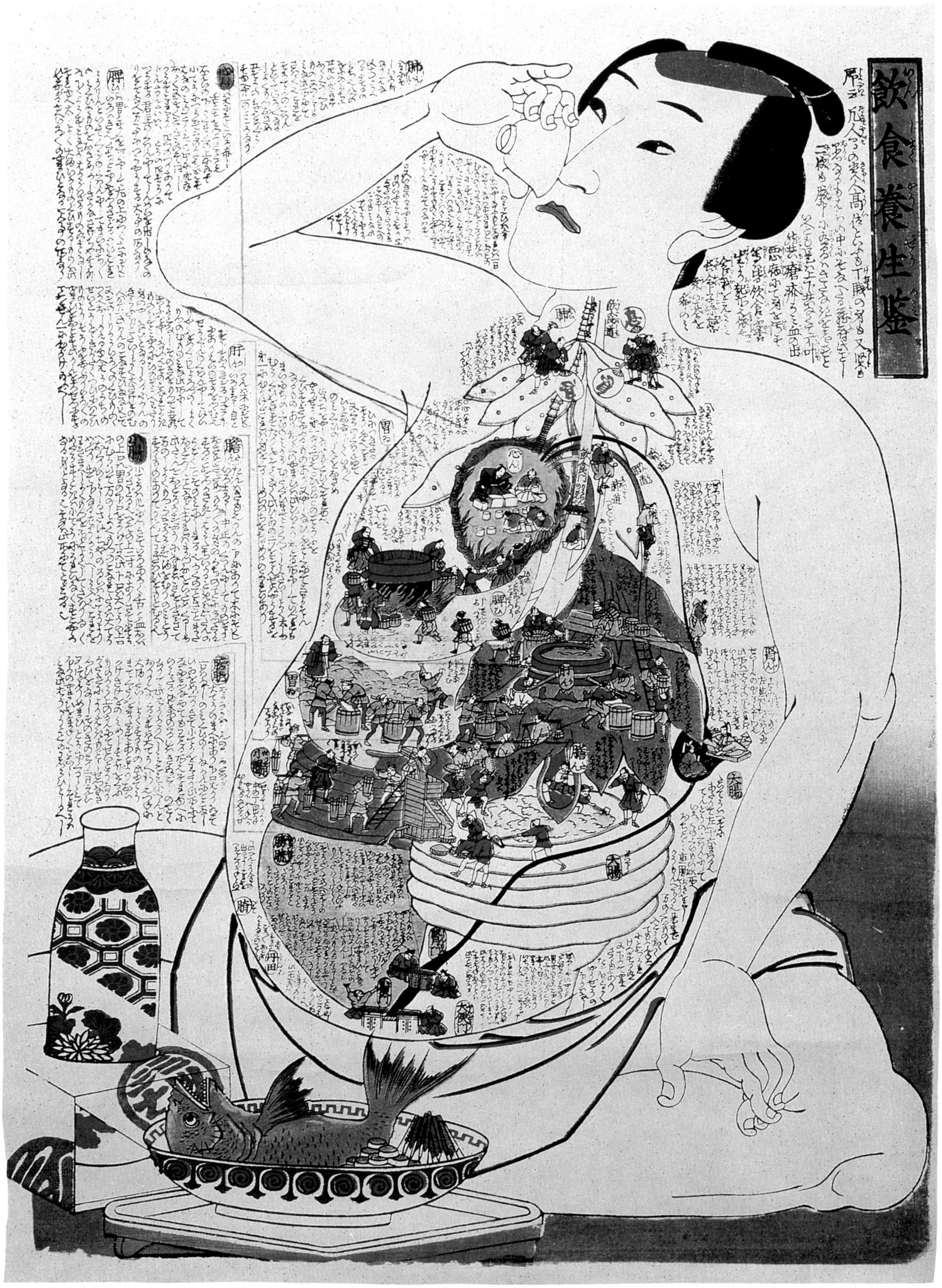

The Rules of Dietary Life, 'Inshoku yōjō', or the means to achieve longevity. The print demonstrates how all skin eruptions are caused by over-indulgence of the senses. Ukiyo-e woodcut print Kunisada Utagawa, c. 1850. Naito Museum of Pharmaceutical Science and Industry, Gifu.

'Hashika karuku hō'. Advice on the relief of measles which prohibits the taking of fish, chicken, mushrooms and eggs for fifty days. Ukiyo-e woodblock diptych by Oju, 1862. Naito Museum of Pharmaceutical Science and Industry, Gifu.

Johannes Pompe van Meerdervoort (1829-1908) with Fuxi and Shennong. He founded the first hospital in Japan. Detail from a scroll painting, possibly by Kuoshoshi 1865. National Museum of Ethnology, Leiden.

Title page of a work on anatomy by Johannes Valverde based on the drawings of Andreas Vesalius and printed by Plantin in Antwerp in 1568.

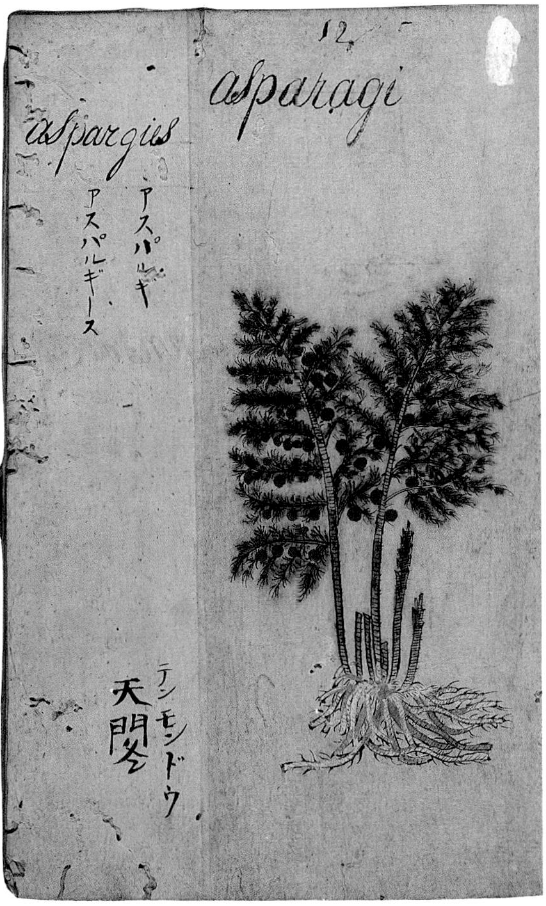

Asparagus plant from a seventeenth century herbal or 'Kruydboek'. The names are given in Dutch and Latin and transliterated into Japanese and Chinese characters. Wellcome Institute, London.

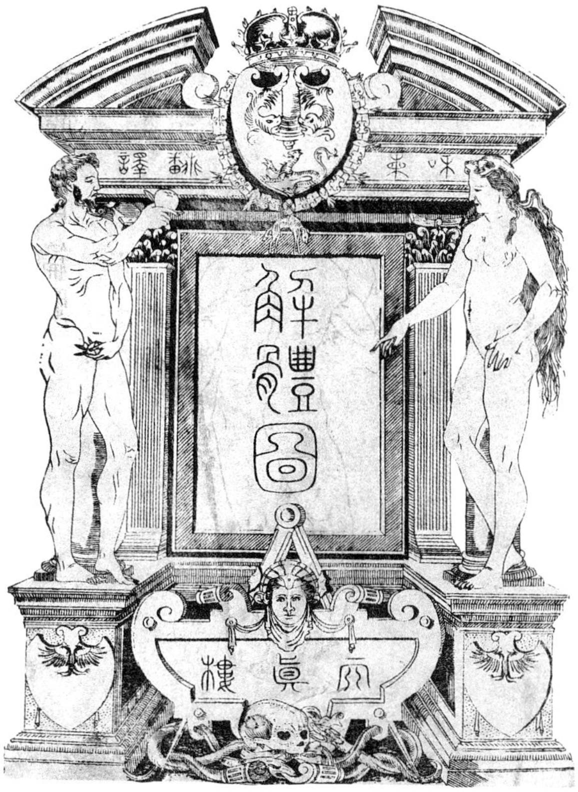

Title page of the 'Kaitai Shinsho', the 'New Book on Anatomy', published in Japan in 1774, where it was to have much influence.

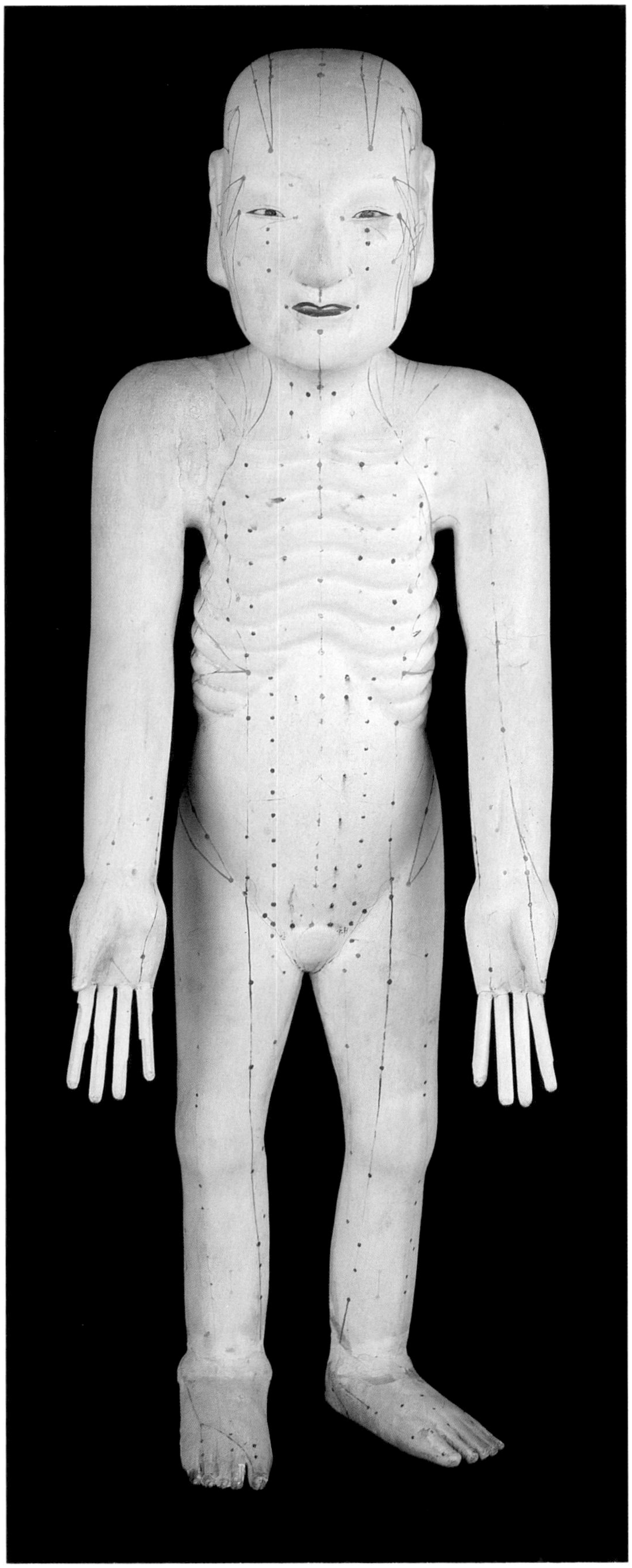

Acupuncture model showing the meridians and acupuncture loci. Japan, early 19th century, collected by Philipp Franz von Siebold. National Museum of Ethnology, Leiden.

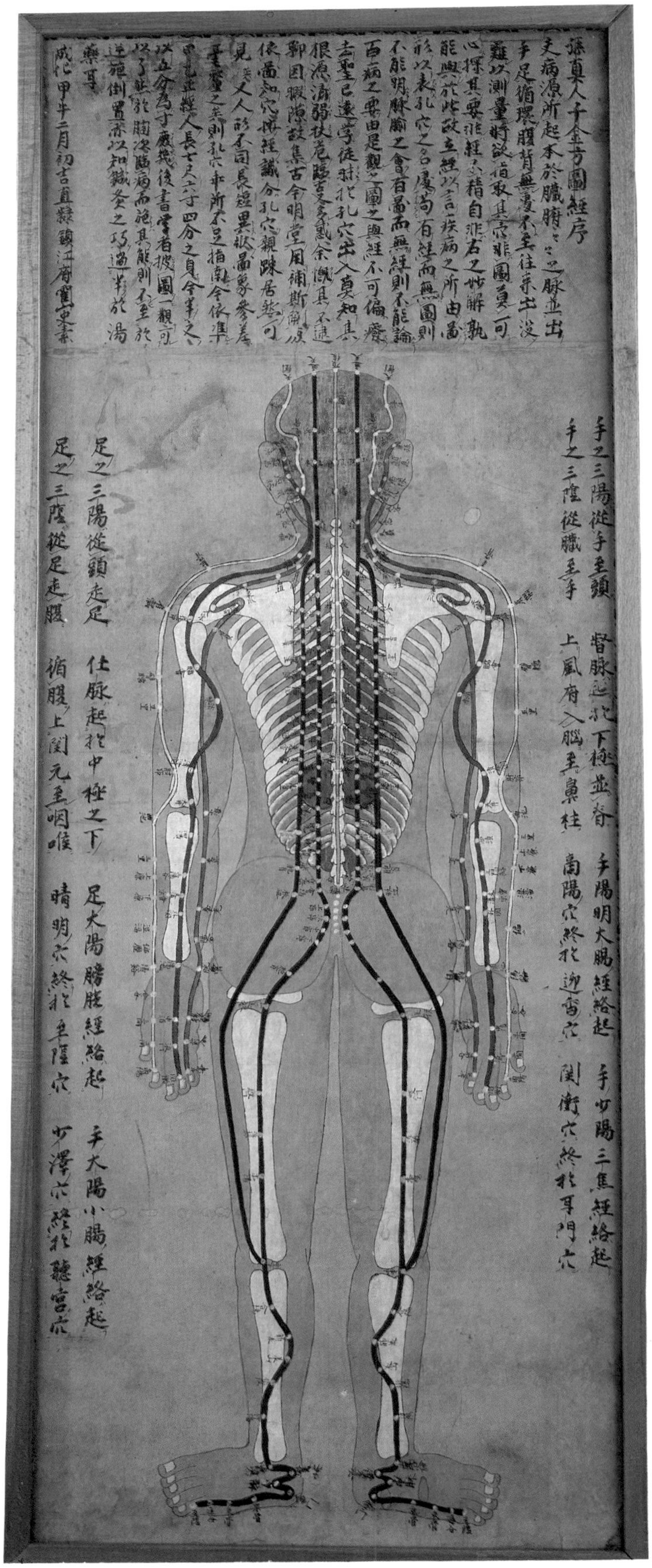

Meridians and loci for acupuncture and moxa treatment, after a Chinese original of 1474, from a work of the same title by Sun Simiao (died 682). Early 19th century. National Museum of Ethnology, Leiden.

Lacquer box for moxa instruments with a polychrome mother-of-pearl inlay illustration of a moxa-doctor with a female patient. Japan, early nineteenth century, collected by Philipp Franz von Siebold. National Museum of Ethnology, Leiden.

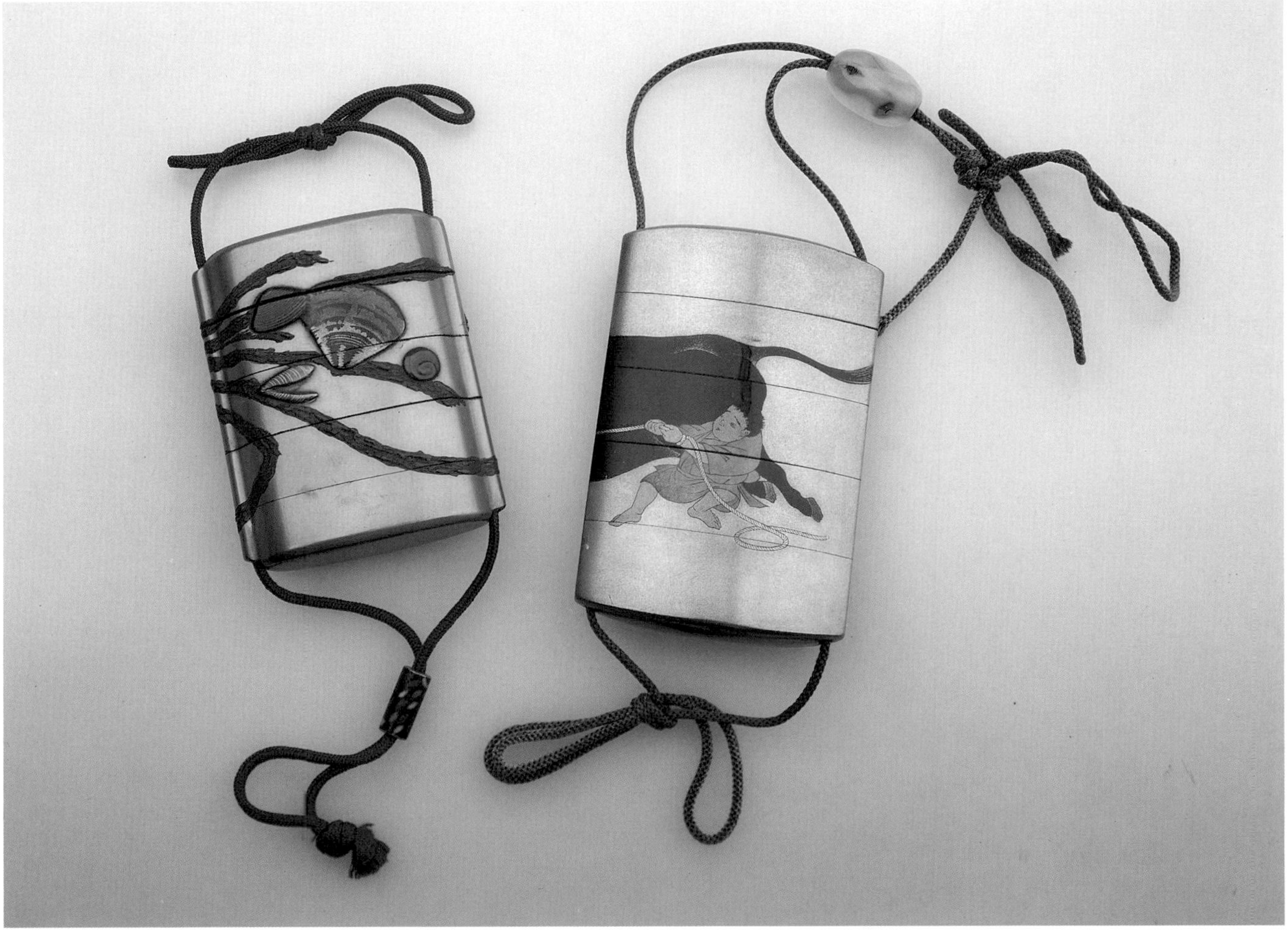

Originally intended as seal containers, Inro have been used since at least the Edo period (1600-1868) as medicine containers. Several neatly fitting compartments, mostly with an elliptical cross section, are suspended with a silk cord and a toggle (netsuke) from a sash on the kimono. Inro on left signed Kansai, late 18th century. Inro on right, unsigned, Someda school, early 19th century. National Museum of Ethnology, Leiden.

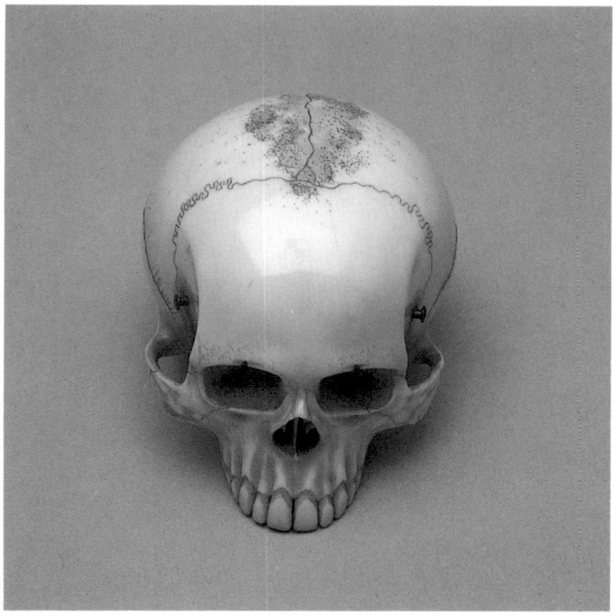

Ivory netsuke of a human skull, carved with the minutest anatomical details. Two character inscription: 'Toko'. Science Museum, London.

Ivory netsuke depicting a Buddhist Arhat (rakan) massaging the shoulders of a demon (oni). Japan 17th century. Science Museum, London.

Signboard for a proprietary stomach medicine 'Kumanoi Mokkōgan' prepared from the gall bladder of a bear, 20th century. Naito Museum of Pharmaceutical Science and Industry, Gifu.

Votive tablet, 'Chichi shibori ema'. Votive tablets were brought to shrines to pray for a cure, in this case 'to make the milk flow easily'. Naito Museum of Pharmaceutical Science and Industry, Gifu.

Portable medicine chest. 'Oshinyo hyaku mi dansu'. Doctors used to visit their patients in palanquins accompanied by various kinds of medicine chests. The names of 130 different herbal medicines are written on this chest. 19th century. Naito Museum of Pharmaceutical Science and Industry, Gifu.

Notes

1 Compiled in 712, the *Kojiki* contains imperial genealogies and successions, as well as myths, legends and songs from the age of the gods until the reign of Empress Suiko (*regn.* 592-628).

2 A kind of bulrush.

3 *Kojiki* (1968), p. 94.

4 *Nihon Shoki* (1985) p. 59, and *Kojiki* (1968) p. 94 n. 8.

5 The oldest extant official history of Japan. Also known as *Nihongi*, the book appeared in 720. The work relates in chronological order the events from the earliest times to the year 697, and includes the genealogy of the imperial rulers, myths, legends and historical tales.

6 In primitive Shintō, the only sin that can be considered as such from an *ethical* point of view seems to have been restricted to incestuous relations between relatives. See G. Kato 1973, p. 145.

7 *Japanese Religion* 1974, pp. 15, 41.

8 M. Lock 1980, p. 25.

9 B.H. Chamberlain 1934, p. 60.

10 M. Lock, *ibid*, p. 24.

11 Y. Fujikawa 1911, p. 2.

12 Tokurai in Japanese.

13 E. Rosner 1989, p. 12; M. Sugimoto and D.L. Swain 1989, p. 44.

14 M. Sugimoto and D.L. Swain, *ibid*, p. 45; *Ancient China's Technology and Science* 1983, p. 351.

15 Kanroku in Japanese.

16 These works include:
(1) *Huang Di Neijing* (The Yellow Emperor's Inner Classic, 3rd century BC) which is subdivided in two parts: *Su Wen* (Questions and Answers) and *Zhen Jing* (Canon of Acupuncture; renamed *Ling Shu* in the 7th century) and which is about fundamental theories of Chinese medicine;
(2) *Nan Jing Ji Zhu* (Classic of Medical Problems, with collected commentaries) compiled by among others Lü Guang in the Late Han era (25-220 AD) which discusses medical theories and a number of diseases besides acupuncture and moxibustion points;
(3) *Shang Han Za Bing Lun* (On Cold Damage Disorders) on diagnosis and treatment, written in the early 3rd century by Zhang Zhongjing;
(4) *Zhen Jiu Jia Yi Jing* (Systematic Classic of Acu-moxi-therapy) written by Huangfu Mi in 282;
(5) *Mo Jing* (Classic on Pulsation) by Wang Shuhe in the second half of the 3rd century;
(6) *Ben Cao Jing Ji Zhu* (Commentaries on Materia Medica), a pharmacological work compiled by Tao Hongjing around AD 500.

17 M. Sugimoto and D.L. Swain, *ibid*, p. 87.

18 *Taihō Ritsuryō* (Taihō Code) was compiled on the order of emperor Monmu (*regn.* 697-707). Including fundamental penal and administrative laws, it completed the Taika Reform edict of 646 which aimed at establishing a centralised authoritarian rule. The Yōrō Code, a revised form of the Taihō Code, was drafted in 718, but was only enforced in 757.

19 Except for the period of study for herb cultivation, which is not specified. M. Sugimoto and D.L. Swain, *ibid*, p. 36, and Y. Fujikawa, *ibid*, p. 8.

20 Y. Fujikawa, *ibid*, p. 8, claims that thirty women were accepted.

21 F. Vos 1991, p. 14.

22 When in the beginning of the 5th century, Koreans and Chinese came to Japan, the Japanese did not have any writing system. Even after the introduction of the Chinese script, they made use of scribes coming from the continent and it was not until the end of the 7th century that some sections of the ruling and intellectual class learned how to write. The mixture of Chinese characters and syllabic *kana* that is used today only came into existence in the 11th century.

23 The text which has come to us would date from the early 10th century. E. Rosner 1989, pp. 24-25.

24 Y. Fujikawa, *ibid*, p. 13, and A. Akihori 1989, p. 19. In his article Akihori points out that the *Ishinpō*, formerly thought to be an inaccurate reproduction full of manuscript errors, actually preserved the original versions after comparison with documents found in recent excavations. The main sources on which the *Ishinpō* is based include *Zhu Bing Yuan Hou Lun* (Causes and Symptoms of Diseases) by Chao Yuanfang in 607, and a prescription book, the *Xiao Bin Fang*.

25 This work is called the *Iryakushō* (Selected Therapies). M. Sugimoto and D.L. Swain, *ibid*, p. 141.

26 The Rinzai Sect is one of the three Japanese Zen sects and made major contributions to the formation of the tea cult as we know it today. In the15th century a priest of the same sect, Murata Jukō (1422-1502), began to set the ceremonial rules for tea drinking, adding Zen flavor to the ceremony. He is considered the founder of the tea cult. His student's student was none other than Sen Sōeki (better known as Sen no Rikyû) who brought to perfection the basic concept of the tea ceremony as expressed in the word *wabi* or quiet taste, the purpose of which is to detach oneself from the troubles of real life in an environment of simplicity.

27 M. Sugimoto and D.L. Swain, *ibid*, p. 147.

28 These had been proposed by Zhang Zhongjing in his 'On Cold Damage Disorders' as methods for examining the patient through the observation of different objective and subjective symptoms. They consisted of *bōshin* (visual examination), *bunshin* (examination by means of the doctor's sense of smell and hearing), *monshin* (questioning about the patient's emotional condition and physical sensation), and *sesshin* (examination by palpation).

29 Even today most of its 113 prescriptions are still in use. M. Lock, *ibid*, p. 54.

30 M. Sugimoto and D.L. Swain, *ibid*, p. 281.

31 M. Lock, *ibid*, p.55.

32 F. Vos, *ibid*, p. 21.

33 R. Ōtori 1964, pp. 30-31.

34 S. Miyashita 1973, p. 278.

35 A translation of the Japanese novel by Arayoshi Sawako on the life and work of Hanaoka Seishû appeared some time ago with the title *The Doctor's Wife*.

36 *Japanese Religion*, p. 143.

References

Agency for Cultural Affairs. *Japanese Religion*, Tokyo, Kodansha, 1974.

Akihori, A. 'The interpretation of classical Chinese medical texts in contemporary Japan: achievements, approaches and problems', in P.U. Unschuld (*ed.*), *Approaches to Traditional Chinese Medical Literature*, Dordrecht, Kluwer Academic Publishers, 1989.

Aston, W.G., (*trans.*) *Nihon Shoki*, Tokyo, Charles E. Tuttle Company, 1985.

Chamberlain, B.H. *Moeurs et coutumes du Japon*, Paris, Payot, 1934.

Fujikawa, Y. *Geschichte der Medizin in Japan*, Tokyo, Kaiserlich-Japanischen Unterrichtsministerium, 1911.

Institute of the History of Natural Sciences, Chinese Academy of Sciences. *Ancient China's Technology and Science*, Beijing, Foreign Language Press, 1983.

Kato, G. *A Study of the Religious Development of Shintō*, Tokyo, Japan Society for the Promotion of Science, 1973.

Lock, M. *East Asian Medicine in Urban Japan*, Berkeley, University of California Press, 1980.

Miyashita, S. 'A neglected source for the early history of anaesthesia in China and Japan', in S. Nakayama and N. Sivin (eds.), *Chinese Science. Explorations of an Ancient Tradition*, Cambridge, MIT Press, 1973.

Ōtori, R. 'The acceptance of Western medicine in Japan', in *Monumenta Nipponica* 19, 1964.

Philippi, D.L., (*transl.*) *Kojiki*, Tokyo, University of Tokyo Press, 1968.

Rosner, E. *Medizingeschichte Japans*, Leiden, E.J. Brill, 1989.

Sugimoto, M. and Swain, D.L. *Science and Culture in Traditional Japan*, Tokyo, Tuttle Company, 1989.

Vos, F. 'From God to Apostolate: Medicine in Japan before the Caspar School', in *Red-Hair Medicine. Dutch-Japanese Medical Relations*, Nieuwe Nederlandse Bijdragen tot de Geschiedenis der Genees-kunde en der Natuur-wetenschappen No. 36, Amsterdam, Rodopi, 1991.

Ricinus communis, the castor oil plant

Leonurus Japonicus, used for female disorders.

Platycodon grandiflorum campanulaceae; decoctions of the roots are used for coughs, sore throat and asthma.

Kanpo: Japanese Herbal Medicine

JONG-CHOL CYONG

Kanpo medicine is the Japanese adaptation and elaboration, over the centuries, of Chinese traditional medicine. Compared to Western medicine, Kanpo medicine acts gently. This does not mean that Kanpo medication always takes a long time to act effectively; it often shows strong effects on acute diseases. Kanpo medicine possesses special characteristics, and it should not be applied to a treatment already based on Western medicine. However, with care, and avoiding an incorrect combination of Western and Kanpo medicine, doctors *can* advance contemporary medicine through a synthesis of the two traditions.

The diagnostic method of Kanpo medicine relies on the five senses and the patient's original pathophysiology. Kanpo therapeutics consists of the formulation of various combinations of crude drugs. The therapeutic approaches of Kanpo in both acute and chronic diseases and the methods of harmonising crude drugs are presented below.

History of Kanpo medicine

Ancient Chinese medicine systematised and developed native medical traditions and those of neighbouring states during the second half of the first millennium BC. A number of invaluable texts have survived to help us understand this ancient world. The *Huangdi neijing* (Yellow Emperor's Canon of Internal Medicine), one of the oldest existing medical classics, was compiled around 200-100 BC. It was highly influenced by Chinese natural philosophy as expressed in the '*In-yō* five element theory' (Ch. *yin yang wuxing shui*). The *Shen Nong bencao jing* (Materia Medica of Shen Nong), the oldest classic on pharmacopoeia, is thought to date to 100-200 AD. Furthermore the third century *Sheng han nan bing lun* of Zhang Zhongjing, is the oldest classic on systematic pharmacological therapy. This extremely practical work remains important for medical practitioners today.

Ancient Chinese medicine was transmitted to Korea, and the medical system that developed in Korea was further transmitted to Japan towards the end of the fourth century. From the seventh century onward there was a mutual exchange of physicians between Japan and China, and Japanese medicine was directly influenced by Chinese medicine. In the tenth century the earliest Japanese medical classic, the *Ishinpō*, was compiled by Yasuyori Tanba.

Kanpo evolved as the core of Japanese medicine, until European medical information came to Japan in the second half of the sixteenth century. The newly emerged Western medicine grew steadily in influence in Japan and competed with Kanpo medicine.

In the Meiji era (1868-1912), the Japanese government favoured Westernisation, even in the field of medicine. Since medical licences were only issued to those who passed the national examination—itself based on Western medicine—Kanpo medicine inevitably declined and took on the role of an unauthorised discipline.

After the Meiji era, great efforts were made to revive Kanpo with the aid of scientific research. In 1950, the Japan Society of Oriental Medicine was established. In 1967, the 'four formulations of Kanpo extracts' were officially approved by the Japanese Ministry of Health and Welfare, and they could be administered through health insurance. Moreover in 1976, 43 Kanpo extracts were first listed by the Price Standard for Pharmaceuticals of the Ministry of Health and Welfare. By 1985, their number had increased to 146.

Today, Kanpo has been revived and it holds a firm place in the modern medicine of Japan. In 1991, the Japan Society of Oriental Medicine was officially approved as one of the Japanese Associations of Medical Sciences, and nowadays nearly 70% of Japan's clinical doctors utilise Kanpo medicine in therapeutics.

Kanpo therapeutics

Kanpo therapeutics has three principles that differ from Western or Chinese medicine.

The first principle concerns the measure of human health. In Kanpo medicine, an individual's current health should always be considered in the light of their entire health history, and the moderate or median state is considered the best. Thus, if a person over sixty looks young and fit, with no white hair, he is not necessarily judged to be healthy, but rather in an unusual—even abnormal—state, a concept which does not seem to accord with Western medicine. Whilst Western medicine might consider someone who remains vigorous after middle age, or free of fatigue after working all night, to be very healthy, the Kanpo system might view such a case as a disorder of the nerves, and crude drug therapy may be required to control an overly active metabolism. In such an instance, Kanpo medication may cause the person to tire more easily, or reduce efficacy when over-working.

This medicine of moderation is based on the intrinsic understanding of *tenju*, or natural lifespan. Kanpo medicine views medical treatment within the context of a healthy daily life in a moderate state, which should culminate with a natural death. Kanpo does not aspire to perennial youth or great longevity, but accepts that each person's lifespan is naturally programmed in their DNA which, for some, makes Kanpo treatment less acceptable. The principles of Kanpo medicine are therefore compatible with the use of drugs composed of natural substances.

The second principle concerns reactivity to drugs. Put simply, it is recognised that the reactivity of a certain drug is not identical for every individual, and that different people may react differently to the same drug because of age, environment, or type of disease, a principle that should always be considered during treatment. In this, Kanpo is unlike Western medical treatment which is based on average reactions, and does not take account of atypical reactions. As Kanpo does take account of individuals' different reactions, it seems more suitable for dealing with variation. In Kanpo methodology, it is also possible to use the same drug for a number of different diseases, thus broadening the drug's range of application. A doctor trained in Kanpo is able to apply Kanpo methods to the use of Western medicines.

The third principle concerns formulations and drug prescriptions, whereby it is essential to consider the combinations and ratios of formulations. Kanpo medicine is not merely a polypharmacy that mixes various crude drugs. Each formulation is composed of a *shang pin* (upper class drug), a *zhong pin* (middle class drug), and a *xia pin* (lower class drug). These classifications are derived from the *Shen Nong bencao jing* (Materia Medica of Shen Nong), and they are also applied to the *jun chen zuo shi* (four regular components in a formulation), discussed below.

A formulation acts as a team for treating diseases as system disorders. *Jun ya* acts as the main drug in a formulation, 'monarch', and might also be likened to the director of a hospital. *Chen ya* is an associate drug that enhances the action of the main drugs. It is the 'minister', and corresponds to the hospital managers. *Zuo shi ya* is an adjuvant drug or messenger drug in a formulation, harmonising the action of the other types of drugs and directing them to the weakened areas. *Zuo shi ya* are the 'workers' and 'assistants', and correspond to the to the medical staff and nurses. Although the participation of the director and managers may not be as visible as that of the staff and nurses, their role is essential and they make decisions that concern the long-term management and clinical services of the hospital.

In many cases, the upper class drug or *shang pin* acts as *jun ya*; the middle class drug or *zhong pin* acts as *chen ya*, and lower class drugs or *xia pin* act as *zuo shi ya.*

The balance of *jun chen zuo shi* or four ingredients within a formulation is respected in Kanpo, and the combination ratio or content, should not be changed unnecessarily. This conviction of Kanpo medicine formulations has made it possible to produce modern Kanpo extracts. When using a decoction, the dose of the crude drugs may be changed, or other herbs added according to the patient's symptoms or the quality of the drugs. This is only done, however, as long as the overall balance within the formulation is not altered. Kanpo holds that the power of each crude drug should not be limited, but that the formulation should respect the role each drug plays in combination with all the others.

Diagnosis

In Kanpo medicine pathogenesis caused by external and internal factors is defined as *byō-ja* (pathogenic factors), as are bacteria and viruses. In ancient times diseases were recognised as being mediated by factors called *ja* (evil). One person might die and another survive as a result of the same kind of evil, yet it was discovered that an individual patient always exhibited a fixed and specific pattern of changes, even when affected by different evils.

Today, Kanpo recognises that a patient's constitution often defines this fixed pattern of changes, and the first step in diagnosis is to know each individual's pattern of changes. Kanpo understanding comes from identifying the physical system most affected. For example, a person with a weak gastrointestinal system will show gastrointestinal disorders whenever he gets a cold, is injured, or is under psychological stress. The diagnostic method of Kanpo relies on identifying the individual's specific reactions.

Kanpo and Western medicine differ in their approaches to diagnosis and treatment. Kanpo diagnosis is closely linked to therapeutics, which aims to tone and support the fragile physical system, but never to fight the pathogenic factor directly. This is in sharp contrast to Western medicine which concentrates on symptoms and attacks the pathogen.

The concept of *ibyō-dōchi* (Ch. *yi bing tong zhi*) entails the treatment of etiologically different diseases with a single formulation. The concept of *dōbyō-ichi* (Ch. *tong bing yi zhi*) on the other hand, refers to the different types of treatment that can be prescribed for one disease caused by the same pathogenic factor.

In cases of acute disease, treatment starts by identifying the stage of the disease, while its progress is determined by observing the symptoms. In chronic diseases, treatment should only be started after ascertaining the abnormality of *ki-ketsu-sui* (Ch. *qi-xue-shui*, see below). In addition, *kyo-jitsu* (deficiency and hyper-function), are also important factors when deciding the therapeutic policy. In the case of chronic disease it is rare for only a single system to be damaged; consequently therapeutics can be very complicated.

Acute fever and disease templates

Acute diseases are treated according to their classified stages. In the case of acute fever, pathogenic microorganisms, or *gai-ja* (external pathogenic factors), try to invade the *gai* (ectoderm), and as a consequence inflammation is caused in ectodermal organs. In Kanpo, *taiyō* disease refers to the injury of ectodermal organs (eg skin, central nervous system, tonsils).[1] Damage to endodermal organs (eg pulmonary epithelia, stomach, bowels), is known as *yōmei* disease.[2] When *gai-ja* invade and injure the paren-chymal organ, circulatory system or bone marrow, *shōyō* disease is caused.[3]

Taiyō, *yōmei* and *shōyō* diseases are grouped together as *yō* (Ch. *yang*) diseases, where physical resistance is stronger than the external microorganism. On the other hand, when physical resistance is lowered, or plural germ layers are injured at the simultaneously, this is generally referred to as *Yin* disease. As specific therapies and formulations are classified for all these stages, one can easily select the appropriate Kanpo medicine if the *kyo-jitsu* (deficiency or hyper-function) of the patient has been correctly determined.

As mentioned above, diseases are classified according to the system infected: ectodermal, endodermal, half-exterior, half-interior. However, the typical textbook progress of a disease is rather rare in clinical practice; its progression can sometimes be very complicated. When a disease is protracted, a patient goes into the *Yin* stage where physical resistance is inferior to pathogenic factors. Moreover, regardless of the stage of an illness, when a patient's internal condition is completely disorganised due to continuous use of potent medicines, the dangerous state of *kai-byō* (atypical symptoms resulting from mistreatment) might develop.

Classics such as the *Shōkanron* (Ch. *Shang Han Lun*) describe the therapeutic methods used for infectious diseases such as typhoid fever. It is also possible to apply such ancient classifications to more familiar and less serious diseases such as influenza or the common cold.

Chronic diseases: the concept of *ki-ketsu-sui*

In Kanpo medicine, protracted diseases can be analysed with the help of the concept of *ki-ketsu-sui* (vital energy, blood, body fluid), a practical concept for effective therapies. When the abnormality in *ki-ketsu-sui* is identified, the most appropriate drug among the series of formulations can be chosen.

Ki (Ch. *qi*, vital energy) is generally understood as 'life energy', but it actually refers to the entire system that produces this life energy. Thus, *ki* involves all the functions for recognising and obtaining food, approaching and eating, digesting and absorbing it. Only when animal cells consume other life forms can they prolong existence. *Ki* must be used for these activities, and it generally corresponds to the nervous and gastrointestinal systems. *Ki-zai* are drugs for modulating psycho-activity and that harmonise abnormal *ki*.[4]

Once the body has become well-nourished by absorbing foreign substances, it must protect itself from attack or it, too, will become food for others. The concept of *sui* (body fluid) involves host defence mechanisms in general, and includes both the immune system and the skin (epithelium). To treat abnormalities in body fluid, *risui-zai*, herbs which promote diuresis, are used.[5]

After the body is nourished and able to protect itself, it also requires internal comfort. The *ketsu* (blood) integrates the functions of *ki* and *sui* and adjusts the information system in order to harmonise the organism's internal functions. The circulatory system and hormones function as this system.[6]

A formulation must be composed of more than two crude

drugs, and specific crude drugs are assigned to the abnormality of *ki-ketsu-sui.* It is exceptional for a formulation to be applied to only one disorder of *ki-ketsu-sui;* most formulations cover multiple disorders.[7] Most formulations have all the factors of *ki-ketsu-sui,* and their composition is well balanced. The pathological concept of *ki-ketsu-sui* aims to make the formulation easy to understand and apply clinically.

Clinical application of Kanpo therapeutics

Kanpo medicine attempts both to cure patients and promote their overall physical and mental health. After identifying deficiency or hyperfunction by means of the four diagnostic procedures, we then diagnose its stage of development in cases of acute disease, or the abnormality of *ki-ketsu-sui* in cases of chronic disease.

Deficiency or hyperfunction can be seen as the reserve capacity for physical strength. When a patient is diagnosed as having a deficient constitution, he shows a small range of reaction. In cases of hyperfunction, the patients are physically well-adapted in the present, but may tend to fall into serious homeostatic disorder in the mid or long-term. Kanpo medicine gives priority to medication when something is wrong with the patient's overall constitution. This approach distinguishes it from Western medicine.

An asthma patient who, over a long period, failed to react to a Western approach, then began Kanpo therapy. It was obvious that the patient had a damaged respiratory system due to the asthma. In fact his gastrointestinal system was weaker than the respiratory system. In this case, treatment of the gastrointestinal system should start with *hon-chi,* systemic meridian treatment according to orthodox theory. Only after this is working normally again, can the respiratory system be treated. The asthmatic condition was considered to have been cured by *hyō-chi,* local and symptomatic treatment. It is often the case that once *hon-chi* is properly completed, the other symptoms disappear spontaneously before *hyō-chi* begins. In such cases one can say that *shō* (diagnosis) is correct and appropriate. *Hon-chi* always takes priority and is characteristic of Kanpo medicine. If symptoms remain after the completion of both *hon-chi* and *hyō-chi,* Kanpo never resorts to another type of *hyō-chi* formulation, but rather returns to *hon-chi* and only then recommences *hyō-chi* once again. After completing systemic meridian treatment using Kanpo formulations, Western medicine could be used in symptomatic treatment.

Kanpo medicines

The drugs used in Kanpo medicine are all derived from natural substances, a situation not remarkably different from Western medicine until about 150 years ago. At present, approximately 40% of Western medicines are still derived from natural origins. Many differences occur, however, when we compare the side-effects and the methods of action and application of the two medical systems.

Classification of drugs: *shang pin, zhong pin, xia pin*

The *Shen Nong bencao jing,* written nearly 2,000 years ago, conceived of a drug as a gathering of various categories that exceeds a single concept. Classification was based not on the drug's effectiveness but on its side-effects and toxicity. Drugs can be generally classified into three groups.

Drugs without adverse side-effects are classed as *shang pin,* ideal or upper class drugs. Such drugs are not required to have strong effects, and even if they have no direct effect but act to eliminate the side-effects of other drugs, they can still be *shang pin.* Non-toxic drugs that have weak side-effects when given in small doses or over a short period of time are classed as *zhong pin*, middle class or moderate drugs. Drugs with a strong effect that often show adverse side-effects are classed as *xia pin*, lower class or slightly toxic drugs.

Western and Oriental medicine define drugs somewhat differently from each other. In Western medicine a drug is defined as a substance having a specific effect and an obvious point of action. Oriental medicine includes as drugs all natural substances that act favourably on the damaged body. Thus on the whole, the drugs of Western medicine correspond to *xia pin* or lower class drugs; whilst *shang pin* and *zhong pin* are not regarded as drugs in the West.

Strong medicine with a specific point of effectiveness can be expected to act in certain ways if it is administered during the short-term. In the case of middle- or long-term continuous medication, however, it can cause detrimental results even though its actions on a specific point of the body may appear effective. Conversely, if a drug lacks a significant point of effectiveness but acts on the systemic body, even if it shows no strong effects in the short-term, it can still create a favourable influence on the body's homeostasis in the long-term. This is especially true when the drug formulation consists of many different ingredients, where each crude drug performs mildly. Each drug acts to create a synergistic effect. For these reasons, Kanpo always adheres to its gentle, formulation-oriented medicine. The crude drugs of Kanpo medicine frequently match or contain elements found in complex drugs, hormones and chemicals that have been analysed in the West.[8]

Kanpo formulations

Evaluations of Kanpo medicine among clinicians vary greatly. A number of cases have been reported where intractable diseases or symptoms have been remitted, seemingly miraculously, by Kanpo medicine. Equally, complaints occur that no effects whatsoever were found in practice. Some over-estimate its effects, while others consider Kampo to be merely a placebo. Neither have a correct view of Kanpo pharmaco-kinetics.

A major indicator of Kanpo pharmacology deals with homeostasis; when homeostasis is maintained, the body shows no significant pharmacological effects after an ordinary dose of Kanpo medicine. However, when homeostasis breaks down due to various reasons, Kanpo acts to normalise the homeostasis. Kanpo medicine is remarkable in that its effects are not visible, unless the body's condition deteriorates, unlike Western medicine which acts regardless of the patient's physical state. The gentleness of Kanpo medicine helps to activate the self-healing potential of the human body. Although it cannot be expected to have any significant effect on DNA-related diseases, it can play an important part in normalising the patient's physical state if there has been a loss of homeostatic balance.

Crude drugs can act to eliminate another drug's side-effects by drawing out and neutralising them; this is achieved by careful composition of a formulation that not only considers the drug's influence on the body, but also its role within the formulation.

In modern Chinese medicine, formulations tend to be defined in terms of efficacy, and the result has been excessive dosaging. By comparison, Kanpo minimises the dose, and it has been rewarded with good results. The technique developed in Japan to make quick infusions from small amounts of a crushed crude drug has achieved maximum effect with minimum dosage. However, Kanpo medicine, forced to practise for a long time in a small, confined environment, came to utilise specific, limited combinations of crude drugs for limited numbers of diseases. Consequently, only about 150 kinds of crude drugs are now used in Kanpo medicine.

Numerous species of plants in Japan can compare with or match the 365 species described in the *Shen Nong bencao jing.*

Entrance to a Kanpo pharmacy in Toyama. Proprietary Kanpo medicines are on occasion most beautifully wrapped.

Kanpo medicines are also presented in the form of herbal cakes and pastries. Kanpo shop, Toyama.

It has been difficult, however, to create new formulations because too much emphasis has been placed on maintaining tradition and the perfect balance of long-standing formulations. It is now necessary to develop new formulations by adding alternative crude drugs to widen the possibilities of Kanpo medicine. These crude drugs and new drugs of Western medicine, should be added to the traditional medical literature to expand the basis of Kanpo therapeutics .

Kanpo medicine has accumulated and systematised the experiences of treatment over centuries. The crude drugs it uses are virtually free from toxicity or adverse side-effects, and doses must be strictly defined to achieve maximum effect. Kanpo established an individualised form of therapy, long before modern pharmacology began to do so.

In Japan, traditional medicine has been revived in clinical practice, although formal Japanese medical education has never dealt with Kanpo medicine. The spontaneous spread and revival of Kanpo depend on its unique philosophy of therapeutics. It is hoped that the introduction of this philosophy to modern cosmopolitan medicine will help lead to a medical renaissance.

Notes

1 *Taiyō* disease appears in the epidermal system, central nervous system, or in the immune system, and results in chills, perspiration, headaches stiff neck, muco- membranous symptoms or swollen tonsils. Allergies can also be categorised as *Taiyō* disease.

2 The symptoms of *Yōmei* disease appear in the endodermal system, such as in the epithelia of the respiratory system, and the gastrointestinal system. It results in cough, phlegm, nausea, anorexia, diarrhoea, or constipation.

3 *Shōyō* disease appears partially in the circulatory system (which belongs to the mesodermal system), and it results in cardiac and blood pressure disorders, dyshemato-poiesia, muscle pain, or parenchymatitis. Immune complex disease with immune disorders are considered essentially a *Shōyō* disease.

4 Abnormalities of *ki* are controlled by the following drugs: *keishi* (cinamomi), *kōboku* (Magnolia cortex), *shiso-yō* (Perillae herba). The formulations *keishi-tō* (Formula cinamomi), *hange-kōboku-tō* (Formula Magnoliae et Pine-liae), *tōkaku-jōki-tō* (Formula Animotionis persicae) are also classified for *ki-zai* use.

5 To cure *sui* abnormality, one can use *bukuryō* (Subterranean fungus), *jutsu*, *takusha* (Alisma rhizome), *chorei* (Polyporus), *hange* (Pinelliae tuber). The formulations *gorei-san* (Pulvis quinque-holen), *chorei-tō* (Formula polypori), *ryō-kei-jutsu-kan-tō* (Formula blycyrrhizae atractyloidis cinnamomi hoelen), *shō-seiryū-tō* (Formula divinitatis caeruleae minor), *bōi-ogi-tō* (Formula astragali et sinomenii) are classified for *Risui-zai*, a treatment to promote diuresis.

6 Some of the drugs that overcome blood stagnation (*ku-oketsu-zai*) are: *tōnin* (Persicae semen), *botanpi* (Moutan cortex), *shakuyaku* (Paeniae radix), *tōki* (Angelicae radix), *senkyū* (Cnidii rhizoma). *Daiō-botanpi-tō* (Formula Moutan et Rhei), *tōki-shakuyaku-san* (Pulvis paeoniae et angelicae), *keshi-bukuryō-gan* (Pilulae hoelen et cinnamomi), *shimotsu-tō* (Formula quandri-medicamentorum) are classified as formulations.

7 For example, *tōkaku-jōki-tō* (Formula animationis persicae) covers both *ki-zai* (drugs for modulating psycho-activity)and *ku-oketsu-zai* (drugs for overcoming blood-stagnation). *Keishi-bukuryō-gan* (Piluae hoelen et cinnamomi) acts as *risui-zai* (a drug to promote diuresis), and *ku-oketsu-zai* (a drug to overcome blood-stagnation).

8 For example, animal hormones such as autacoids (which produce effects between hormones and neurotransmitters, e.g. prostaglandin and serotonin), neurotransmitters and intracellular secondary transmitters are found among crude drugs used in Kampo medicine. They sometimes have the same structural formulae. For instance, cyclic AMP and cyclic GMP are found in *taisō* (Zizyphy fructus) and a large amount of cyclic GMP is also contained in *goshuyu* (Eviodiae fructus). Synerpherine, adrenergic agent, is also contained in *goshuyu*, and ephedrine, another popular adrenergic agonist, is the main ingredient of *maō* (Ephedra herba). Large amounts of diosgenin, androgenic hormone analogue, is contained in *sanyaku* (Discorea rhizoma). Many kinds of steroid hormones, including oral contraceptives, are produced by chemically modifying the diosgenin obtained from *sanyaku*. *Kyōnin* (Armenicae semen) contains both estrogen and serotonin. The ingredients contained in these crude drugs are classed as *shang pin* or *zhong pin*, and could control the neurotransmitting systems of the body . Though these ingredients might act in cell-to-cell recognition, it is impossible to identify the specific organ point that is affected since they are spread so widely throughout the body. For instance, if functional disorders occur in the nervous, immune, gastrointestinal system or kinetic system, the drug ingredients are thought to have the effect of adjusting the system. Sennoside, found in *daiō* (Rhei rhizoma), and aconitin in *bushi* (Aconiti tuber) are fairly definite in their site of action and mechanism; these are generally included in the crude drugs classed as *xia pin*, lower class drugs. Kanpo medicine relies on multi-ingredient types of drugs that affect various sites, every ingredient having a systematic effect. Moreover, one crude drug has more than two kinds of neurotransmitters and the substances in it occasionally have the contrary effect. Therefore the reverse effect can occur depending on the combination.

Appendix
Three Healing Deities of Asia

A Brahmin priest in front of the Viśvaṁbhara temple in Kottakal, Kerala. Dhanvantari is known as Viśvambhara in Kerala, the lord of the three powers; knowledge, action and volition.

Dhanvantari

JAN VAN ALPHEN

Dhanvantari is the heavenly physician of the Hindu gods and is generally considered to be the one who brought the knowledge of Ayurveda to mankind. His name is derived from the Sanskrit verbal root *dhanv* which means to run or to flow. The noun *dhanvan*, meaning a bow, is derived from this root. *Dhanvan-tari* means 'moving in a curve'. His name suggests the parabolic flight of an arrow, and in an early stage he was identified with the sun which also moves in an arc. He is referred to in several of the eighteen *Purāṇas*, the 'ancient books' that describe the history of gods and kings in India. In the *Bhāgavata Purāṇa* (I.3.17) Dhanvantari is called the twelfth incarnation of Viṣṇu:

> *In the twelfth incarnation, the Lord appeared as Dhanvantari, and in the thirteenth he bewitched the atheists with the charming beauty of a woman and gave the demigods nectar to drink.*

In the same *Purāṇa* (II.7.21) it is stated:

> *The Lord in his incarnation as Dhanvantari very quickly cures the diseases of the ever-diseased living entities simply by the power of his fame, and it is only through him that the demigods achieve long life. Thus the person of the godhead is for ever glorified. He also exacted a share of the sacrifices, and it is he alone who inaugurated the science and knowledge of medicine in the universe.*[1]

After introducing the forefathers of this heavenly physician, the *Vāyu Purāṇa* (30.1-26) and the *Brahmāṇḍa Purāṇa* (17.1-26) contain almost identical verses on the origin of Dhanvantari. Here are some verses of Chapter 17 of the *Brahmāṇḍa Purāṇa*[2]:

> *King Dīrghatapas was the ruler of Kāśī (Benares) and the son of Kāśya. Dhanva was the son of Dīrghatapas and in turn the scholar Dhanvantari was born to him. In his old age, at the completion of his penance, this brilliant son was born to the intelligent king.*
>
> *The sages said:-*
>
> *"Who is Dhanvantari, the lord who was born among human beings? We wish to know this. Tell us, O scorcher of enemies?"*
>
> *Sūta replied:*
>
> *"Let the origin of Dhanvantari be heard, O Brāhmaṇas. He was born when the ocean was first being churned, for the sake of nectar. At the outset, he was born before the Kalaśa (the pot) and was encircled by a halo of glory". Viṣṇu, on seeing him accomplish his task, said; "You are born of water". Hence, he is remembered as Ab-ja (water-born). Abja said to Viṣṇu; "O lord, I am your son. Grant me my share and place in the world, O excellent god."...*
>
> *The lord said: "In your second incarnation you will be famous ... Brāhmaṇas (and other twice-born ones) shall worship you with the mantras from the four Vedas, ghee offerings and Gavyas (milk products). You will once again introduce Ayurveda, the Science of Medicine"...*
>
> *Lord Dhanvantari was then born at his abode. He was a great king, the ruler of Kāśī , the dispeller of all ailments. He learned the science of medicine, Ayurveda, along with the therapies from Bharadvāja. He classified it into eight sections and taught them to different disciples.*[3]

Dhanvantari is known as the god who arose from the primordial milk-ocean together with the nectar of immortality in the famous story of the Churning of the Ocean (*samudra manthana*). The *Bhāgavata Purāṇa* (VIII.8. 31-34)[4] recounts as follows:

> *O king, thereafter, while the sons of Kaśyapa, both demons and demigods, were engaged in churning the ocean of milk, a very wonderful male person appeared.*
>
> *He was strongly built; his arms were long, stout and strong; his neck, which was marked with three lines, resembled a conch shell; his eyes were reddish; and his complexion was blackish. He was very young, he was garlanded with flowers, and his entire body was fully decorated with various ornaments.*
>
> *He was dressed in yellow garments and wore brightly*

A statue or painting of Dhanvantari is found at the entrance to most Ayurvedic hospitals and pharmaceutical companies. He has four arms, like Viṣṇu, and holds, besides a conch and a disc, the vase containing the nectar of immortality in his left hand and leeches for bloodletting in his right. Podar Ayurvedic Hospital, Bombay.

polished earrings made of pearls. The tips of his hair were anointed with oil, and his chest was very broad. His body had all good features, he was stout and strong like a lion, and he was decorated with bangles. In his hand he carried a jug filled to the top with nectar.

This person was Dhanvantari, a plenary portion of a plenary portion of lord Viṣṇu. He was very conversant with the science of medicine, and as one of the demigods he was permitted to take a share in sacrifices.

The 'churning of the milk-ocean' is a well known story that introduces the tortoise incarnation (*Kūrma avatāra)* of Viṣṇu into popular Hinduism. In the cyclical creations and destructions of the earth and the universe Viṣṇu appears each time in one or another form in order to save the universe and humanity. In this story, gods and demons start to churn the primordial milk-ocean (*kṣira sāgara*) in order to cause all the good things that had sunk to the ocean depths to rise up. Mount Mandara served as a churning stick while the snake Vāsuki was used as the rope. The gods tugged the rope in one direction, the demons in the other. Viṣṇu incarnated himself as a tortoise and placed the Mandara mountain on top of his shell to prevent it from sinking into the ocean. On churning the ocean, many splendid things arise from the depths and are reinstated in the new era, such as the science of healing which was brought up by Dhanvantari as the vase containing the nectar of immortality.

It is with this story that Dhanvatari's reputation and fame were established. He became the celestial guardian of the north-east. In some myths Dhanvantari is referred to as an aspect of Viṣṇu, in others as a disciple of Śiva, and in still others as a pupil of the eagle-god Garuḍa [5].

The name Dhanvantari was frequently adopted by or given to famous Ayurvedic doctors. There is the well-known case of a Dhanvantari as one of the 'nine gems' at the court of king Vikramāditya (fifth century) who is believed to be the author of the medical botanical lexicon *Dhanvantarinigaṇṭum*.

According to Suśruta, the science of medicine was created by Brahmā who taught 100,000 ślokas, arranged into eight sections (the eight disciplines of Ayurveda), to Dakṣa Prajāpati. Prajāpati transmitted this to the Aśvins who brought it to Indra. Finally Indra taught it to Dhanvantari and he passed his knowledge on to Suśruta. (According to Caraka however, Indra bestowed his knowledge on Bharadvāja who passed it on through Atreya Punarvasu and Agniveśa to Caraka).

Dhanvatari's iconography closely resembles that of Viṣṇu. He is depicted with four arms and the emblems of Viṣṇu such as the conch shell and the *cakra*. But he always carries the vase containing the nectar of immortality, and very often he holds a pair of leeches in one hand, the method of blood-letting still practised today in Ayurvedic medicine.

Notes

1 A.C.B.S. Prabhupāda, *Śrīmad Bhāgavatam*, The Bhaktivedanta Booktrust, New-York/ Los Angeles/London. nd.

2 *The Brahma Purāṇa*, translated by Vasudeo Tagare, Motilal Banarsidas, New Delhi 1983, and H.H. Wilson, *The Vishnu Purāṇa*, Punthi Pustak, London 1840, Calcutta 1961, p.324-328.

3 Concerning Dhanvatari in Kāśi, *see*: Margaret and James Stutley *Harpers's Dictionary of Hinduism, its Mythology, Folklore, Philosophy, Literature and History*. Harper & Row, San Francisco 1977, p.75.

4 See note 1

5 Benjamin Walker, *Hindu World, an encyclopedic survey of Hinduism*, Munshiram Manoharlal Publishers, New Delhi 1983, p. 274.

Shennong, the Chinese deity of medicine, pharmaceutics and agriculture. Seated at the mouth of a cave, he wears a leaf skirt and holds a branch with leaves and berries. Watercolour, Shanghai, 1920. Wellcome Institute, London.

Shennong

Jan Van Alphen

Shennong, the legendary founder of Chinese medicine, is said to have been an emperor who reigned in the middle of the third millennium BC and one of the famous 'Five Emperors': Fuxi, Shennong, Huangdi, Shao Hao and Zuan Xi.

Emperor Fuxi discovered the 'Eight Trigrams'. His successor, Shennong, extended these to sixty-four hexagrams. Fuxi, Shennong and Huangdi preside over the Taoist Ministry of Medicine. Shennong and Huangdi are also known as the 'Red Emperor' and the 'Yellow Emperor' respectively.

Legend has it that Shennong's mother, princess Anteng, conceived on seeing a dragon. The child, with bovine head, was nurtured by wild beasts in the Lie Shan mountains.

A priest (some sources mention a ghost), Zi Songze, taught Shennong everything about agriculture, magic and medicine. Together they gathered all kinds of herbs on the mountain-slopes. Later on Zi Songze disappeared in one of the inhospitable caves of the Kunlun mountains.

Shennong is said to have moved Fuxi's capital from the province of Henan to Qufu in Shandong. This probably has some historical basis, as two forces arose in China at the same time in the latter half of the second millennium BC. One was the Shang Yin kingdom of the Proto-Chinese Xia tribes, and the other was composed of the Proto-Tangut tribes of Jiang. These Jiang had been previously assimilated into a Central-Asian nation of twelve tribes. They supposedly invaded China as part of the Zhou confederation around 1100 BC. As the first force was based in Henan, the arrival of the second may have been the reason why the capital was moved from Henan to Shandong. Historical studies have shown that Shennong was a leading deity of the Proto-Tangut Jiang tribe, where he was associated with fire and known as the 'Flaming' god of agriculture.

China, an agricultural society until recent times, has always paid great attention to the rituals associated with the god of agriculture. Each spring at the capital's temple of agriculture, the emperors carried out the 'ploughing ceremony', a ceremony which was thereafter repeated throughout the provinces. Shennong is worshipped as the inventor of the plough and was specially venerated at an altar to the west of the Temple of Heaven in Beijing on the Third Moon, when the ceremony of 'breaking the soil' was performed.

Shennong and attendant, both holding rice stalks, seated amidst other Taoist and Buddhist deities in the Fuhegong temple in Taipei.

As the founder of the sciences of botany and medicine he is reputed to have tasted a hundred medicinal herbs and is said to have written the first work of *materia medica* in China the *Bencao* or 'Essential Herbs'. Shennong tamed and trained six to eight dragons to pull his carriage in which he traversed the earth to measure its dimensions.

Shennong is mostly depicted as a pot-bellied old man with a massive head, a long beard and two protruding rudimentary horns. He wears a skirt of green leaves, like the taoist immortals, and is often depicted chewing on a medicinal leaf or writing the sixty-four hexagrams on a tablet.

Bhaiṣajyaguru, the Master of Remedies or Medicine Buddha, holds the fruit of the myrobolan plant, a universal panacea, in his right hand, and a bowl containing the elixir of immortality in his left, and is accompanied by the two Bodhisattvas Sūyaprabhā (with the emblem of the moon) and Candraprabhā (with the emblem of the sun). The eight Medicine Buddhas are placed on the left and right borders, and the lineage of transmission of the medical teachings with, in the middle, Avalokiteśvara Saḍakṣari, at the top of the painting. Tibetan painting of the 14th century. Musée Guimet, Paris.

Bhaiṣajyaguru, The Medicine Buddha

CHARLES WILLEMEN

Buddhism is the path leading to perfect rest which in Asia is a common interpretation of *nirvāṇa*. In perfect rest one no longer performs intentional actions, the formations (*saṃskāra*) are allayed and the cycle of birth and death has ended. A Buddha, an Awakened One, is liberated from the suffering of existence. As long as perfect rest is not achieved, one dwells in suffering. Although one may be called ill, the cause of illness is actually ignorance or delusion. Buddhist doctrine does away with the cause of suffering and thus provides the remedy for illness.

When Prince Gautama Siddhārtha became Buddha Śakyamuni, he awoke to the Four Noble Truths, and expounded them for the first time in the Deer Park in Benares. One tradition, a revised Singhalese calculation, holds that Buddha may have died, to have entered into *parinirvāṇa*, in 480 BC. Another tradition, based on Sanskrit texts and on Chinese sources, places him in the fourth century BC. He may have lived some decades before Alexander the Macedonian was in India from 327 BC.

When Buddha turned the wheel of the doctrine for the first time in Benares he provided a remedy for illness. The doctrine, that is the Four Noble Truths, is the true medicine, the remedy for suffering. The first truth says that the very nature of existence entails suffering, a fact which is established empirically. The second truth states the cause of suffering, providing the aetiology. The third truth speaks about healing suffering, doing away with its cause. The fourth truth provides the therapy, the Noble Eight-fold Path.

The therapeutic itinerary provides a cure for the whole person, not simply for a specific illness. Illness, after all, is a result of previous *karma*, of former actions. The Jātaka Tales, amongst other texts, make it clear that illness serves to admonish, and to instruct in right behaviour. If the ultimate cause of suffering is ignorance, Buddha taught how life may be lead in a healthy manner. Perfect rest, *nirvāṇa*, is also interpreted as the absence of illness, *ārogya*. When he left his father's palaces for the first time, the young Siddhārtha encountered sickness, old age and death. The fourth encounter was with a *śramaṇa*, an ascetic, showing that a healthy life may be realised when abandoning worldly occupations. However, the Buddhist ideal, perfect rest, may best be realised in a monastic environment. A layman can indeed achieve perfect rest, but he is likened to an old horse; a monk is a thoroughbred on the path to the place of perfect rest.

Buddhists believe that physical illness is closely linked to the condition of the mind. They treat the whole person, especially his mental state, not just a particular physical ailment. Of course, people fall ill and die and a doctor cannot change this karmic causality, but he can alleviate suffering. The ideal is that people will not suffer again through further rebirth. Buddha himself died at the age of eighty, suffering from food-poisoning, but he had left *saṃsāra*.

The Healing Buddha in Mahāyāna Buddhism

The Buddhist path and community spread through Central Asia eastward as far as Japan, adapting everywhere to geographical, local and historical factors. Buddha's doctrine and the different schools which came into existence soon after his death were later called the 'Lesser Vehicle' (*Hīnayāna*). Today the term 'Vehicle of the Hearers' (*Śrāvakayāna*) that is of disciples, is often used. In Thailand, Burma and Sri Lanka it is known as the 'School of the Elders' (*Theravāda*) with Pāli as its canonical language. East Asia's most influential *Hīnayāna* school is the *Sarvāstivāda*. Its own canonical language was Sanskrit, and its texts originated in Gandhara and Kashmir.

The beginning of the common era witnessed the development of a new trend within Buddhism. Devotionalism, and the need for saviour figures such as altruistic *bodhisattvas*, who postpone their entry into *nirvāṇa* while saving others, characterised the rise of the 'Great Vehicle' (*Mahāyāna*). While Śrāvakayāna is characterised by the individualistic arhat, a holy sage, *Mahāyāna* is represented by an altruistic, compassionate *bodhisattva*.

The Master of Healing, Bhaiṣajyaguru, belongs to *Mahāyāna*, as does Amitābha, sovereign of the 'Pure Land' of the western paradise. Just believing in the later is karmically wholesome and after death he welcomes pious devotees to his paradise. The *Tathāgata* Master of Healing rules over the eastern paradise, 'Pure Lapis Lazuli', and he is there to help the living, who are ill.

These two Buddhas belong to *Mahāyāna*, but *Mahāyāna* is renowned for its *bodhisattvas*. Avalokiteśvara, Guanyin (China) or Kannon (Japan), the god(dess) of mercy, are household names in East Asia. During its spread eastward

Gilded bronze image of the Medicine Buddha, Bhaiṣajyaguru, holding the myrobalan fruit in his right hand. Wutaishan, China.

Buddhism assimilated many indigenous beliefs and practices considered helpful in attaining enlightenment. Indeed, Central Asia is often mentioned as the place of origin of a number of popular Buddhas or *bodhisattvas*. In Tibet we find that Buddhism absorbed many local deities, while in China even Confucius became recognised as a *bodhisattva* in the course of the Qing Dynasty (1644-1912). In Japan there is the influence of Shintō, the local pantheism, both on orthodox Buddhism and on syncretic teachings.

The role of healing was central in the transmission of Buddhism to China and Japan. The task of the Tathāgata Bhaiṣajyaguru is to inspire the right method, the search for the right cure, for the main illness is ignorance, and the Master of Healing eliminates ignorance. He does not tell us precisely what to do when we are ill, but he shows us the way.

Even though the medical profession was first denied to *bhikṣu* or monks, this rule came to be changed. Monks could, and indeed should, help each other when ill. Medicine was one of the four requisites carried by any roaming mendicant or bhikṣu. The Mahāvagga VI of the Vinaya, the corpus of monastic rules, contains a list of essential items used in healing, which could be stored and preserved. But the most common, the five medicines, are not to be stored. These are *ghee* (clarified butter), fresh butter, oil, honey and molasses. A rice gruel with honey was especially beneficial. It is clear that the main medicine to be prescribed was that of a healthy diet. Herbal remedies could be used when a dietary cure was not sufficient.

The pragmatic Chinese and Japanese were interested in healing practices and the Master of Healing became one of the primary objects of worship. The biographies of the early masters in China show that their healing powers largely contributed to their success. An example is An Shigao, a Parthian who settled in Luoyang in 148 AD, where he initiated the translation of Buddhist texts. It is probable that Buddhism became accepted in Japan around 600 AD because of the therapeutic abilities of the first Buddhists, and because of its message of spiritual healing.

Texts of Central Asian origin, such as the Lotus Sūtra with its famous simile of the Buddha as a physician in chapter 16, were very popular in East Asia. This text propagated the names of the bodhisattvas, the brothers Bhaiṣajyarāja, King of Healing, and Bhaiṣajyasamudgata, Supreme healer. Another popular text of Central Asian origin is the Sūtra of Golden Radiance, Suvarṇaprabhāsa. This contains two chapters on healing and medicine, claiming that Buddha studied medicine in a past life, thereby justifying the pursuit of medical studies. Another popular text in China is the Vimalakīrtinirdeśa, in which the sick sage Vimalakīrti has a discussion with Mañjuśrī, Bodhisattva of Wisdom. Vimalakīrti explains that his illness is the result of a bodhisattva's pledge to save all beings, and he himself is ill because all sentient beings are ill.

Bhaiṣajyaguru and his representations

In the Lotus Sūtra, and not only there, we read of the *bodhisattva* Bhaiṣajyarāja, King of Healing, who heals through his exposition of the doctrine, and who came to personify the doctrine. His younger brother, the *bodhisattva* Bhaiṣajyasamudgata, the Supreme Healer, often appears in later literature. In the Lotus Sūtra they appear together. Neither *bodhisattva* seems to occur in Indian Buddhism, but they are known in China and Japan through the Lotus Sūtra.

The rise of Bhaiṣajyaguru may be considered to be a later development. In China he is called Yaoshi liuliguang Rulai, Bhaiṣajyaguru the Lapis Lazuli Radiance *Tathāgata*. He is mentioned in Chinese translations from the third century onward. A wide range of names is given to him, indicating a link to the earlier worship of Bhaiṣajyarāja.

The early Chinese texts emphasise the Buddha's royal nature. The popularity of Bhaiṣajyaguru, the Lapis Lazuli Radiance *Tathāgata*, is certainly connected with the transmission of the so-called *Bhaiṣajyagurusūtra*. The first translation into Chinese is traditionally said to be the work of Śrīmitra from Kucā and was made in Nanjing in Southern China, in the early fourth century. The most popular Chinese version of the *Bhaiṣajyagurusūtra* was made by Xuanzang in the seventh century. Moreover, there are many sixth and seventh century manuscripts of this *Bhaiṣajyagurusūtra* recovered from Dunhuang. Manuscripts of the Sanskrit version were found in Gilgit (Kashmir) in 1931. N. Dutt dates them to the sixth, or possibly seventh century. The Sanskrit text is in accord with Xuanzang's version. The language of the manuscripts indicates Central Asian or north-west Indian origin. There are also Sogdian and Khotanese fragments. The Tibetan translation was made by Jinamitra, Dānaśīla, in the ninth century.

It is possible that the *Bhaiṣajyagurusūtra* came into existence in Central Asia or northwestern India, possibly in Gandhara, close to the main source of the dark blue lapis lazuli, *vaiḍūrya*, at the Badakshan deposit, in the mountains to the north of the Hindukush in northeastern Afghanistan. It must be said that some scholars translate *vaiḍūrya* as beryl, which is pale blue in colour Bhaiṣajyaguru, however resides in his eastern paradise which is called 'Pure Lapis Lazuli' which presents some similarities with the cult of Amitābha, who dwells in his 'Pure Land' in the west. In China, and also in Japan, there are Śākyamuni-triads where Śākyamuni is flanked by Bhaiṣajyaguru and Amitābha. Prayers for the living are addressed to Bhaiṣajyaguru, who prolongs life. One commonly says: 'Homage to the Buddha Bhaiṣajyaguru who annuls disasters and lengthens the life span'. Prayers for persons in the spirit realm are addressed to Amitābha.

There are no early Indian statues of the Master of Healing, at least not earlier than the time of Śrīmitra in China, which is the fourth century. The so-called metal reliquary of Kaniṣka (late second century) from Gandhara may show a representation of Bhaiṣajyaguru, the Master of Healing, flanked by his two attendants, the *bodhisattvas* All-Pervading Solar Radiance (Sūryaprabhā) at his right, and All-Pervading Lunar Radiance (Candraprabhā) at his left. The metal reliquary may date from around the time of the composition of the Bhaiṣajyagurusūtra.

In China and Japan Bhaiṣajyaguru is often represented flanked by the bodhisattvas Sun and Moon. Sun's mount is a horse, and his attribute, the sun, may appear in his crown or on a lotus support. Moon's mount is a goose, and his attribute, the moon, may appear in his crown or on a lotus support. Below the triad, twelve *yakṣa*-generals may be found, representing the twelve time-periods of the day (each of two hours). They relate to the zodiacal signs and the twelve months. The twelve astrological signs, the sun and moon, and the blue hue of lapis lazuli, all convey a profound image of time and space in harmony.

Since the eighth century, that is since Tang times, there has appeared a series of seven healing Buddhas, seven brothers: Bhaiṣajyaguru, Abhijñārāja, Dharmakīrtisāgaraghoṣa, Aśokottamaśrī, Suvarṇabhadravimalaratnaprabhāsa, Ratnaśikhin, and Suparṇkīrtitanāmaśrī. The names of six of them, especially of the last two, may vary. In images from Tibet and Nepal, Śākyamuni may be placed in the center and Bhaiṣajyaguru at the top, bringing the total to eight. A typical representation of Bhaiṣajyaguru has him holding a lapis lazuli medicinal bowl in his left hand in *dhyāna* (meditation) *mudrā*. The right hand makes the *varada* (wish-granting) *mudrā*. The Tathāgata does not cure directly, but inspires the application of the right remedy. In his right hand he may offer the healing fruit, holding the branch of the yellow myrobalan (*harītakī*).

In Tibet Bhaiṣajyaguru is called sMan-bla and he is represented in much the same manner as Śākyamuni. Only his attributes, the medicinal bowl, and his *varada mūdra* are typical. He may hold the myrobalan. In fact he does not differ from the Chinese representations. In Tibet, where Bhaiṣajyaguru was introduced much later than in China proper, the Master of Healing is often represented as one of a group of eight Buddhas. He cures not only physical illnesses, but also the three main mental defilements: desire, hatred and ignorance. The group of Healing Buddhas shines in all directions. Bhaiṣajyaguru's celestial palace, his retinue and his excellent teaching (*The Four Tantras*) are the subject of a series of 77 Tibetan paintings of the seventeenth century which were used for training doctors.

Gilt bronze statue of the Medicine Buddha Yaksa Yorai (Bhaiṣajyaguru) from Korea, 9th century, 25 cms. National Museum of Korea, Seoul.

Seated Buddha in front of a painting of Bhaiṣajyaguru. Chikji-sa Temple, South Korea.

In Japanese art there are some statues of Bhaiṣajyaguru making the *abhaya* (fearlessness) *mudrā* with the right hand. Indeed, he rescues beings from the nine untimely deaths, the nine hardships. In Chinese painting from the ninth century, and also in Japanese esoteric art, Bhaiṣajyaguru is sometimes represented as a monk holding the *khakkhara*, a caduceus-like staff, in his right hand, and a blue medicine bowl in his left, accompanied by his two attendants, Sun and Moon.

Opposite: The Buddha Yaoshi (Bhaiṣajyaguru) accompanied by two monk attendants, possibly Ānanda and Mahākāśyapa. Tang Dynasty painting on silk (2nd half of the 9th century) recovered from the Caves of the Thousand Buddhas, Dunhuang. The Medicine Buddha is shown walking and in half-profile. The cartouche on the right states "An image of the Buddha, Master of Medicine, executed for my late daughter Li, and offered for ever and as an expression of felicitation". Musée Guimet, Paris.

Index

urine production, 235

vaccination. *See* inoculation
Vāgbhaṭa, 22, 48, 72, 74, 76, 77, 80, 90, 95, 114
vaidya, 27. *See also* phycisian
Vaidyajīvana, 22
Vairocana, 112, 114, 141
vāta, 83, 85, 88, 89, 90. *See also* doṣa
venepuncture, 90
vessels *See* mai
Vietnamese medicine, 209-216
vipāka (post-digestive effect), 79-80, 103
virilisation *See* rejuvenation
vīrya (potency), 79-80
viscera, 117, 123, 129, 132, 134
Von Siebold, 235

Wang Shuhe, 161
wastes, 74. *See also*, residue, tissues and wastes
water
  as a healing substance, 20
  as anupāna, 88
  element, 39, 71, 73, 123. *See also* elements; shui
  injections with, 36
Western medicine, 56, 63
  Ayurvedic influence, 27, 99
  and Korean medicine, 226
  impact on Unani medicine, 54-57
  influence on Ayurvedic medicine, 30, 33
  influence on Tibetan medicine, 110, 112
  in Japan, 234-235
  in Taiwan, 205
  Unani influence, 46
wind, 175, 180 *See also* air; elements; feng; humours
wounds, 20, 43, 88, 192, 218
wuxing, 159, 167-168, 169, 191. *See also* five agents; huo; shui

xin, 165, 167, 168, 176. *See also* heart-mind
xue, 161, 165, 179, 183, 188, 189. *See also* body: apertures of the

Y duong an tap and Y am an tap, 212
yang, 164, 167, 175, 180, 189, 218, 220, 247, 249 *See also* yin and yang
yangsheng, 161, 162, 176, 192, 194 *See also* health
Yellow Emperor, 14, 159
Yijing, 166, 167
yin, 167, 175, 180, 218, 220, 247, 249
yin-yang, 159, 163, 164, 166-167, 169, 173, 180, 182, 200 *See also* ûm-yang; in-yō
Yin-Yang School of Chinese medicine, 167
yoga, 123, 124, 125, 192
  principles of, 105
  school of philosophy, 103
  tantric, 31
Yuanqi Lun, 169, 192, 194
yukûm oegam, 218
Yunji Qiqian, 169, 176, 194
Yuthog the Elder, 109, 114
Yuthog the Younger, 112, 114, 116

zang, 180 *See also* zang-fu
zang-fu, (storage-places) 165, 167, 169, 170, 175, 176, 193, 215. *See also* diagnosis: by reference to zang and fu
zao (dryness) *See* liuyin
Zhang Zhongjing, 159, 212, 219, 244, 247
Zhuangzi, 157, 158, 176, 193
zodiac, 46 *See also* horoscope; astrology and medicine
Zuozhuan, 157, 193
Zur school of Tibetan medicine, 116, 118

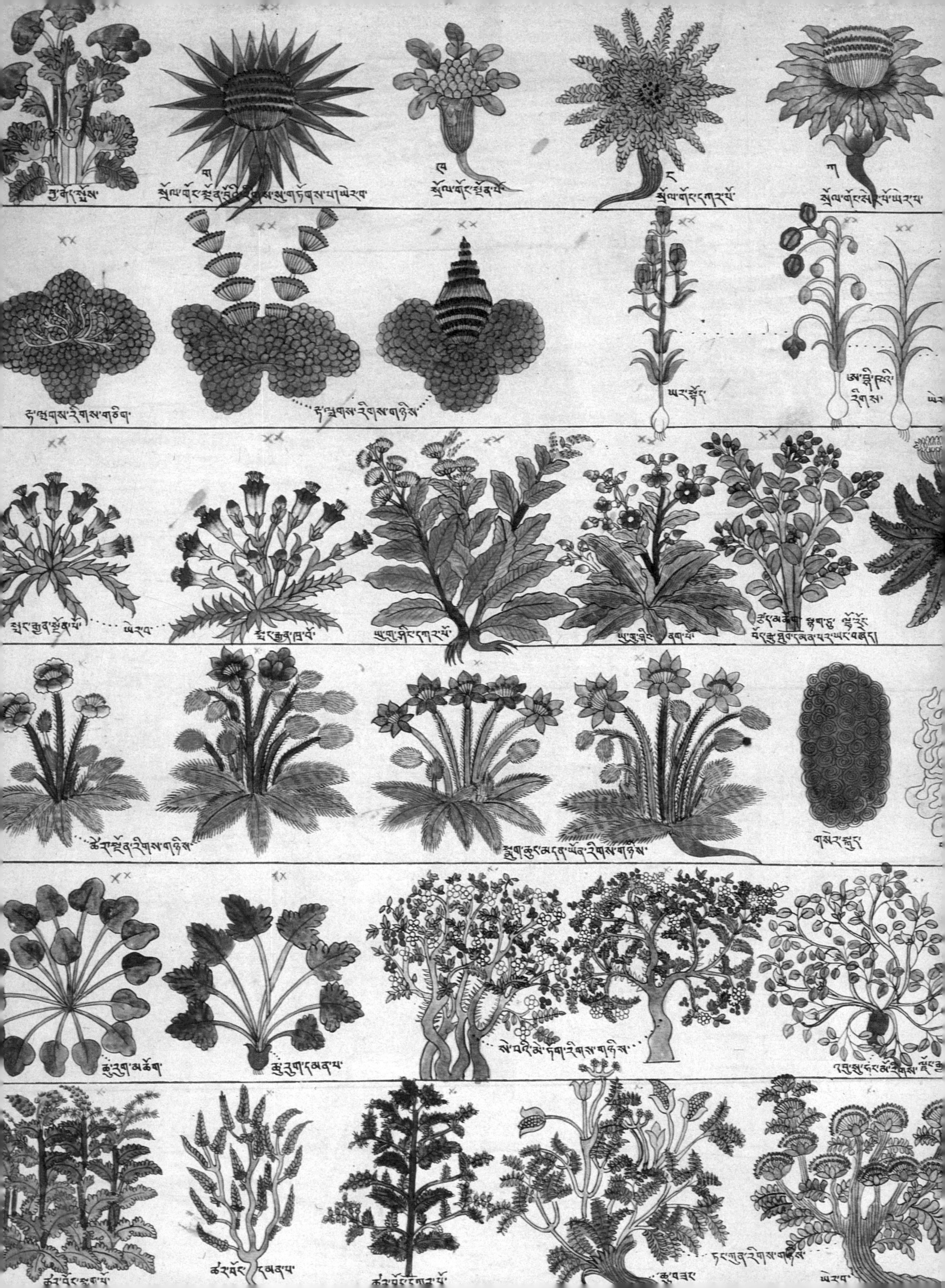